Talk That MUSIC TALK

PASSING ON BRASS BAND MUSIC IN NEW ORLEANS
THE TRADITIONAL WAY

A COLLABORATIVE ETHNOGRAPHY

by Bruce Sunpie Barnes & Rachel Breunlin

PARTNERSHIPS

Talk That Music Talk was generously supported by the New Orleans Jazz National Historical Park, the Surdna Foundation, and the Louisiana Division of the Arts, Office of Cultural Development, Department of Culture, Recreation and Tourism, in cooperation with the Louisiana State Arts Council. It was also supported in part by Community Arts Grant funding made possible by the City of New Orleans and administered by the Arts Council of New Orleans.

   SURDNA FOUNDATION

ART & PHOTOGRAPHY PARTNERS

A significant portion of the historical photography was donated by Black Men of Labor Social Aid & Pleasure Club, The Historic New Orleans Collection, the Louisiana State Museum, the Hogan Jazz Archive, Tambourine and Fan, the Archives and Manuscripts Department, John B. Cade Library, Southern University and A&M College, Baton Rouge, the Amistad Research Center, the New Orleans Museum of Art, and *The Times Picayune*. Their parternships connected important visual archives to the story of passing on music and parading traditions in New Orleans. Title page sign by Charles Otis.

  LOUISIANA STATE MUSEUM

HOGAN JAZZ ARCHIVE
304 Joseph Merrick Jones Hall
6801 Freret Street
Tulane University
New Orleans, LA 70118-5662

   NOMA

The Times-Picayune

Published by the Center for the Book at the University of New Orleans

© 2014 by Bruce Sunpie Barnes and Rachel Breunlin

All Rights Reserved

Graphic Design by Gareth Breunlin

Cover photograph: Benny Jones, Sr. teaching Sidney Bradford IV how to play the snare drum. Photograph by Bruce Sunpie Barnes.

Back Cover group portrait: The New Orleans Young Traditional Brass Band, by Eric Waters. ***Back cover left:*** Kenneth Terry and John Michael Bradford. ***Right cover right:*** Aurelien Barnes and Oscar Washington. Photographs by Bruce Sunpie Barnes.

Library of Congress Cataloging-in-Publication Data

Sunpie (Musician)

Talk That Music Talk: Passing on New Orleans Brass Band Music the Traditional Way/Bruce Sunpie Barnes & Rachel Breunlin.

   Pages 312

ISBN 978-1-60801-107-0

1. Brass band music--Instruction and study--Louisiana--New Orleans.
2. Brass band music--Louisiana--New Orleans--History and criticism.
3. Neighbors--Louisiana--New Orleans--Interviews. 4. New Orleans (La.)--Social life and customs--Anecdotes. 5. New Orleans (La.)--Social conditions--Anecdotes. I. Breunlin, Rachel. II. Title.
  ML3508.8.N48S856 2014
  784.9'1650976335--dc23

DEDICATION

To the spirit of the city that gave birth to jazz:
If you want to have good Creole tomatoes,
you have to raise them yourself.

ACKNOWLEDGEMENTS

Talk That Music Talk grew out of a partnership between the National Park Service's New Orleans Jazz National Historical Park and the University of New Orleans, which was established in 2012. The list of people and institutions that have helped make this book come true is long and travels across many parts of the city and region. Thank you:

At the National Park Service...

To the leadership at New Orleans Jazz National Historical Park for funding the Music for All Ages (MFAA) over many years, and for bridging the world of interpretation and ethnography to create this book. We would especially like to recognize Superintendent Lance Hatten, Assistant Superintendent Joe Llewellyn, Chief of Interpretation and Education Nigel Fields, and Anthropologist Allison Pena. Special thanks to Southeastern Regional Ethnographer Antoinette Jackson for all her guidance in developing our methods of collaboration across disciplines and institutions.

To the coworkers at New Orleans Jazz National Historical Park for all their support of the project over the last few years: Matt Hampsey, Tran Paul, Reginald Galley, Michael Crutcher, Wanda Releford, Karen Armagost, Leonard Rose, and Prudence Grissom.

To all the tremendous supporters of the MFAA program: Gerard Jolly at the National Park Foundation, UPS, and the African American Experience Fund for the initial grant that launched the program. To all the members of Black Men of Labor (BMOL) for their mentorship of the Young Traditionals on the streets of New Orleans. And to Don Marshall, Scott Aiges, and the staff at the New Orleans Jazz and Heritage Foundation for operational support for the program.

To Jane, Terry, and Barry Taylor for financial support as well as weekly Saturday drives from Albany, GA to attend the MFAA program, and an invitation to play in Albany. We will never forget the Seventh Ward Creole gumbo. To Nancy Moultrie for generous donations and weekly support.

To Jennifer Pickering and the staff at Lake Eden Arts Festival (LEAF) for helping us buy the first instruments for the students, and for continued support in both New Orleans and at LEAF. To the staff at Quantec for creating a model for how to sustain a lasting program and for joining us at the BMOL parade. And to Bethany Bultman and the New Orleans Musicians Clinic for free health screenings and generous donations.

To the people behind the scenes at festivals in New Orleans who believed in promoting music by young people and showcased the New Orleans Young Traditional Brass Band over the years: Karen Konneth at the Children's Stage at the Jazz and Heritage Festival, Marci Schramm and Greg Schatz at the French Quarter Festival and Satchmo Summer Festival, and Kenneth Ferdinand and Amy Kirk at the French Market Association.

At the Neighborhood Story Project...

To the Center for the Book at the University of New Orleans: Abram Shalom Himelstein for ten years of creative partnership through thick and thin, G.K. Darby for working with the unruliness of a collaborative ethnography, Jen Hanks and Katie Pfalzgraff for copyediting, and Alex Dimeff for taking on transcribing countless hours of oral histories, copyediting, and making the index. And special thank you to Katherine Hart and Michael Crutcher for helping us through the last rounds of editing.

To Gareth Breunlin for working with us to create a book inspired by a long history of jazz and portrait photography as well as the parading arts of BMOL.

To Lucas Allen, and Seth Welty and Emilie Taylor of Collectivo Design/Build for helping us create a portrait studio inspired by natural light. To Fred Johnson, Jr. and Todd Higgins for sharing the fabrics from BMOL for the backdrops. Thanks to Helen A. Regis for sharing fabric from Senegal (on Kenny and John Michael's chapter) and Dave Spreen for the contemporary black and white (on Ray and Xavier's) and black silk backdrops.

To the Surdna Foundation's Thriving Cultures and Strong Local Economies programs for partnering with the Neighborhood Story Project on this project, and the Arts Council of New Orleans for much needed operational support during the process.

To the Neighborhood Story Project Board: Corlita Mahr-Spreen, Troy Materre, Helen A. Regis, Petrice Sams-Abiodun, and Susan Krantz for their deep patience on this one.

To the Department of Anthropology at the University of New Orleans for being a wonderful home for the practice of collaborative ethnography. David Beriss, Steve Striffler, Jeffrey David Ehrenreich, Ana Croegaert, and Ryan Gray.

To Kevin Graves, Interim Dean at the College of Liberal Arts, and Dean Darryl Krueger at the College of Education for their ongoing commitment to the Neighborhood Story Project, and President Peter Fos and Vice President of Business Affairs Greg Lassen for reinvesting in UNO's public humanities press.

And in the creation of the book.....

To New Orleans CORE members Jerome Smith and Doratha "Dodie" Smith Simmons for sharing how the Civil Rights Movement has been intimately connected to jazz.

To BMOL members Fred Johnson, Jr., Gregg Stafford, and Tyrone Calvin for contributing life histories to the book.

To the young people and their families for growing up with a book in their lives: Will Hightower, Jose Bravo Besselman, Jeremy Jeanjacques, John Michael Bradford, Doyle Cooper, Xavier Michel, Aurelien Keenan Baaba Barnes, and Thaddeaus Ramsey.

To the mentors who shared their pasts and presents: Will Smith, Benny Jones, Sr., Anthony Bennett, Joseph Torregano, Kenneth Terry, Woody Penouilh, Ray Lambert, Oscar Washington, and Julius Lewis.

To the friends and family who contributed interviews: Ray "Hatchet" Blazio, Roger Lewis, Johnny Vidacovich, Kirk Joseph, Al Kennedy, Donald Harrison, Jr., Wesley Schmidt, Leslie Cooper, Melvin Washington, Caleb Windsay, and Ashton Ramsey.

To all those who donated photographs from their personal collections: Jenny Bagert, the Barnes family, Anthony Bennett, the Besselman family, BMOL, the Bradford family, Ray "Hatchet" Blazio, the Cooper family, Jeff Day, the Hightower family, Donald Harrison, Jr., Anthony "Meathead" Hingle, Cayetano Hingle, Fred Johnson, Jr., Benny Jones, Sr., Julius Lewis, Wylie Maerklein, Kate McNee, Ed Newman, Woody Penouilh, the Nation Institute, Ashton Ramsey, Doratha "Dodie" Smith Simmons, Wesley Schmidt, Ayo Scott, Charles Silver, Jerome Smith, the Smith/Michel family, Matej Slezak, Gregg Stafford, Joe Torregano, and Oscar Washington.

To Eric Waters for donating time, images, and mentorship in the art of street photography. In your dedication to capturing cultural history at F-stop 250, you've been an inspiration.

To the F&F Botanica, Prime Example, Vaughn's Lounge, Bullet's Sports Bar, the Candlelight Lounge, and Preservation Hall for allowing us to photograph in their spaces.

To the Editorial Board for providing critical feedback to drafts of the book: Michael Crutcher, Antoinette Jackson, Leroy Jones, Bruce Boyd Raeburn, Helen A. Regis, Nikki Thanos, and Joseph Torregano. We couldn't have pulled it together without you.

To Doratha "Dodie" Smith Simmons, John "Kid" Simmons, and Matt Sakakeeny for reading over drafts of the first sections of the book, and to Angie Bradford, Edna Smith, Dawnis Michel, Bill and Cathy Hightower, Odilee Kelsey, and Kate McNee for reading drafts of other chapters.

To the Louisiana State Museum for the use of the New Orleans Jazz Club's photography collection. Special thanks to Greg Lambousy for believing in the project and generously donating his own time, and Anna Gospodinovich for helping us organize all the images.

To the inspirational team at the Hogan Jazz Archive—Bruce Boyd Raeburn, Lynn Abbott, and Alaina Hébert—who all provided enthusiasm and critical support for the photography and oral histories in the project. And down the hall at the Southeastern Architectural Archive, thank you to Keli Rylance for helping us find Alphone Picou's funeral.

To the Historic New Orleans Collection for many years of collaboration between photography collections and storylines in NSP books, and for housing the master tapes and transcriptions of the New Orleans Jazz National Historical Park's oral history collection: Goldie Lanaux, Alfred E. Lemmon, Daniel Hammer, Jude Solomon, Becky Smith, Jennifer Navarre, and Ann Robichaux.

To Barry Martyn, Jack Stewart, and the oral history team who worked with the New Orleans Jazz National Historical Park for interviews with Uncle Lionel Batiste, Waldren "Frog" Joseph, Placide Adam, and others.

To StoryCorps, Henry Griffin, and Kate McNee for permission to publish an excerpt of an interview of Hart McNee.

To Christopher Harter at the Amistad Collection, Angela Proctor at the Archives and Manuscript Department at Southern University, Baton Rouge; Marie Page Phelps at the New Orleans Museum of Art; Cynthia Sesso for Herman Leonard Photography LLC; and Quo Vadis Hollins at *The Times Picayune* for opening important archives up to the project as well.

To Maria and Analina Barnes for spending countless Saturdays giving rides to students, and supporting Aurelien in his musical development in the house, in the street, and in the classroom.

To Cynthia, Douglas, Kate, and Lucy Breunlin for visits in and around this book. To the wonderful Pagoda Cafe. And to Max Omar Etheridge. Last time the NSP books came out, you were nine months old, and crawled all over boxes of books as we opened them for the first time. Now you and Simone are working on your own. Proud to raise y'all in the trade.

The next generation. Artwork for Black Men of Labor created by Melvin Reed. Photograph by Bruce Sunpie Barnes.

TABLE OF CONTENTS

Kenneth Terry working with the trumpet players in the Music for All Ages program. Photograph by Bruce Sunpie Barnes.

MUSIC FOR ALL AGES

TOWARDS A COLLECTIVE VOICE

In the early 1900s, jazz was created in New Orleans. Soon afterwards the fear began...it's moving away, it's going to die out, it needs to be preserved. Yet each generation has put time and energy into making sure the roots of the music stay strong in the city. This book is about the history of that kind of organizing work, and what happened when the New Orleans Jazz National Historical Park brought together a new group of young people to learn traditional brass band music from older musicians and the Black Men of Labor Social Aid & Pleasure Club.

The New Orleans Young Traditional Brass Band sponsored by the New Orleans Jazz National Historical Park at a Black Men of Labor second line parade. *Front Row:* Jawansey "NouNou" Ramsey, Austin Campbell, Thaddeaus Ramsey, Jeremy Jeanjacques. **Back Row:** Jose Bravo Besselman, Gerid Gibson, John Michael Bradford, Will Hightower, Doyle Cooper, Aurelien Barnes, and Gabriella Butera. Photograph by Eric Waters.

For their fifth year anniversary, Black Men of Labor hosted an event at the House of Blues in New Orleans honoring traditional jazz musicians. The San Jacinto was a club In Tremé known for its live music. Image courtesy of the BMOL archive.

INTRODUCTION
BY

Bruce Sunpie Barnes,
Interpretive Park Ranger
New Orleans Jazz National Historical Park

&

Rachel Breunlin,
Co-Director
Neighborhood Story Project

Bruce: Music is about emotions and memories. When people talk about New Orleans jazz—what it does, how it feels, why it's different—it's possible to put it in technical terms, but it also comes down to the raw emotional value of the music itself. People have developed a very exciting, driving way of playing in the city. It's open. And it captures people's imaginations very quickly.

Recognizing the world-wide significance of the music, the United States Department of the Interior created the New Orleans Jazz National Historical Park in 1994 to support the development and progression of jazz music through stewardship and education. That same year, Black Men of Labor Social Aid and Pleasure Club (BMOL), an African American benevolent society with roots in the Civil Rights Movement, was formed to keep traditional brass band music alive in the streets of New Orleans.

In 2005, I brought the two organizations together when the National Park Service announced a "Call to Action" for parks around the country to develop intergenerational programs with kids under 18 and adults over 50. As a musician and an interpretive park ranger, I thought it was a great opportunity to start a music program to teach young people how to play traditional brass band music by working with professional

3

People who study jazz have heard that musicians in New Orleans are open to sharing their music in many different settings. It's not uncommon for out-of-town musicians to sit in on gigs or join brass bands playing parades. Not only do these opportunities give them a chance to get to know the people who are dispelling the information, it also allows them a chance to get into the more esoteric parts of the music. *Above:* Midway through Dizzy Gillespie's (*on right*) career, he traveled to deepen his understanding of different styles of music. His travels to Cuba to study with Mango Santamaria and Chano Pozo developed a new genre of music called latin jazz. Gillespie also traveled to New Orleans to study the roots of jazz, and played a funeral with the Onward Brass Band. Photograph courtesy of the Jules Cahn Collection at The Historic New Orleans Collection, 2000.78.1.107.

Left: Constantin "Tin" Dangermond and Emmanuel Mitchell, Jr. playing the trumpet at the MFAA program.
Right: Benny Jones, Sr. teaching Sidney Bradford IV how to play the snare drum. Photographs by Bruce Sunpie Barnes.

bands. There are many ways to learn the music, but I decided to focus the Music for All Ages (MFAA) program on "ear training." This method of playing music teaches you to listen to a piece of music and figure out what key it's in, then learn how to play the sounds you hear with your fingers or your lips and wind. When you're reading music, it's a dictation. But learning to play by ear teaches a musician how to negotiate a moment with others—how to work together to produce a body of sound. You're going to have to compromise.

I learned early on that when a musician is trying to transfer the spirit to you, you have to be open to receive it. Understand that it's you and me, and I'm fixing to show you how to play something. I'm going to give it to you, but I want you to be open to catch it all, not just part of it. Notice how I tap my foot, when I talk out of the side of my mouth. Be open to the whole embodiment of what the music is. When you play it back, it's not going to sound exactly like me. It's going to be in the same spirit, but it's going to sound like you. And that's what passing music on in the city is about—developing your own voice and being able to make your own mark.

Bruce Sunpie Barnes (*on far right in park ranger uniform*) leading the New Orleans Young Traditional Brass Band in a parade. Photograph by Ashton Ramsey.

As part of the program, I also wanted to teach students how the music functions in the city—how the repetoire of songs and the etiquette of being a brass band musician works in different social settings, including participatory parades sponsored by social aid and pleasure clubs called second lines. I had recently joined BMOL so I decided to ask them if they wanted to partner with the Park Service on the program.

As I was working on the proposal in late August of 2005, I had an unsettling dream that New Orleans would flood. I wasn't sure what to make of it until Hurricane Katrina grew to a Category 5 storm, and barreled down on us. I called Gerard Jolly, the grant manager for the National Park Service, and said, "Hey man, I'm not quite done writing the grant, but our world is about to get blown away down here. Will you hold it for me?" I faxed in the application and evacuated the city.

Needless to say, Katrina was a serious delay, but if there was ever a time to invest in holding onto the musical traditions of the city, it was after the storm. When the

program was funded, I began meeting with BMOL to figure out how to begin. We discussed whether MFAA should target "at-risk" children in New Orleans or be open to all kids. We decided to open the doors to any child between kindergarten and 12th grade. We knew that access to this way of learning music comes from neighborhoods and networks of musicians around the city. In the case of jazz and brass band music, we understood that the true "at-risk" children were those who didn't have access to these places. With people scattered all over the country, the neighborhoods themselves were "at risk" as well. Members of BMOL talked about the lack of understanding many politicians have about cultural organizations that parade, and agreed that having a diverse group of kids who had been raised in the tradition could be a powerful way to extend the network of people who care about the music and the street culture built around it.

We started MFAA on January 7, 2006 at the National Park Service's site in Dutch Alley in the French Quarter. Four bands well versed in the traditional brass

band repetoire rotated monthly Saturday residencies—the New Wave, the Tremé, the Royal Players, and the Storyville Stompers. Members of these bands learned from legendary brass bands like the Olympia, the Onward, and the Doc Paulin Brass Bands. Then they went on to form some of the most famous modern ones in the city, including the Dirty Dozen, the Chosen Few, the Pinstripe, and New Birth Brass Bands. Having traveled the world playing music that spanned over a century, each band had developed a distinctive sound when it came to trad jazz.

A core group of 10 to 15 students came to the program regularly, along with 200-300 park visitors who came to watch. The first group of kids, from neighborhoods around New Orleans as well as the suburbs, didn't have any real music backgrounds—nothing beyond first-year learning—but sitting in with the bands helped them develop quickly.

The kids had to play in front of an audience, which was nerve-wracking, but once they got over the fear of it, they were able to open up to the music. Sometimes I slowed the songs down if I thought the program was becoming more of a performance than a lesson. The people in the audience were cool with that because they got to see the process of learning the songs. It dispelled the myth that music either "bubbles up from the street" or you to have to practice until your knuckles bleed and your sight reading is perfect. Having different bands to play with helped the students quickly learn that there are many ways to interpret the music.

Out of the regular students in the program, I started the New Orleans Young Traditional Brass Band. My hardest challenge was to have girls join and stick with it. A number came to the program, but they did not stay with the band, which was unfortunate because it was with the band that the students got a chance to experience playing the music in the city the way that professional musicians do.

Bruce Sunpie Barnes, Arthur "Mr. Okra" Robinson, Fred Johnson, and members of the New Orleans Young Traditional Brass Band in front of Sweet Lorraine's at 1931 St. Claude Avenue. Photograph by Eric Waters, courtesy of the BMOL archive

Members of BMOL dance through the streets. Photographs by Eric Waters, courtesy of the BMOL archive.

Parading

The New Orleans Young Traditional Brass Band played the BMOL parade for many years. Before the first one, I tried to get the kids to get a little taste and feel of what it was going to be like. They had done a bit of parading around, but now they were going out on a four and a half hour sojourn, which was a whole different experience. It was hot. 103 degrees, and the club was wearing red. Smoking heat. BMOL had decorated the whole corridor along St. Claude Avenue, and there were flags made with African fabrics representing each year the club had paraded. On the side of Sweet Lorraine's, there was a mural of a group portrait from the previous year, and if you looked closer, the other years behind it.

The kids were walking into this history. Their parents were concerned about how long the parade was going to be but I said, "They are going to make it. You can't walk in the parade, you are going to be on the side." They were about to grow up really fast. They were about to get baptized in this thing.

BMOL always comes out the door dancing to a spiritual. This is the root of the music because a lot of songs came out of the churches. The band will play *The Old Rugged Cross*, *Jesus On the Mainline*, or *Lily of the Valley*. The kids got to see us dance to songs that were from a different era. When we dance in a circle, single file, or in figure eights, it looks like one body of movement. And people will yell out from the sidewalk, "Dance that old style, man!"

When you are watching a club interact with a brass band, they will clap on a two and four count, but dance on the one and three. Within this basic structure is the improvisation. The bass drummer accents, or plays an extra-syncopated rhythm, between the three and four, and then has to quickly turnaround to get back to a strong "one" count. These accents are what people really feel the strongest when they are dancing or even just following a brass band. It puts a hump into the music that dancers interpret in their own ways.

When you are dancing, you follow the bass drummer and sousaphone player. As they add or subtract accents, you have to move with them. You can try to count it out, but it is very difficult to feel the music that way.

You have to open yourself up to being inside the music. You have to join it, and learn to distribute the rhythms through your body. Once you have it, you can lock into it. When you are dancing inside the music, you are in sync with the band, you are riding the wave of the energy and it makes everything very easy. It takes all the stress off your body, and your mind is free. And whatever direction the music goes, your body will interpret that. Feet, head, arms—all of it.

The kids got a chance to experience the interaction between the band and the dancers, and the way the musicians played with each other. It was hard for them to be near the adults playing instruments because they could feel all that energy. It was voracious. They wanted to be able to keep up, but they had to learn their role was playing underneath the band—supporting it and learning the timing of walking and playing. A trumpet player like Kenny Terry is one of the most powerful on the street—he can't be beat. I guarantee you. Listening to him gave the kids something to reach for. He put his sound in their ears, and it gave them a direction to point to: This is where I want to go.

The kids survived the parade, and the club thought it was great. It answered something they felt should happen. We are a social aid and pleasure club, so for people in the communities we parade through, they got a very strong message. You see kids dancing with second line clubs, but it hadn't been since the days of Danny Barker's Fairview Baptist Church Band and the Bucketmen Brass Band that real young kids were dressed up in black and white playing traditional music in second line parades.

Like these earlier bands, the New Orleans Young Traditional Brass Band gained a reputation around the city. They started playing for social events, parties for judges, and political rallies. They were featured at the Jazz and Heritage Festival, the French Quarter Festival, and Satchmo Summer Fest; they took a road trip to Georgia to play the Homecoming parade for Albany State University. They were featured everywhere from local TV shows to *The New York Times* and *W Magazine*.

Left and right: Ray Lambert, snare drummer of the Storyville Stompers Brass Band, and trumpet player Xavier Michel discuss their experiences in the MFAA program. *Middle:* Anthony Bennett and Joseph Torregano met in Andrew J. Bell Junior High's band in the 1960s, and have been friends ever since. They have taught together in MFAA program with the Royal Players Brass Band. Photographs by Bruce Sunpie Barnes.

Ensemble Playing: A Collaborative Book

It was great to have this kind of publicity for the program, but it didn't capture the deeper significance of what was going on around the musicial mentorship—how learning music "the traditional way" was shaping the lives of the young people. After seven years, the students were growing up fast. The oldest student had graduated from high school and enrolled in a music education program in college. The other students had been accepted to high schools with strong music programs, were starting to join brass bands themselves, and seeking out other mentorship programs.

It was the right time to step back and record what had happened, but I knew some kind of professional spirit organizer would be needed. I talked with the Neighborhood Story Project, a collaborative ethnography organization based out of the University of New Orleans.

Since 2004, the co-directors, Abram Himelstein and Rachel Breunlin, had produced a series of books with different cultural groups and public schools about communities around the city. I decided that partnering with them was the best option in creating something that would tell a more inside story. I asked Rachel if she would work with me on the project.

Rachel: In New Orleans, there is an important canon of autobiographies by jazz legends such as Louis Armstrong, Sidney Bechet, Danny Barker, and others where the significance of brass bands and street music is mapped out. When we began the project, we thought about adding to this body of literature by using a writing workshop model to make the book, but decided to record interviews instead so that we could share the "music talk" that happens in conversation. In

the introduction to *Mr. Jelly Roll*, Alan Lomax wrote:

My notion was that the great talkers of America could, if lovingly transcribed, contribute enormous riches of prose styles and varied points of view to literature. What they had to offer was not literal history, as so many oral historians have mistkenly thought, but the fruit of their lifelong experience, the evocation of their periods, and their imagination and style—the things that every good writer brings us...editing aimed to transfer the surge of speech into the quieter flow of type could, I found, sometimes produce prose as graceful and finely-tuned as the best of written literature. Its originality in music and point of view was boundless.

Inspired by this call to literature created from the spoken word, we decided to ask members of BMOL, and the musicians who had participated in the MFAA program how they would like to make a book together. In March of 2012, we gathered at one one of the Jazz Park's sites, Perserverance Hall No. 4, and held a story circle where everyone talked about their inspirations for music. Todd Higgins, the time keeper, had a hard job. The group got excited and told long stories. Todd would call time and he'd get overruled. That was good news for a book project because we needed to have a strong investment to get through it.

As we talked about why a book like this would be important, the president of BMOL, Fred Johnson, said it was important for the book to connect the broader social and political contexts around race and social justice. The older musicians agreed that the music came out of a struggle for equality, and were also adamant that playing music had helped shape their lives for the better. In the large group, the young musicians didn't say anything, but you could tell it wasn't because they didn't have an opinion. We decided to break into two groups, with members of BMOL and the older musicians going in one and the younger musicians in the other, to write out questions that they would ask each other in the interviews. On their own, the younger musicians opened up about the legacy they were a part of:

You can celebrate history, but you have to learn different types of music. Every generation goes through the process of changing.

They want to preserve the music, but you can't just be in a bubble.

Yeah, they lived in a different time period.

I don't want to limit myself. I want to be able to develop.

They are the ones who told us not to copy cat.

After listening to members of BMOL and all the musicians, we decided we were really embarking on a two-part project. The first was to trace how MFAA fit into a lineage of music education programs that have seen passing on traditional brass band music as a way to invest in the social and political well-being of the city. The second was to work with the musicians to tell their own stories about how music has shaped their lives.

With these goals in mind, we spent the next two and a half years recording interviews, looking at pictures in personal and archival collections, and attending a lot of performances. As we learned about the deep friendships around music, we extended the initial conversations to include other interviews that could help us illuminate the call and response of music and art in the city. When someone important to this history had already passed away, we used oral histories that were archived with the New Orleans Jazz National Historical Park and the Hogan Jazz Archive.

Bruce: As the chapters started coming together, Rachel worked with everyone to edit their interview for the wider world to read, ponder, and enjoy, and I photographed the years we all spent together.

Left: Bruce Sunpie Barnes photographing at Preservation Hall. Photograph by Rachel Breunlin. *Right:* Rachel Breunlin looking through photographs with Ashton Ramsey. Photograph by Bruce Sunpie Barnes.

The rich layering of fabrics and textiles in portrait photography can be found on both sides of the Atlantic Ocean. *Left:* Benny Jones, Sr. poses before a BMOL parade. Photograph by Eric Waters, courtesy of the BMOL archive. *Right:* Portraits from Seydou Keita's Bomoko, Mali studio, courtesy of the New Orleans Museum of Art.

Jazz Photography

Rachel: Although I was a bookmaker and Bruce was a musician, we had come into this project at a time when photography was on both of our minds.

Bruce: In the year leading up to the book project, I had a series of dreams that I was photographing musicians around city with what turned out to be a Leica M9 camera. I had no idea what this camera was, but I decided I'd take the dreams seriously. I bought the camera, and started wandering the city taking pictures.

Rachel: Around the same time, I was working on an article for *African Arts,* and came across the photographs of Seydou Keita, who had a portrait studio in Bomoko, Mali. I fell in love with textile backdrops, and got inspired to build a portrait wall at the Neighborhood Story Project. I thought of it as a new method of collaborative ethnography.

Bruce: When we started working on the images for this project, Fred brought over the BMOL's archive of photographs taken at parades by the club's official pho-

tographer, Eric Waters. Before the parade begins, all the club members gather to take photographs in front of backdrops of the textiles, flags, and artwork that are put up for the occasion.

Rachel: Looking at the way the club used the backdrop of buildings for their own portraits immediately took me back to the Bomoko studios. We already knew that we wanted to photograph the musicians in MFAA together, and Bruce proposed that we use the Neighborhood Story Project's studio. Inspired by the

12

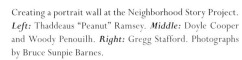

Creating a portrait wall at the Neighborhood Story Project. *Left:* Thaddeaus "Peanut" Ramsey. *Middle:* Doyle Cooper and Woody Penouilh. *Right:* Gregg Stafford. Photographs by Bruce Sunpie Barnes.

aesthetics of BMOL, we created backdrops to honor the relationships built around the program.

Bruce: One of the other things I wanted to show with photography was the movement of musicians around the city—be it a brass band funeral, a group of musicians playing at Jackson Square for tips, or a concert in a formal setting. Photography is very much like music in that you must learn to improvise. To capture the spirit, you have to open yourself up to the universe and be a part of something rather than circling and stalking around it. The thing I loved most about making photographs was the challenge of dealing with available natural light to give viewers a real sense and feel of a moment.

Rachel: The photographs Bruce took over three years are in dialogue with the history and ongoing art form of ethnographic and jazz photography from people like Ralston Crawford, Michael P. Smith, Jules Cahn, and Eric Waters, as well as from personal collections.

Bruce: In the chapters that follow, I provide brief introductions, and then the cultural activists and musicians involved in the project will tell their own story.

Rachel: The chapters gradually build on each other, but the book can also be read like you would play albums—finding individual stories you like, skipping around, and making connections. Like a traditional brass band that has played in the city for a long time, you will encounter many of the same songs, places, and people, but never the same way twice.

13

The backdrop for the 2013 Black Men of Labor parade at Sweet Lorraine's. Photograph by Bruce Sunpie Barnes.

ORGANIZING IN NEW ORLEANS

LIFE HISTORIES IN SOCIAL JUSTICE, ART, & COMMUNITY-BASED MUSIC EDUCATION

New Orleans Is MUSIC Is New Orleans

Note! The essential spirit of our city is Echoed in the daily courtesies of "Good Morning" and "Good Evening".
This gives GRACE to the place we call New Orleans.
These sounds of spirit make us a Musical And Blessed People."

"Good Morning" and "Good Evening" are Synonym for Caring.
Caring is a Recognition of And the Commitment to the Humanity of each Other.

Left: Jerome Smith standing on St. Philip Street in Tremé in between Joseph A. Craig Elementary School and the Tremé Community Center where he was director for many years. He is holding a picture of himself playing at Uncle Lionel Batiste's jazz funeral with young musicians who were in the MFAA program. Photograph by Bruce Sunpie Barnes. *Above:* Curriculum from Tambourine and Fan situates music as part of social relationships in New Orleans. Image courtesy of Jerome Smith.

JEROME SMITH

Bruce: When I first began working at the New Orleans Jazz National Historical Park and started thinking about music education in the city, musicians and community activists were constantly directing me to Jerome "Big Duck" Smith. For more than 60 years, he has been a cultural investor. He created a curriculum for understanding how music, street culture, and social justice are connected in New Orleans, and then taught it by example. One of the co-founders of the New Orleans chapter of the Congress of Racial Equality, a nonviolent direct action civil rights organization that helped dismantle Jim Crow segregation in the American South, he took the principles of civil rights organizing into Tambourine and Fan, a community-based organization in the Sixth and Seventh Wards of New Orleans.

Through Tambourine and Fan, Jerome helped to create the Bucketman Social Aid and Pleasure Club and an annual parade called Super Sunday that brought the young people into the street with brass bands and Mardi Gras Indians. In preparation for the parades, children learned that the music of people like Louis Armstrong came out of similar neighborhoods. When Louis traveled the world as the United States' Ambassador of Jazz, and people asked him about his music, he always told the stories of growing up in New Orleans, and the people and institutions who helped him become an icon.

Left: Plarine [*Praline*] Seller in New Orleans, circa 1895. Photograph by George Francois Mugnier. *Right:* Pork Chops and Kidney Stew tap dancing in the French Quarter. Images courtesy of the Louisiana State Museum.

Introduction: Where You Hear Music

Jerome: I'll ask kids, "Where you first hear music?" They'll say, "On the radio!" "In the choir!" I say, "No. That ain't the truth. You know where you hear music at? In your mama's womb. You hear her heartbeat. And then you come attuned to your own creation."

Some of us come out there and can hold onto it, but everybody comes with it. Some places help you hold onto it easier than others. Some kids are lucky to grow up in New Orleans around music—they are fortunate enough to be in situations where they can hear it, and then see it celebrated. Other kids have to seek the music out. If you want it, you can come from anywhere. If you love something, you can find it.

When I was growing up in New Orleans, the streets were so swollen with the music. You had the ragman with his cowbell buying old rags. There was the lady coming around with the pralines. You had to deal with the lottery man, selling the gigs like 4-11-44. There were the produce peddlers. Hobo Gable would come through with his wagon singing, and I used to work for Fred Johnson's father with Tom, the mule. He was one

of the top peddlers. We used to have some fun on that wagon because he could rhyme for days. They had certain streets he would come down. It would be mostly Italian ladies, and he knew how to give it to them:

Watermelon, watermelon, red to the rind. Come here pretty lady ain't nothing sweeter than mine!

That was his magic. His magic wasn't his produce. The magic was him. He'd sing about the okra and potatoes. It wasn't like they were buying, it was like he was bringing them gifts because of the way he would handle the music.

And then you'd be passing by the jukeboxes in the clubs, and on Sundays, before Indian practice, there would be a band—a piece of horn, a half a drum—before all the tambourines. Pork Chops and Kidney Stew would be on the corner tap dancing before they went into the French Quarter. And you had all the conversations on the street.

The saying of "good morning" and "good evening" is New Orleans music. That is to say, everyone is an instrument. Their voices enter into your creativity as

an artist. Part of Louis Armstrong's music is the way he said, "Good evening, everybody!!!" These greetings mean that you care for the other. That's what I teach with these youngsters—recognize the humanity of the other. That's a healthy thing. It has to do with a decency of spirit and it's reflected in the song of saying, "good morning" and "good evening."

Life-Giving

When I think about brass band music in New Orleans, I think of how the music was tied into all these other sounds of the neighborhoods, and how it was part of community rituals. We can call it traditional, but what we are dealing with is sacred sounds. I would say it "is the is." Danny Barker often talked about "the root music." When you say "root," you can identify with a tree. It is anchored and can spread.

For many people in New Orleans, and then all over the world, the music is a synonym for life-giving. As a teacher, someone who wants to pass it on to the next generation, you have to find ways to hold the spirit of where it came into existence. It came from this city, which had a different social fabric than the rest of the South—the rest of America. From its inception, black people used the streets and the music they created to express themselves. They invented something that prevented us from committing suicide.

Holding on to tradition means holding onto the rituals that gave the whole thing its life. The power in ritual is passing on inheritances from generation to generation. A branch can come off here, come off there. But it "is the is" of sounds. That's why the dirges are so beautiful. It's the sound, but also the rituals connected to it. I remember going to hear John Coltrane and Rahsaan Ali in New York, and all of a sudden, I jumped up and almost started second lining. After the set, I said, "There was something in there that brought me back to home."

Rahsaan said, "Where are you from?"

I said, "I'm from New Orleans." He said, "That's it. Coltrane's been experimenting with traditional jazz."

In my youth, I heard those songs in jazz funerals that would pass by Joseph A. Craig Elementary School. Once in awhile, my friends and I would roll out of the first-floor window and follow the processions. Coltrane was dealing with the bottom of this spiritual music in New Orleans, too. He was fascinated by how musicians here kept time without using numbers. They could do an emotional count. Coltrane's experimentation shows that the branches can spread out when they have strong roots. It is the first step of what is and what will be.

Something Bigger Than You

In the 1990s, a group of children in Tremé had their little parade, grabbing anything they could for instruments. They called themselves the Box Band because the boxes were the dominant instruments. The kids were doing it for play because they saw the music all around. They grew up in a place where if somebody hit the beat with the bass drum, the next sound they heard would be the shutters. The shutters on the front windows of houses would start opening, and the youngest to the oldest would be looking out for the band.

That's the kind of thing that made it so easy to teach the kids more. We saw it all the time with Troy "Trombone Shorty" Andrews' desire to participate. He saw the power of the music, and the way it brought people together. Sometimes when he would be out on Dumaine Street with the Box Band, Uncle Lionel Batiste would come around there, take one of them boxes, and play with them. Herlin Riley sat on the block and said, "Give me a box, too." Guess what the little bass drummer put around his wrist? A piece of wire because Uncle Lionel wore that watch.

If I caught one of the kids on the street, I'd say, "What you got? Where's that mouthpiece at?" If they have it, I give them a few dollars. And if they don't, I punch them in the chest. But, you know, that's a traditional thing, too. There were men who would do similar things with us. They'd put something on your mind. They would applaud you and punish you. They wanted you to feel connected to something bigger than you.

My whole life I've watched the connections between New Orleans and jazz musicians considered to be the best in the world. In New York, I went to see Herlin's uncle, Melvin Lastie, play with Willie Bobo. Miles Davis was on the corner. A man comes up with a group from overseas. "I want to introduce you to the greatest trumpet player of all time." And Miles cuss a lot, I won't cuss now. He reprimanded him, "No, you mother— I'm not the greatest, but I'm not the worst. There ain't no such thing as the greatest. Pops done did it all, man. Pops done did it all." Oh, that was something to hear because you get caught up in that whole public thing. He could have shaken the man's hand and went on with it, but he checked that. He was humble, and honored Louis Armstrong and the music of New Orleans. Serious jazz musicians will tell you they honor the source.

One time the saxophone player Rahsaan Roland Kirk, who was blind from an early age, was following our second line parade for the Bucketmen. He was balancing himself between the people. And then for a few blocks he put his head down close to the ground. I was hitting the band marshal to check on him because I thought he was going to fall. He was listening to the sounds of the dance steps. Each step is a sound, and it's just like your fingerprint. When you had all those people dancing, with all these different sounds, he couldn't stay away from it. He was hip to that. And then he'd yell sometimes. He had a free spirit, that rascal.

The Box Band at WWOZ, the community radio station. Photograph courtesy of Jerome Smith.

Seeing More

I got introduced to the drums early at Craig Elementary. I was always doing something with my hands on the desk, tapping out a rhythm. My teacher said, "I'm going to put you on the bass drum." Bass drum!? I wanted something pretty! She said, "No, you gonna play the bass drum."

At the time, I had serious impediments to speech. I felt my speech was like a car wreck, and I didn't think I would be able to participate in the theatrical production of the year. But my teacher had a plan. She gave me a word, and I had to pronounce the word on the beat of the bass drum. It started building up my confidence. The sound of the drum protected me from being criticized if I stumbled with my speech. Ultimately, when she noticed I was consistently pronouncing my words with some clarity, she gave me a word outside of the beat, and put that word into the script. It gave me a means of participation with putting on that play.

My father, Walter Smith, was a seaman, and he traveled the world. He used to tell me, "Anywhere man lives, they are going to tell stories about themselves. Shakespeare and all them fellas, why do they get all the promotion?" You know, that don't mean writers like Shakespeare aren't giving something you can't appreciate. But you can't appreciate it if your own sense of self is going to be denied. There ain't no fairness there.

Every night when my mama, Leona JuLuke, would come from work, she read to me about black performers like Paul Robeson and Marian Anderson. She used to tell me, "You are black and you are poor, but you will not be dirty or dumb. And they are not better than you." She read all kinds of poems, but I had to pay a price. I had to make up poems, too. My favorite was Henry Wadsworth Longfellow's "The Village Blacksmith." I thought of it when I went to the International Longshoreman's Union Local 1419's Labor Day parade each year. The men put on overalls and had all this music. I looked down the line and saw all these hands, all grotesque and swollen up big from that hard work:

The smith, a mighty man is he,
* With large and sinewy hands;*
And the muscles of his brawny arms
* Are strong as iron bands.*

I was impressed with that and developed an emotional attachment. It was the poem that allowed me to see more.

Footwork at a second line parade. Rahsaan Roland Kirk studied New Orleans music and incoporated it into his own. Some of his best interpretations can be found on *The Man Who Cried Fire*, where he tells the crowd, *I'm going to play some real vintage music at this time. This is some real music that if you are ever in New Orleans, and you were very fortunate—I mean, this might sound sort of strange—if you are ever fortunate to be invited to one of the funerals...because if a guy leaves New Orleans and he's been accepted, he goes out the right way. I mean, really. They really give him a nice way to go. They don't tamper with his mind—they play what he would really like to hear.* Kirk goes on to say *New Orleans Fantasy Part II* is for his own funeral. Photograph by Bruce Sunpie Barnes.

Associating

A key piece of my education occurred in the third grade when my teacher taught us the word "association."

A year later, my fourth grade teacher told us we were going to a concert at the Municipal Auditorium. She took us down to the pecan yard a block from school. They used to have a lot of birds in the trees. She said, "Every time you hear a bird chirping, raise your hand and follow it." To ourselves, we might be saying, "Ms. Lawrence, something wrong with her!" We were in that yard there, and I don't know why we were waving our hands.

We got back to class, and Ms. Lawrence asked us if we knew of any music about cowboys and Indians. We said, "We listen to Tonto!" We didn't have televisions but we followed Tonto, the Indian, on the radio show *The Lone Ranger*. She said, "Okay, next week we are going to a special kind of concert, and before we go, we are going to define the word "symphony."

At the auditorium, this is where the word "association" took off in my life. When the conductor pulled up that baton, we associated it with that pecan grove, and as the orchestra started playing the first selection, the *William Tell Overture*, we realized that it was the theme song for *The Lone Ranger*. Ms. Lawrence had locked us in. We were conductors.

Now we gave complete attention. We are going to move from that number to discover something else we feel good about. We came back to class and she said, "That was European classical music." She got out a map and showed us. She said, "You know our thing in New Orleans is jazz," and she started playing Duke Ellington and Fletcher Henderson.

I started to make these associations between my experiences and the rest of the world, and it's followed me throughout my life. At Clark school, we had to read *Macbeth* and write a paper. Parroting my daddy, I told my teacher, "I'm not writing it." But on the way home, I ran into the funeral procession for a man in the neighborhood named Booty. I'm sitting on the curb on North Robertson, and both sides of the street were saying, "That no good, low down something, he should have been dead." I said, "Oh! Wait a minute! That's like the chorus in *Macbeth*."

I wrote my paper and my teacher said, "You didn't do this!" I said, "Yes, I did!" I was being a little bit belligerent because I actually did it. She took me to the principal and told him I sassed her. He said, "I'm surprised because you don't give no trouble. You are always quiet." I explained I knew how to associate.

He gave me a double A and told the teacher to apologize. I didn't expect that! He also told me, "One of those As was for the teacher whose class you come out of at Craig." There were connections between the neighborhoods and the school. If we don't have it, we can become strangers in our own space and that ain't no good.

When I got to have a chance to go to New York and be around Broadway, none of the drama measured up to the experiences I had in New Orleans. See, the dynamics of drama were engrained in our socialization, and the emotional improvisation was spontaneous.

During Mardi Gras, we weren't allowed to go to parades like ride along Canal Street. It was only for white folks. But I learned that Rex was stagnant compared to what I was coming up around. When I was a young boy, I saw Louis Armstrong out in front of the Caldonia when he was king of Zulu. Louis didn't have a horn, but the crowd was yelling, "Please Louis! Come on, Louis, please!" He started scatting off the float, and the people were dancing. Then he started calling names out of the crowd. Man, that was it! He was a great man and was recognizing people he grew up around. "Louis still know me!" Oh, my goodness! Rex couldn't beat that. There ain't no way.

LOUIS ARMSTRONG
THE WORLD OWNS IT

Louis: *When I go back to New Orleans, half of the places I called home are all torn up, but there's still the old women down there saying, "Come here, boy! You know I raised you."*

The Carnival was something to remember. Everybody masked, and the Zulus paraded. I have Africa in me. When I was a kid, my great-grandparents instilled in me that they brought that rhythm from Africa to New Orleans. My grandmother Josephine had been a slave, and remembered Congo Square. She told me all the slaves came in their finest clothes. The women mostly had on calico dresses, and their hair was bound in tight bandannas. Some colored musicians played African music, and we would dance the Bamboula or the Cajole until we had to

go back to our quarters...One would beat the drums, another would scrape a cow's horn with a key, a third would blow into an instrument with slides, a fourth sat on his haunches and rang bells. And I saw it when I went to Africa. The different tribes, everyone had a different rhythm.

Of course, you know I was born in Jane's Alley, that's Back-a-town in the rear of the city. It's one street with everything—honky tonks, churches, and gambling. I was just a kid, but I remember all of that. Then we moved to Perdido and Franklin, where there was the heart of the little honky tonks, and even a schoolhouse. My mother she taught us the real things. You might not be rich, but you always have health. We didn't need

a whole lot of money. Mama could take 15 cents and cook a big pot of red beans and rice and a slice of salt meat, and two loaves of bread—a day old for a nickel.

I always could sing. My mother took my sister and I to church. This is what they call rock 'n' roll today. We used to hear that same kind of music in Sanctified churches. At the age of 12, I was playing in a quartet. I was singing tenor at the time. We'd go around the gamblers and the hustlers and pass our hat. I could help my sister, my mother, myself to have a new shirt or new shoes for myself.

It never dawned on me that I was going to blow the horn. I second lined behind Joe Oliver. In the parades, he was always my idol. I'm just a kid. I didn't want to go with the other children to go up to the other schools and fight. I remember when Oliver's Onward Brass Band was playing in the Labor Day parade, and they've got 15 bands. All these bands had to open up for Joe Oliver and his brass band to come in.

I got to the age where I noticed everybody celebrating Christmas and New Year's Eve with pistols, roman candles, shotguns, and cannons. Anything they got in their possessions, they shoot it up in the air. I didn't know there was a law against it. But if you can get away with it, all right, see.

I kept finding my stepfather's old .38 gun. Mama kept on hiding it and I kept finding it. New Year's Eve, coming into 1913, I had this in my bosom, and we were going down Rampart Street singing My Brazilian Beauty—*that was an early tune:*

My Brazilian Beauty down on the Amazon
That's where my baby's
Gone, gone, gone...

There was another little kid with a six-shooter on the side of the street, dying dying dying to celebrate. They all know I had this pistol. They all called me Dipper back then. They say, "Get him, Dipper!" When I looked around, these two arms were hugging me. I said, "Oh, Lord!" I cried like a little baby.

I went to the Colored Waifs' Home for shooting the pistol, and I stayed in there a year and a half. There was a teacher there by the name of Mr. Peter Davis, and it was a long time before he would even look at me, you know, because of the neighborhood I came from. He figured I was one of those bad boys, too. One day, Mr. Davis came and made me the bugler of the institution, and showed me how to bugle. I played all the chords, and boys had to drill, eat, and go to sleep by the bugle. I used to hold that mess call by about five minutes and them cats all wanted to kill me!

Finally, the little cornet player in the band went home, and they put me in the brass band. When they gave me this cornet in the orphanage, I recalled all the things I had listened to, and I loved the horn. We had to play The Saints Go Marching In every Sunday for the boys to march to church. Most of my life was in this institution, and when I got out, I went right to Joe Oliver. Joe would give me lessons, and I used to run errands for his wife, Ms. Stella Oliver. I was always there when she'd make red beans and rice.

I knew the life of the riverboats before I got on the Steamer Sydney, where Fate Marable used to play the calliopes. Before that, we used to unload cotton and banana boats. But this was an excursion boat. And when I got in that band, I had the feeling that I was high up on the horse.

I didn't worry about whether I was going to be a big shot because we weren't taught that. Everybody was good in New Orleans. I left in 1922 when I went to play second trumpet with Joe Oliver at the Lincoln Garden in Chicago. I had just finished a funeral with the Tuxedo Brass Band, Celestin leading, and they took me to the station telling me not to go: "Joe Oliver scabbing, man!" I said, "What is a scab? I just want to blow with Joe." I knew nobody else was going to help me get out of New Orleans but Joe Oliver. I used to see so many of my friends come back after running away from home—they so hungry, raggedy, don't have a quarter. I said, "Well, I don't want to do that."

I stayed with Oliver a long time. We got so wedged in together making duets, musicians like Bix Biederbecke and Paul Whiteman and all them people couldn't understand how we played so well together. Joe got ready for a break, I had every note in the duet, and we'd sit right there and didn't say nothing to each other, that's how well I loved him. In those days, musicians didn't take care of their teeth, well that's Joe's downfall. Quite naturally they wanted to take his teeth, but he couldn't do that if he was going to play trumpet.

Most of my education is observing. There were several trumpet players who instilled things in me that I admired and I never forgot. How do we know who owns? If it comes out, the world owns it.

This edited transcript was composed from interviews with Louis Armstrong recorded from 1960 to 1962, and archived at the Hogan Jazz Archives, except for the passage about Congo Square, which comes from Armstrong's own writings quoted in *Louis Armstrong: An Extravagant Life*, by Laurence Bergreen.

Louis Armstrong and his band posing in front of picture of the Colored Waifs' Band he was a part of as a child. According to jazz historian Will Buckingham, at the Waifs' Home, *Peter David taught instrumental music and directed the band, choir, and singing quartet at the Home. He was an eclectic musician. He was proficient on..a number of instruments...and had a deep knowledge of European art and music and contemporary brass band and dance music. He is described as "very ecccentric" [and should be remembered as someone who] "gave his entire life and almost every waking moment of his day to working for music for young people.* Ralph Ellsion wrote in "Living with Music" that when jazz musicians: *expressed their attitude towards the world, it was with a fluid style that reduced the chaos of living to form.* Photograph courtesy of the Louisiana State Museum.

The Language of Masking

Jerome: When Louis Armstrong introduced the solo in jazz music, it was clear that everything wasn't what it was supposed to be no more. He flipped that world but also maintained the structure. Everyone followed him.

The Big Chief of Yellow Pocahontas, Allison "Tootie" Montana, was a special kind of person, too. As I grew up, he changed the language of masking as a Mardi Gras Indians by having such intricate costumes for Carnival. He had confidence in what he was doing and was incredibly consistent. He had this craft as a lather, and could get constant employment, which made a tremendous difference in terms of being able to devote himself to designing and sewing Indian suits.

I knew Tootie as a person, but got a deeper connection to his gang when my *nannan*, Ruby, became his queen. That's when I got a chance to go his house and meet all the people who sewed. I got addicted to that sewing because I was able to see something coming from something mysterious from the self—and give that gift.

Allison "Tootie" Montana (*right*) walking with the Yellow Pocahontas during a Tambourine and Fan parade, circa 1990. Photograph by Michael P. Smith © The Historic New Orleans Collection, 2007.0103.4.208.

On Carnival morning, people would come to his house just to see one section of his suit. You would have folks from every division of the human experience—the worst of the worst and the holier than the holier. Some dressed in their church clothes. They had nuns and preachers, and some of them evil spirits would be around there, too. And when they would lower that crown down you would hear, "Oooooo" from everybody. You would have people crying.

All those old men who had masked with Tootie's daddy would be standing out there looking at him, and they would blow a kiss with two fingers to send him off. Before he opened up for the day, Tootie would leave his house and go back on Pauger Street. He spoke Creole—a language the older generations still spoke,

but only in private. He would step from the street onto the banquette to speak to his grandmother's friends. Some of them would be way up in age. Sometimes they said a prayer for him because they related to the times when his father was masking and the streets were really dangerous. It was an honor before he got back into the street.

There were other chiefs who had great presence and leadership that met Tootie at his level. Lawrence Fletcher masked with the White Eagles. During that time, people from Uptown and Downtown had a limited association, but Tootie and Fletcher had a powerful relationship. They respected each other's work, and it was special to see their friendship on the

street. You knew when they were coming because they would talk with their flags. Make conversations. Tootie would have about 200 people behind him, and Fletcher would come with an even number. When they met, nobody crossed the line. They played the principles of the rituals, and then greeted each other. It was not about the spoken word, but still a sophisticated embracement of the other.

One Carnival, this white woman came to see our gang with her family. She was a tourist and she heard something about the black Indians. She was out there with her family when we were coming down a dirt road in the Seventh Ward called New Orleans Street. I don't know how she found us because the blocks were tight in there. She may have caught the sound of the tambourines. She jumped out of the car and went to hollering to her children, "Come see!" To this day, I still remember what she said: "Oh my God! This is like a devastating beauty!" Now that's the reaction you want! Understand?

But the police came when they saw the white woman. They went to put dogs on Tootie. And then she went to screaming and crying, "Oh no! On no! Don't do that!"

It was long before I got in the civil rights movement. A man she was with intervened, and they pulled the dogs back. All those years, that moment was locked in my head.

The Movement

At Joseph S. Clark Senior High, I was the drum major in the band under Ms. Yvonne Bush. I also played a little saxophone. I was more of a saxophone holder than a player because they have bad boys that be out here. I don't want to talk too loud! Ms. Bush had us so well trained, you couldn't cheat on practice because the section leaders would eliminate you. We used to be on the telephone practicing. We won state championships a few years in a row, and I decided to join Southern University's band after high school.

When I got to Baton Rouge, I was focused on the music. I used to leave the dormitory and go into the middle of the football field to practice on my horn. I wanted to play against Florida A&M band. Really, I wanted to be able to play in the chopping sessions after the game. I knew we were going to have a rough time dealing with them Rattlers during the half-time show. They had great musicians down there like Cannonball Adderly who had tremendous talent and creative abilities. But one thing they didn't have, they didn't have the Sixth Ward! We were going to put it on them, because we know there were certain places they couldn't go with

it—they didn't know how to improvise like we did.

But then I got involved in the Freedom Struggle. I had been thinking about my father and enrolled in a history class. When my daddy came back from being overseas, he always wanted to discuss something. He mentioned this fella named Nelson Mandela. In 1962, he had been put in jail for trying to overthrow Apartheid in South Africa.

At Southern, I wasn't with my history professor more than four weeks and he changed my whole perspective. He brought me into the Movement. He taught us to put our books down. "Let's go walk on the campus." He said, "You try to compare the physical structure of Southern to the largest college in this area." That's LSU. "Tell me what differences do you see." And then the thing becomes, "Why?"

Congress of Racial Equality

I was 19 when I quit school, moved back to New Orleans, and started working on the banana boats. They had this great labor leader at that time named Dave Dennis. He was president Local 1419 and was a powerful man of great influence. One time he came out there, and stopped everything on the river because the rules of the contract were being violated. I was impressed with that, and thought I should get involved.

The Consumer's League of Greater New Orleans, organized by Reverend Avery Alexander, A.L. Davis, and Henry Mitchell, was boycotting the businesses on Dryades Street in Central City and picketed in front of a grocery store that, even though the majority of the clinetele was black, didn't have blacks working on the cash register or in management. I went and joined the line. I didn't know what my place was, but I didn't have to define it before I made a contribution. It was like being at a family dinner, and that's how I saw myself—around my elders. I learned so much from them, and

The "For Colored Patrons Only" sign marking the day-to-day realities of Jim Crow segregation. Photograph courtesy of The Charles Franck Studio Collection at The Historic New Orleans Collection, 1979.325.6222

got a chance to meet other students like Rudy Lombard. The student component emerged out of those boycotts. We met with Jim McCain, a representative of the Congress of Racial Equality, at the YMCA on Dryades and decided to organize a local chapter. As we started that nonviolent, direct action in the city with the sit-ins and voter registrations, we used to go by a joint across the street from the YMCA, Big Time Crips. I used to sit in there and read. It felt good to have a place that was supportive of our cause.

And then the moment came for us to step it up. The Freedom Rides started in Washington, D.C. in May of 1961 and were supposed to travel through the South and end in New Orleans. It sent me back to riding the streetcars during my childhood. One time, my father and I rode on one that was basically empty. He took the screen down that said "For Colored Patrons Only" and put it on the floor. He told me to take a seat. There was no reaction to that. The white folks didn't tell him anything. They might have thought he was crazy or drunk.

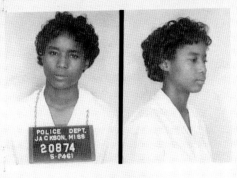

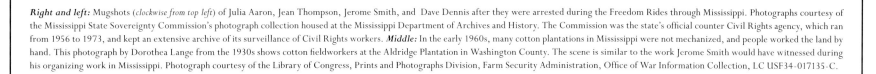

Right and left: Mugshots (*clockwise from top left*) of Julia Aaron, Jean Thompson, Jerome Smith, and Dave Dennis after they were arrested during the Freedom Rides through Mississippi. Photographs courtesy of the Mississippi State Sovereignty Commission's photograph collection housed at the Mississippi Department of Archives and History. The Commission was the state's official counter Civil Rights agency, which ran from 1956 to 1973, and kept an extensive archive of its surveillance of Civil Rights workers. *Middle:* In the early 1960s, many cotton plantations in Mississippi were not mechanized, and people worked the land by hand. This photograph by Dorothea Lange from the 1930s shows cotton fieldworkers at the Aldridge Plantation in Washington County. The scene is similar to the work Jerome Smith would have witnessed during his organizing work in Mississippi. Photograph courtesy of the Library of Congress, Prints and Photographs Division, Farm Security Administration, Office of War Information Collection, LC USF34-017135-C.

One day, when I was about ten, I was on the streetcar by myself and I imitated my father. I didn't know nothing about no civil rights. I put the sign on the floor and the white folks went off from there. They started calling me all kinds of n-words. An elderly black woman came from the back and slapped me on the back of my head, grabbed my shirt, and told me not to disrespect them white folks. She said, "I'm going to get him. I'm gonna beat him." And they were telling her, "Yeah, Mama, beat him. Kick him."

She took me off the streetcar and took me on St. Claude and St. Bernard where there was an auto supply store. I go around there now a few times a month and meditate. I've left the Black Men of Labor parade to go by that spot, because it's a sacred for me. The woman hugged me and told me never to stop. She was crying and said prayers for me. I didn't know then that I would join an organized movement that would test the same kinds of laws.

Freedom Rides

Members of CORE in New Orleans were selected to go on the first Freedom Ride, but Julia Aaron and I were in Orleans Parish Prison after some demonstration. That bus was bombed and burned in Alabama by the Klan, and they had to call off the rest of the trip.

The group reorganized in Montgomery a few weeks later and when we got out of jail, they sent us there with students from Fisk University. In practice, you couldn't tell the difference between the CORE workers and the Fisk students because we had the same attitudes about determination. We were daring. A little stupid, but still productive!

Dr. King was at the bus station to send us off when we left Montgomery. I remember Julia Aaron asking him why he wasn't coming with us. He had a tear in his eye as he said her strength made him know we would be successful. We rode to Jackson, Mississippi and attempted to integrate the white-only waiting room of the bus terminal. They arrested us. John Lewis and James Forman were my cellmates. When I was in jail, I started to hear other stories about Nelson Mandela. I remembered what my father had told me from his travels, and those times in jail became spiritually connected to other parts of the world, and what he had fought as well.

A Black Hand in the Field

Going to jail was not the most significant thing to me. The most significant thing was when that bus was slowing down. I was sitting next to Doris Castle. She was about 17, and I wasn't much older. We were passing on the outside of a cotton field, and they had some workers in this field. I noticed this hand.

This lady, she raised her hand just a little. I could see she was struggling with it. But then she just let it go, and raised it all the way to wave at us. She let us know she was with us. She wanted to be free. They could have hurt her bad. That made me know that the risks we were asking people to take in places like Mississippi were greater than the risks I was going into. I said, "This is it, man. If I reverse it, I don't know if I would have been able to do that on solo."

My strength came from the collective and the goodwill of people around the country. We had all those folks in Mississippi who were not as educated as some of us, but were much stronger than many of us. Afterwards, Ms. Fannie Lou Hamer heard what happened and called for me to come to Rulesville to do some work with her. She was a sharecropper and serious freedom fighter. When I shook her hand, it looked like that hand in the field was hers. It came right back to me.

Many of the Civil Rights workers could leave and come back to New Orleans where a lot of people had experiences living together, but people like Ms. Hamer were forced out of their home for speaking up. Still,

Gene Young, an active member of the Movement when he was in elementary school, joins SNCC and CORE members meeting in Greenwood, Mississippi: John Lewis, Matt "Flukie" Suarez, Jerome Smith, and Dave Dennis. Photograph courtesy of the Civil Rights Movement Veterans Archive, Tougaloo College, Jackson, Mississippi.

she ain't never stopped. I remember growing up, the white kids played with us until their parents came and got them. They'd be raising hell because they wanted to stay. That's their natural spirit—they're emotionally comfortable—and I saw that. I also spent time at my friend Bitsy's house. He was a white kid who was a boxer and lived near me. His father had been in the war with black soldiers, so he was fair. He didn't agree with that race thing.

McComb, Mississippi

The first Freedom Rides forced the Interstate Commerce Commission to integrate interstate bus transit and abolish segregation in bus terminals. But then

we had to test it. We knew that McComb was rough, rough, rough. An NAACP volunteer named Herbert Lee had been killed. The Student Nonviolent Coordinating Committee had been based there but under the premises of our work, if you weren't able to elevate the consciousness of the people to invest in the struggle themselves, then you were just leading them into dangerous situations. SNCC decided they would have to withdrawl. The folks in CORE kept saying, "Some people have to go. They have to go." We started speaking amongst ourselves and decided to go, even though others thought it wasn't a good idea. It was Doratha "Dodie" Smith, Alice Thompson, Thomas Valentine, George Raymond, and me. We broke it open.

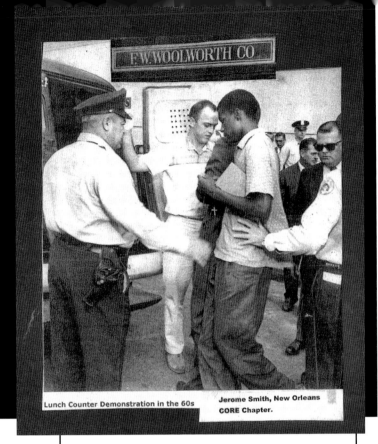

Lunch Counter Demonstration in the 60s

Jerome Smith, New Orleans CORE Chapter.

Tambourine and Fan curriculum shows Jerome holding prayer beads as he is being arrested. Before the sit-in, an Italian woman came up to him and gave him the bead, saying, "You're right, son." In day camp, students are asked to think about how the spirit of a moment sometimes inspires gestures in people that go against the institutions they are a part of. Image courtesy of Jerome Smith.

We got off the bus in McComb, and I told this white fella, "Good morning, how you do?" He looked back at me and he didn't say nothing. I don't know. Something happened with his face where he could feel the moment in history. Something beginning to shift.

The group went into the bus station separate than me. I was the observer. If somebody got jammed, I was supposed to intervene and try to separate them. At the counter, the white folks determined I was with the group and they swung on me. I got jammed in a corner, and they were banging on me. If George Raymond didn't intervene, I wouldn't be here today because

they were coming with brass knuckles. George was jumping all over the place. They were trying to deal with him. It worked, and I got outside the station, and started running.

A black man had a pick-up truck full of pig slop. He drove up close and said, "Can you hear me?" I mumbled something. He was the kind of brother they would say he was an Uncle Tom in his physical appearance, but it had nothing to do with his spirit. If he didn't say, "Just roll over into the truck," I would have been in trouble. He came back and got Dodie, and I gave her a private number to call the U.S. Attorney General, Robert F. Kennedy, because I was in and out of consciousness. She called and he picked up the phone. Kennedy tried to get us to take a flight to New Orleans.

The story was all over the national news and when my friend Bitsy found out I was hurt, he wanted to drive from New Orleans to Mississippi to get me. We decided, "We ain't budging. We're going back. We're going to finish this!" But they closed down the station, and we had to get the bus out on the highway.

Service of Social Justice

In New Orleans, I tried to go to Flint-Goodridge Hospital that was run by Dillard University on Louisiana Avenue, but we were told there were no doctors on duty! We went to some of their houses, but people were frightened and didn't let us in. I was treated at Charity Hospital. I started having tremendous headaches. It kept feeling like my eye was going to come out of my head, and I had moments where my balance wasn't stable, but I didn't want to leave the Movement. We were tough. I'm not going to say the word me. *We* were tough.

I traveled around the South with CORE. In South Carolina I was on a picket line with Ike Reynolds, who

had been on the first Freedom Rides that had been bombed, when someone threw powder dust on us. It was a chemical similar to Agent Orange. See how my fingers are black? That comes and goes but it will never leave my system. I wasn't doing well physically. I still wanted to fight, but it was clear I was in no condition. I was sent to live with Quakers in Pennsylvania. They taught me how to fast, and that helped. You can do a whole lot with your body if you believe in it.

News of the Freedom Riders traveled around the country. In New York, we were invited to stay at James Baldwin's brother, David Baldwin's house on 110th Street. His house was a Freedom House for people involved in the Movement. Lorraine Hansberry, who wrote *A Raisin in the Sun*, became one of my mentors. She would tell me to go to back to school. I still had a speech impediment, and she'd say, "If you you have something good, write it down." We met movie stars and musicians. I remember this one particular lady was fascinated with George Raymond because he was hell of a dancer. She was Frank Sinatra's girlfriend, Ava Gardner. She always wanted to be dancing with George.

Often I was asked to speak on panels. One time, during a question-and-answer period I spoke of my great-grandmother who was always surrendering or giving up on self. I felt this was what we should do in the service of social justice. It touched someone in the audience, and awhile later, I was told this person wanted to support me going back to college.

I said, "I'm beyond that, I don't think that's going to happen at this stage."

"Well, they wanted you to have this." They gave me $30,000 in the 1960s. It sounded like a movie. They never wanted their name mentioned because they thought it took away from something spiritual. I was grounded in a spiritual application of service, too. I thought that being given this money was a test.

Big Time Crip. Photograph by Michael P. Smith courtesy of The Historic New Orleans Collection, Gift of Master Digital Corporation, 2011.0307.14.

Top: Children parading on North Claiborne Avenue with Tambourine and Fan carry pictures of Malcolm X. *Middle:* Tambourine and Fan's key messages about history, music on the streets, avoiding drugs, and protecting young people. *Bottom:* Taju Smith (*in middle singing*) at an Indian practice, with Fred Johnson and Anthony Hingle to the immediate right. Photographs courtesy of Jerome Smith.

I went back to New Orleans and met with Tootie and my friend Ray "Hatchet" Blazio. When I told them about the money I had been given, Hatchet thought that we should buy a pool room so that we could have an income stream, but I was thinking about doing something with kids. I didn't have a business sense of how to keep the money circulating like Hatchet did. I always felt that my purpose was collective.

Tambourine and Fan

I went back to Big Time Crip. The bar had moved into a different building, but it was still important place for me. I started associating activities that were like emotional tattoos on people, and came up with the name Tambourine and Fan. The tambourine symbol-izes Mardi Gras Indians, and the fan is that artifact popularized in the street parade. But both connect to the church, and spirituality. My thing was, throughout my life there was always someone lifting me up. Our kids are going to stumble, we've got to build wagons around them and help them get up again.

I wanted to create an organization out of children's play and Civil Rights—use their fun time for social aware-ness and historical linkages, especially to the music. I wanted the organization to create things that would electrify their senses—electrify their spirit. We'll give birthday parties and have eight or nine conference tables with nothing but birthday cakes. That's magic. They will not forget it! That becomes engrained in that spirit. Where else are they going to see that? Nowhere else.

Left: Milton Batiste playing with the Olympia Brass Band. Photograph courtesy of the Jules Cahn Collection at the Historic New Orleans Collection, 2000.78.1.347 *Right:* Tambourine and Fan logo by Doug Redd, courtesy of Jerome Smith. In 2006, Doug Redd talked to Kalamu ya Salaam about making art for the organization: *In college, you are confined to a certain environment—in terms of painting, designing, that kind of thing. But the cultural environment in New Orleans is so rich, they produce their own artists; people who grew up in the culture like Melvin Reed. When I worked with the Yellow Pocahontas, we became like a work crew. We would go from Indian to Indian and hook up what we needed to hook up and give them what they needed to get on the street.*

When I started working with Tambourine and Fan, everybody was looking to Africa and trying to find a context in which to live and do their work. The thing you always heard about Africa was that artists were an essential part of the community—that art had a function in society. Tambourine and Fan and the second line groups gave me a way to feel and understand that, cause you were creating for the community. I was never doing art work for myself. Just working for, you know, the people. For my folks.

The youngsters around us knew they were protected. That's the truth. My son Taju and his little friends were ridiculous around that Indian thing because they came up around all these great men like Hatchet, Franklin "Wingy" Davis, and Anthony "Meathead" Hingle, and then they had Fred and others who were closer to their age to cushion them. They could go anywhere in the city with their costume, and I don't care what they were doing, nobody would touch them because they knew how we felt about children. It's not like we were super people, but the neighborhood had something. That's hard to achieve now that it's been ruptured by years of disinvestment and now gentrification.

A Moving Classroom

Before they had the expressway on North Claiborne come, we'd run up and down the neutral ground. It was a safe place to play. Now it was covered in concrete, but there was a piece of land at St. Bernard and Claiborne under one of the off ramps that had a grassy area. I said, "Them children need somewhere to play. Let's go take the land." We squatted on it, and then went down to City Hall and took it over with 400 children. That's how Hunter's Field, under the I-10 overpass on St. Bernard and North Claiborne, came about.

At that time, the neighborhood was so tight, and the music was too. Danny Barker had relatives around Tootie's house, and he would come sit around the old timers. Harold Dejan, the leader of the Olympia Brass Band, stayed across from Sidney Bechet's old house on the 1700 block of Marais. I bought a house not too far away at 2258 North Robertson Street, and rented a house for my own family. Everyone involved in Tambourine and Fan called it "the Building." We became more than an organization. We were a tribe.

Many of the young people involved with us got involved with the Yellow Pochahontas. This is how Fred Johnson came into the picture when he was a little dude.

Hatchet, who was the lead man for the gang, was telling me Fred wanted to mask Indian. When they were sitting around at Hatchet's house sewing, I was looking at Fred. The thing about him, he was always anchored. He wore shoes like an old man. That meant he had balance. He wasn't flashy; he was rooted. His commitment bred determination. He became one of the best in masking Indian, and then one of the best running Tambourine and Fan. We believed in giving kids the same kind of authority and responsibility that they could get on the street, but on the positive. The other kids can't always see me all the time. They've got to see somebody that they're near to. That's how you bring them in.

Soon after Danny Barker came around and helped to develop a music program for the kids, Milton Batiste and Harold Dejan formed the Junior Olympia. Milton was a fun person—with his style, he could relate to the children. They were our library to teach the kids about traditional jazz.

The Olympia Band also did a lot to help us financially. They played gigs for us and didn't take the money, or they'd get the gig, and give us the money they were paid. That's how we paid for the kids' uniforms and we chose the same colors as theirs—red and goldish yellow. The Olympia played at their Little League football games. All that's special. Milton developed a serious interest in passing on the music.

Left: A Tambourine and Fan banner advertising the Bucketmen, courtesy of Jerome Smith. *Middle:* Members of the Bucketmen honor the Longshoremen's Union Labor Day parade by wearing overalls. *Right:* The Bucketmen Brass Band at a Tambourine and Fan parade. Photographs by Eric Waters.

Around this time, my brother Walter and our friend Morris were beaten by the police so severely that Morris eventually died of complications from his injuries. At his funeral, we got a band, took the flowers from the service out into the street, and had a parade. Afterwards, we decided to form the Bucketmen and lead a second line parade. The parade brought together many different components of the day camp, Hunter's Field, and traditional brass band music that the kids were learning from older jazz musicians. We saw the parade was a moving classroom. As a club, we were dedicated to having all the great brass bands in the city, but we also wanted the kids to play as well. They formed the Bucketmen Brass Band and paraded with us. When we would do parade rallies beforehand, we would wear the overalls in honor of the Longshoreman Association's Labor Day parades. We took the artistic talent that went into building Mardi Gras Indian suits and put it into the parade, and created different social messages for the students to learn about as well.

Doug Redd was an artistic anchor to everything that we did—he gave us a visual definition. Everything that the children carried and made symbolized something in the struggle. The first parade we had, we had banners up that honored the civil rights workers Michael Schwerner, Andrew Goodman, and James Chaney who were killed by the Ku Klux Klan during the Mississippi Freedom Summer in 1964. Another year, before Apartheid in South Africa was overthrown, the children made fans that said, "Nelson Mandela for President."

We lasted a number of years as the Bucketmen, and then Tambourine and Fan created Super Sunday to elevate consciousness. We invited Indians from around the city to meet at Bayou St. John and parade with us to Hunter's Field. When Fred and them were young boys, we had to go against the police to do it. We painted yellow bricks that we used in the day camp and brought with us to the bayou. Each brick

was some country where children were suffering—the Palestinian, the Jewish, the Irish children—and behind the bricks we had a sign that said, "The tears of the child is a man's shame."

But in the midst of everything we were doing at the parades, nobody in the audience seemed to pick that up. They'd compliment the kids' dancing. Come talking about their footwork. But they don't ever come talking about their fan that had some statement on it. That discouraged me, and made me want to do something else. I'm still thinking about it.

I've been a witness but I think it will be up to the next generations to be able to look at what they've inherited, what they grew up in, and bring all those pieces together in an even deeper way. The struggles are important, but so is the art, the music, and drama embedded in the improvisation of life. The expression of self with humanity is, ultimately, an emotional story.

I'm a Bucket Man —
From the Promised land. — Repeat

I'm the fashion Plate
From the Seventh ward —
When I play, I Play real hard.
I'm a money waster.
A good time Cat —
Where things Jump
That where I'm at

I'm a Bucket man
From the Promised land. Refed
got a hundred dollar hat
On the top my head.
Alligator shoes —! that special made
fifty dollar shirt
ten dollar socks
I drink my scoth
on top the Rocks
I'm a Bucket man
From the Promised land. — Repeat
Vof. Vip vop — Vip vop. Vip Vop
Let em Roll — Let Roll — Repeat

Left: A song written by Danny Barker about the Bucketmen was most likely inspired by the songs he heard the young people in the Bucketmen Brass Band sing. Barker also recorded Mardi Gras Indian songs with Ray "Hatchet" Blazio and other Mardi Gras Indians that he turned in recordings like *Tootie Ma Is a Big Fine Thing*, which incorporates tambourines and other percussion with beautiful saxophone and piano solos. Image courtesy of the Danny Barker Collection at the Hogan Jazz Archive. *Below:* Bucketmen and BMOL member Tyrone Calvin dancing in 2012. Photographs by Bruce Sunpie Barnes.

Tyrone Calvin: *Second lining, brass bands, and Mardi Gras Indians make us all touch. It all runs through the music. I first joined a procession when I was three years old. My uncle Edward Perkins masked Indian with the Yellow Pocahontas. Come Mardi Gras, he was very upset that I complained the whole day about how my crown was too tight.*

The Indian thing didn't work out too well for me, but when I saw my uncle parade with the Square Deal Social and Pleasure Club, I loved it. When I heard the music, it took over my soul. My uncle was the type of person, if you were going to hang with him at the second line, you were going to do everything. You're a little boy? He's gonna turn your cap backwards and you're gonna have your little tennis shoes on. He's got you by the hand, but once you get by the music, you're gonna dance—you gonna do something!

I always wanted that opportunity to join a club. Then, when I was about 17 years old, an organization in my neighborhood, Tambourine and Fan, came out with their own second line club.

We lived right off of St. Bernard, and when I was on the bus coming home from work, I saw little eyes on the telephone poles: "Watch out for the Bucketmen." Who the hell are the Bucketmen?!

In October, this big parade started on Hunter's Field with the three bands of music—the Tuxedo, Onward, and Olympia Brass Bands—and there were children everywhere.

I wanted to be part of something good. Let me tell you, the first time I paraded with the Bucketmen—when I walked out on that field and saw all those people—I went to getting the shakes! Jerome said, "Tyrone, take your fingers out of your mouth now." I was just in awe of all of these people. That's where my inspiration went, and it's still there with Black Men of Labor.

Left: Oliver "Squirt Man" Hunter at a Tambourine and Fan Super Sunday parade, by Eric Waters. *Right:* Squirt Man at Satchmo Summer Festival's annual second line in 2014. Photograph by Bruce Sunpie Barnes.

Fred Johnson, Jr. standing in front of Packy's Grocery Store at the corner of Pauger and North Villere (now called Mike and Ike's), where he worked as a child and later ran a Mardi Gras Indian practice for the Yellow Pocahontas. The mural painted on the side of the wall is a tribute to this history. Photograph by Bruce Sunpie Barnes.

Fred in his Indian suit, courtesy of Anthony "Meathead" Hingle.

FRED JOHNSON, JR.

Bruce: *Fred Johnson grew up in the Seventh Ward masking as a Spyboy for the Yellow Pocahontas Mardi Gras Indian tribe and working for Tambourine and Fan. In Fred, Jerome Smith found exactly who he needed: Somebody who was into the group process and could see a project through from start to finish. Fred's a field general, and he loves his job. He is a community builder and real eclectic funky collage maker. Fred and Jerome helped each other out a lot, and have loved passing those values on to younger people.*

In Fred's life history, he interviews one of his other mentors, Ray "Hatchet" Blazio, who was the Flagboy for the Yellow Pocahontas and one of the grand marshals of the Bucketmen. Listening to Ray talk and sing—he's got that slow Creole phrasing, and it's always on time. If a hurricane hits, if anybody is swimming and coming out on the other side looking good, it is Ray. I don't know how he does it. That's all a secret unless you come through Ray's school. Fred went through it. He learned how to run at it as hard as he can. And when you stop, folks aren't going to forget you.

Introduction: A Man-Child

Fred: I was born and raised in the Seventh Ward at 2120 Pauger—right in the heart of the Yellow Pocahontas' neighborhood. In the 1950s and 60s, fruit peddling was a big deal. The French Market wasn't far from our house and it was for real. You had trucks coming in every day from all over the South with fresh vegetables and fruit. My dad, Fred Johnson, Sr., was one of the youngest peddlers in the city. He had a very good work ethic, and very good hustling skills. He started out with a horse and wagon, and established a big route. Then, in the early 1960s, he bought a brand-new red Chevrolet truck.

My father rolled around the Seventh, Eighth, and Upper Ninth Wards, and when he'd turn a corner, he didn't blow the horn, he sang, "I got tomatoes! Apples, oranges, peaches, and bananas!" He wrote their orders down on paper bags, and his penmanship was exquisite. He grew up in a time when it was a struggle for black people to have a good education. They really put an emphasis on handwriting. When you came to school, they made your ass make As and Bs for days—big ones, little ones! My dad had that down to perfection, and the dude could count. I've never seen anyone count so fast.

He made a lot of cash money, but he had two vices—he was a heroin addict and played a card game called cotch. The dude didn't put the money on the table at home, and when he did, it came back short. I loved him, but I hated how hard he made life for us. It wasn't until I became a man that I was able to understand that he had a sickness. When our lights were turned off and I had to go around the corner and buy the kerosene oil, that was embarrassing. When that kerosene got on my hands, I couldn't wash the scent off. Our saving grace was my mama, Eva. She said, "That's your dad, no matter what he do."

Out of the six of us, I was the oldest. In a lot of ways,

that forced me to become a man-child at a very early age. The love of my mom made me do a lot of things. At ten years old, I had a job. I had a *real* job. I was working a few houses away in a grocery store on the corner of Pauger and North Villere called Jack's. When Mr. Sidney went to Café du Monde to bring us some beignets and café au lait, I'm going to steal the staple items that weren't in the house. When my mom asked me where I got it, I said, "Mr. Sidney gave it to me."

Madly Bit

On Sundays, there was an Indian practice held at the Crocodile, a barroom on Derbigny and Pauger that was across the street from my mama's mother, Viola Campfield Jackson's, house. She would say, "Boy, go in the back before they start fighting and shooting." But I could hear these tambourines. And then, when I was 12 years old, Demetrius White's Uncle Ed and them made him an Indian suit. He lived in an apartment complex right next door to me, and when he put that suit on for St. Joseph Night, I followed him with the Yellow Pocahontas.

At the end of the night, I was madly bit. It was like a Dracula behavior—once they bite you, you were bit! I was taken over. Once that became my thing, I was in the deliverance of the suit. My goal was to make sure that I could get on the street Mardi Gras Day. First, I had to figure out a design and a color scheme. Tootie had a big gang. There were two and three of everything—Spyboys, Flagboys, Wildmen. If he had 30 people in a tribe and had to instruct them all on how to put together their suits, it would take away his time from building his own, which was the centerpiece of the whole gang. To take the position of Big Chief required an unbelievable amount of discipline. He bent his life around this discipline. After work, while other people had the freedom of how they wanted to spend their time, he was limited because, as the song says, if you want to mask Indian, you've got to sew.

Top: Fred dancing as Spyboy. ***Bottom:*** Fred and Anthony "Meathead" Hingle with other members of the Yellow Pocahontas. Photographs courtesy of Anthony "Meathead" Hingle.

That's where Melvin "Left" Reed came in. He took the Spyboys and the Flagboys who wanted help and put their suits together so Tootie didn't have to worry with that. He worked at Swiss Bakery making and designing cakes, and had a natural knack for how to draw and put things together. He interchanged all of those techniques when it came to using canvas, wire, cardboard, and glue to build Indian suits. Some guys in the tribe made their own suits, but if they needed help, they went to him. If you wanted to mask in peacocks, you could bring him a book with pictures of them in it, and he'd draw them so you could sew them into designs.

Melvin lived in the next block from me. He was older, but he knew me because he was friends with my dad's brother, Roy "Sundown" Johnson. I went to him, and said, "Man, I want to mask Indian." He said, "You know how to sew?" I said, "No, but I'm willing to learn."

I told him I wanted to mask in black and yellow butterflies. He drew me up some butterflies. I went to Greenberg's, a bead store on North Rampart across from Congo Square and the Municipal Auditorium, where all the Mardi Gras parades ended and krewes had their Carnival balls. I couldn't get the yellow sequins in time, and I was anxious to get started, so I changed to black and white. Making a suit taught me not to be locked into my own fear. I couldn't have inhibitions because they stopped creativity from flowing.

It was through Melvin that I met Ray "Hatchet" Blazio, the Flagboy of the Yellow Pocahontas. I sewed over by his house. Hatchet kept saying, "Jerome need to bring his nappy-ass head here. The white people beat him up in Mississippi, and he crazy, but he need to come here and bring the feathers, beads, and sequins from New York." I was just a young boy coming up in this. I didn't know nothing about the Civil Rights Movement, or how it was connected to the YPH. I didn't know Jerome had gotten his ass beat in McComb, Mississippi trying to integrate a bus station during one of the Freedom Rides.

Left: Melvin Reed at BMOL's gala in 2012. *Right:* Jerome Smith, Fred Johnson, and Rudy Lombard before the 2013 BMOL parade. Fred is wearing artwork by Melvin Reed. Photographs by Bruce Sunpie Barnes.

When Jerome Smith came in the door, I'll never forget how intrigued I was. Man, I'm looking at this dude and he's got a natural. Hair sticking up! It wasn't cut and groomed, but it was naturally even, and he looked like he was seven feet tall. He had a black pull-over mockneck shirt, black, small-leg mohair pants, a whiskey colored jacket with zippers everywhere and a pair of boots to match it. Motherfucker was smokin! He stood at the door and said to Hatchet, "Who needs what to mask?"

He went around the room asking who needed what. When they got to me, I said, "I need 90 yards of marabou and it cost 110 dollars."

Every zipper on Jerome's jacket had money it. He reached into one of the pockets and gave me a 110 dollars on the spot! I couldn't go get that from my mama and daddy—not for no marabou. He did that because of his endearment and love to see Tootie Montana have a strong gang—he knew that it would make Tootie's gang stronger to have more Indians. I said, "Hey, man, whatever you want to do, I'm down with you. You know, let's do it."

Mentors

Jerome introduced me to Rudy Lombard. They had been in CORE together. Rudy was quiet, but he carried a big stick. He didn't say a whole lot, but when he did, it was worth listening to. He was fearless. He was a warrior. When we think about how the Movement played out—there were people who went in one day. They came out, and they never went back. And there were people like Rudy, Jerome, and others who went day after day.

When Jerome and Rudy started Tambourine and Fan, heroin was heavy. Heroin was running like the Mississippi River. They decided to start an anti-drug program for kids, ranging in age from four to 14. They wanted to have them consumed with enough activities that they would not have enough time to go towards drugs. In hindsight, it was also another way to keep out the FBI and other governmental organizations because the moment they said, "This is an all-black group for this and for that," then you've got all kinds of issues with agents. But through this cultural process, the kids were learning about the spirit of Civil Rights

The Malcolm-Martin Football Classic sponsored by Tambourine and Fan includes Mardi Gras Indian flags and signs that say "Keep Dope Away From Our Children." Collage courtesy of Jerome Smith.

activists like Martin, Malcolm, and Medgar Evers.

I had been smoking a little weed, but my peer group was doing heroin. I'm like, "You got to be crazy!" I'm looking at how the drug use played out in my house, so I know I don't want to go down that road. Maybe that's why, of all the guys my age, I showed the most interest in getting involved in Tambourine and Fan. The other guys wanted to coach football, baseball, or play sports. I didn't want to do any of that. I wanted to do the business part of the organization. When Rudy and Jerome looked at me, they said, "Listen, this little dude have a work ethic." They're looking at me, and would call me by my nickname. "Listen, let Molo do this. Molo, handle this." And I know they were testing me. Tootie noticed my work ethic, too. He would always say, "You're a little man. I like the things you do with and for your mother."

Tambourine and Fan and my friendships in the Yellow Pocahontas helped support me in so many ways.

When my mother moved to the Florida public housing project, I still hung in the Seventh Ward. Jerome and Rudy had done a lot worldly things and showed me how to look beyond my immediate environment. I never met men like that. What did they do?! They were flying in and out of New York and talked about what it was like to function there. Since they were teenagers, they had not been afraid to challenge the system. They taught me the system never changes unless you make it change. And somebody has to be willing to make that sacrifice to force that change. It reminds me of the meeting between Franklin Roosevelt and A. Philip Randolph. Randolph said to Roosevelt, "Mr. President, the Negro people need this. Mr. President, the Negro soldiers need that." And Roosevelt said, "Mr. Randolph, I don't disagree with you. Now make me do it."

At Joseph S. Clark Senior High, I was part of a group that started an Afro-American Society. We read different books, listened to albums, and had conversations. In the Desire projects, not far from my mother's apartment, the Black Panthers had moved in, and began a free breakfast program for the children of the neighborhood. In 1970, they got into shoot-outs with the police, and Chief Joseph Giarrusso rolled out a tank in an attempt to kick them out.

The Afro-American Society discussed all of the events, and wanted to be involved in change, too. The group decided to pressure the school board to create a holiday for Martin Luther King. At the time, all public school students had to honor the benefactor of the school system who made his fortune off slavery during John McDonogh Day, but there was no holiday in honor of equal rights.

Jerome and Rudy gave me insight into how to deal with the school and the administration. We organized all of the high schools and went down to the school board's office on Carondelet Street. But I was also uneasy. I would come home to my mother's apartment in the Florida projects, and sleep in the living room. I kept the music on her hi-fi stereo on all night, but it didn't stop nightmares about the police kicking in the door of our apartment because I was speaking up.

I told Jerome about my dreams, and he said to Rudy, "Maybe we ought to start a little dojo at Tambourine and Fan's building." There were about six to eight people who came regularly, including Melvin Reed. People think martial arts has to do with fighting, but it's about developing internal strength and discipline. At the same time, Hatchet showed me how to play Indian. He was serious about it. He wore a nice shirt, shoes, and dress pants. Diamond rings and big gold chains. We would ride in his white Impala that we called the Tender Trap, and he showed me how to keep the spirit strong so you can prepare for Mardi Gras Day.

It's a hell of a thing to put a wig on and paint your face red. Most people put on a costume like that, they're transformed. Once you come out on Carnival day, you got six to eight hours to show and tell, so you better be about the business of it. If you're not a man, you're gonna be a man now because you just stepped into a man's shoes. Nobody's holding your hand. This ain't no nursery. This is real time. You couldn't come whimpish and crying—you're scared and you're nervous—they're gonna bat the piss out of you. You're looking at these dudes and you want to be what they are. You better follow them.

Left: Ray "Hatchet" Blazio. Photograph by Bruce Sunpie Barnes. *Middle and right:* Photographs of Hatchet masking as Flagboy for the Yellow Pocahontas. Photographs courtesy of the Blazio family.

RAY BLAZIO
TRANSFERENCE OF THE SPIRIT

Fred: I'm glad we got to do this, man. I tell everybody what I learned from the game, I learned from going to practices with you and Jerome. You were the baddest Flagboy who ever lived. Ever lived! Listen, I never told you this, but what I was taken by was how everywhere we went, they respected you. There wasn't no bullshit.

Ray: I wouldn't trade it for the world. I loved that game. Jerome and I came up around it because our families lived on the same block as Tootie on Marais Street. Right on the corner was the Monogram Bar. The first tribe that Tootie started was called the Monogram Hunters because a lot of the people who were driving trucks for that company were in his gang.

I lived on Annette between Marais and St. Claude, and tried to go by my Uncle Howard when they had Indian practice at the bar. Tootie said, "Don't stand on the corner, the policeman will come and want to fool with y'all and then they will want to fool with the practice." Me, Paul, Honore, and Cake-Eater stood on the side, and Tootie opened up the gate. We'd go into the barroom and dance. In 1953, a fella across from my house, Charles Fauria, was Tootie's first Flagboy. He was try-

ing to hook up a suit for me, but he didn't get it together for Carnival. And so the suit was together for St. Joseph Night. I walked with them and we all went to the San Jacinto Club on Dumaine Street, and had a dance there. That was the first time I met Fletcher, the Chief of the White Eagles.

Fred: Fletcher and Tootie always had a thing about who would be the prettiest?

Ray: Fletcher was supposed to be one of the best crown-making chiefs from Uptown. They made crowns out of plumes and we made crowns out of feathers. When we got in the San Jacinto, Fletcher clowned with me. I hollered back and clowned with him, and he told Tootie, "He ready. He ready."

Fred: So, Ray, how many years did you mask after that?

Ray: I didn't mask anymore until I was 21 when I was able to make my own suit. I worked by the Circle Food Store, bagging groceries for 30 cents an hour. But the thing was, you could always bring people's groceries to the car and they'd tip you more than that. 50 cent, some time a quarter, and all that little change. But it wasn't expensive to make an

Indian suit like it is now. You could buy beads for ten cents a tube at Woolworths.

I started masking in 1961. I wore a headband with one plume and a cape—yellow, trimmed in black. I tried to meet Powder Blue and Red from the Creole Wild West, but he wouldn't meet me because I didn't have no crown. I said, "Maybe he heard from somewhere that they got a rule like that not to meet someone who had no crown."

Fred: Not only that, but their egos not going to let that happen.

Ray: Correct. The second year I masked in red trim and white. That crown I made, I didn't know really what to do. I had set it with feathers, but I didn't know that I was supposed to cut them. I had them going all kinds of ways, but it served a purpose. The third year, I masked in all black. When Jerome came by and seen that he said, "Get some lace on there." My companion, Viola, fixed the lace, and gathered it. In 1964, Jerome helped me with a peacock suit.

Fred: Yeah, that was a pretty suit. That peacock suit.

Ray: *Noonut sewed my crown. I watched him take my crown and he had it up so straight. He clipped it all the way around. I said, "Oh. That's how you were supposed to do it." I had the plume tips and put them around, even, and I had done sewed plenty of little small designs to put all around that crown. Getting ready, the Monday before Mardi Gras is one of the fastest days on earth. It pass so fast. And then Carnival...*

Fred: *Ooooh!*

Ray: *It passes even faster. You done sewed all that time, and you can't hit that street, it's something else, brah.*

I Sew to Meet Indians

Tootie had a man who had a stop for him in the Eighth Ward, and we saw the Creole Wild West down there. Powder Blue and Red said, "You're pretty, but you got too much red on your face."

I said, "Look at them boots, look at that!"

Noonut seen me, and he said, "Don't worry about them, you got them. Come let Donald see you." I went to let Donald Harrison, Sr. see me, and said, "Tootie coming with that turquoise five point crown." Afterwards, I asked Tootie, "Chief, are we going Uptown?"

"Yeah, we're going, we're going. Go ahead straight up Claiborne." Shit. I looked back, and I ain't see no Tootie. I kept going. I sew to meet Indians.

It was me, Jerome, Rudy Lombard, and his brothers Edward and Bo. All of us went Uptown, and Bo messing with me going over that overpass. He said, "Man, they got a dude up there so pretty." I said, "Yeah? I don't want to hear it. Don't tell me how pretty he is, I want to see it." And when we got to Washington Avenue, brah, we tore it up. We were rolling. I had a big second line.

Fred: *They were waiting on your ass.*

Ray: *They're instigating.*

Fred: *"There he come! There come Hatchet!" "They ain't gonna beat that! Them boys Downtown got something for their ass up here!"*

Keeping the Gang Alive

Fred: *Tootie didn't have many men masking with him.*

Ray: *Yeah, when Tootie changed to the Yellow Pocahontas, it just started dying out, like.*

Fred: *Jerome Smith started helping Tootie have more Indians in the gang. Smith was instrumental in encouraging guys to mask. Keep the gang alive. A lot of people was like one-time masking. They mask this year, they don't mask next year. And the day after Carnival, everybody's masking. Everybody.*

Ray: *Oh yeah.*

Fred: *"I'm coming next year!" But back to back to back? You might get a handful of people who will do a ten year run. No bullshit. Just on it like Christmas or Thanksgiving. They make a point to weave it into the fabric of their life, because that's the only way you can do it. But that stick-to-it on the Indian game side, that don't work for everybody. Everywhere I went with him he'd be telling someone, "Hey boy, you masking huh? You getting ready?" He'd be egging you on. And some guys would break it down, "Yeah man, I got my front apron." He used a couple of us to draw others in and at one point, man, they had 40 or some people in that gang between men and children.*

Ray: *Like we did when we started out the Bucketmen. We'd have practice in the Building that Jerome got for Tambourine and Fan in the Seventh Ward, and have the children sewing and people helping them.*

Fred: *When Tambourine and Fan had the summer day camp, we'd make the sewing part of the camp. We'd buy the feathers and this and that and you'd have a whole bunch of children sewing or putting something together. But that was another way Jerome...*

Ray: *Was trying to get them interested in it.*

Fred: *Jerome was using some the same tactics they'd use in the Civil Rights Movement. Now, sometimes you'd start out with 50 and we might end up with 150 or we might not have more than five, but five is greater than zero.*

Decorations for the Bucketmen parade at Hunter's Field. Photograph courtesy of Jerome Smith.

Back then, we never would turn on the TV. We'd be listening to Ray Charles, Aretha Franklin. You get some food—butter beans and bread pudding—and good conversation and we'd go seven or eight hours on that. You learned how to get organized so you weren't running all over the place looking for needles and threads. Making an Indian suit is really about how well you can organize time.

Ray: *That's right. I always did learn how to organize myself.*

Fred: *Yeah, like when you got dressed in your civilian clothes.*

Ray: *I be dressed. I like to get clean. I always had the Indian stuff in my blood, but in 1969 I done changed my lifestyle. I started running a card game in bars around town, and couldn't be involved like I used to. I came back again in the 1990s with my own gang, the Wild Apaches, for a few years.*

Fred: *When you stopped masking it looked like a lot of weight started shifting to me.*

Ray: *When I stopped masking Flag, the spirit went through you, and you are carried the spirit on. You kept rolling. You were well known just like I am.*

Word Got Out

Fred: My boys-to-men moment came when I wasn't more than 20 years old. I had to meet our rival gang, the White Eagles, out of the Sixth Ward.

Their Spyboy, Nat, had masked with Big Chief Jake Millon for years. Beautiful personality. I mean, they don't even make people like him no more. But when he put that suit on, and you had to meet him, you had to bring your ass. We were on the railroad tracks at Lafitte and Galvez, and let me tell you something, I was a rookie.

And goddamn. Listen. We're about 300 feet apart. They've got a group of dudes around Nat and Jake is a distance behind him. Tootie is behind me. When you get into the street, you are representing your gang—all this work. I got all these people behind me saying, "All right Molo, we got to meet. We got to meet them."

We were on the track for an hour plus. Nat's playing Indian. He's bent down with his arms around his body—damn near folded up like an envelope. He starts creeping up, dancing and jumping, and his plumes are going up and down—like an octopus. He's calling, "Spyboy! White Eagle! Coochie Mally!" And I'm hollering back. Oh, he's clowning so bad the asphalt's shaking. And here I am on the other end. I said, "Oh man. I got to meet this dude, brah." Everybody around me done fired me up. I knew I didn't have a choice because I had to go home with my gang. I couldn't back out.

I didn't disappoint them. When Nat didn't back down, I didn't care if he had 20 cannons. I had a 12-gauge shotgun covered in a beaded sleeve and wrapped in marabou. Nobody suspected that I had it—not even the guys on my side. I let it into the air. *Boom-boom!* Feathers go flying! Oh, we're rolling.

We opened it up. Nat ran back, but he did it with

Fred Johnson with Tootie Montana. Photograph by Michael P. Smith © The Historic New Orleans Collection, 2007.0103.3.32.

style. He stayed on top of his game. He ran up again, and when I met him, it was clean. We embraced each other. He said, "You a bad mothefucker. Boy, I love you." Because I didn't *hoombah*—back down.

That was a pivotal moment. The people I was with were proud of me. Nat was older than me. He was more experienced than me. But by catching him with the element of surprise, I showed that even though I was young, I had the heart for the game, too.

The word got out that Montana had a strong front. That shit spread like YouTube because you've got a lot of people following the Indians. They're with this tribe because they want to see them meet as many other tribes as they can meet and bust their ass in a positive way. They don't want to miss that history.

A Proposal

Yellow Pocahontas didn't have a practice. Anthony "Meathead" Hingle and I had Indian practice on the corner of Pauger and Robertson. Outside! It was cold as a motherfucker, so I went to Jerome and told him we needed a real practice. He said, "Go talk to Chief."

Tootie explained why he stopped the practice. Years before, when he was living in the Desire project, he didn't drive. On a Sunday evening, he'd stop sewing, get dressed, and catch two buses to the practice at the Crocodile Bar. It was the same bar that was across the street from my grandmother Viola! The practice was supposed to start for six, guys don't come until nine. Well, by nine, he was ready to stop the practice because he got to get up at 5:30 to be at work at 6:30.

Chief want me to do." That's a wrap. Success always breeds envy, but it was all right. I represented my gang, so they couldn't dispute that. I masked one year and I didn't even have a back apron. My helper, Java, got drunk and he didn't finish it. I said, "Forget the back apron. Let's go anyway." Say brah, when you are a part of a group, you don't make any excuses like, "Oh this don't match, I'm not going to do this." Make the day. If you don't make the day, nothing else matters. That's a Tootie Montana lesson.

Making a Phone Call

Tambourine and Fan decided to start the Bucketmen Social and Pleasure Club with adult and children's divisions. It was linked to Civil Rights and the fostering of self-pride. It was my job to hire and pay the brass bands. I would find them at the clubs they played in on Bourbon Street. I was also the one to get all the hat and shoes sizes for the members. Listen, I had 48 men on that list. Back then, they had a thing called making a phone call. And when you made a phone call, you don't stop calling until you talked to that person. That's the definition of making a phone call! So they can't say, "I didn't know. I didn't get the message. Brah, you screwed over me." I'll call you at one in the morning and apologize. You gonna be mad, but I got you!

I was told, "Molo, put the divisions together with the children." There were a minimum of 40 of them. I showed the girls how to dance like girls and the boys to dance like boys with a Eureka Brass Band album. Then I showed them how to line up in a division.

I knew how to do it by watching my uncle Sundown

Right? He was very disciplined. I said, "Well, damn Chief, I was right across the street!" That was the beauty in connecting moments in my life. "I heard y'all when I was a little boy."

I made a proposal, "If you let me start the practice, I assure you, you won't have that problem."

And he did. We were able to have a practice at Packy's grocery store—the same grocery and barroom that I used to work in as a kid. A black guy named Packy bought Jack's from Mr. Sidney and renovated it. He opened up the back barroom. The place was huge with beautiful terrazzo floors and a fireplace. We had the hippest, most spacious Indian practice in history!

We played with nothing but tambourines. No bass drums, no microphones. The only person who was allowed to come in with something different was Lionel

---

"Bird" Obicheaux—Wildman for the White Eagles. Bird would come in there with two white buckets, and he turned them over, and he'd be rolling on those buckets.

Running the practice ties into the other two disciplines I had learned from sewing and martial arts. They roll together. I came on time, I wasn't drinking or loaded, and I stayed in the circle from start to finish. Listen, when Tootie came in that practice, he was elated. All his life all he wanted to do was to be a chief and have somebody to start practice so when he got there, the practice was in full swing. The drums would be jumping in there, and he'd be fired up! That created a strong bond between us, but I also caught a lot of flak for running the practice. Other guys in the tribe said, "Fred want to be the chief."

"Never! All I want to do is be Spyboy and do what

Left: The Bucketmen parade coming down the Claiborne overpass, headed Uptown. Photograph by Eric Waters. *Right:* Tambourine and Fan curriculum reminds children that the music and dancing are part of their "moving classroom." Image courtesy of Jerome Smith.

when he was in a club called the Sixth Ward Diamonds. When I was ten years old, I saw him with his umbrella, and said, "Okay, I know what time it is."

I didn't say anything. I just followed Sundown on Claiborne Avenue when it was lined with beautiful oak trees to Holly's at Orleans and Villere. That shit was overpowering. You were on that, in that, with that, by that. I learned how to put a division together by watching his club the whole day. How they lined up, how they danced.

When a parade is done in its correct form, the pageantry is just beyond belief. It could be a grand marshal with anywhere from two to 12 people in a division. You've got to pay attention to the grand marshal. A good one is going to keep that parade moving. He's going to keep the division active. You are paired off,

and the grand marshal calls the signals. If he says, "Single file!" that division got single file! If the grand marshal says, "Put 'em down," that means if you have an umbrella or basket, you put them down. Then he might say, "Dance around it." He could tell you to crisscross, skip around, or sidestep. You keep that middle open, and wherever your partner goes, you go.

At the same time, Danny Barker was creating the Fairview Baptist Christian Band to teach young people how to play traditional jazz. We asked him if he would help Tambourine and Fan start a brass band with the help of John Longo.

New Orleans is one of the few towns where you can have a participatory parade. Every other city in America, you stand behind the barricade and you watch the parade go past you. That's not the nature of second

line culture. You may have an invisible line of demarcation, but you don't have where the whole route is barricaded. No. The parade is created so that, if you want to get in and dance, you get behind the band and dance. You want to walk and play the tambourine, the cowbell, you can get behind the band.

Once a division starts it could start off really lightly, but it's going to have a groundswell. It's going to pick up, and you want the followers. You need them because if it's only the division and the band, people would say, "Damn. Well, nobody like that group." And you know, it would not be pleasant to put in that much work, time, energy, braintrust, and money and come out the door to a lukewarm crowd. You want the biggest crowd you can get, the most festive crowd you can get, but you want a crowd that respects the division and the music.

Tambourine and Fan curriculum, courtesy of Jerome Smith. At the beginning of the day camp, students are often asked to recite the lyrics to Abel Meeropol's poem *Strange Fruit,* which was turned into a song recorded by Billie Holiday: *Southern trees bear a strange fruit / Blood on the leaves and blood at the root / Black bodies swingin' in the Southern breeze / Strange fruit hangin' from the poplar trees.* Children discuss what lynching is, and talk about the concept of "self-lynching."

The Bucketmen would go all the way Uptown to Big Time Crip's where Jerome and Rudy used to meet with other CORE organizers, and then come back downtown. Crip had one of the hippest jukeboxes in town, and played all jazz. It was the first barroom where I heard "Moody's Mood for Love."

There I go, there I go, there I go.

Land and the Landless

I masked with the YPH and worked with Tambourine and Fan for 17 years. You got to understand, when Jerome gave me the money in Hatchet's house, I was game. I was cool with that as long as it wasn't stagnant. If we're growing, we're good. If we ain't growing, we ain't no good. As an organization, I knew we had the culture down—nobody was going to beat us on the cultural side—but within the organization, Rudy began to talk more about how we needed to create an economic side, or we would always have to keep begging people to help us to do what we should be able to do ourselves. We didn't want to become a welfare group. We wanted to create some financial independence.

Rudy got sick and left the organization. He took a job at Howard University in a drug program. Then one day he sent me a letter that said, "Man, I'm going to come back home. My brother gonna run for mayor." White flight, not just in New Orleans, but all over America, meant that the more African American the urban inner city became, the larger the voting population became, which made it much easier to elect African American officials. It had already happened in New Orleans with Ernest "Dutch" Morial. And when his terms were over, there was a question of who was going to take his place. When it seemed like Morial wasn't going to back Rudy's brother, he decided not to run. Rudy said, "I don't want to run, but if my brother doesn't want to run, I'm going to."

I said, "Listen, we need to grow and move. If you run, I'm going to support you." I trusted him with my life. I sat down with Jerome and said, "Listen, Smith, I'm not sure where you are going to be at with this, but let me tell you where I'm with this. Rudy going to run. I'm going to endorse him." I wanted him to get that from me, not from anyone else.

It was 1986. I ended up being the driver for Rudy. Everywhere he went—whether it was gay people, Uptown Jewish people, Italians, whoever, I was sitting in the room. I had to change all my clothes. I had all recreational clothes. I've got to go get a tie, a shirt, a jacket! Every constituency came to the table with money and a demand list. They wanted to know how their interests were going to be protected. It was an education that I couldn't get in any of the universities because this was real time—going down, right here, right now. We had a good platform, but Rudy only won 2.4 percent of the vote, and Sidney Barthelemy had to go up against William Jefferson in the run-off. He won by appealing to white voters.

We hadn't won the election. I had done my time with Tambourine and Fan. On the back end of the campaign, we had come out with this wealth of information about housing demographics. Tim Will, one of the guys that volunteered in the campaign, said, "Why don't we start a first-time home-buyer training program?"

When they said this, I didn't know anything about housing. Nothing. I come out of a house where we would be put out because the rent wasn't being paid. Didn't even know how to spell mortgage. But one thing you're going to know: Rent doesn't decrease, rent increases. A mortgage has a beginning and an end. Rent has a beginning, but it has no ending.

I was on a learning curve. I wanted to give it 300 percent. I stopped all my cultural stuff because I

Fred Johnson holding up a photograph of himself masking with the Yellow Pocahontas that is at his office at the New Orleans Neighborhood Development Foundation in 2014. Photograph by Bruce Sunpie Barnes.

wanted to be focused. Masking Indian, I put a lot on hold. Now it was time for me to start moving them. I needed to buy a house. I had to put my daughter through college. None of those things was happening as long as I was masking Indian. I changed my work schedule so I wouldn't have time to sew a suit. I got to work at nine and I don't get off until ten at night. My underpinning was Malcolm X's sermon where he said in every war that's been fought in the annals of history it's been the landlord against the landless. Land is the basis of all independence.

A lot of people thought that success was buying a house outside of the old city. When I bought a house, I wasn't going to move to the suburbs because I wanted to be where if I don't have a car—I can walk or get a taxi. I don't want to cross no high rise bridge every day. I'm urban. I'm fucking urban to the core. Now, I'll go out for a little while, but I'm a homing pigeon—I'm coming back. I like the sirens, the loud music. I want to walk out the door and somebody is speaking to me. I don't want to be stuck out somewhere that's so quiet you can hear your heartbeat. No. I want to be able to walk out of my door where there's life. I look at some subdivisions and there ain't nobody moving—like a cemetery for living people!

There's no tambourine ringing outside the city. Now, I'm not knocking the people who live there. I'm just saying that ain't for me, and people should consider what they have given up. Why does everybody come this way for Mardi Gras? If it is so *all that*, why you're coming this way? And now the white people are buying up the urban city. That's where the synergy is.

I'm a YPH until the day I die. When I was doing that, I did that. I represented that gang, and my chief.

I still like going to the Indian practice to get my spirit on, to feel the rhythm of the tambourines. When the tambourines and singing are right with the beat, the dancing is that much slicker and smoother. There's that's call and response back there:

Going uptown
Two way pock away.
Nobody kneel down
Two way pock away
Nobody hoombah

Which is like the church, you know. There is a lead and then a response from the second line, and you dance with your partner to the beat of the drum. When it's done beautifully, it's going to electrify the practice.

In or out of a suit, I fired Tootie up, because we had that kind of rapport. When I wasn't masking, I would always go to him and say, "Listen Chief, today is Friday before Mardi Gras, I'm gonna be here with you Friday through Tuesday." You can't buy that. He knew if he gave me his apron, I knew what to do. It's called experience. I know how to tack it down. He don't have to worry about that. Give me som-ething else. And if I tell you I'm going to be here, I'm going to be there. I'm not drunk. I'm not smoking weed. I'm sitting here, and I'm going to give you five or more hours each night.

I always looked forward to the Sunday before Mardi Gras. It was the last practice of the season. The old timers in the Yellow Pocahontas would get dressed up to celebrate that we were bringing it to a close. Cats would put on a suit and tie, and spiff it up a little bit. The next time, when they came together as a group, it would be Mardi Gras morning, and they would have a totally a different suit on. A costume.

Fred dressed in a suit on the Sunday practice before Mardi Gras. Photograph by Michael P. Smith © The Historic New Orleans Collection, 2007.0103.4.194.

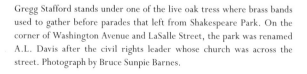

Gregg Stafford stands under one of the live oak tress where brass bands used to gather before parades that left from Shakespeare Park. On the corner of Washington Avenue and LaSalle Street, the park was renamed A.L. Davis after the civil rights leader whose church was across the street. Photograph by Bruce Sunpie Barnes.

The Dew Drop Inn was located just up the street from Shakespeare Park at 2836 LaSalle. The Dew Drop Inn's music venue supported jazz and R&B, and was frequented by black and white patrons. The owner, Frank Painia launched his own protests against city ordinances that enforced Jim Crow, and at one point went to jail for violating segregation laws. Photograph by Ralston Crawford, courtesy of the Hogan Jazz Archive.

GREGG STAFFORD

Bruce: Gregg Stafford is a trumpet player and bass drummer who has played with brass bands all over the city, including the E. Gibson, Doc Paulin, Fairview Baptist Church, Hurricane, Onward, and Young Tuxedo. Many of his mentors were the musicians who created the New Orleans Jazz Revival period, and he has been a bridge from old to young. He sat for thousands of hours with older musicians and learned how they played. Gregg can be stern about keeping the music true to an older era, but he's also very funny. Sidesplitting funny.

For years, he also played with Danny Barker and the Jazz Hounds. At a gig, Danny would wear a bowler hat, two-tone shoes, pinstriped pants, and a checkered jacket. He cocked his banjo down to the left. He strummed and told stories. He dropped jokes, one-liners. He would seamlessly put anyone in the room into a song, and keep it rolling. He could tell who was really interested in the music. Before you could get to him, he got to you: "I see you studying up over there with your notepad." Of all the people who studied with him, Danny entrusted his band to Gregg. A public school teacher, Gregg is also the leader of the Young Tuxedo Brass Band, and the Heritage Hall Jazz Band.

Left: Reverend C.C. Taylor, minister of St. John IV Missionary Baptist Church, was the leader of the Freedmen's Association and the Ideal Missionary Baptist and Educational Association. He died in his early 40s, and Reverend Dr. Earl Willie Horsey took over the church. Photograph courtesy of the Stafford family. Right: Mural portrait of A.L. Davis in Shakespeare Park, which was renamed in his honor. Davis' family followed the migration of many black families in the area, moving from Bayou Goula on River Road to Central City. As minister of the New Zion Baptist Church, he hosted the Southern Christian Leadership Conference's first official gathering on February 14, 1957. Photograph by Bruce Sunpie Barnes.

Introduction: Central City

Gregg: My story starts where I was raised up in New Orleans on Second and Freret. A lot of black families from the plantations on River Road and south of New Orleans moved to this part of the city. Many of the men worked on the riverfront, and many others played music. A lot of legendary jazz pioneers lived in that area, from Kid Ory to Buddy Bolden to Doc Paulin.

My family came from Lockport, Louisiana. My mother, Helen, was primarily a domestic homekeeper. When I was young, she worked on St. Charles Avenue cleaning people's houses, and then stayed home with us. My father, Amos, was a longshoreman. We lived across the street from the original Snug Harbor. On Friday nights my parents, two sisters, and I visited our great aunts on the 2400 block of Second Street because that was fish fry night, and our entire family would gather. We enjoyed riding down Freret Street, making that turn towards LaSalle, and passing the Dew Drop Inn. In the 1950s, the Dew Drop was popping—people would be standing out in front of the place to see Ernie K-Doe or Lee Dorsey.

When I was seven years old, we moved next door to our great aunts. The 2400 block was full of black children like myself, and the 2300 block of Freret that intersected our street was highly populated with white kids. We played football, shot marbles, rode our bikes together. But, according to the institutions, when it was time to go to school, they went one direction, we went the other direction.

Church was another place where there was often strict racial divide. All over Central City, there were small black Baptist churches. When we moved to the neighborhood, I was baptized at St. John the IV Missionary Baptist Church—the same one that Buddy Bolden attended. For many years, my mother's cousin, the Reverend C.C. Taylor, had been the minister. He was a mentor for other preachers like A.L. Davis.

We stayed only one block from Shakespeare Park, which was the setting for so many social gatherings. There was an Olympic-size track with bleachers that could hold at least 800 people. During the Civil Rights Movement, people would gather to listen to Ernest Wright. He was arrested more than 60 times

Shakespeare Park is also an important meeting place for Mardi Gras Indians who gather there on Carnival, St. Joseph's Night, and Uptown Super Sunday (*shown here in 2012*) organized by the Mardi Gras Indian Council. Photograph by Bruce Sunpie Barnes.

for speaking out against Jim Crow segregation. After Martin Luther King Jr. was assassinated in 1968, the religious and civic leaders had everyone come to the park to keep the peace in the community.

On Sundays, it was also the beginning of all kinds of parades hosted by churches and organizations that went around the neighborhood. That's where I really became aware of second lines, and the Masonic and Eastern Star parades. There were Baptist churches all over the area that also hosted parades. Many of the them finished at St. John IV Missionary Baptist Church.

When I was seven, we were walking back from church near the Magnolia housing projects, and people were watching a parade. I peeked through the crowd, and the first thing I saw was this beautiful burst of color—powder blue and pink—with tall men with fans and baskets. I had never seen anything like that in my life. I was just stunned. I couldn't move. And they had happened to stop there, and they were dancing in a little formation, with big smiles.

Left: In 2012, a Palm Sunday parade sponsored by Holy Trinity Church moves through the Broadmoor neighborhood with a brass band playing spirituals. Photograph by Bruce Sunpie Barnes.

Instrumental Music

My mother and father started going through some problems, and they separated. I kept to my books. I went to school right next to the park at Carter G. Woodson Middle School. Under the direction of Walter Harris, our band had won state championships year after year. I wanted to join the band, but when I brought home the consent form, my mother said, "No, no, no." Looking at running a household on her own, she didn't feel like she could afford to buy me an instrument. She had to get a job, and when she found one at Woolworths on Canal and North Rampart, she moved downtown to be closer to work.

I moved with my mother, but I wanted to go to high school Uptown at Walter C. Cohen. I stayed out of school for about six weeks, trying to get into school. My mother thought I was trying to drop out. When I got in, the principal stated that I could only have the choice of taking instrumental music, vocal music, or home economics for an elective. I wasn't sure what I was going to take, but I knew I wasn't taking home

Walter C. Cohen's Marching Band, with Gregg Stafford in the front row on the right. Photograph from the high school year book.

FRONT: Elard Phillips (Drum Major), Kevin Barnes, Nedra Charles, Leroy Williams, Tyrone Watson, Clarence Jackson, Van Odom, Larry Jefferson, Odilee Elias, Alma DeLandro, and Marsha Williams.
CENTER: Harold Carter, Albert Ransom, Henry Johnson, Gregory Jones, Joe Hardy, Harold Joseph, Tyrone Ellis, Debra Nolan, and Gerald Hawkins.
BACK: Albert Jack, Curley Cosey, Antoine Duncan, Ralph Caesar, Samuel Evans, Moses Gordon and Rodney Bridges and Richard Porter.

FRONT: Michael Patterson, Shelia Sutton, Reginald Walker, Debra Parnell, Mack McLaurin, Emel Hunter, Gregory Stafford, Sandra Thompson, Jerald Smith, Cornell Coulon and Dwight Clark (Drum Major).
CENTER: Michael Washington, Bruce Lee, Levi McCaskill, Gwendolyn DeCoud, Joshua Clark, Alvin Cooper, Michael Converson, Terrence Young and Bruce Blanchard.
BACK: Bonita Saulsbury, Luther Doss, Byron Rousell, Norman Caesar, Joseph Mayfield, James Sterling and Robert Butler.

economics! But if I knew then what I know now, I probably would have taken that class.

As I walked out of the office, the band director, Solomon Spencer, came up behind me and tapped me on my shoulder. He had been listening to the principal and said, "Open your mouth and grit your teeth." I'm looking at him. "Just do what I say." I gritted my teeth. He said, "Take instrumental music."
"I don't have an instrument."
"Don't worry about it, I'll give you one."

I pretty much knew my mother wasn't going to be okay with that, but I when I got home I asked her anyway. "No, no, you're not taking music. You can't take music."

"Well, the band director said he would give me an instrument."

"No, I'm not signing that paper."

I had to go back to school the next day and explain she said I would probably lose the instrument and then she'd be responsible for paying for it. He said, "Don't worry about that. You won't be held responsible for it." Despite reassurances, my mother still refused. I cried all night. And you know, she got up the next morning and said, "Okay, I'm going to sign this paper."

Solomon Spencer told me, "I'm going to give you this cornet." It was green, tarnished, and banged up. I said, "I can't play that instrument!" I'm more concerned about my health because the horn was so old and hadn't been touched in years. And it smelled bad.

My band director said, "I'm going to give you some polish. You are going to clean this up, and you are going to use this horn." I said, "Well, I want to play tenor sax anyway."

He said, "No, you're not. You're going to play cornet." I started in the beginner's class, and was told if I did well, I would be placed in the band the next year. I studied hard. I would go home every day and build my chops up, learn my scales, and before I went into my junior year, I got into the band. Right around this time, my mother had a heart attack. She never fully recovered and had to go on disability. She saw that I loved music, but it worried her. She wanted to make sure I'd be able to support myself.

Union and Scab Bands

I got my first break into the professional world of music after Cohen played the homecoming parade for Tulane University. Julius Lewis, a saxophone player, and I were walking back to the school bus with some of our other band members, and we walked past some guys affiliation with the E. Gibson Brass Band standing in the parking lot. In those days, there were union bands and nonunion bands. The union bands were the Tuxedo, Onward, Olympia, and Eureka. They played mostly all the big time brass band jobs. The other bands were called nonunion bands, or scab bands. They were the bands that were underbidding the union bands. Doc Paulin's band, E. Gibson Brass Band, and John McNeal's Reliance Brass Band. Most of the bands would parade Uptown.

Johnny Winberly, the bandleader of the E. Gibson Brass Band, called out, "Excuse me. You saxophone players, would y'all be interested in playing this kind of music?"

Those saxophone players had R&B and funk bands that were inspired by groups like the Meters. High school students all around the city had their own groups.

Downtown, they had groups called Sage and Chocolate Milk. Uptown, Julius played for a group called Sound Corporation, and there were other bands called the Blue Pearl and MG Funk. During the day, they played for their school bands, but at night they played club gigs with false identification cards. Julius and the other sax players declined the offer, but I said, "I would be interested in playing."

He looked at me and said, "We don't need any trumpets."

I started walking away and he called out, "Hey, wait a minute. Give me your number anyway. If something comes up, I may give you a call."

Two weeks passed. He called me, "Look, I've got an Elk's parade coming up at the end of the month. I'm gonna have two bands and I was thinking about you, so if you can make some of these rehearsals, I'll put you in with the band." Antony "Tuba Fat" Lacen was already a member of the E. Gibson Band. We lived a few blocks from each other so he gave me a ride to the practice. I learned songs like *Bye and Bye*, *Lord, Lord, Lord* and *Just A Little While to Stay Here* to play in the Elk's parade that started at Shakespeare Park.

The Elks were one of the oldest clubs with a big membership. Prior to the insurance industry coming in, that's how members paid their medical bills and funeral costs. Some of them belonged to two or three organizations like the Masons or the Odd Fellows. A lot of people don't really know about the history of all that, but those people were proud of what they were about. They had parades for their members' funerals. They marched so proudly. It could have been a regular carpenter, a laborer, but when he died, it was like a homegoing for a president.

Some of these people belonged to three or four organizations. They all came out with their own bands for

that one individual. The memberships stretched five or six blocks long with their beautiful uniforms— dark navy blue serge suits, each member wore a sword, and their beautiful hats with the plumes. Elk's members had royal blue and khaki colored suits with gold threading. I started playing these these gigs more regularly, but I didn't know why they included brass band music. No one ever explained to me where it all came from.

Nearby in the Irish Channel, there were white social clubs like the Delachaise Marching Club, Pete Fountain's Half-Fast Marching Club, the Buzzards, Frankie and Johnny's, and the Lyon's Club. They were social and pleasure clubs for white people, but they hired black brass bands for their parades. On Mardi Gras, we had to be at the Delachaise Marching Club's clubhouse at Eighth and Chippewa for five in the morning. We would march all around the Irish Channel, criss-crossing with other bands like Doc Paulin or the Tuxedo. Over a span of 12 hours, we paraded all the way to Canal Street and back Uptown.

The Civil Rights Movement brought in a lot of change that broke up cultural aspects of the music from a number of directions. After integration, people could buy insurance through big companies like Prudential. There was less need to become members of these organizations. At the same time, after the integration movement, all the marching clubs of the Irish Channel went with the white flight out to suburbs like Metairie and Chalmette.

In 1969, the American Federation of Musicians forced the local black and white musicians unions to merge. At first there was a dual presidency, but, eventually, Ted Weinstein became president and Louis Cottrell, Jr. became vice president. Some people expect it just to be that way. Still to this day, there are a lot of things going on around race in New Orleans that are not right. I guess Mr. Cottrell was very noble. I don't

Top: The Elks lodge members in the late 1940s. Photograph by J.V. Myers, courtesy of the Hogan Jazz Archive. *Middle:* The Delachaise Carnival Club in 1963. Photograph by Jack Hurley, courtesy of the Hogan Jazz Archive. *Bottom:* The Excelsior Brass Band, courtesy of the Jules Cahn Collection at The Historic New Orleans Collection, 2000.78.1.33

think he was the type of guy who was willing to fight or challenge that.

Southern Activism

After I graduated, I majored in elementary education at Southern University of New Orleans (SUNO), a historically black university by Lake Pontchartrain that was actually created after *Brown v. Board of Education*. Some say it was created to prevent integration on a deeper level, but it also created a more affordable alternative to HBCUs like Dillard and Xavier.

In 1972, I attended the Southern Christian Leadership Conference in New Orleans. Their organizing had helped lead to things like the Voting Rights Act, but that didn't mean that there was equality in the support of black education, health care, or housing. They organized a parade from St. Bernard and North Claiborne at Hunter's Field all the way to Shakespeare Park, and I got a chance to hear the Fairview Baptist Church Band perform. Now second lines and Baptist churches in New Orleans do not always mix. Many preachers did not want to associate themselves with social and pleasure clubs because they hosted their parades at the same time as church services were going on. Some preachers I was raised up around did not think of dancing in the street as the right political or spiritual statement. I thought it was interesting that the Fairview was a church that was supporting traditional jazz. I knew I wanted to meet that group of young musicians at some point.

It had been more than a decade since students in Louisiana started the Louisiana Chapter of CORE. Black students were still protesting. On November 16, 1972, Students United at Southern University in Baton Rouge protested against the inequity in funding between the Southern and Louisiana State University systems, and demanded more say in the curriculum.

During protests at Southern University in 1972 by Students United, the Baton Rouge police officers used tear gas to disperse the crowd, and are suspected of the rounds of gunfire that left two students dead. Photograph courtesy of the Denver Smith and Leonard Brown Collection, Archives and Manuscripts Department, John B. Cade Library, Southern University and A&M College, Baton Rouge.

Two students, Denver A. Smith and Leonard Douglas Brown, were shot and killed.

SUNO was funded even less than the main campus. Throughout the fall semester of 1972, students were leading boycotts and demonstrations to demand equality in education. After the students were killed at the main campus, they demanded a full investigation into the shootings and organized a take over of the SUNO administration building. The chancellor and the dean of academic affairs were rolled out in their chairs, and I joined hundreds of students who moved into the building for a few days. We were told that the National Guard was going to come in and remove us. We tried to stand our ground through the feeling of fear—not knowing what was going to happen after the shooting in Baton Rouge. The Louisiana Board of Education started claiming that if we didn't return to class they would close down the school. Some of the ministers in New Orleans brokered an agreement, and classes resumed.

To support myself through school, I worked the graveyard shift at Perky's Pancake Parlor, an all night diner on the 500 block of Bourbon Street in the French Quarter. See this place, most of the musicians would come there and have breakfast after they'd get off. People like Louis Prima, Thomas Jefferson, and a trombonist named Show Boy Thomas would come every night, and we would talk music. He worked with Danny Barker at the Maison Bourbon with George Finola's Band. I told him I was playing in brass bands Uptown. He said, "Oh, you're a young man, you might be interested in my friend Danny's band. He's got a young church band."

Meeting Mr. Barker was my chance to get involved. He said, "Yeah, I got a band. Young cats your age. We rehearse on Thursday nights. Come on down and meet the guys, and see if you'd like to be a part of it."

DANNY BARKER
A CULT ONTO ITSELF

Danny: *My name is Daniel Moses Barker, Jr. My mother met my father, and of that union, I was born into this world against my will—this cruel world!—on 1909, January 13. I was raised between two Christian religions. My father's people were Baptist—hard-shelled Baptists. And my mother's folks were lukewarm Catholics. I was baptized in St. Louis Cathedral.*

Until I was six years old, I lived with my grandparents in a tenement at 1027 Chartres Street in the French Quarters. New Orleans had apartment buildings before people in the rest of the country knew what they were. I lived there until I was six years old, and then I moved with my mother into the Seventh Ward on Bourbon, which is called Pauger now, and St. Claude.

In the Vieux Carre, I'd hear these workmen passing in front of our tenement singing blues and laments, and gypsies sing-ing their music. Every Sunday morning, this old colored lady would stand near the St. Mary's Catholic Church on the corner of Chartres and Ursulines selling callas. In fact, I used to buy some from her and got a good look at her. She was extremely old and small. She was real dark with kinky white hair covered in a tignon, and she had sky blue eyes. That's what used to fascinate me.

Down By the Riverside

My father's father came from Kentucky. It's a mystery to me how he came down South and didn't go North. I think he was employed on one of the riverboats and he settled in New Iberia, where he met my grandmother. She bore him four children and moved to New Orleans with him. He worked as a longshoreman on the riverfront, and she was a marchande *lady—a merchant. The first music I remember hearing her voice, singing such classics as* Down by the Riverside *while she was doing her work around the kitchen. "I'm going to lay my burden down." That's what she would sing. If you ever hear Bunk Johnson's version it's, "Down by the riverside, I'm going to lay my weapons down."*

From our apartment, I could hear these long, drawn-out steamboat blasts at the arrival and departure of the boats, and all kinds of weird whistles from those river pilots. My young cousins and I would help my grandmother with big baskets of food full of red beans and rice, and hot biscuits. Around 11:30, we would leave for the river just as the whistle would blow for the gangs to break. She would find cotton bales and place all the food on top.

On a payday, the blind men would come out and play the guitar for the workmen as they gathered around to get paid. One named Blind Tom was sensational. News would spread, and in 15 minutes you'd have 200 people gathered around. The first time I had to push through the crowd to see what was the excitement. Who was sitting on a crate but this old blind man in his 50s playing these blues on the guitar and singing the Ballad of the Titanic, *because the men on the river knew about boats. He sang about the millionaires who were cry-ing and screaming that they didn't want to go down with the boat. He described the iceberg, and how all these women were going down in the salt of the sea to waste where them sharks were going to eat them up.*

Once, I was on the riverfront, and the newsperson said, "Here comes that Bald Eagle!" It was the last of the river rogue—like some kind of pirate ship—with a rugged crew. I looked up and the Bald Eagle was steaming down the river like a bat out of hell. Both of them chimneys throwing sparks and steam. And the captain didn't seem like he cared about no captain on the river. He passed close to the excursion boats, and in its wake, would leave cinders flying all over.

Most of the riverboats had calliopes. It's similar to a piano, but it worked by steam with copper keys on it. You had to play it with gloves on, and a raincoat and a rain hat over your uni-form because the steam came from all directions. The keys get awfully hot, and you had to hit them staccato. Long, whole notes would scorch your fingers. It was a real haunting sound before the city got so commercial with electric wires. Without the noise of the trucks, you could hear it real clear. When I was about ten years old, Fate Marable used to give a half-hour concert around seven o'clock before the boat would depart. I think he was one of the greatest calliope players of all time.

The Onward Brass Band

My mother, Rose Barbarin, was the daughter of Isidore Bar-barin, who was the original leader of the Onward Brass Band. The brass band was a cult onto itself. A lot of those guys used to love that music for the fun of it. The money wasn't too much. It was hard to make a living. My grandfather worked as a coachman for undertakers.

Spasm bands in New Orleans, circa 1910s. Photographs by Dan Leyrer courtesy of the Hogan Jazz Archive.

become accepted with the older musicians. They give you a break. They call a youngster who they know who's competent to sit in the band and let him play. That was before the unions became powerful.

I had three uncles who played drums: Paul, Louis, and Lucien Barbarin. Naturally, I'd sit behind Lucien's drums and play during intermissions. My Uncle Paul went up to Chicago with King Oliver and came back in 1921 with a clarinet. He suggested I take some lessons. I took half a dozen with Barney Bigard, who told me to leave the clarinet at home and come get the notes first. I drifted off from it because I wanted to blow something right away.

Around 1923 was the Charleston era, and everyone was buying ukuleles and balloon skirt dresses. My Aunt Theresa bought a banjo ukelele. She tried it for awhile and she left it around the house, so I started fooling around with it. She didn't mind. I started acting like it was mine. She said, "Where's my uke?"

"It's at home."

She told me, "It don't belong to you." I said, "Well, would you sell it to me?" She said, "Yeah, I paid seven dollars for it." I said, "I'll pay you on an installment plan." She said, "No, give me one dollar and you can have it."

I didn't know how to tune it. There was a guy around the corner from me named Ashton Murray, who was a piano player and a school teacher. I knocked on his door every evening and asked him to tune it for me. Finally, he told me to listen to the tone of the strings, and I could learn to tune it like that.

I organized a little tramp band. It was four of us. Along with my ukelele, it was a little guy made up a jive set up drums with washboard and little contraptions, a kazoo player, and another guy with a makeshift tambourine. I called the group the Boozan King. Boozan means "good time" in patois. It was a very popular word. "I'm going over to so and so. They are having a boozan over there."

My daddy separated from my mother. She remarried, and my uncles used to take me up to get some coins from my daddy. He owned a bar in the red light district above Basin Street. There was the other section above Canal on Franklin and Gasket. Ever heard of that street, Gasket? That was a notorious street. I got a chance to see the painted ladies in the evening and hear the noise out the jukebox. I saw the organ grinder on the street. He went from barroom to barroom playing the melodies of the day: China Town, Alexander's Ragtime Band, St. Louis Blues.

My uncles knew a lot about music, and whenever a band was parading because my grandfather knew about it—at least Downtown. They would second line and take me with them.

My uncles would always stick with the band—they wouldn't be with the second liners—because they were curious to see who was playing. All the kids idolized the jazzmen. There were dozens of bands in dozens of halls in all levels of society. Like most kids today, you see them everybody interested in the football or baseball teams. But in New Orleans, the kids were interested in the bands. Whose band was great? Around the 1920s, a lot of the trumpet and clarinet players became famous and left New Orleans. You heard about them having success away from here and that inspired you to learn to play an instrument.

Some kids they learn real fast—they're real apt and they're diligent in their studies so they improve right away they

About seven o'clock at night, we used to sneak off to the District and go into the barrooms. I'd go and ask the bartender if we could play a couple of tunes—Little Liza Jane, My Blue Heaven—and pass the hat around. In other words, we'd hustle. The group got popular. We played on the stoop after school and all the kids in the neighborhood would congregate. We'd have our rehearsals in the street, and it would be a nice thing. We organized a little club with about 18 members and started giving parties. And then other kids would hire us to play for their parties, and we became very popular.

When I was about 14, there was an advertisement for Kid Rena's band on the corner of Marais and Annette. Sun Thomas was supposed to be playing the banjo, but he was drunk so the band sat him in the back corner of the furniture wagon with the drums. One of the musicians was sitting on the tailgate, and said, "Hey little Barbarin. Can you play banjo?" I said "No." He said, "Come up here." I climb up in the wagon and sat down. He said, "I'll tune it for you." I sat in the band. All the people in the second line watched me play, and I was like a hero because the banjo is real important in a band without a piano.

I had a little reputation from that. "This kid could be a wonderful banjo player if he had a banjo." My Uncle Paul was back in Chicago with King Oliver, and when I told him what happened, he sent me a banjo. I worked with bands around town until the Depression hit New Orleans. A lot of musicians were leaving because there weren't no money. I had a wife, a house, and a houseful of furniture. My Uncle Paul was in New York and asked me, "How you doing?" I said, "I'm not doing. I'm not working! Bills piled up on me." He said, "Well, come up to New York, there's plenty of work up here."

New York City

In New York, I started playing in big bands. They were arrangement conscious. Everybody wanted to have a special type of arrangement so they'll have a different sound from somebody else. When you hear a record, you can tell it's a Glen Miller sound, a Duke Ellington or a Count Basie sound.

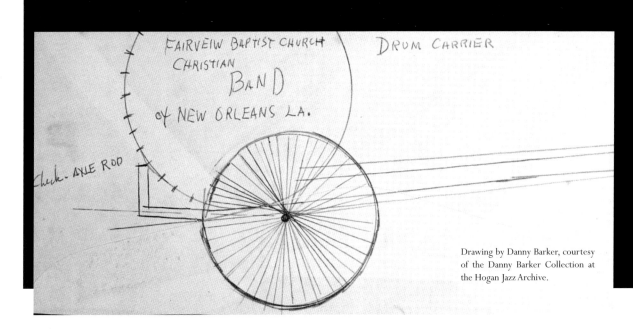

Drawing by Danny Barker, courtesy of the Danny Barker Collection at the Hogan Jazz Archive.

That's how you had to make it. You had to have something individual. You couldn't sound like somebody else.

I went with Cab Calloway's band in 1939 and stayed with him for nine years. My wife, Blue Lu, is a singer, and she made some records for Decca which were quite popular with the black populace. They were called Race Records and they played them on black jukeboxes. She recorded my tune Don't You Feel My Leg, but the federal government made Decca Records stop pressing those records because they were considered risqué.

I left Cab Calloway's band in 1946 and formed a little band of my own, which was quite a problem trying to get booked because there's so much keen competition in New York City. There's just thousands of people trying to do the same thing you can do. Sometimes they can do it better than you can do. I went through this bag, running to agents, playing jobs, and just barely making it.

A New Dress

In the early 1960s, my wife's mother had taken sick so she left me up there in an apartment while she came down to New Orleans for nine months. And she said she liked it. She never liked it before. She didn't want to come back here because they had all these Jim Crow laws, these signs you had to abide by: White only, black only. But with the Civil Rights Act all that was broken up and it gave you some relief. The pressure was somewhat off because it was a nuisance man, all these signs around. So I said, "Well, I suppose I come on." She said, "All right, pack the things up."

And this is about the best time I've had since I've been playing music. Since I've been here, it's been relaxed. No pressure. And I got a reasonable amount of work. New Orleans jazz was at the beginning and it'll always be here. Eventually, they'll put it in the schools where the records will be available to youngsters in the bands. The whole rigamarole of jazz, all the way from the beginning from folk and work songs to ragtime to jazz. All that music has been well documented by the original people who created it. In the future, the youngsters will be able to pick up like the Europeans are doing now. It will be a vintage thing, like old cars. You can't expect it to stay in the forefront because there's always music piled on top of it, but you can always take the music and give it a new dress.

This edited transcript comes from an oral history with Danny Barker conducted by Richard B. Allen in New York City on June 30, 1959, and a transcript for the movie Red Beans and Ricely Yours, archived at the Hogan Jazz Archive.

The Fairview "New Orleans" (1)
"Jazz" Institute—

Organized 1971 — — by Danny Barker
at the suggestion of Rev. Andrew Darby
Pastor of the Fairview Baptist Church —
Danny, Rev. Darby and Charles Barbarin
whose two young sons Charlie and
Lucien — and grand children Jerry and
Deanna — were the first members of
the Fairview band. —
— The Idea of reviving the ~~interest~~
interest — of young people — musically
inclined — to learn and play Jazz —
The traditional Jazz of King Oliver
Buddy Bolden Jack Carey — Bechet
Louis Armstrong — composers Clarence
Williams, Jelly Roll Morton, Spencer
Williams — and hundreds others many
Innovators forgotten —
The musicians who still continued to
~~was~~ present and perform, playing the
~~if catenory~~ outdoor street marching
music — rarely encouraged Youngsters
to join — the ranks — — playing the
street music — One of the most

Left and right: Writings from Danny Barker outlining a music program for young people to learn traditional jazz. Image courtesy of the Hogan Jazz Archive. Many of the musicians that Danny calls out started playing when they were teenagers. *Clockwise above:* Buddy Bolden (*with cornet*), Jelly Roll Morton, Kid Ory (*playing the trombone with his legs crossed*), and Sidney Bechet. Kid Ory was leading a little orchestra in Woodland Plantation out in LaPlace when he was only 13 years old. He said, *We made a homemade violin, bass viol, guitar, banjo, played on a chair for drums. We saved all the money we made, except for 15 cents a piece for carfare, so we could buy good instruments. We used to go round crowds and hustle. We saved the money and I decided to give picnics with beer, salad—15 cents to come in and dance...We used to go down to New Orleans on the weekends to hear the different bands that played in the parks.* Photographs courtesy of the Louisiana State Museum.

captivating, exciting scenes the eyes
ears, legs, feet — the heart —
Every moving part of the
restless body — have got to
pulsate — vibrate — "Dance that thing"

If you are serious, observant look
about and you will also see dogs
out there — in the midst —
"Dancing and doing that thing"
I had been wondering about the
plight of New Orleans Jazz —
considered — old. out of date. — passe
I would hear all these chicky —
Exclamations. — But that's
the mental attitude attitude of each
emerging — generation — —
The U.S. is geared — mentally
restless for the new thing — in some
The latest new car.
The ... new Clothes.
            Hats shoes — food,
attitudes Did you see the new dance
the sparse clothes the girls are
wearing —
From my serious observance of
Bands, dancers — atmosphere create
by the music —

I've recalled the 3 scenes, the Brass
bands create especially after
the dead are released and the huge
crowds get geared up — then explode
bedlam, charged up by the the
rythm. and sounds of the Brass bands.
Poor Willie is gone — He troubles
are over — He gone to Glory.
Give the happy noise unto the
"Lord"
Oh what dancing
            & Prancing.
            Wiggling —
What strange expression of the dancers
            faces.
You'll see peoples of all ages
out there dancing — Dozens dancing
prancing strutting wobbling — They are
doing dances of their time — age etc.
These dances have names — the dances
will swear by the names origin — etc.
Yeah. yeah — but old folk looking on
seriously observing — will grunt that
that's the Zoobeedoo — We used to do that
dance 80 years ago — Same thing cooked over

THE FAIRVIEW BAPTIST CHURCH CHRISTIAN BAND OF NEW ORLEANS

Left: Community outreach for the Fairview Baptist Church Christian Band organized by Danny Barker gives a brief history of the band and its affiliation with the church. *Right:* An early publicity photograph of the Fairview that Danny Barker kept in his personal files. Images courtesy of the Danny Barker Collection at the Hogan Jazz Achive.

The Fairview Baptist Christian Band

Gregg: Mr. Barker started the Fairview in 1971. There were 12 of us who would meet in Leroy Jones' mother's garage. Mr. Barker would give us lectures about older musicians like Freddie Keppard or Buddy Bolden. He was directing us so we would understand where the music came from.

Then he brought in records by the Tuxedo and Eureka Brass Bands. He'd say, "If you don't know the song, just listen. And when you feel like you can play it, play." You could learn the melody of the songs, but if you kept listening, you could also hear the differences in the way that musicians played their instrument. On the Eureka Brass Band's version of *Joe Avery's Blues*, Kid Shiek played a lot of blue notes, then he'd lay out and come back in with something else. It was different from Percy Humphrey, who played flowing melodic lines. When you studied it closely, you could pick them out at parades, too.

Lucien Barbarin's father, Charles, was Mr. Barker's personal assistant. The two of them really supervised the band. He was a musician who had stopped playing music because he had some problems with his health, but being with Mr. Barker gave him a purpose. He was very much involved in scheduling and making sure we had rides. If Mr. Barker couldn't make it, he'd tell us, "I won't be there, fellas. Charlie's going to be there for y'all."

The band became so popular that young kids came from all over the city. It grew to 30. Mr. Barker told us to teach the new players, and we learned how to share songs. The band got so big he had to split us up into three different bands for gigs. He'd give me a band, one to Leroy with Lucien, and one to Herlin Riley, who was playing trumpet at the time. There were all these independent filmmakers coming in from Japan and Germany, and we became very important.

Sometimes he would tell me, "Look, I'm doing something over there with Jerome, Fred and them, can you meet me over there, and we'll try to teach some of these kids some of these songs?" I went over to work with the kids at Tambourine and Fan, and we played in the Bucketmen's parade. We got so popular to where some of the older musicians were responsible for breaking up the band. They felt like these young kids were beginning to get their work—it was a threat.

A Lot of Wind

The Musicians Union had a strong foothold in all the social activities—the conventions and the nightclubs, the bars. You had to have a union card to get those gigs, and they used to have delegates walk around to check. If you were perceived to be undercutting union bands, you could be brought before the Musicians Union Board, and that's what eventually happened with Mr. Barker. With the merger of the black and white unions, Louis Cottrell, Jr. was now vice president, but he was still considered the pope amongst black musicians and got plenty of respect. He was also the leader of the Onward Brass Band. Mr. Barker was the grand marshal for the Onward. The two men knew each other very well. When it came to evaulating what was going on, honestly speaking, Louis Cottrell was a fair person. He understood the need for younger musicians, but had to pretty much uphold the union's rules and regulations—the bylaws. The union told Mr. Barker if he did not cut ties with us, he would be fined.

Mr. Barker told us, "I can't have nothing to do with y'all now. Y'all need to go out on your own." He went and got cards made that said "Hurricane Brass Band," and put it in Leroy Jones' name.

Leroy and I used to run the band. The other members were Lucien and Charlie Barbarin, Kevin Harris, Tuba Fat, Joe Torregano, Gregory Davis, and Darryl Adams. I had a little yellow sports coupe Camaro, and that was our means of transportation. We were

Left: Danny Barker as grand marshal of the Onward Brass Band. Photograph courtesy of the Jules Cahn Collection at The Historic New Orleans Collection, 2000.78.1.151. **Middle:** The Fairview with Leroy Jones as leader. Songs in their repetoire included hyms like *Down by the Riverside*, *Just a Little While to Stay Here*, *The Saints*, *Just a Closer Walk with Thee*, *God's Going to Set This World on Fire*, and *Lord, Lord, Lord*, as well as other songs such as *Bourbon Street Parade*, *Battle Hymn of the Republic*, and *Joe Avery's Blues*. Photograph by Michael P. Smith © The Historic New Orleans Collection, 2000.0130.4.379 **Right:** Tuba Fat with the Hurricane Brass Band. Tuba explained his involvement: *By the time I got in with Danny Barker and the Fairview band, I was a grown man in my mid 20s. What happened, Gregg Stafford came to me. Danny needed somebody to play tuba with the band; the kids couldn't get the tuba together. So I shaved my beard off and went down there.* Photograph courtesy of the Jules Cahn Collection at The Historic New Orleans Collection, 2000.78.1.75.

the first young band on the street in a long time, and we added to the music based on what else we were involved in. A saxophonist, Leroy Robinet, wrote a song called *Leroy Special* as a gift to Leroy and the band. That was unprecedented. At the time, the Indian song *Hey Pocky Way* was popular. During a street parade, Tuba Fat started playing this riff off the song, and another saxophonist, Hank Freeman, fed Leroy and me horn riffs to go with Tuba's bass lines. We called the song *Tuba Fats* and started to play it on the street.

The Hurricane Brass Band lasted from about 1974 to 1978. Starting in 1976, Leroy took on six nights per week gigs on Bourbon Street—first with singer Lee Bates at La Strada, and then with Hollis Carmouche and his jazz band at the Maison Bourbon. Some members of the Hurricane were upset, but you can't be mad when musicians move on to something else. Leroy was a young budding musician—he was the talk of the street, and started his own quintet, New Orleans Finest, in 1978. We watched each other grow in our way, in different directions. As older musicians saw we could play the music, too, we were asked to join other bands.

Around this time, I got a call from the leader of the Tuxedo Brass Band, Herman Sherman. He was an alto saxophonist with a day job working for an office supply company. He was probably one of the first band leaders to start hiring young, white musicians from Europe like Clive Wilson and John "Kid" Simmons. They had come to New Orleans to learn the traditional style in the 1960s, and worked with the Tuxedo Brass Band. When he saw that Danny Barker was bringing up these young black musicians, he wanted to support us, too. He brought Joe Torregano, Lucien Barbarin, and Tuba Fat.

It was the weekend before the Bucketmen parade, and Mr. Sherman said, "Look, I need a trumpet player and you know some of those old songs." I was excited but didn't want to cause any more problems. I said, "Well, I'm not part of the union." He said, "Don't worry about that. I'm going to pay for you to be in the union so you can be in the band and make this parade."

After joining the Tuxedo Band, I started paying my own dues and was able to work with the Olympia

and the Onward Brass Bands. In my early 20s, if I got behind in my dues, Louis Cottrell would call my mother's house and tell her. I was playing trumpet, sousaphone, and bass drum. When I worked with the Louis Cottrell's Onward Brass Band, I mostly played bass drum while Placide Adam or Freddie Kohlman played snare. Mostly with the Tuxedo Band or the Olympia Band, I played trumpet.

My mother saw I was working a lot and was kinda like, "Huh. You really surprised me." She still felt that I needed to get a real job. Through connections with New Orleans music, I was lucky enough to have had an opportunity to be introduced to some people who worked in the field of television. Jules Cahn, who was a good friend of mine who took pictures of second line parades and produced the Leroy Jones Hurricane Brass Band album in 1975, had a brother who was on the board of directors of PBS in New Orleans, Channel 12.

The production manager said, "Well, I'll tell you what. I'm gonna hire you, but you've gotta get in and learn this stuff fast because we have people who are graduating in communications. Good thing you have a degree in education." They brought me in as a production technician. When I started working for Channel 12, boy, my mother was so excited. "You're a what?! You're a TV cameraman?!" I said, "Yeah, a real job." She said, "Yeah, that's what you need, a real job."

Fellowship

I was working the station and working my gigs afterwards. My college sweetheart, boy, she left me because I chose music over her. She said, "It's either me or the music. Me or the horn." I said, "Well, baby, you got to go."

It wasn't just playing music, it was the fellowshipping between musicians. When I was young, it was the side of musicianship that I learned to really appreciate. We helped each other. When I'd be leaving work, the banjo player Emmanuel Sayles would sometimes be standing at the bus stop at the corner of Canal and Galvez. I'd blow the horn of my Camaro sports coupe. I said, "Come on, man. Get in the car." I'd bring him home.

It was the same thing when I was working regularly at Preservation Hall. Jeanette Kimball and I both lived Uptown. I'd pick her up, and bring her to work.

And when I'd come into play with Sweet Emma Barrett, she'd ask, "How're the Skirts?" I'd ask, "The Skirts?" She'd say, "You know what I'm talking about. The girls. How is the girls?"
"The girls okay." She would tell me, "You're lucky. If you were around during my time, you'd be my man. I love some trumpet players."

When I wasn't working, I'd go to the Hall a few times a week to listen to trumpet players. A lot of jazz is the individuality of the person playing the instrument.

Lifetimes in music. **Left:** George "Kid Sheik" Colar at an Elks parade with the Eureka Brass Band in 1953. **Right:** "Kid" Thomas Valentine singing at Speck's Moulin Rouge in Marrero, Louisiana in 1955. Photographs by Ralston Crawford, courtesy of the Hogan Jazz Archive.

You had to make yourself available to be around those people to know what they sound like. If you never went to check it out, to listen at their phrasing, you would never know who it is. George "Kid Sheik" Colar played on a Tuesday. "Kid" Thomas Valentine played on a Thursday, so those were the two nights that I normally would go. I had listened to Kid Sheik on the Eureka Brass Band albums Mr. Barker had played for us. It was interesting to compare his style to Kid Thomas. He had a very fascinating way of playing his horn. He was able to do a lot of nice little things with his mutes and he plays so quietly and softly. And he had a way of working the wah-wah mute. It was just beautiful.

The Firing Line

I worked in television for almost ten years—Channel 12 for maybe three years, and then Cox Cable came to the city. I had started with the company from the beginning when there were just five of us in the office at One Shell Square. As part of the Cox Cable contract, they were supposed to have a public access studio, but it took a few years to get started so they brought me in as a field engineer. Then I went into programming. My idea at that time was to become a director for Cox.

But that didn't work out too well because my boss and I butted heads. It was a very bitter thing.

At that time, they were going to do the big connection from New Orleans to Algiers. It wasn't feasible to run a cable line under the Mississippi River, so they had to go up a pylon and run cable lines underneath the span bridge. They brought somebody in, and fired all of my coworkers who were engineers. Wiped the whole slate and they only kept me.

I didn't like the way they fired everybody in the department, and I had a decision to make. If I wanted to advance with the company, I was going to have to go with the company somewhere else like North Dakota. I was very active, not only as a brass band musician, but also as a regular club performing musician. I was working a lot with the Onward Band and the Tuxedo Band, but I had also started working with Mr. Barker at places like the Maison Bourbon—playing in a sit-down, cabaret style band. I was also working with Teddy Riley a lot. I couldn't find that in North Dakota so I said, "I don't think I want to move on."

I started teaching in 1985. I chose to teach at Craig Elementary because I lived in Tremé at 1227 Marais

Teachers participating in the strike protesting at Duncan Plaza in front of City Hall in 1990. Photograph by Ellis Lucia, courtesy of *The Times Picayune*.

Street. Teaching was fun because when I went into the classroom, all the kids in the neighborhood were there. Corey Henry was one of my students. Derrick Tabb was one of my students. And by me playing in all the parades and funerals, everybody knew me in the community. George Lewis' great-granddaughter, Bianca, used to come knocking on my door, "Mr. Stafford!"

I said, "Girl, get away from my door. Today is not a school day. Today is Saturday morning. Go home."

I taught sixth grade at Craig for five years. We were like family in that school. The faculty was mostly in their 30s and we used to have some fun. We'd have Christmas parties at a hotel and go to another teacher's house until six in the morning, still partying.

The last Orleans Parish teacher strike was held in October of 1990. Almost the entire faculty at Craig was on the picket line. That's the kind of solidarity we had. The strike lasted for several weeks. I was one of the ringleaders of the strike line and I made up all kinds of songs while we marched. I'd be leading the line with 40 of us chanting:

Two bits, four bits, six bits, a dollar.
Everybody grab a scab by the collar.
Scab in the morning,
Scab in the evening.
Once a scab, always a scab!

We had some fun on that strike line.

The kids in the windows, looking out.
Oh, teachers on the strike line, sticking it out.
Scab in the morning,
Scab in the evening.
Once a scab, always a scab!

Some principals were cool, because they understood the larger point, but there were just some principals who took it so personal. The union knew that some teachers were gonna be put on the firing line. The principal at Craig was angry. He threatened me, "When you get back in here, I'm gonna get you."

I Got Your Back

I had just purchased my house Uptown. The principal from my old school, Woodson Middle, called me up and said, "Well, look. I hear you're having problems at Craig. I need teachers. I have an English position open. Eighth graders." I said, "That's great. I need to get out of here because it's going to turn into a bad situation with my principal."

The first day I started, the principal said to me, "Mr. Stafford, I'm gonna tell you something. I have lost five teachers in the last six weeks. I'm just letting you know in advance. Now, fourth period, the class right after lunch period? That is the worst." I said, "Okay, it's cool."

I introduced myself during homeroom and by lunchtime, everybody knew there was a new teacher at the school. I'm in my early 30s, but the kids are thinking I'm fresh out of school. They figure they're gonna run me.

The teacher in the room that was adjacent to mine was a very stern, strict teacher. She had told me, "Mr. Stafford, you need any help, just knock on the door. I'll come over. I'll straighten things out." I said, "No. It's gonna be all right." I had blackboards all around the room covered in work and some pages for them to do.

That fourth period bell rung. And oh, I can hear them coming down the hallway. When they first came in the room, they were sliding books across the floor, throwing paper at girls, running around. I'm sitting there, looking. I ain't saying nothing. I mean total chaos.

I said, "Now that I know where all the damn fools are, I'll tell you one thing. I heard you ran five teachers, but I ain't the one to run. Your work is on the board. Now, if you have any idea of moving forward to the next grade, leaving Carter G. Woodson to go to Walter C. Cohen or Booker T. Washington, I can tell you right now you're gonna have some hard days in here. Your work is on the board. I'm not gonna say anything else. I suggest that you get busy." It got quiet. They went to writing. And I went back to my seat.

My sixth period class had 48 students in the room—I mean, the kids were sitting on top of each other, but I didn't have as much trouble with the 48 as I did with fourth period. The principal used to say, "Mr. Stafford, I promise you after October the 1st, I'm gonna get another teacher. I've just got to keep the numbers right."

It turned out I had four kids who were too old to be in fourth grade so they socially promoted them to the eighth. They acted up because they were so far behind. We had a little incident in the classroom which required the parents to come for a conference. When I came to school early the next day for the meeting, a friend of mine's little brother was at the school. I said, "What you here for?"

"Oh, my son, he got into trouble with some teacher."

"What teacher?"

He said, "I don't know. His mama called me. We're not together. She said I need to get over here to check on him." I said, "Mitchell's father?"

"Yeah, yeah."

I said, "I'm the person you've come to see." He said, "Man, what he did? What he told you?" I said, "I was at the board writing and somebody threw a piece of paper. And as the paper was coming at me, a voice was saying, 'Hit that M-F. I got your back.'"

He was outraged: "Let me tell you something. If he ever do anything like that again, if you got to take your shoe off and hit him on the top of the head, you got my permission." I said, "No, Mitch. I'm not going to do that. Come on." We went to the principal, and I said, "Look, don't suspend him. His father is the younger brother of a friend of mine. I'm going to take care of it." The next day, all the kids were wondering why he was the only one not suspended.

I said to the class, "The incident that occurred yesterday, I'm sorry that happened. Y'all got to see a real bad side of me. I grew up in this community. I grew up a block away from here at Second and Freret, and went to this school. When I first came here, I told you I probably know your aunts, your uncles, your mamas, your daddies, your grandmothers, because I grew up in this community.

"Now, Mitch, he's going to tell somebody he got their back, but I'm gonna let him come up to the board and explain to you how closely and how well I know his family." Now he started grumbling and saying he didn't want to do it.

"No, no, no. Come on up here."

He walked up to the front. He didn't want to say anything. I said, "See? I know his pride got the best of him, but I'm gonna explain to you. I used to help his daddy cross the street to get snoballs. That's how well I know him, but he got somebody's back? And then the strangest thing is that when his uncle got married, I was the best man and he was the ring bearer. He was the little boy. So let this be a lesson in life for you all. You never know about certain things in life."

He was still grumbling, "Oh, man. You didn't have to tell them all that." But after that incident, I had no more problem with the fourth period. They fell in love with me. The day after report card conferences, one of the kids said, "That man knows everybody. He know everybody!"

I said, "I told you all." That's one of the most beautifulest things about working in your community. It's important. It helps.

I used to go see my good friend Big Al Carson play around town. When I was active in the Masonic Hall, one of the members was running Colt 38. My lodge brothers and I used to hang out there on Sundays and listen to Al's band. For Christmastime at Woodson, I brought him in to play. That was my gift to the school and to the students. Boy, they had a ball. Then the next thing you know, Big Al had parties coming from all the schools. They'd see him on Cox's cable access channel and the next thing you know, all the principals are calling him.

Dedicated Service

I stayed at Woodson two years and then I decided I wanted to go back to primary grades. I had enough of junior high school. It got to a point I was teaching kids who would come in without any homework. I was keeping kids after school, and I was very stern about what I was doing. You can't do that now because all the kids are not neighborhood kids. They get bussed in. I said, "You all don't understand. You can't come to school and just take it as though it's a big playhouse. When I get up in the morning, I come here to teach. I'm not here to babysit." They got tired of detention. But I got tired of dealing with teenagers. I went to Crocker Elementary on General Taylor and Liberty, just five blocks away from my house. I was there all the way up until the storm.

One of the most rewarding aspects of playing music is getting to share it with my students. I tell my kids about my traveling experiences. I had all different types of monies I showed them—Japanese yen, Russian rubles. For holidays, when I travel back and forth to Finland, I come back with Finnish money, and share it with them.

"Mr. Stafford, that looks like food stamps!"
"No, this is a Finnish mark. It's not food stamps."

Then I have a little celebrity status. I show them I'm on the front page of the paper in Finland. I'm on the front page of the paper in Norway. Oh, they get excited. That creates a feeling of belief in what you're doing. They begin to understand and they respect you more because they know that you're not lying. There's the proof right here before you.

As I went along with music, I started wearing more hats. I became the leader of the Young Tuxedo Band, and Teddy Riley's Heritage Hall Jazz Band. And before Danny Barker died, he told Ms. Lu to turn the band over to me, so I became the leader of the Jazz Hounds. And it was all due to the fact of my service throughout the years. Dedicated service. You know, that's how you establish a reputation.

Portrait of Danny Barker and a list he wrote of work he did to preserve traditional jazz in New Orleans. Images courtesy of the Danny Barker Collection at the Hogan Jazz Archive.

PREPARING A FUNERAL

Bruce: *When Danny Barker returned to New Orleans in 1965, he not only played and taught music, he also got involved with organizations dedicated to preserving and documenting jazz. He was concerned that organizations like the New Orleans Jazz Club only had white people in them, period, and that black folks did not have any editorial input in publications that were coming out, like* The Rag *and* The Second Line. *These publications wielded power by directing how people thought about the history of jazz, and Danny thought that the people who were playing the music needed to be more involved. But instead of just complaining about it, he said, "I'm going join the Jazz Club."*

He soon became the Director of the Jazz Museum—giving tours, amassing one of the most significant collections of jazz instruments in the country, and working on book projects like Bourbon Street Black: The New Orleans Black Jazzman, *a study he did with a sociologist, Jack V. Buerkle, that was based on extensive interviews with black musicians about playing music in the city.*

Like Louis Armstrong, he wrote all the time. Sometimes he called himself a frustrated writer, but he produced one of the most significant jazz autobiographies, A Life in Jazz, *with Alyn Shipton. He talked about the many historians of jazz who were suspicious of musicians telling their own stories. They wanted to know what day something happened was, what time. But Danny felt that if you only looked for hard physical evidence of the past, you could miss the spirit. He told me one time, "I was standing on the corner when jazz came dragging its poor ass down the street." A musician's musician, when he died, the whole community wanted to be part of sending him off the traditional way. In the following conversation, members of BMOL talk about what it was like to put together his funeral.*

Fred Johnson: On March 13, 1994, Gregg called me and said, "I've got bad news."

"Man, what's the matter?"

"Mr. Barker just passed."

I said, "I'm on my way."

By the time I got to him, Gregg was sitting on the bumper of a car in front of Mr. Barker's house. He explained to me, "Mr. Barker became disenchanted by some brass band's behavior that he felt had nothing to do with the beauty and the pageantry of the brass band music. He was very broken-hearted about it."

Gregg Stafford: One time he was on his way home and he ran into a funeral procession of a young kid who was murdered. He got out to view the funeral, and saw people pouring wine on top of the hearse, jumping on top of the hearse, dancing and doing all kinds of things that just weren't right—according to what he thought.

Fred: Mr. Barker had told his wife, Ms. Lu, "I don't want no brass band funeral.'" When people had heard the news, they started milling around outside of Danny's house, but nobody wanted to go inside and challenge Ms. Lu about having the funeral. And then the press started calling. They knew what it meant in New Orleans when a musician of his stature dies. They were asking when the service was going to be because they were coming down. Ms. Lu said, "All right, let's meet tomorrow at three o'clock."

The house was packed with people both her and Danny respected. Most of us were sitting on the floor. Ms. Lu talked about Danny's displeasure with what he had been witnessing and how he didn't want that foolishness. Gregg stood up and said, "I can assure you, I will take full responsibility for the musicians showing up in black and white."

I've never told Gregg this, but I was elated. I guess I was worried about somebody else standing up and not

being sure whether they would be willing to put their heart into it to make it right. And I never said this to him, either, but I will now: He not only knew it, he acted on it! A lot of times we know, but we don't act!

Gregg: I saw so many of the parades stretch from five blocks to one block to no more members at all. All of this lives through me. I got all this in my soul.

Fred: It gave me the confidence to stand up, too. I was in a group called the Family that organized Lundi Gras balls. I said, "Well, Ms. Lu, I will make sure we have 12 men dressed in suits and ties to marshal the funeral." Now, the reason I said suits and ties was because people were showing up any kind of way to funerals. And in the tradition of burying people, what you look like, how you put it on, all that's important. I wanted Ms. Lu to have that level of comfort. The rest of the room went in unison. My feeling was like this. "This is what you brought to us. This was your objective. You wanted to train some younger musicians to make sure the tradition lived on. This was our gift back to you."

Grand Marshal

Gregg: I proclaimed myself the Commissioner of Jazz Funerals. If you want to be part of Danny Barker's funeral, you must wear black shoes, black hat, black pants, black coat, white shirt, and a black tie. Alfred "Dut" Lazard was a cousin of Mr. Barker. He pulled me to the side and said, "Look, man, Danny and I related. When that body hits the door of that church, I want you to give me full permission to be able to be the real grand marshal and bring my cousin's body. If you don't do it, I'm gonna kill you!" He said it so seriously!

The grand marshal has to be someone who has to be proud of what he's doing. Dut has been to a lot of funerals, and paraded with a lot of groups, so he understood.

Fred: It's kind of like a peacock. They open up their tail and say, "Beat this!"

Gregg: Some grand marshals have their own way of stepping.

Tyrone Calvin: The beauty is everybody has their own way of moving to the beat.

Gregg: Some of them lean all the way back, and walk. Some of them stand tall. You have to have a grand look about yourself. You don't have to have a stone face, but you have to have a very proud face, and you have to sway your shoulders, and your feet have to be in the rhythm.

Part of the custom is related to the sound of the drums. On a snare drum, there is a slot on the side that you twist, and you can change it from snare to tom-tom—which has more of a tenor sound. You turn it on tom-tom when you playing the dirges to the cemetery.

When you play on snare, it is almost a ragged sound. There are little springs at the bottom of the drum. When you are playing on the head of the drum, you can hear the metal rattle of the snare underneath—almost like the scratching on a washboard. On the tom-tom, there is no snare sound. It is just a deep rumble of the drum. You are playing a press roll on the tom-tom with that deep sound. And then when the bass drummer hits, then you start walking on your left foot. You are walking in time with the drum.

Tyrone: The timing is very important. If you are trying to bring the body down, it's the drums that drive you.

Gregg: The grand marshal knows that when that drummer hits the head of that drum, it's gonna be on one. You better not be stepping on two or three!

A grand marshal is expected to lead two parts of the jazz funeral—the somber dirges leading to the cemetery, and the joyful celebration after the body is cut loose. In this case, photographer Micahel P. Smith's archive shows the arc of a life in the tradition. Matthew "Fats" Houston leads George Lewis' funeral in 1969 with the Olympia Brass Band, and is then celebrated by his community at his own funeral in 1981. Images by Smith © The Historic New Orleans Collection, 2007.0103.4.403; 2007.0103.4.427.

People will be saying, "Get him out of there! What he doing?! Where did y'all get him from?!"

Fred: Oh! That's a terrible sight to see! I hope I never see that! In addition to that, you have to have a respect for history. In order to have a respect for history, you have to respect the people who come before you.

Tyrone: When I think about grand marshaling, the first person that comes to my mind is Mr. Fats Houston. I watched him do it so much. And I know he did it with a lot of respect.

Gregg: Fats Houston was one of the greatest of all, because he had that big round face, he was about 300 some pounds, but he was light on his feet. He wore that homberg. He kept his head to the side and trembled as he walked.

Just a Little While to Stay Here

Gregg: The morning of Mr. Barker's funeral, we met three blocks away from St. Raymond's Catholic Church on Paris Avenue in Seventh Ward. The band assembled away from the church so that we could go pick up the body. We marched there playing, *Just a Little While to Stay Here.* The musicians were looking at each other and we were in approval of each other. "Oh, we gonna do this today! We gonna do this today."

Everybody was on the same foot, the lines were straight.

We began at full volume, but as we got closer, a block away, the music came down, real soft. That's such a sweet thing to hear. Inside that church, you can hear that band coming in a distance. The minister knows the band is on the way, and everybody in the church can feel that sound of the music. It's in your bones, and you can feel a chill.

When we got to the church, some of Danny Barker's family came out and weren't sure what was going on. They told me to cut the music off. I had to tell them, "Look, you don't know nothing about this. You didn't grow up in New Orleans." I reassured them, "We got this. This is how it's meant to be done."

When it was time to take Mr. Barker out of St. Raymond's, we played *In the Sweet Bye and Bye.* As we were marching out of the church, we passed by Ms. Lu standing with Milt Hinton. He was a bass player who had been friends with Mr. Barker for years. They were both in Cab Calloway's band together. I didn't know he was in town. I mean, big tears rolling down his eyes. He came in just for the funeral.

Fred: Mr. Barker's funeral came out on Paris Avenue to where it ran into St. Bernard. They stopped the funeral, put everybody on busses, they brought the funeral to St. Bernard and North Derbigny and put the funeral back on the ground.

Gregg: We made that turn up Claiborne, and we started playing dirges again. Now, we kind of broke the rule, just a little, when we almost got to Orleans Avenue because we had to pick the pace up. We played the tune, *Lily of the Valley*. We wanted those people who weren't at the church to feel the beauty.

Fred: And then we proceeded to go to St. Louis Cemetery No. 2. And let me tell you something, Danny could not have been more proud. I saw some guys who I know like to buck jump, they had to get off the street on this one. It went old school.

Gregg: Once you come out of the cemetery, we played the lively music again. No more tom-toms anymore. The drummer switches back to the snare, and you roll it off. The band leader will call a song to celebrate the life of the deceased. You know he's gone off to a better place. His reward is in heaven, and everybody now is joyful. If the deceased was a member of an organization, you flip the banner from the black side to the colored side. For Mr. Barker's funeral, we didn't have no banner. We just stepped back onto Claiborne Avenue and marched to the Tremé Music Hall.

Fred: Mark Cerf, a former Spyboy with the Yellow Pocahontas, had opened up a bar on the corner of North Robertson and Ursulines in the Sixth Ward.

Danny Barker's funeral on March 17, 1994 going under the I-10 overpass on North Claiborne Avenue. Photograph by Daniel C. Meyer, courtesy of the Hogan Jazz Archive.

Back in the day, it was run by the famous clarinet player named Alphonse Picou.

Gregg: You know one of the greatest compliments I got the day of that funeral? Right before I was leaving, Willie Humphrey—one of the pioneers of the music, clarinetist who was around in King Oliver time—came up to me and said, "I understand, young man, that you put all this music together." I said, "I had some help, but I supervised." He said, "I'm so proud of you. The music was so strong. It was a beautiful procession."

Fred: When we were coming out of the cemetery after burying Mr. Barker, Tyrone said, "Say, brah, we need to do this again." I said, "Not with a body!" Everybody was starving for it, saying, "Now that's what we grew up on!" I said, "All right."

BLACK MEN OF LABOR

Bruce: After Danny Barker's funeral, Black Men of Labor was founded by Fred Johnson, Jr., Gregg Stafford, and Benny Jones, Sr. They all have had extensive experience in passing music along in the city. Benny, the leader of the Tremé Brass Band, is an institution by himself. When he decided to go back to playing trad jazz, it made a difference in the social fabric of New Orleans. Not a whole lot of talk; a lot of action. Benny and Gregg are likeminded in their commitment to holding the tradition together. They know there aren't that many people who are playing the trad music who were raised in the trade.

They teamed up with Fred who brought in his experience with the art and organization of the Yellow Pocahontas and Tambourine and Fan. Pulling together their resources and talents, they created their own institution dedicated to traditional second lines and jazz funerals, with a special emphasis on the parading arts that came out of the Sixth and Seventh Wards. While Fred makes sure the art changes every year, Benny puts together a band that showcases the history of traditional brass band music in the city.

The co-founders of BMOL: Benny Jones, Sr., Fred Johnson, Jr. and Gregg Stafford. The first years of the BMOL second line parade began at the Tremé Music Hall on North Robertson and Ursulines, which was run by Mark Cerf, a former Spyboy with the Yellow Pocahontas. Jerome Smith's brother, Walter Smith, is credited for setting the stage for decorating the building, which over the years has become a backdrop for portraits of club members. Photograph by Eric Waters, courtesy of the BMOL archive.

The BMOL banner in 1997 was designed by Douglas Redd, who worked closely with the Yellow Pocahontas and Tambourine and Fan, and went on to co-found the Ashé Cultural Arts Center in Central City. Photograph by Eric Waters, courtesy of the BMOL archive.

Fred Johnson, Jr.: I hadn't fully devoted myself to something culturally since I stepped back from masking Indian, but Danny's funeral inspired me to return to the street. As I had worked my way up through the business and nonprofit world, I had observed that many middle-class black folks felt that once you got to a certain quality of life, you don't need to participate anymore—you are beyond that, you are above that. I wasn't buying into that perspective. I believed you could make a good living and still be part of the culture that you grew up in. Tootie was a very good counter-example. The man worked every day. He wasn't in and out of jail. He paid his bills, and he made that costume.

The problem with integration is that it brainwashed black people into thinking that somebody's ice was

colder than theirs—that being part of white people's organizations was somehow better than holding onto your own. When I thought about starting a club, I believed social aid and pleasure clubs were something about and for black people. When I grew up, the parades they hosted were part of our own salvation.

Now everybody don't see history the same way and everybody tell their own story. But I know you can't love nobody else if you don't love yourself. The whole experience here has to do with self-pride. If you don't have pride in you, why should anyone else have pride in you?

I spoke to Gregg and Benny and said, "Let's do a Blue Monday and talk about what we want to do." The three of us sat down at the Praline Connection, had

some red beans and rice, chicken, and a couple of beers. The one thing we agreed on was that the club's parade was going to be around the traditional music.

Coming out of the Bucketmen and Tambourine and Fan, I already knew how to make phone calls. I had that training. I began by calling all the former members of that club to see if they wanted to join, and expanded from there. "Say, brah, we gonna put a parade together. We want to put a band with the tempo we want on the street and have a good time. You interested? Tremé Music Hall on Saturday." Before I knew it, 40 people showed up.

When we talked about our vision for the club, the musicians in the group had white friends that they wanted to include in the organization itself. I'm not

Left: The first year of the parade, the club wore overalls in honor of the memory of the Longshoremen's Labor Day parade and the Bucketmen's second lines.
Right: In the following years, they wore suspenders in the style of older parading organizations. Photographs by Eric Waters, courtesy of the BMOL archive.

opposed to that for other groups, but I believed there was power in keeping it an all black organization. I wanted to reinforce what the generations before us started—to let them know there are some of us who respect the fight, the blood, the loss of life that they went through the sacrifices they made.

I had to look in the audience and figure out how not to alienate my musician friends. Why don't we consider our name? I said, "Why don't we name it Black Men of Labor?"

One, black men always get a bad rap about how they don't take care of their business or their house. I said, "That's not true for most of us." Now, let's go on the other side—the labor part. The biggest organization that ever hit the streets was the Labor Day parade from the Longshoremen's Association. We used to honor them with the Bucketmen. Let's take some inspiration from that organizing and extend it to all kinds of labor. Cats in the club did all kinds of things. They were bus drivers, construction workers, musicians, managers in hotel security, sanitation truck drivers. Other guys worked in hospitals, city hall, and the court house. My brother worked for Proctor and Gamble going all over the world. Bruce works for the National Park Service, I work for an organization that does first-time home-buyer training programs. Let's put a parade together close to Labor Day and we can give respect to the black men who work.

My other suggestion was that this is a culture that came out of Africa. Why are we in denial about it? Let's just use African fabric in this parade so that we can say to the social scientists—the historians and the anthropologists—we understand the connectivity. We know who we are. We don't need you to tell us who we are. We're telling you we know who we are.

Melvin Reed adjusts Ricky Gettridge's streamer during the BMOL parade in 2012 while Gregg Stafford looks on. Ricky was a Spyboy for the Yellow Pocahontas, and has worked with Melvin for decades. Photograph by Bruce Sunpie Barnes.

Left: In 2008, BMOL came out in boubous from Senegal. Photograph by Charles Silver. *Right:* Seguenon Kone, a griot from Ivory Coast, performed before their parade. Photograph by Bruce Sunpie Barnes.

The Art of a Parade

Setting a date was important. If you set the date, you are supposed to do everything in your power to make the date. It's a weight around you because you know you will never get to full completion, but you also have to know that unless it's really glaring, the audience won't be able to tell what's missing or incomplete. In a parade outfit or an Indian suit, the only people who know are the people who are putting it together.

I assembled a team that went back to the days of the Yellow Pocahontas and Tambourine and Fan. From my very first Indian suit, I never did anything culturally that Melvin Reed wasn't a part of. He's quiet, and in a lot of respects he's an introvert. But when it comes to creating suits or decorations for a parade, he's a fucking genius. He helped us with our regalia. At first, I didn't ask Tootie to do any work because I was mindful that it could take away from his time sewing, but his belief in the integrity of the artwok inspired me. He used to always say, "You've got to beat yourself." Over the years, that is how the clothing, the colors, and the artwork of the parade continued to transform while holding onto some core values.

What's important is: One, we're uniformed. Two, I'm always concerned about the pageantry of it, and what stands out in the pageantry is color. It all starts with the fabric. The stronger the fabric is, the stronger the message is because it is the foundation of the parade. Once I get a piece of fabric, I can tell you what that parade is going to look like. I can take it and move it all over the body—in all the places where it needs to be—and I can see the clothes before they're even made.

When we decided to do this, I went up to New York and talked to Rudy Lombard about the fabric options. He said, "Hey, man, go in that store in Manhattan called Homeland Fabrics. They got all the fabric you could ever want." When I went in that store, I met this guy named Abdullah Diaw. We started doing business, and a few years went by. One day, I'm talking to Doug Redd, and he says, "Well, listen, all of primarily what we do is out of the West Coast of Africa. It comes out of Senegal."

I pick up the phone and I call Abdullah, and I say, "Abdullah, where did you say you was from?" He said, "I'm from Senegal." I'm like, "Wow, this is strong." Of all the Africans that I could've been doing business with, I end up with one that is Senegalese. We just kept building the relationship, and he's provided services for all 20 years.

As the parade progressed, Tootie had been watching me. He had watched me mature and grow over the years, and felt that if I was involved in something cultural he should have a hand in it, too. By the fifth year, he was saying he wanted to make the streamers because he wanted to keep them traditional. I was overjoyed about it. I had best of both worlds in terms of decorative skill sets.

One of the lessons I learned from him is that an anniversary year should always be above a normal year—it's got to rise above. I first saw Kente cloth in New York with Rudy more than a decade ago. For the 20th anniversary, I knew that we couldn't find anything

stronger. In the copy world of second line parades, nobody was going to imitate that.

Todd Higgins is a member of BMOL and my business partner. He travels to Africa on a regular basis for his work in international trade and wanted to us to make a trip together to get the fabric for the parade. We found it on Lundi Gras in Kumasi, Ghana. We hired two women as interpreters, and got in a raggedy cab that looked like the driver got parts from everywhere. We went down a red clay road. Dust flying up. And they got kente cloth everywhere. I hadn't seen poverty like that before. Tin roofs. Nothing like New Orleans.

We get to a little shop, and a young guy and an old dude welcomed us with open arms, but the old dude wanted $26 a yard for this fabric. We tried to tell him we needed 800 yards. He said, "Well, the lowest I'll go

is $24." I understood his position. I didn't agree with him, but I understood how many people—the Europeans and everyone else—had come there and tried to bargain the price down. The dude took a hard line. He said, "You want it, pay for it. If you don't want it, fuck it." After three hours, I was feeling like we needed to get out of there. I bought a few pieces of cut off fabric just to smooth it over: "Man, I thank you. We appreciate it." The young African looked like he was about to cry.

We got back in the cab, and we rolled a few blocks, made a left turn and went into a village. There was a whole art school. We found the fabric. Homeboy come out and said, "16 dollars a yard!" My man! Now you talking!

Inside the school, they were making the fabric. They had a loom that looked like a hand with thread around

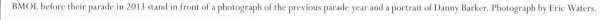

BMOL before their parade in 2013 stand in front of a photograph of the previous parade year and a portrait of Danny Barker. Photograph by Eric Waters.

BMOL members dressed in Kente cloth mingle with their second line crowd on North Galvez. Photograph by Bruce Sunpie Barnes.

about our heritage, I had the evidence to back it up. Not only are we saying it, but we are doing it.

Routes

When we gather people together, and then lead them through the streets, we think ahead of time about what's been significant to us. We want to tie it to history. We wanted to share the connections between the traditional brass music that's been on the streets of the Sixth and Seventh Wards for nearly a hundred years and the people who have come together all of these years to celebrate it. The neighborhoods have changed a lot since we first began parading. A lot of the bars that kept live music close to people's lives are gone from both gentrification and neglect. Our parade brings people back together.

The traditional music brings out both black and white folks. Everybody operates in their own personal comfort zone. A lot of white people come to the beginning of the parade. Their comfort zone may be to follow the parade up North Rampart, and then make a left turn into the French Quarter, but others follow the whole route. You can stay four blocks or you can stay 400 blocks—it is a street parade and you are welcome to come and have a good time.

From Rampart, we turn into the Sixth Ward, go through Tremé, past Little People's Place, and up North Robertson, and then turn on to Orleans Avenue. When we get to North Claiborne and head towards the Seventh Ward, most of the white folks have left the parade. The second line becomes predominantly black. Just imagine how beautiful it would be if you turned onto Claiborne and that median was still lined with live oak trees. But Claiborne still has a history that the interstate can't delete. I did so many events with Tambourine and Fan under the bridge, and met many different Indian tribes with the YPH.

each of the six fingers. On the other end, they had the string tied to a tree. They walked down to the tree and came back over and over again. I thought this was amazing because, just like where I am from, sometimes the poorest people make the richest shit. It reminded me of making an Indian suit. It's piece by piece. They made the patterns, then they made the strips. They make another strip, and they sewed them together. They keep going until they make a piece three yards wide, and 12 yards long. You are either going to make it by hand, or it's going to be straight imitation. It's like sewing and gluing beads. Two different worlds. It was cold-blooded.

People go to Africa all the time, but most of the art that they bring back go in their homes. My thing was, we are going to put it on the street. We are going to make a street museum of it. We are going to put it on blast so that everybody gets to say, "Wow, where did they get that from?"

Coming out the door at Sweet Lorraine's in the Seventh Ward of New Orleans, that fabric made me feel fortified in my statements about the social scientists and the historians. When you see this fabric, it is not Chinese or Persian silk. There isn't but one place in the world that's going to string that thread together like that—line by line. Not only was I making statements

Members of New Orleans CORE and BMOL pose in front of Sweet Lorraine's with a mural designed by Ayo Scott. Photograph by Eric Waters, courtesy of the BMOL archive.

Parading Honors Civil Rights Histories

Since Rudy and Jerome used the methods of organizing they learned in New Orleans CORE in Tambourine and Fan, I've thought about the way we honor the freedom to assemble and move through time and space together. Fifty years ago, the group of people who come to our second line could have been arrested for spending an afternoon together, but because of the men and women who fought, bled, and died to make a way for equality, we are able to share it today.

In 2011, we honored them at our parade because we don't want to take it for granted. A lot of accomplishments that have taken place today are on the shoulders of people like this and the the history books don't tell that story. These are everyday people who were walking around here that fought not just to change New Orleans but to change America. A lot of people don't know that the New Orleans chapter of CORE was very instrumental in giving direction to the rest of the country during the Freedom Rides, and the Freedom Summers that followed. They stepped up. One of the messages that we have wanted to highlight in our parade is that many people involved in New Orleans CORE have also been involved in preserving tradtional New Orleans jazz. They have seen their work in Civil Rights and music as interconnected, and so do we.

Masking Indian and running a second line are two different assignments with different agendas and behaviors. It's damn near two different worlds, even if they take place on the same streets, because there is a different chemistry involved. The engagement with the public is different. With Indians, you are meeting and challenging other tribes to see who is the best dancer, singer, and who sewed the best costume. You can't talk your way through this now. You've got to meet and show them. The crowds on both sides are going to be the ultimate decider about how this played out.

In the parade, you don't have to meet another club, but you have ongoing interaction with the crowd. I always call it a Moving Broadway Show. There are some other people who will walk the whole parade with you from the beginning to the end as your support system—*Do you need a beer? Water? You want me to hold something?* They treat you royal. There are other people on the sidelines who want you to know they see you, and they want you to know that they are present in their support. A lot of those greetings are confirmations: *Job well done. Keep up the good work.* Somebody's holding up the "blood-stained banner" because when they come in and look at the division, they see things that make them happy that they live in that neighborhood. Towards the end of the parade, we come down St. Bernard, and turn back to Sweet Lorraine's. That's how I've always been taught to do it—bring the parade back to where you started.

DORATHA "DODIE" SMITH SIMMONS & WILLIAM SMITH

Bruce: *It was great for the New Orleans Young Traditional Brass Band to parade with Black Men of Labor the year we honored New Orleans CORE. It gave them a direct route into understanding how people who had supported the Music for All Ages program were directly connected to this history. Almost every Saturday, a prominent local CORE activist, Doratha "Dodie" Smith Simmons, would come to the program with her husband, trumpeter John "Kid" Simmons, to listen to the kids perform. They would sit towards the back, and when they knew where they could make a suggestion, Dodie would write some songs out on a piece of paper and whisper, "Here are some tunes they might want to play." John was even more hands-on. He played at the Park Service on a regular basis, and if he had a concert, he'd invite the kids to come and let them sit in. Dodie's youngest brother, William Smith, was a member of the Tremé and Storyville Stompers Brass Bands, so the kids were also getting to know him as a teacher.*

I know they were aware that Dodie, John, and Will were related and had a special relationship to the music, but I'm not sure if they ever realized how. Dodie had been the secretary of New Orleans CORE before committing herself to traditional jazz music by working for years with Preservation Hall and the New Orleans Jazz and Heritage Festival. What I always saw in Dodie was someone who was not rigidly dogmatic, but held a deep belief that people should have the right to choose their own lives—to have their own pursuit of happiness. That's what the struggle should afford you, and she passed it on to her younger brother in music and life. Will grew up playing at Preservation Hall and with the Fairview Baptist Church Band, and has played with Lil Rascals Brass Band, Tremé Brass Band, the Storyville Stompers, and the PresHall Brass Band. Dodie taught him about being a full, actualized human being and not having to worry about other people's thought processes. Her family's support of the program hopefully taught the kids something similar.

Introduction: For Us, By Us

Dodie: The Black Men of Labor's parade dedicated to the Freedom Riders touched my heart. These are young—I say "young" because they are younger than me—black men who thought enough of what we did. They didn't have to honor us, but they felt they had to. Their parade meant more to me than going to the Freedom Riders convention in Mississippi where we were given an award shaped as a bus. For me, my involvement in the Civil Rights Movement led me to Preservation Hall and a rich life in music. Their parade honors the same origins. Now the young people may talk about traditional jazz and say, "Oh, that's Uncle Tom." But I say, "Ain't nothing Uncle Tom about this music. This is FUBU music: For Us, By Us." I want them to know the history behind the music they are trying to play.

When I talk about traditional jazz, I always say "New Orleans music" because that's what it was called by the old timers. It was not jazz. A white musician named Johnny Hyman told me that when he was growing up, the word jazz came from white folks calling it "jack-ass music." In polite society, when there were women around, they called it jass. Johnny loved it, but when he played New Orleans music, he couldn't use his own name. When he played music he was Johnny Wiggs.

From Yazoo County to the Ninth Ward

I was born May 30, 1943 in Benton, Mississippi. I've been in New Orleans since I was two and a half. There are ten of us—five girls and five boys. I helped raise my youngest brother, William. He's a trumpet player and has played all over the city with traditional and modern brass bands.

Will: I came along in 1962.

Dodie: Our daddy, Sam Smith, is from Lexington, Mississippi. Our mother, Gladys Smith Smith, is from Benton. They were farmers.

Will: In fact, our dad's family was one of the few families that actually got their 80 acres. Even so, our family grew up in sharecropping environments, and there was really no money involved. They may have gotten a lot of crop for themselves, so part of that crop was usually exchanged for meat. And they also raised pigs, chickens, and other livestock to sustain themselves.

Our parents grew up 20 miles apart. Our dad tells stories of having met my mother at church. Real Southern Baptist. He's deeply religious. I've seen few people that exemplify a Christian life more than him. He can't read or write. If he told a lie, he didn't know it. He wouldn't take something from you under any circumstance. When he got to go court my mother, he had to wait for the day that they didn't use the mule to plow with, and he'd go 20 miles down an unpaved road. Still no paved roads there now, so when a car goes, man, it's just dust. You can't see anything. Our father rode on a mule to go sit on her porch. Her dad and mom would sit, too, and watch them. They got married and had three kids in Mississippi before they decided to move to New Orleans.

Dodie: Our mother's sister, Dickey, already lived here with her family. When we moved to New Orleans, we stayed with her family on Louisa Street and Industry.

Will: Aunt Dickey was an absolute whip. Of all our aunts, she was the most worldly, most city, most flashy, flip-mouthed. In fact, none of our other aunts were anything like her. She'd wear a short dress when the rest of them would be saying, "You see her?!" I came along a lot later after she had gone on to Chicago.

Dodie: From kindergarden to eighth grade, I went to Johnson C. Lockett. I never had a new textbook. We

The front cover of a CORE pamphlet, courtesy of Dodie Smith Simmons.

Top: Oscar "Papa" Celestin, by Ralston Crawford, courtesy of the Hogan Jazz Archive. *Bottom:* Roosevelt Sykes, by Michael P. Smith, courtesy of Dodie Smith Simmons.

got all the hand-me-downs from the white schools, and they were torn and already full of answers, but we had great teachers. They talked about how music has always played an important role in the freedom of black people. They told us about how Harriet Tubman helped slaves escape through the Underground Railroad, and how people would change the lyrics to the song *Swing Low, Sweet Chariot*. The slaves were not singing "chariot," but "Swing by, Sweet Harriet." Songs became codes, telling us where to go.

Will: A lot of my early experiences with music I heard in our house in terms of the call and answer kind of singing that my dad did. He's been described as a born witness. If you've ever been in a real kind of holiness old style Baptist church, the preacher preaches, but there's always somebody that's responding: "Amen. Say it, Preacher. Amen. Preach. Preach." That was our dad. Every Sunday when the altar call, my dad was the person who went down and prayed out loud to the whole church.

When our mom moved to New Orleans, she got involved with the African Methodist Episcopal Church. It began in Philadelphia with Richard Allen, who was a black, popular person in the church. Blacks weren't allowed to go to the altar. One day, they staged a protest, went to the altar, and were all kicked out of the Methodist Church. Thus you have the African Methodists, which you'll see still today as the "AME Church." Hugely into education. They're completely different from what you call fundamental kind of holiness Baptist churches. That's not the AME Church. They raise money and give scholarships. You're not liable to see a lot of people catching the Holy Ghost running through the aisles. They're looked at as the uppity black church. Our family helped start St. Luke AME, which is at 2500 Louisa. Our mom's name is on the cornerstone. She was also the choir president until they made her retire.

Dodie: Our dad worked at the Lone Star Cement factory. Every spring, they had a picnic, and they would hire Oscar "Papa" Celestin's band to play. On one side of this big field was the white area, and on the other side was the black. But we all heard the same band. I remember everyone ran up to sing *Marie Laveau*. The music drew us together. We didn't care who we were standing next to. When Papa Celestin would sing *Oh Marie Laveau*, and the whole crowd would join in:

The Voodoo Queen,
Way down yonder in New Orleans.

At the house, we had a piano that nobody played, but when we moved to Metropolitan Street, Roosevelt Sykes lived around the corner from us on Louisa Street. When we needed to raise some money, we had a fish fry, and brought the piano out for him to play for tips in the yard. For 50 cents, you could either have chicken or fish, potato salad, green peas, one slice of white bread cut in half, and piece of pound cake. We put chairs and benches around the yard, and people ate, listened to the music and danced. We took the music for granted. I think this is true for a lot of kids who grew up in New Orleans.

Will: On Metropolitan Street, people owned their houses. These were people who were in a position to do things for their family, but if you crossed Louisa, you entered into a different world of the Desire public housing project. I didn't really understand community living until I had a few friends in the project. I went over there and thought, "Goddamn. Everybody lives here." It was different than in my house where there was a traditional structure. It's mom, dad, and the kids and chores and everything that they brought with them from rural Mississippi. Those values were strictly enforced.

Dodie: In the summer, at four o'clock in the evening, you had your bath, put on clean clothes, got your hair combed, and went to sit on the step. You better not move. You didn't get off the step and go running around the yard. In the Ninth Ward, some kids thought we were trying to be cute. They called us "The Smith girls with the long hair." They thought we were trying to be more than we were, but we were just doing what our mother told us.

Leaving the Neighborhood

Dodie: For ninth grade, there was a school right on Franklin Avenue that I could have walked to, but it was a white school. Instead, my older sister Dorothy and I had to take two buses to Andrew J. Bell Junior High and Clark Senior High in the Sixth Ward. Bell school was on the platoon system. Half the kids went in the morning and half went in the evening. All my classes were in the evening except for PE, which was at ten in the morning. When I walked into the class, I said, "Oh, Lord, I'm in the wrong place." In other cities you had "black" and "white" but here you had Creole as well. The Creoles were very proud of that, and at that time, don't make a mistake and call them a Negro. All the Creole students went to school in the morning session, and the darker kids went in the evening.

I was so nervous because living where I did, you may have seen one or two Creoles, but this was a whole classroom full of white folks as far as I was concerned. It wasn't until another classmate who was a lot darker than me came in that I started to think, "Maybe I am in the right place." Many of my classmates became my best friends. My friend Barbara's grandmother was the organizer of the Creole Fiesta Society. One day she asked me if I was going to the football game. I said, "If I can get bus fare to come back." She said, "Why don't you just come to my house and we'll go to the game together?"

We walked down North Miro to Columbus. When I got to Barbara's house, her mother and grandmother were sitting on the porch, so I said, "Good evening." I don't know what they were saying because they were speaking French, but they went into the house. Barbara and I went inside and they called her to the back. When we had dinner, Barbara was served on a plate, and I was served on a napkin. It was worse than the white folks treated me. We were getting it from both sides.

I kept taking the bus to the Sixth Ward to go to high school at Clark, until 1958 when the School Board opened George Washington Carver down the street from where I lived. My sister was offered the choice of finishing up her senior year at Clark, but our mom said, "Finance-wise, you need to stay in the neighborhood," so she went to twelfth grade at Carver. That year, the NAACP was recruiting students to desegregate LSU-NO, which later became the University of New Orleans. They were picking the brightest of the bright, and recruited my sister. She was a good student, a wonderful seamstress, and worked at Charity Hospital in the kitchen after school.

The NAACP Youth Council

Dorothy joined the NAACP and took the bus to their meetings at at the Mount Zion Baptist Church in the Sixth Ward on Dumaine and Galvez. My mother told her, "When the meeting is over, you come straight home." If Gladys Smith said come home, you came straight home. One thing you didn't do in my family was lie.

One day, I walked back into our bedroom and I heard her on the phone saying, "Yeah, after the meeting we're going to the Golden Pheasant." I knew about the Golden Pheasant. It was a black club on Claiborne Avenue. They liked to dance, so did I. They wouldn't serve you alcohol, but they had a jukebox and for 25 cents you got six tunes and could dance the night away.

I blackmailed her. I said, "Next time you go to the meeting, you are taking me, and you are paying my bus fare both ways. And you are going to pay my dollar to join the NAACP Youth Council or I'm going to tell Mama." She knew if I told mama she would tear her tail.

Will: Our mother was fond of wearing Daniel Green slippers. It's a slipper that was also a fashion social statement. If you had a pair of Daniel Greens, you were accomplished. You didn't have those Kmart slippers on. If she said, "William, empty that garbage," and I ignored her, the next time I'd hear her, she'd have taken off that slipper and, oh, the motion was great—Whap!—"Empty the garbage." Before I looked up, she would have put that slipper back on.

Dodie: My sister Dorothy and I took the bus up to the church. The NAACP's thing was go through the courts to end racial segregation. They didn't believe in direct action, so their meetings were a lot of talk, talk, talk. I sat in the church bored to tears, waiting for it to be over so we could go dance. It was a bunch of girls, and we had the greatest time playing Ben E. King and Jackie Wilson records. When we got home, our mom would say, "You're mighty late getting in." We told her, "We just missed the bus and the other bus was so late coming." I thought, "Lord, if Mama ever finds out the truth!"

But then things got more interesting. Later in the fall, CORE started to have sit-ins at Woolworths and McCrory's on Canal Street. One night, Rudy Lombard and Jerome Smith, the chairman and the project director of CORE, came to our meeting to ask us to help them with their picketing and sit-ins. And we did. After a couple of weeks, one of the adult members of the NAACP came and said, "If you go to jail, we will not get you out." And I'm not the type of person who likes to be told what to do—except by my parents who I wouldn't dare! We all got up and walked out.

Dorothy decided not to join CORE, and my mom said, "I don't think you should join either." I'm asking her why. She said, "Because the first time somebody looked at you the wrong way, they got a fight on their hands." That year, Dorothy started at LSU-NO and it was its own struggle. She had a horrible time, and didn't finish.

CORE Offers An Answer

WHAT CORE WANTS is no secret. Nor is it anything strange or new. CORE simply wants for all Americans, regardless of race or creed, their constitutional rights and guarantees. But it wants these as more than words in law books. It wants them as a reality in terms of jobs, housing, education and a fair chance at all the opportunities of American life.

A century ago, after the Emancipation Proclamation, Wendell Phillips said, "The proclamation frees the slave but ignores the Negro." CORE says, "The Negro will no longer, can no longer, be ignored." CORE seeks not only an end to the formal segregation practiced in the South, but to the de facto segregation that exists in the North. It wants an America in which race or creed will be neither asset nor handicap.

There's an old saying, "Wanting won't make it so." CORE was founded in 1942 to translate "wants" into action. In the words of James Farmer, CORE's founder and now its national director, its purpose was "to substitute bodies for exhortation." Its special technique has been a militant non-violence. The effectiveness of this technique, in compelling action to end discrimination, was demonstrated by CORE in dozens of communities before it attracted national attention by the CORE-led Freedom Rides, the lunch counter "sit ins" and the massive Birmingham demonstrations.

CORE does not advocate demonstrations for their own sake. It aims always at tangible results. CORE victories have included desegregation of bus lines and terminals, lunch counters, theatres and swimming pools — many of these in the deep South. It has broken through the color barrier in housing developments, and its action program has persuaded numerous firms to open jobs to Negroes. Its activities, often unpublicized, crisscross the country, from Mississippi to Chicago, from New York to Los Angeles.

CORE's major emphasis is on the fundamental problems of voter registration, Negro employment and integration of schools and public accommodations. As a result of a voter registration campaign in South Carolina, Negro voters in one precinct elected 16 of 17 representatives to the Democratic county convention. In Columbia, the Negro vote was decisive in defeating a segregationist candidate for mayor.

MILITANT non-violence has transformed the whole struggle for Negro equality. It has extended the struggle from the courts to the streets. It has enabled a large, and steadily growing, number of people, Negro and white, to participate in the struggle in an important and useful way. As a result, barriers, once considered so formidable, are now beginning to crumble all over America. But obviously much remains to be done. CORE invites your participation.

CORE is an inter-racial organization without religious affiliation. It is open to anyone who wants to fight discrimination and who will adhere to CORE's rules. The only people not welcome in CORE are "those Americans whose loyalty is primarily to a foreign power and those whose tactics and beliefs are contrary to democracy and human values." CORE believes that militant non-violence, to be effective, must also be responsible. It expects all

members to respect these basic action principles:

● Investigate the facts carefully before deciding whether or not racial injustice exists in a given situation.

● Avoid malice and hatred toward any group or individual. Never use malicious slogans or labels to discredit an opponent.

● Meet anger in the spirit of good will and creative reconciliation. Submit to assault without retaliation. This is the essence of non-violence.

CORE believes that equality for all is a cause that demands the support of all Americans, Negro and white, who value the democratic principles on which this country is founded. It is not someone else's responsibility. It is ours, whoever we are.

"We better know there is a fire whence we see much smoke rising than we could know it by one or two witnesses swearing to it," Abraham Lincoln wrote. "The witnesses may commit perjury, but the smoke cannot." The smoke of Negro protest is now rising all across the American horizon. Only the foolish will wait to see the flames.

CORE

CONGRESS OF RACIAL EQUALITY
38 Park Row, New York 38, N. Y.

 490

Nonviolent, Direct Action

On Thursday nights, CORE had their meetings at New Zion Baptist Church on Third and LaSalle. We all showed up at the meeting and joined the organization. But you just don't become a member, you have to go through training. We had to learn Gandhi's philosophy on nonviolence and the techniques of direct action.

Will: One of my main ways of remembering Dodie as a kid is sitting somewhere with a book. She's a very well-read woman. She may not act like it all the time when you see her on the street second lining like she's trying to sweat, but she has always been. I think that's where she gained motivation to get involved in that whole Civil Rights Movement.

Dodie: In the middle of the winter, we fasted outside of St. Aug on London Avenue. We were allowed to bring one blanket or quilt. We had our overcoats and gloves, and we spent the night outside in the cold. We didn't talk. We just sat there. That's how we learned how to become disciplined.

On a national level, you don't hear much about what New Orleans CORE did. People ask, "Why haven't we heard of y'all?" We weren't looking for recognition. There was something that had to be done and we did it. A lot of that work is credited to the Student Nonviolent Coordinating Committee (SNCC), but, actually, on the Freedom Ride from Montgomery to Jackson approximately 40 percent of the people who went to jail were trained by New Orleans CORE. Jerome Smith, Dave Dennis, Julia Aaron, and Doris Jean Castle got out of jail and set up training sessions here in New Orleans, Nashville, and Montgomery. They wanted you to know exactly what may happen to you, so you don't think,"Oh, we're just going to sit down and be arrested." No. In the training, we slapped them, and not lightly. Wack! Dumped them out of chairs. Kicked them, and called them names.

Will: When I was a little kid, I remember looking at pictures of Dodie in the newspaper. I couldn't understand why she would get dressed up to go get beaten up.

Dodie: It started before Will was born. I remember we left for the campaign in McComb on November 29, 1961, and I didn't have anything ready to wear because I didn't like washing, and I didn't like ironing. Dorothy had just made this blue wool pleated skirt, and bought a nice white sweater to go with it. She had it hanging up to go to work with a chain necklace with a pearl ball at the end. She was still sleeping when I was getting picked up about 5:30 in the morning. I put on her clothes, and thought Dorothy is going to kill me when I get home.

When we went on a testing campaign, we had testers and observers. At the Greyhound Bus Station in McComb, the testers were myself, Alice Thompson, George Raymond, and Thomas Valentine. And Jerome was the observer. He went to the ticket counter, and didn't look at us. The four of us went in and sat at the lunch counter. George Raymond said, "May I have a cup of coffee please?" The manager said, "Greyhound does not own this building."

George said, "May I have a cup of coffee please?" A young white guy filled a cup of coffee, walked behind him, poured the coffee all over his head and hit in the base of the neck with his cup. At that time, Jerome signaled for Alice and me to come to the waiting room, and that's how other people in the station connected Jerome to us. This guy started beating him with brass knuckles yelling, "I'm going to kill him! I'm going to kill him!" Some other guys jumped in and were beating on him, too.

There was a glass partition around the lunch counter. Other white folks came around chasing George, and he jumped over the glass partition, and ran around the counter. It looked like a scene out of *The Three Stooges.*

They'd run after him and he'd jump over the counter again. Thomas Valentine was a little slight guy. They picked him up off the stool, threw him on the ground, and he was up again right away. They grabbed him and threw him down again. Up again.

On campaigns, I'd always take a note pad, and I began writing: *George is jumping over the counter being chased. Alice and I can only sit here and watch the guys get beaten.* As I'm writing all these notes, and I sang in my head:

We are not afraid. We are not afraid....

That kept me sane.

When we finally got out of the station, Jerome and I started running. I was behind him trying to keep up in high heels. A pick up truck pulled up, Jerome jumped in, and was gone. I said, "Oh my God, what am I going to do?" I looked back and saw Tom being kicked as he tried to get into a cab. I didn't know what happened to George and Alice. I ran around the side of the Greyhound Station to the Colored Entrance, and these black folks just encircled me. I stood amongst them trembling like a leaf in the wind. I said to myself, "You are going to calm yourself down, you are going to walk out of this crowd, and walk up the hill like you are going to clean Ms. Ann's kitchen, and when you get out of sight, you are going to run like hell." It didn't dawn on me that I was in a white neighborhood...where was I going to run to? An 18 and a half year old girl, never been in a situation like this before, and that's what I did. Then I heard, "Dodie!"

I said to myself, "How do these white folks know my name?" I ran faster. I was thinking, "They are going to have to catch me. I'm not just going to stand here and let them kill me. And they are going to do some speeding to catch me." Those heels were not touching the ground. I was flying. I think of this song that we sing,

If they ask you tell them I'm gone.
Tell them I'm gone.
If they ask you, tell them I was flying, boy.

Then I heard my name again. The adrenaline had kicked in and I ran even faster until the truck passed me up and I saw it was Jerome.

Will: I used to think Dodie had no fear. After McComb, she kept going. I think she saw Civil Rights as her way out. Like people saw they had to get out of rural Mississippi, she saw it as her way out of the Ninth Ward. Because the Ninth Ward actually wasn't just a place. It was that state of mind that people accepted that this is where they belonged.

Dodie: The first time I went to jail, three white Freedom Riders had gone to a black family's home for dinner. The police dragged them out of the house and beat them. We did a protest. We had a sit-in at Orleans Parish Prison at Tulane and Broad. We were singing, and the police came out and said, "Stop the singing. You are disturbing the communication center." We sang louder: *Ain't going to let no police man turn us 'round, turn us 'round, turn us...*

The police came back and said, "I told y'all, stop the singing, you are interfering with the communication center." We sang louder. They brought the police dogs, and we started to sing,

Ain't going to let no police dogs turn us round.

They brought the dogs closer. *Turn us round. Turn us—closer—round. Ain't going to let no police dog turn us 'round.* They brought them as close as they could without the dogs biting us, and when they saw that they weren't going to deter us, they arrested us. They put the nine females in a cell for two so we sang all night because we had nowhere to sit, nowhere to sleep. Then Oretha Castle, who we didn't know was pregnant at the time, got out, went home, and had a son! He was almost born at Tulane and Broad.

SUNO and the Kitchen Cabinet

In 1963, I was sitting home watching the news, and there is Doris Castle and Sandra Nixon being carried out of City Hall on chairs, and Reverend Avery Alexander being dragged up the stairs. I thought, "When did they discuss that? I'm the secretary! I don't know anything about this." But, see, there were three CORE organizations being run. Oretha was at Southern University of New Orleans, so she would have her group at SUNO; there was the regular Thursday night meetings at New Zion; and then she had what I called the Kitchen Cabinet at her parents' house at 917 North Tonti.

Oretha and Doris' mom, Virgie, worked as a waitress at Dooky Chase's and their dad, Johnny, was a longshoreman during the day and a cab driver at night.

Their house in the Sixth Ward had three bedrooms, a living room, a kitchen, a bath, and a little enclosed porch in the back. There were always people involved in CORE all over the place. When people would come in from the field, they would get something to eat, take a shower, sleep. Sometimes we would leave Thursday meetings and go by their house to continue strategizing. It would get too late to go home so we slept in these wonderful quilts that their grandmothers made. When Larry McKinley, who used to frequent Dooky Chase, found out how Virgie was taking care of everyone, he told Louis Armstrong, and he wrote a big check to help support CORE.

With three different parts of the organization going on, there were a lot of people that I didn't know. I figured if I really wanted to keep abreast of what's going on I better go to SUNO, too. September rolled around and I said to my mom, "I'm going to SUNO." She said, "You got the money?"

I said, "No ma'am." My parents had to stretch, but they came up with the money. $33. Then came the books. All my books were second-hand. After I spent 75 dollars and I needed another book, she said, "There ain't no more money." I had to drop that class. Thank God the next year CORE was doing a scholarship fund. I applied for it and got the Elenore Roosevelt Scholarship. That's how lot of other people finished school all over the country.

Preservation Hall

At the time, the only white people that I associated with were involved in CORE. One day I was working at the office on Dryades Street, and some of the volunteers, Carol and Tim Heaton, said they would give me a ride home, but were going to stop by Preservation Hall on St. Peter Street in the French Quarter. It was a music venue that had recently opened to support New Orleans music.

Left: Judy Nussbaum and Dodie Smith during the CORE years. *Right:* Dodie at Preservation Hall. Photographs courtesy of Dodie Smith Simmons.

The first night I walked into the Hall, I could tell the volunteers from CORE were a bit nervous because white and black people were not supposed to be socializing together. At the Hall, black musicians played for white audiences. Not by choice, but by law. In fact, when a white musician, Charlie Dufour, played with one of the bands, everyone was arrested.

I didn't know the recent story behind the place. Larry Bornstein had been hosting jam sessions out of his art gallery, and then, for awhile, leased it to Ken Mills. One time when Bornstein went to Mexico to buy art for his gallery, they helped to form an organization called the Association for the Preservation of Jazz. When Bornstein found out, he went crazy. In the meantime, Allan and Sandy Jaffe came down for their honeymoon, and start going to the sessions. Bornstein took a liking to them and decided they should run the space. Allan Jaffe was a smart businessman. He got his degree from the Wharton School of Business in Philadelphia, and Larry was very shrewd. He saw the potential of it. Ken was paying four hundred dollars a month. Larry doubled the rent on him, which forced the Society out, and the Jaffes took over.

A few years later, I had my own issues with rent. My friend Judy Nussbaum—a white woman from New York—and I were CORE Task Force members. We got $22.50 every two weeks—if the check came. We decided to rent an apartment together Uptown on Annunciation on a white block. Judy moved in before me and the house was broken into. We didn't want to stay there and decided to break the lease. Another CORE member, Ike Reynolds, said we could stay at his place in the back of the Castle's house on North Tonti and Dumaine.

We didn't have very much money and both relied on our parents to help make ends meet. I'd go home and steal food out my parents' freezer, and Judy's parents would send her a $100 a month. Most nights, we would walk to the Quarter. It was probably crazy, but we just never thought to worry about it. We would always walk past Preservation Hall, listen to the music for a while because they opened up the shutters and you could hear the musicians play for free. Then we would walk down by the French Market by the vegetable venders, go have coffee and beignets, and swing back by Preservation Hall on the way home.

One night, we decide to go in. We took out our dollar and put in the basket, and Mike Stark asked, "Are you students?" Well, I was, but Judy wasn't, but I just said, "Yes." So he gave us back 50 cents each, and we thought, "Woah! That's the greatest thing." We stayed all night. When we got ready to leave, Mike said, "If you ever want to come back, you can come back as my guest." Why did he say that? We went every night. It was so fun, we would go sit right upfront on the cushions. Bornstein would tell him, "Here come your salt and pepper friends."

At the beginning, I think I was an oddity to most of the musicians—to have this young black girl sitting there was unusual. We became friends. The only songs that I knew were the hymns like *A Closer Walk With Thee* that I had heard in church, and Judy had never heard the music before, but we started to get familiar with it. One time we went to Bogalusa, Louisiana to hear Dick Gregory. When we came back to the Hall, Sweet Emma's band was playing, and she started playing *Bogalusa Strut*. It was the last number of the set. Jaffe told us the name of the tune afterwards.

After a few weeks of going every night, Jaffe offered us a job on the weekend. We did the Babe Stovall concerts on Friday and Saturday afternoon and then worked the night. Babe was known for playing in Jackson Square for tips, and could play guitar really well by himself. A few months later, Judy moved back to New York and Sandy got sick and went back to Philadelphia. Jaffe asked me to work every night. I said, "I don't know about that." I had moved back with my parents and was catching the Desire bus home. I didn't want to do that every night. He said, "If you work, I'll give you a place to live for free."

Worldwide Appeal

For a number of years, I lived above Preservation Hall, and got to know the band leaders who played there: Punch Miller, George Lewis, Sweet Emma, Percy Humphrey, Billie and De De Pierce. Many nights, an artist from Mississippi named Gail Sams, the jazz historian Bill Russell, and I had to be the audience because not many people came in to hear the music. During that time, Jaffe often paid the band out of his

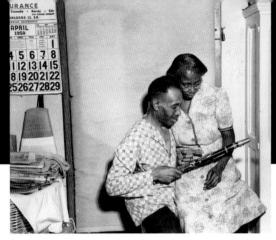

From left: George Lewis and his wife, by Ralston Crawford, courtesy of the Hogan Jazz Archive; Joe Watkins; Dodie with Sylvester and Julius Handy, and Lars Edegran; Captain John Handy. Photographs courtesy of Dodie Smith Simmons.

own pocket, and he'd pay above union wages.

My friends didn't understand why I wanted to hang out with these old people, but I thought, "You know, this is something that is great. They aren't here much longer. And if I don't hear it now, I'm never going to hear it." I wasn't hanging out with anyone my age except Gail Sams, the musicians who came to the Hall from Europe and Japan, and my girlfriend Lorraine. If I was upstairs when George Lewis' band was playing, I knew when she walked in the door because he would play *Sweet Lorraine*. I put George on the level of Frank Sinatra—he was so sophisticated. When he spoke his voice was very low. You almost had to strain to hear what he was saying. I used to like to watch him play the clarinet at Your Father's Mustache. It was simple and it was beautiful.

I just had no inkling that these musicians had a worldwide appeal. That blew me away. There were musicians from England, Greenland, Australia coming to study the music. In 1966, when the Hall celebrated the fifth year anniversary, I remember lying in bed and hearing this clarinet player. I thought it was George. I

threw on some clothes and went downstairs to see if he wanted to come up and have some coffee. But when I got there, it wasn't George—it was the clarinet player from Japan from the band the New Orleans Rascals. He sounded just like him.

The Hall started getting national attention. *The Huntley-Brinkley Report* on NBC did a show on the Hall, and there were articles in national publications. Tourists who used to walk past us to go to Pat O'Brien's started coming in. At the same time, photographers began to document what was happening at the Hall in this timeless way. Lee Frielander and Ralston Crawford did a lot of the pictures. If you look at them, the musicians look like they've lived a lot of life. I think Jaffe tried to keep that vintage feeling, even if the musicians themselves were interested in, like they said on their band cards, "Music for All Occasions."

I remember one time, Gail and I cleaned the Hall. We spent our money to buy the supplies. We cleaned the windows, scrubbed the floors, and fixed up the musicians' bathroom. When Allan got back, he was just outraged. I couldn't understand it. I thought we were

doing the musicians a favor, something wonderful. He was mad as hell. It was part of the appeal of the place to keep it looking old—a part of another era. But I knew there were a lot of things about that time that shouldn't be held onto.

After awhile, I got to book a band once a week when a band was out on tour, and I would hire people who didn't normally play there. Captain John Handy lived in Pass Christian. I'd never heard him before. He came to the Hall one night when the Jaffes were not there, and was playing *Ice Cream* on alto. I got so excited. I said, "Why hasn't he been playing here before? Who is this man?" I started to hire him and his brothers.

I also started a jam session at the Hall to get Joe Watkins back playing the drums. It evolved to getting other musicians who hadn't played in a long time. It made me proud to see how the sessions helped them relaunch their careers. We had these wonderful sessions and I thought, "Am I lucky or what?" I would go with people like Lars Edegran, Keiko and Yoshio Toyama, and Jane Julian to pick up them up, and bring that over to the Hall. That's how I met my husband,

From left: Will and his cousin in front of Preservation Hall; John "Kid" Simmons and Dodie in front of the Hall; Will (*on far right*) watching the band play at John and Dodie's wedding. Photographs courtesy of Dodie Smith Simmons.

John "Kid" Simmons, in 1966. I didn't like him then. I thought Englishmen were too opinionated. But he came to one of the sessions again in 1967, and we got to know each other.

924 Orleans

During these years, I always brought Will and my nieces and nephews his age into the Quarter to experience things that I didn't get to see when I was young. We were not allowed in the Quarter—you better not unless you were a waiter, a musician, working in somebody's house, or waiting for the bus.

Will: By 1970, the economic, social, political climate of the Ninth Ward was in turmoil. Civil Rights had turned into the Black Power Movement and the Black Panthers were all in my neighborhood. Not at all viewed as a negative entity. Not at all. That was the only place you could go in the park and they had

stuff to eat. When they had the shootout, of course the whole neighborhood was polarized. In fact, two of my friends' parents were killed in that incident. Just innocent people in their houses who got shot.

In 1971, John and Dodie got married. On top of all this involvement in all the Civil Rights activities, she's gonna marry a white guy from England. He didn't relate to the premise of racism. He grew up in a sort of space where he didn't get to get exposed to it, so his eyes were like most black people. He was like, "Where does this come from?"

Dodie: We had the wedding reception at the Autocrat Club, which was one of the premier Creole clubs in the city known for the "brown paper bag" test where you couldn't be any darker or you couldn't get in. By that time, the club had changed and opened up. Now everybody is invited. Kid Sheik Colar was the best man and Sweet Lorraine was the maid of honor.

Will: Talk about a strong dude. I've seen people walk up to John and punch him in the face, spit right in his face, call him nigger lover, push him while he's trying to hold my hand and walk with me. I'm a kid. My sister would be just like, "What an asshole," and then they'd just keep going. I found that strange, too. I felt like, "Why don't you all pick up a bottle and bust him in his head." I didn't give a shit if he was white, black, whatever, but they never did.

Dodie: We moved into an apartment at 924 Orleans that Jaffe owned. We were the first ones in the building, and stayed there for 34 years. It was full of people who loved music.

Will: When I got to be going into fourth grade, I went to live with Dodie until I started high school. I think that is what saved me because when I think about it, all the kids that grew up on my block, they're all dead or in jail.

Top: Jim Robinson being interviewed by Dodie and Bill Russell. *Bottom:* Will, "Kid" Sheik Colar, and John "Kid" Simmons playing at Ms. Carrie White's funeral. Photographs courtesy of Dodie Smith Simmons.

I went to school at McDonogh 15 Elementary in the Quarter. Dodie had to go through detailed explanations to our parents about the improvement I would get in not just an education, but also just in exposure. She had no kids at the time, and so she made me her personal project. I was exposed to everything. I had gone to school with all black kids, and then when I went to McDonogh 15, it was completely diverse.

We lived on the third floor of the building on Orleans, and on the first floor was a huge apartment occupied by Bill Russell. From the front to the back there were shelves filled with boxes, violin cases, basses. Just a hermit kind of musician with an extreme intellect and a memory like nobody I ever met. Everything looked random, but if you asked him a question about a song, he could go right to a box and find the answer. And not only that, then he'd go get a violin and play it. We often talked about the transition from the violin to trumpet. That was sort of my fascination with having read some books coming up and having seen a lot of photographs of how initially the bands were all string bands.

A very old lady named Carrie White lived in an apartment in the back of the courtyard. When I was eight years old, I would imagine that she had to be in her mid-80s. Her face was thin but round, quite wrinkled, but she never wore glasses. She had what we used to call "good hair." It didn't seem very kinky even though she was old, so you could tell she had probably had it straightened up a lot over the course of her lifetime.

At night, she smoked cigarettes on the stoop. She became like my mom away from my mom. She had been a maid for one of the most famous madames in Storyville, Lulu White. She wouldn't let me listen to the stories too much. Sometimes they would say, "Tell him, Ms. Carrie, what used to go on." And she'd say, "Send that boy in the house." She was quite strict on me. If Dodie said I could go out in the Quarter after I did my

homework, I'd go listen to musicians in the Square for awhile but would have to be back before the church bells at St. Louis Cathedral started ringing. And if I was late, I heard about it from Dodie and Ms. Carrie.

Learning the Trumpet

Dodie: William's been around the music since he was a little boy, so he knows the old style.

Will: My brother-in-law John was my idol. I listened to him practice every day, and was intrigued and fascinated by the trumpet. I was always saying to him, "Let me try. Let me try. Let me try." I wanted to play trumpet like him. The school sent home this form for you to join the band and you were supposed to circle the pictures of the instrument you wanted to play. I circled trumpet. But when it got delivered, it was a trombone. I started crying. "I didn't want that! That's not what I circled!" Boy, I cut up.

When they got it switched to trumpet, John used to challenge me. He'd say, "Well, that's only four notes of the scale. You gotta learn the whole scale." Or he said, "Oh, the D is probably too high for you." Soon as he go out the room, I'm back at that. I would try, try, try. And then he'd say, "The E is too high for you."

I'd say, "All right. Go ahead. Go take a walk. Go wherever you're going." And then after that, it got to be the same thing with songs. Lionel Ferbos probably knew the most melodies, but John is probably a close second. There's few melodies you could call a traditional music that he can't play.

Another huge impact on me was Preston Jackson, who also lived in the building. He played many years with Louis Armstrong. You'll hear on Louis' recordings sometimes, "That's old Brother Jackson there. Take it, Preston. Take it. Take it." He taught me a lot of the melodies to the songs, too.

When Dodie went out of town as a road manager for Preservation Hall, I'd get dropped off back at my parents' for the weekend. My friends started treating me a little different, saying I was getting white. I think I'm too much. I remember they used to ask me questions about my school. They saw me as different, and I saw them as different because I knew that half of them hadn't been across Canal Street, and that was true. That was true.

Dodie: The Preservation Hall tours took off. The band played *The Saints* as the last song, and went out in the audience to encourage them to dance a second line with them onto the stage. Nobody gets on stage at Carnegie Hall, but when they played, Jim Robinson probably waved and said, "Come on." The people got on stage and there was nothing the Carnegie Hall could do about it. When I wasn't on tour, William got to be around the older musicians all the time

Will: Part of that was from going to the Hall and part of it was from hanging out at Buster Holmes on the corner at on Burgundy and Orleans. The restaurant was famous for their red beans and rice. For a one dollar bill, you'd get a oval shaped plate of the best beans in the world, and for $1.50 you'd get a huge chunk of either smoked or hot sausage. On the table was just huge containers of French bread and pounds of butter with butter knives. That was it. There was nothing else that they sold. I ate there twice a week. And if got my own dollar, I might sneak in there and eat again.

It was a favorite spot of the musicians to hang out. Any day of the week you'd go there and the Humphrey brothers might be hanging out. Percy Humphrey took to the fact that I had got the trumpet, "Yeah, you did." He would give me scales that he wrote for me. Also Paul "Polo" Barnes actually wrote out songs for me, which Dodie still has and won't give back to me.

The Second Wave of the Fairview

The first band I ever played with was the Fairview. Dodie told me all about Danny Barker. I had listened to his records and knew he had played with people like Louis Armstrong. We went to a second line, and Dodie tells me, "Boy, now you're gonna get to play with the band." I'm standing there wide-eyed holding a trumpet, and the band's coming. The parade stops on Orleans, and she pushes me up in the band. They all knew, "Oh, that's him," And in that band was Tuba Fat, Leroy Jones, Gregg Stafford, Lucien Barbarin, Charlie Barbarin, Herlin Riley, Darryl Adams, Raymond "Puppy" Johnson, Henry "Hank" Freeman, and Gene Mims. A huge band.

That was my most concrete moment of when I thought, "I'm never gonna stop doing this." When I had reached the fulfillment of what I feel my life was about. I started practicing with the Fairview in a trailer that the church maintained on Sere and St. Bernard. At this time, I was 11. A new set of kids was beginning to come in and the older guys were beginning to get other work. Danny had been real hands-on with all the first guys, and I got to see that. At practice, he'd stop right in the middle of the song and say, "All right. No." If one of the trumpet players was having a problem he'd say, "What note is that he ought to be playing, Leroy? Get him straight on that part of the melody." Then they'd start up again. If he had a problem that one of the older guys couldn't solve, he pulled out a banjo and would say, "Play this: *Ding, ding, ding, ding, ding.* That's you: *Ding, ding, ding.*"

Right alongside him was Lucien's dad, Charlie, who was really the person who was in charge of us. After the first group left and there was a whole set of us

who had learned enough and was sounding good that he kept interest in us, we'd go with Charlie on an old raggedy bus to different churches to fellowship, and we'd play our little one song. From what I understand Charlie was a trumpet player but I only once heard him play once and that was only because somebody was daring him. However, he knew every scale and all the songs. He would show it to you by fingering it. "Look." I'd say, "Oh yeah."

After gigs, the band often got dropped off at the Barbarins' house right on Galvez and Orleans across from the Lafitte Project. And boy, we learned a lot right there. Little Jerry Anderson and his twin sister Deanna were raised up with their cousin Lucien. That's where they learned how to second line in front of the band. Deanna could second line, and that was really great because people liked to see that. There were no little girls doing this. And so our act was: Whenever we stopped in front of people, Jerry would take the drum off and walk up like he was challenging her, and then Deanna and him would cut up. They would cut up.

Right around that time, Charlie died, and we started to call ourselves the Charles Barbarin Memorial Brass Band, which was just the Fairview Band that felt, "We're not really associated with the church no more. Let's change the name." But the purpose of the Fairview was to stay along long enough to get to a the level where we can go on to do other things. And it worked.

Passing on Traditional Songs

By the ninth grade, I was playing professional gigs with Doc Paulin's band. Doc talked so hard in broken French, and he was as black as your shirt. The band was mostly his children. When you had a gig with Doc, you had to meet him at his house an hour early, and everybody sat on the porch because you got an inspection before you left. When he finally comes out ready to go, first thing he's going to do is look at you,

but I'd already been checked out. Ms. Carrie used to say, "Come here, boy" and she'd give you the inspection, much like my mom. She'd pull your shirt right, look at your shoes.

Doc's song list was completely different than what we were doing with the Fairview. We played *Tulane Swing*, *Let Me Call You Sweetheart*, *Bye Bye Blackbird*, and songs he played for all those Irish groups Uptown. Doc was not a person to abide you coming back twice not knowing something. I remember the first time he called *Margie*, and I didn't know it. He said, "William, you come back, you don't know that song, you'll be in trouble." I said, "All right."

Luckily, the musicians who knew the music were Dodie and John's friends. That's who we hung out with—who we'd eat dinner by. I remember the distinct smell of old people. I got to hang out with Louis Keppard many, many times while they fixed his food. He was blind by then. His brother was called the original jazzman, Freddie Keppard. And also that happened with Billie and De De Pierce.

Dodie: I liked to listen to Billie and De De tell stories, and listen to Billie play those low down dirty blues that she didn't sing in public. I'll never forget when Bishop Perry was made the first African American bishop, Jaffe invited him to the Hall because Billie and DeeDee were Catholic, and then he came over to their house. Billie cooked for days—there was food for an army—and then she got to the piano and started playing *In the Racket*. I said, "Oh Lord!" But he enjoyed it, and when she finished, she was laughing.

Will: When I started teaching with the Music for All Ages, I felt like it was really a culmination of what my life is. I saw myself in the role of the facilitator. I understood what needed to be done from having seen it before.

Portrait of Billie Pierce, courtesy of Dodie Smith Simmons.

We were training the kids by ear. They weren't reading a sheet. You're strictly going on the strength of your ear to be able to catch what's being played. My focus was the melody. I realized I could help them by doing the Charlie. I can stand in front of the trumpet players and they'll know, "Yeah, that sounds like he's playing an E, but I can also see he's playing E." I saw progress, and that fed the natural kind of teacher in me. I also started to find a joy in myself in looking at it as very segmented. "Let's take the A section and half it." That's just what Danny did, too. He'd say, "What's the point in going on? You don't get this part." I started seeing my own success.

Dodie: I did some recordings of the old time brass bands, and gave copies to the kids in the program at the National Park Service, because they need to hear it. Even if they never play the music, know what it's like. My husband and I always have arguments. He wants it to stay the old way. I say, "Now, you don't think Kid Shek was playing the way that Buddy Bolden played, or Bunk Johnson?"

Will: Everybody's trying to push forward. I really like to forge backwards. I still got a gazillion songs I'm holding onto that I heard as a kid. What's behind, there's so much beauty and prettiness in that.

Will plays with the PresHall Brass on Friday nights at Preservation Hall. Members include: Richard Anderson (*trombone*), Kerry Hunter (*snare*), Cayetanio Hingle (*bass*), Will Smith (*trumpet*), Jeffrey Hills (*tuba*), Daniel Farrow (*leader and tenor sax*), and Darryl Adams (*alto sax*). Photographs by Bruce Sunpie Barnes.

LIVING IN TRADITION

A man can make a whole lot of music to himself, but what growing the music does, what arriving and what becoming arises from it, that only happens when musicianers play together—really play together with a feeling for one another, giving to one another, reaching out to one another and helping the music advance from what they're doing together.

—Sidney Bechet, Treat It Gentle

BENNY
JONES, SR.
&
WILL
HIGHTOWER

BENNY JONES, SR.

Bruce: *Benny Jones, Sr. is a snare drummer, the leader of the Tremé Brass Band, a founding member of Black Men of Labor, and the first musician I talked to when I wanted to get the MFAA program started. I've always been impressed with the ease at which he plays his music and likes to make it happen for people. I watched him play at the Glass House with the Dirty Dozen Brass Band, and at second lines with the Chosen Few. I'd see him relaxing at the Petroleum Lounge or at a Mardi Gras Indian practice after a gig. What I remember was how kind he was when you saw him. I soon learned he took care of everything and everyone around him. At the end of a night, his truck would be loaded with people he was giving rides home to. If you want to know what's happening in the city, call Benny Jones. He knows. People tell him. His thumb is on the pulse of street culture in the city. For a lot of cats, he's a safe haven.*

Uncle Lionel Batiste, the bass drum player for the Tremé, was Benny's main running partner. A very magnetic character, when he was dressed in the traditional black and white with his band hat and walking stick, he was something else. The kids in the program were fascinated by him—especially the little bitty ones. He had a very light voice and used to them tell, "Come here, stand by me." They'd check him out, and in no time flat, they were all trying to dance and dress like him.

Benny and Lionel worked in tandem. They taught the kids the different ways you can make a roll off—the count or cadence to begin a song. The snare starts every song, except on a dirge, which begins with the bass. They showed the kids the tempos of the songs and their rhythmic patterns. Many of them sound similar, but they aren't the same. If you are playing snare, you have to play some part of the melody to make the song happen. Lionel taught them all the lyrics to the songs, and showed them how to make all the timing accents on the bass drum. He also showed them how to parade—how to line up and sway to the music as a band. When he passed, the kids played his jazz funeral.

Above: Portrait of Benny Jones, Sr. standing in front of an old sign for Ruth's Cozy Corner on the corner of North Robertson and Ursulines in Tremé, where family and music blended together in his childhood. Photograph by Bruce Sunpie Barnes. *Right:* The Olympia Brass Band plays a jazz funeral for a member of the Jolly Bunch Social and Pleasure Club in front of Ruth's Cozy Corner in 1970. Photograph courtesy of the Jules Cahn Collection at The Historic New Orleans Collection, 2000.78.1.885.

Photograph of Benny Jones Sr.'s father, Chester Jones (*left*), by Ralston Crawford, courtesy of the Hogan Jazz Archive. Growing up in the same neighborhood as his dad, Benny learned to play music just like he did—from paying attention to the musicians around him. Chester Jones explained: *I was born the first day of March, 1913. It was always my ambition to play drum. Nobody taught me how to learn this. I learned on my own. I've been around St. Philip Street all my days. I stayed a few blocks from Economy Hall, and all the kids and everybody'd gang around and listen to the bands because they'd play the first few numbers on the street. I used to grab the drummer's drum to help bring it up the stairs. I used to run behind the trucks with the bands playing music—jump on the back and get to close to the drummer where I could watch him.*

Introduction: You Can't Get Lost

Benny: I'm a self-taught musician. All of my friends wondered how I did that. My thing was, I never did practice playing like nobody else. If I got hooked on playing like this one, I'm going to forget about myself. I can't forget about myself. I have to create my own style. Cause once you play like yourself, you can't get lost.

If you don't be quiet and listen, you are going to miss it.

I went around to other musicians—all the grown-ups. Sometimes, when nobody was around, I'd go on the porch or the backyard by myself and be playing on the pots and pans. If everybody around, I sit under a tree by myself and be practicing.

I come from a very, very poor family. My family never ever sent me nowhere unless it was down the block and back, but my dad, Chester Jones, always used to tell me about all his friends overseas. He played the bass drum with Placide Adam's Onward Brass Band, and Harold Dejan's Olympia Brass Band. He brought musicians from Japan by our house, and they'd sit in the yard, drink, and talk about their trips. Or sometimes they'd go to Buster Holmes' bar and restaurant, talk that music talk and have a jam session.

When he marched on the street, my daddy had the big drum with that old deep, deep sound. I used to listen to him play in the French Quarter and watch how those ladies would be dragging those long dresses and hitch them up to dance. If he hit his drum on the back end of the Quarter, you could hear *Boom, boom, boom* on Canal Street.

Ms. Panola and Mama Ruth

I was born in the heart of Tremé in the summer heat of August 1941. My mother, Panola George, raised me at 1024 1/2 North Robertson. It was a mixed neighborhood. We've got black and whites, we've got Mexicans all renting old double shotgun houses. We used to play together. Fight together. We were together every day on the corner next to Ruth's Cozy Corner. We did everything but go to school and church together.

My mother was quiet, very low key, and used to dress old-time. She had all them kids, trying to raise them by herself. She was together with my daddy for some 20 odd years. He was a hard-working man. He kept a day job as a harbor police out there on the river, and also at Lincoln and Pontchartrain beaches. He stayed busy, but he was running around on the side. Even when we were teenagers, we didn't know what was going on. I still respect him. He lived just two blocks over from us with his first wife, Ms. Fanny, and their two children.

My daddy was born in Cut Off, Louisiana around 1913. His family moved to St. Philip Street in the Sixth Ward when he was just one year old. He was raised up on the same block as the Caldonia. Later on, he also courted the club's manager, Mama Ruth Queen. They had a son together, Chester Jones, Jr., who was the drummer with Clarence "Frogman" Henry for a long time. The neighborhood people would always go to the Caldonia. The Olympia and Onward Bands started the funerals and parades at the club, and the social and pleasure clubs made the bar one of their stops on their second lines. And let's say a big dance was going to be happening in the neighborhood. The band would put a big poster on the side of the truck, and put the band in the back. They went around to the different clubs and played in front of the door to advertise. I've been working on trying to bring that back.

When the city tore down the Caldonia to build Armstrong Park, Mama Ruth decided to get her own club. She opened up Ruth's Cozy Corner on Ursulines and North Robertson, and I grew up next to a corner barroom just like my dad did. She was also a member of the Lady Jolly Bunch Social and Pleasure Club, and hosted their meetings at her bar. A bunch of my relatives would go there and have their little meetings. On Sunday morning, I noticed they opened the bar up, put a sheet over their liquor, and had church service. Mama Ruth stayed on the same block as the bar and shared a yard with my family. We lived in the back and Mama Ruth lived in the front. My mother was a lady that never worried about going to the street too much, but Mama Ruth liked to go all over. I guess it made sense for my daddy. He didn't want two of them making noise—then you wouldn't be able to hear yourself!

My mother always got along real good with Mama Ruth. In the evening time, they would be sitting out drinking their little beer, talking all kinds of trash while listening to the fights on the radio. Only thing was, the mosquitoes used to be bad. You listening to the fights, fighting mosquitoes. Young kids couldn't go around grown folks when they're talking. "Y'all go catch up with your gang. Go play. Shoo fly." But they took care of us.

When I was about 14 years old, my mother took sick with cancer. She just went on down, started losing weight, and after about a year or so, she passed away. My older brothers, sisters, and I had to look after the younger ones. My dad would come check on us. The rest of our aunts, and people in our neighborhood made sure we had what we needed, that we were on the right path. Mama Ruth looked out for us, too.

A Little Hustle

I was a young man who tried to keep a job, a little hustle. I palmed up the red brick used to scrub front steps and sold a can of its powder for 25 cents. When the wintertime comes, I would work for the guys to sell coal to warm their houses. George and Mayo Clivens, who lived next door to us, had a peddling wagon. From when I was about ten, I worked with them, going around selling fruits and vegetables to people's houses. In my teenage years, I would come out to the French Market and throw watermelons in the truck. My good friend, Jake Millon, who was the Big Chief of the White Eagles, used to work on his father's peddling wagon as well. I used to play tambourine in his gang. If you grew up around the songs of the street vendors, you knew how to think up rhymes in the Indian songs.

I started to move out on my own in my early 20s. I drove a produce truck for the French Market. I always kept my truck nice. I would go around and clean people's yards or cut grass. A lot of people used to know about me. Smokey Johnson and James Black lived in the Sixth Ward, and, through those guys, I got to know Mr. Dave Bartholomew, who is like a father to me, too. My dad was a pretty good boxer, and he told me Mr. Dave used to play music between the bouts.

Mr. Dave would tell me, "Oh Benny, I got my house on Marais Street, I want you to come move some stuff for me." I said, "Okay, I be there tomorrow." As time went on, whenever he needed something moved, he used to call me. He'd give me keys and say, "Look, go over there and check on my property." And told me about his own musical career.

Verna's Family

I got my own little apartment on North Robertson and Governor Nichols, and started courting my wife, Verna Mae Shezbie, while she was still at Clark Senior High School. Her people were from the Sixth Ward, and our families grew up together. Verna's dad was away in the service, and when I met her, she was living with her aunt and uncle in the Ninth Ward. Uncle Lionel's oldest sister, Miriam, and her husband owned a double house there, and so Uncle Lionel was living on the other side with his first wife.

Uncle Lionel was a musician and he could draw and sew pretty good. When we was coming up in the 1960s and 70s, guys used to wear pimp shoes. They were black shoes with hearts, diamonds, and spades cut out of them. You wear them with white socks and then you can see the design in the shoes. Verna was kind of shy, but as far as music, she could dance. Her aunts and uncles sung all them Creole songs. She would be in the kitchen listening, and knew them word for word. She lived with Uncle Lionel most of high school, and then one day she came over to my apartment after school, and I said, "You better go home or Uncle Lionel and them are going to be looking for you." She decided she wanted to start staying with me.

She said, "When my daddy get home, we gonna get married."

I said, "Okay."

Left: The Dirty Dozen Kazoo Band, with Alfred "Dut" Lazard holding half a mannequin with underwear on. Photograph by Eric Waters. Besides the kazoo band, Benny paraded with a number of different social and pleasure clubs. The Sixth Ward Diamonds started at Ruth's Cozy Corner and lasted more than ten years. He paraded with Sixth Ward High Steppers and an Uptown club called Scene Highlighters, and was a co-founder of the Money Wasters Social Aid and Pleasure Club in 1976.

We lived at 811 Marais Street. We had a room and a kitchen. Her sister and mom used to come stay over night. I told them, "Y'all get in the bed. I'll sleep on the floor. In a couple of hours, I'm going to work." Every morning, I got up at to be at the French Market by three. I used to work 12 to 14 hours a day. We weren't making that much money. We were working for 75 cents an hour in them times. Yeah, and those were long hours, but I had to do it.

In the 1960s, I joined the Dirty Dozen Kazoo Band, which was made up of a lot of Verna's family—her Uncle Lionel and Aunt Miriam, and them. We were just learning. We weren't professionals. I'd be at my in-laws on St. Philip Street and Marais with a snare drum, and they'd be playing the kazoo, the banjo, the comb, or the washboard. We'd come out in the neighborhood on St. Joseph's Night or Halloween and play old Creole songs.

The Dirty Dozen

Around the same time, the Olympia Brass Band used to call me for certain gigs. By me parading with social and pleasure clubs, I knew how to dance and how to walk in front of a band. Harold Dejan also knew I could play drums. Tuba Fats played with the Olympia, too, and we did a bunch of gigs together. Tuba loved to play his horn. He used to play the church music. He played the brass band music. He also knew the rhythm and blues, and could sing pretty good, too. Then he also masked Indian and also paraded social aid and pleasure club. When the young guys saw Tuba with the Olympia Brass Band, they said, "Oh, I wanna be like Tuba Fat." The tuba players come around and he'd say, "Don't steal my notes!" Then, before you knew it, he'd be on the side, teaching them how to play the sousaphone.

When I branched off from the kazoo band, that's when I started to talk about building up the brass band. I got it with Tuba and Charles and Kirk Joesph, Rio Salavand. We started off playing little gigs like parties. Then we started picking up a couple of parades through the Young Men Olympia Benevolent Society. Tuba said, "Look, Benny can hook them up for you." We used to play for the First Division.

I learned from Harold Dejan to put two or three bands together. I take my time and figure out who I want to put in a band. I try to get guys who been around the music a while and know the tunes that we going to play. I'll put the Dirty Dozen Number 1 and Number 2. And that's how I started building the Dirty Dozen Brass Band through the social and pleasure club. I was always a man trying to keep a job and support my family. I was driving a truck for an electrical company in Metairie, Fisk Electric. Sometimes I used to go all the way down to Mississippi. I did that for about 15 years while staying out until two in the morning playing music. But I did that because I have kids, and I want to make sure that they go to the school, get the right education, make sure my family have money, and pay bills. I was dedicated to my family.

On Thursday night at Hardin Park in the Seventh Ward, the Dirty Dozen played because they have the baseball game. The guys used to be playing and wear dresses to have fun. We'd go down in the bleachers, and the band played. When the game was over, we'd do a parade from Hardin Park to Darrell's, on St. Anthony Street between Miro and Tonti, and play for about an hour or two. We'd come back and do like two sets on a Sunday.

One time this guy I knew from parading Uptown with the Scene Highlighters came all the way down by Darrel's Bar. He used to mask Indian, and he knew me from Indian practice, too. In the early 1980s, he said, "Benny, I need to talk to you. Man, I want you to come help with my club." I said, "Well, where's your club?" He said, "Down on Saratoga Street. We call it the Glass House." I said, "Yeah, I'll come talk to you." It took me about two weeks or three weeks. I'm thinking, "What is this here guy talking about? He sent for me. He must need help." I said, "Okay, we'll come on a Monday night." I always get there first to set up. We started at about ten o'clock. I had to be on my job by seven in the morning so I couldn't drink.

By ten, you can't get in the Glass House. You can't get in that whole block. Our music was real up-tempo music.It was a like a dancing contest every time we'd get there. They got a couple of guys, one was named Sugar Slim. He be second lining. He swing out, swing out. They had another one called Ice Cream. He come there and dance all night. Another thing we used to do, we used to throw tunes at the Glass House. We used to make up tunes, and then during the week we would go rehearse the tunes at practice. We weren't doing traditional music because they wanted to do something different. We're doing *Night Train*, *Kansas City Blues*, and Thelonious Monk tunes. They went to another level with the music. We stayed there about ten years on a Monday night. It was bringing the brass band music to younger people.

Plenty of Gigs

The Dirty Dozen started traveling a lot—going out for a month, coming back in, and going back out. For me, it wasn't going to happen. I had to back off on the traveling on account of my job at the electrical company. I could only take off so many days at one time. I had to back off. My electrical job was paying all kinds of good benefits, so I stick to that and make that work for me. It wasn't that hard. I caught up with the music when I could. I got back in the traditional music when I started the Chosen Few with Tuba. He didn't like fooling too much with that modern music. He'd been around with traditional music all his life. He was known for that. It was a good step for me, too. We had plenty of gigs around the city.

The Tremé Brass Band got started in the mid 1990s. A friend of mine named Darnell Washington owned the club Sidney's Saloon. On a Tuesday night, they had seafood night, and I used to go down there. I told

Benny in 2012 at Sidney's Saloon at 1200 St. Bernard Avenue in the Seventh Ward where he started the Tremé Brass Band. Over the years, his band has gone on to help establish a scene for many neighborhood barrooms. Most recently, he helped keep live music in Tremé by playing at the Candlelight Lounge, and has helped Kermit Ruffins reinvent Antoinette K-Doe's (wife of famous R&B singer Ernie K-Doe) Mother-in-Law Lounge on North Claiborne and Columbus in the Seventh Ward. Photograph by Bruce Sunpie Barnes.

the manager Calvin Vincent, "Let me bring the band down there one night, and audition." He said, "Y'all come down here next week, we'll see what happens." During the weekday, I called all the musicians and said, "We have a big jam session at Sidney's Saloon." About 30 musicians came around. We put something on top of the pool table and had musicians all around the sides— oh, we played!

They liked it and said, "Look, I want you to come here on a Tuesday night. What kind of money are you going to charge me?" I said, "You know, every one of these musicians has a price. A couple of them will sit in with me, but this money here, it ain't going to go that far." I worked out a price with them, and I broke the band down, and told who all was going to be in it.

Uncle Lionel was the bass drummer from the beginning, and he was a great influence on the band. Everybody loved him because he would sing songs and at the end of the night, he would get up there and dance for the people in the audience. He didn't drive, so whenever he had to go on a gig, he would ride with me. Many times we would knock off at midnight. I'm thinking I'm going home, but I have to drop him off, and he's going to dance and make a party until three in the morning. People don't want us to leave. And when I get home, my wife's looking at me like I'm hanging in the street, but she knows we've been together.

Come Sit In

Wherever I go, I invite musicians of all ages to my set."If you ain't doing nothing on a Tuesday or Wednesday night and you're free, come sit in and play a few numbers with us." It gives them an opportunity to try to play the music. They ain't gonna learn it overnight, but they get a chance to get one foot in the door. Learn some of the changes in the song as they go.

The Tremé Brass Band at Bullet's Sports Bar at 2441 A.P. Tureaud Avenue in the Seventh Ward in 2013. *Left:* Terrance Taplin playing trombone while Kenny Terry sings. *Middle and right:* Benny playing snare drum under the glow of the neon lights with saxophonists Roger Lewis (*on alto*) and Cedric Wiley (*on tenor*). Photographs by Bruce Sunpie Barnes.

One Thursday at Bullet's, my little trombone player, Terrance Taplin, said, "I got my little partner from Baton Rouge gonna come and sit in," and I said, "Yeah, come on, man." Nice youngster—quiet. He was sitting on the sides and explained, "Well, Terrance is my mentor. I've been watching him. Next set I'm going to come up there." We broke down the first set. The second one, they were swapping licks, and then he did his own thing. I mean, that little guy could play some trombone. I said, "Man, you are always invited to play with this band."

All of that helps the band out and makes the musicians proud because everybody's gonna tell the story about who played with Benny, and when they get a chance to tell all their other musician friends and say, "Man, y'all oughta go down there. If you feel like playing, they've got a hot jam session." It reminds me of the Dew Drop Inn. Cats get off their gigs and say, "We're going down by the Dew Drop for the jam session." It makes it a wonderful night. And I get a chance to play and learn other stuff I haven't heard before—what they are doing.

Benny's snare drum resting on top of his Cadillac in 2012. Photograph by Bruce Sunpie Barnes.

In My Spirit

Whenever I get a phone call, I don't know what it's going to be about—could be a jazz funeral, a wedding for a close friend or someone I don't know at all. It is all part of my business and I have to keep it in my spirit. One of the most touching experiences was when they buried all the people from Hurricane Katrina back at Charity Hospital Graveyard. People had lost their loved ones and couldn't find them; their bodies were held for so long. We had to get up around six in the morning. Hearses and limousines brought all the bodies to Canal Street, and we had to march them to their graveyard to put them in tombs. We must've been out there about four hours, and buried about 100 people in that one morning. I never did that in my whole life of fooling with jazz funerals. I've played for family,

friends from my neighborhood, musicians, Indians, and members of social and pleasure clubs.

When people call me today about a funeral, the first thing I ask them is, "Is it a young person?" If they say it is, I say, "Well, I tell you, we can play all kinds of music, but we play kind of old music, traditional music. If you've got a younger guy out there, you might want to get a young band. You do what you feel, but I'm just giving it to you because I don't want to go out there playing our music, and then I've got to get all those people on the sidelines."

I played for the Lady Buck Jumpers years ago down on Earhart and Broadway. A lady in there said, "Will you play for my parade?" I said, "Okay, Celia, we'll be up there." Here come the band. We get up there half an hour before the gig starts—taking our instruments out of our cars—and the little guys on the sidelines are talking their trash. "Oh, here comes Pop and them. Oh, Pop and them are going to play that old traditional music." Well, see, I don't get involved with that talk on the sideline. I said "Okay." We struck up the music. We're coming out. We are here on Washington Avenue around Rocheblave. I called a couple tunes, and I changed the music on them. We started playing some of that modern music. Next thing you know, they was all changing their tune, "I told you Pops and them could play!" Whatever funeral it is, I always try to do my very best because I know I'm here on a visit. When my time comes, I can't tell them, "Pass back, I'm not ready." When my time comes, I've gotta get on out of here.

Left: Uncle Lionel Batiste at St. Louis Cemetery No. 2. *Right:* Uncle Lionel passed away on July 8, 2012. Despite torrential rain, musicians paraded after his funeral at the Mahalia Jackson Theater for Performing Arts in Louis Armstrong Park on July 20th. The group included Gregg Stafford (*bass*), Kerry Brown (*snare*), Benny Jones, Sr. (*snare*), and Woody Penouilh (*sousaphone*), with Jose Bravo Besselman (*bass*) walking behind them. Photographs by Bruce Sunpie Barnes.

UNCLE LIONEL BATISTE, SR.
ST. PHILIP STREET

Uncle Lionel: *I was born February 11, 1932 on 1403 St. Philip between North Liberty and St. Claude. My mama's name was Alma Trapagnier. She was born and raised in the Tremé area, and my dad, Walter Louis Batiste, Senior, was from New Roads, Louisiana.*

In our neighborhood, everyone had aliases. They used to call my daddy "Papa" and my mom "Cairo." Mama had her children by midwives. I was the youngest of 12. My dad raised us working at a bakery shop. He played every instrument there was except the harp, but he did it mostly to entertain his family. He didn't worry playing in no nightclubs. He showed George Lewis, who is his nephew, how to play clarinet off a nickel flute.

My mama had a real strong voice and liked to have her children entertain her. In my parents' house, my mama would teach us to dance, and my dad was a good dancer, too. I can jitterbug, slow drag. And I like to waltz. My mom and them would go to the dances at the San Jacinto Club and waltz around the whole hall.

My mama was also the founder of the Dirty Dozen Baby Dolls. She would do the sewing. I would make the hats. It didn't cost nothing to buy your own material. A few nickels. As a young kid, I played music with them on Carnival Day in order for them to dance. People would be waiting to see us come out. We had the kazoos. I played the banjo, and I'd have it hooked up so I could play it the kazoo, too. I like the sound of the banjo, but it's a lazy instrument. You have to whip it. The baby dolls would stop at one of their members' house.

When they would come out again, they would come out as the Million Dollar Baby Dolls, and they'd have the lace stockings stuffed with money. If you reach up one of them women's legs, you're in trouble.

In the evening, the women in the neighborhood would sit on the steps with a bucket of beer and talk Creole. Musicians like Kid Howard would be coming down the street playing music and singing on their way to the French Quarter. They would stop there and serenade the ladies one or two numbers. And me, I would follow them, but I knew how far to go. When I hit St. Claude Street, I knew I had to turn around, but I would stand there and listen as long as I could hear them. I lived right across from Joseph A. Craig School on the 1400 block of St. Philip. When the band started rehearsing upstairs on the third floor, they would open the windows. I would play on the steps of our house until the band director's sister looked out the window and saw me. They gave me a white, blue, and gold uniform. And they gave me a hat. I wound up playing a hand-me-down snare drum.

One time the bass drummer was out and we had to do a parade. They had a huge drum, and hooked me up. I cried, "I'm too small to carry this bass drum!" The fella in front of me would hold it for me. Once I started playing, any time a second line come about, that's where I was, following drummers like Mr. Willie Parker and Mr. Emile Knox. They would take me under their wings. When I was about ten, I followed a second line, a little further, a little further, until I was way cross Gravier on the other side of Canal Street. Man, it started getting dark, and I started getting nervous. Where the hell am I? I remembered my parent's phone number. I called the house. My daddy answered the phone so I just hung up. I called again. It was my mom, so I hung up again. I passed in front of the train station three times. I went to the police, and they brought me home.

A lot of Dancing

The shoeshine box was one of my hustles. I also did a lot of dancing. I liked the way Fred Astair danced, and it's a blessing from God to give me the strength and memory to do these things. Even on St. Philip Street, Pork Chops and Kidney Stew, who were well-known, nice comedians and dancers, lived on the same block. Around the corner, Jim Crow and Jim Robinson both played the trombone. They would get in the yard and play that instrument. I used to take Coke tops or a piece of wood and grip them with my feet, barefoot, and tap dance. Later, when I was working down on Bourbon Street doing porter work, and I'd knock off work with this fella Lionel "Bird" Obicheaux—we called him Bird. We used to dance from my job all the way to my house. People would throw nickels and dimes.

Left: After Uncle Lionel's funeral on July 20th, children stood in front of Craig Elementary School to watch his procession. They wore memorial T-shirts and carrying fans organized by Tambourine and Fan. **Right:** During another jazz funeral on July 23, 2012, a horse-drawn carriage leads Uncle Lionel's casket down St. Philip Street past North Villere Street where he grew up. The house was torn down in the 1960s as part of the city's urban renewal project that ultimately led to Louis Armstrong Park. The Tremé Community Center is now located there, across from Craig Elementary. Photographs by Bruce Sunpie Barnes.

Dancing helped with the way I play music because you are following the rhythm of the drum and the bass. But times have changed. As of today, if you were to reach into your pocket and give a teenager $3,000 to waltz, they wouldn't be able to do it. That's true. What they are doing today with brass band music, they are jumping. The tempo is faster, and they're dancing by themselves. They cannot hand dance. They will get on the floor and do the alligator. That's not dance. That's called alligator.

Now I remember one time I was dancing, and I actually slipped onto the floor. And when I slipped, I had to do it again to make it seem like it was part of my act. But ask me if I didn't feel it later.

This edited transcript comes from oral histories with Uncle Lionel by Jack Stewart on September 6, 2001 for the New Orleans International Music Colloquium and Barry Martyn on April 17, 2004 for the New Orleans Jazz National Historical Park and the New Orleans Jazz Commission. Both interviews are archived at the Hogan Jazz Archive. Portions of Martyn's interview were previously published in Mick Burns' *Keeping in the Beat on the Street.*

Uncle Lionel Batiste's jazz funeral on July 23, 2012. *Left:* Oliver "Squirt Man" Hunter. *Right:* Oswald Jones, the father of trombonist Corey Henry, has been a grand marshal with the Tremé Brass Band for years. *Next page:* Norman Batiste dancing at his brother's funeral. Photographs on both pages by Bruce Sunpie Barnes.

Will Hightower at Roger Lewis and Mari Watanabe's house. The musicians are good family friends who have helped shape Will's understanding of New Orleans music. Photograph by Bruce Sunpie Barnes.

Will and Julius "Jap" McKee at a BMOL parade, courtesy of the Hightower family.

WILL HIGHTOWER

Bruce: *Will Hightower is a clarinet and saxophone player. In the MFAA program, we don't give out awards, but if we did, I'd say Will would receive the one for "Most Improved." When he first came, he did not want to get on the stage at all. I used to sit out in the audience with him and encourage him to try. You could see he was sparked by it, but he didn't want to put his hands in it. That was for crazy people.*

When Will finally came up, his clarinet would squeak and squawk like a baby goose. He started coming early and working out with musicians like Bruce Brackman, Joe Torregano, and Julius Lewis, and began to smooth things out. Then we didn't see him for a while, and when he came back, he had made a quantum leap. He was handling that horn. He was playing blues and swinging it.

One of Will's main musical connections outside the program was his relationship to Roger Lewis and other members of the Dirty Dozen Brass Band. One of the most traveled bands in the world, the Dirty Dozen continually challenge themselves to play everything from Thelonious Monk to Robert Johnson to Jelly Roll Morton. Roger is a saxophone player with a background in R&B and trad jazz, too. When he is at home, he loves to play with Benny and the Tremé Brass Band. In this interview, Benny and Will talk about their overlapping histories and friendship with the Dirty Dozen, and how to keep rooted in New Orleans music.

Introduction: In and Out of New Orleans

Benny: Where did your family and you grow up?

Will: I grew up in Metairie, but for the first four years of my life, I mainly stayed with my mom's grandmother because both my parents had to work. My dad worked as a drafter for an architectural firm, and my mom worked at an auto parts store.

My great-grandmother was really, really old. She lived over on Orleans Avenue right over by Bayou St. John next to the American Can Company. My mom tells funny stories about her. How she used to walk with an umbrella every day to get to her work because she was Spanish and she didn't want her skin to get any darker.

This was a time when, if you were a certain color, they wouldn't let you work at certain places. My memories of her are walking into the back of an old shotgun, and this decrepit woman is making food that smelled good in a kitchen that's got that yellow glow to it. She probably talked to me, but I remember visual images more than I remember hearing anything.

During Mardi Gras, her house was on the way to the Endymion parade route. It's like you're sitting on the porch with your great-grandma and you have double decker floats that are about the size of 18-wheelers coming down the street. It's a giant show of grandeur, and at four years old, you're like, "Oh! I feel tiny."

I think my great-grandmother passed away when I was about five. They still had to work so my mother's father, Frank Cole, started taking care of me more often. My grandpa was an old Spanish man. He had a full head of silver hair. It was freaking hilarious! He had raised my mom in Gentilly, and worked for an electrical company.

For a long time, he installed telephone poles and phones in white and black bars around New Orleans.

In the late 1960s, he moved his family out to Metairie. He was told by his superiors that black people were coming to take his job because of the integration with African-American culture. He got scared and was like, "Well, if that's gonna happen, then I might as well just move and get a job out in Metairie." There was a certain element of the "white flight" in there, but it wasn't driven by a dislike of people. My family, we don't really care. My grandpa was accepting of everyone. He still loved the city and its music. He was also really big into traveling. He had a map that he showed me and he had little red dots over every place he had been. He showed me pictures he'd seen like penguins in Australia.

He wouldn't crack a joke often, but he created a funny environment for you to be in. We used to go to Lakeside Mall. He would wear an alligator claw, and would walk around while he'd talk to old people. I would be bored out of my mind! And then he would go outside and smoke and it was just like, "This smells frickin awful!" But thinking back on it, those are some of my favorite memories of growing up.

Saxophones

I met Roger Lewis, the saxophone player with the Dirty Dozen, when I was about six. He is married to Mari Watanabe, a piano player from Japan. They have a daughter named Maya, and I took karate lessons with her at the Louisiana Karate Association. It was just down the street from my house. My first thought when I met Roger was, "Who is this old guy with this little hat?" I had never seen a kufi prayer hat before. To me, he looked like a cartoon character. Maya used to come over while Roger and Mari would hang out with my parents. He would always have something to say about

Top: Will's grandfather, Frank Cole, holding an alligator that he used to keep in the back of the family house on Orleans Avenue. *Middle:* Roger Lewis and Mari Watanabe's daughter Maya with Will (*next to each other on bottom right*) at karate class. Photographs courtesy of the Hightower family.

Above: Portrait of Roger Lewis, circa 1984. Photograph by Michael P. Smith © The Historic New Orleans Collection, 2007.0103.4.347. *Right:* Julius "Jap" McKee playing the sousaphone in Jackson Square, by Bruce Sunpie Barnes.

where he'd been on tour, but I didn't realize how big of a musician he was. I was a little kid; I didn't know what was going on. I was just like, "Duh," dazed.

Benny: When Roger Lewis first started with the Dirty Dozen he was playing tenor saxophone. One day we were doing a jazz funeral back on Orleans Street headed towards the bayou—right near your great grandmother's house—and we were getting ready to cut the body. Roger took one of the long solos. He took us so low, so long, and everybody got up and danced. Then, next time he started bringing the baritone saxophone. He's been on baritone every since. He

plays tenor every now and then, but he loves to play the baritone saxophone. Sometimes at certain gigs he will bring his alto. I never did hear clarinet. I don't think he liked clarinet. I ain't never seen him!

Will: Sometimes we go by Roger's house and work on some stuff. He is always asking me to give him a clarinet lesson! I think he wants to understand it more than play it.

Benny: What kind of music did you like to particularly play?

Will: I originally wanted to play saxophone. Maybe because of Roger and all the R&B music I was around as a kid. My parents had me growing up on Fats Domino, Marvin Gaye, and Al Green. You always hear the saxophone in the back. It's like, "Oh yeah, this is excellent. This is cool."

Benny: Yeah, when I was growing up as a kid, I used to like Motown music. I always liked to go to dances with R&B bands. When Ray Charles, Jackie Wilson, or Dave Bartholomew used to come to the Labor Union Hall, Jerome Smith and I would pay a $1.50 to go to their dances. We bought tailor-made pants and three quarter length shirts. During that time in the Tremé, old people could sew. You could buy material and tell them what you wanted. They used to have a bunch of tailor shops on Rampart Street, too. On Sunday nights, we used to dress up and swing out all night long. Everybody knew how to dance. If not, they knew how to dance by the time they left the Labor Union Hall!

Will: I was a really off-balanced kid. I was clumsy as hell. I couldn't walk straight.

Benny: What made you get involved in music?

Will: Before I started playing music, I had a hard time

in school. Both of my elementary schools were pretty awful because many of my classmates were, I guess the word would be "close-minded." They'd hear what their parents, who were really right-wing racists, said and immediately they believed them instead of saying, "Well, maybe someone else has something to say that's right." I didn't feel like being in these small classrooms where if you weren't friends with some people then you're not friends with a lot of people. I felt out of place and ostracized. I thought I'd joined the school band because I didn't like to play group sports. It's a terrible excuse, but I just needed a way to get out of P.E.

Benny: That's one way.

Will: When I told my teacher I wanted to play saxophone, she gave me a clarinet. I thought my teacher gave it to me as a way to scare me off! I'm like, "Oh, my God. This isn't fun. This thing's torture!" It ended up being a good thing because the clarinet is the grandfather of all the other woodwinds. You get clarinet down, and the saxophone is easy. But when I think back on it, deciding to play music had a lot to do with what was going on at my house. I got to know the music Roger had been playing for years.

Music at Home

After Katrina, I appreciated the effort that people put into things, and how quickly it could be taken away. I'd read a book and think about how much work went into it, just like how much work was going into rebuilding the city. But then my grandfather, this major figure in my life who had raised me, died and I was just like, "Oh, God! I don't wanna think about this."

We used to have a tenant who lived in a side apartment of our house, but he had a heart attack, and passed away, too. My parents kept that on the "hush, hush," because it was so tragic with my grandfather, but I knew what was going on.

Left: Bruce Brackman showing a young MFAA participant fingering on the clarinet. *Right:* Will playing with Julius Lewis on saxophone. Photographs by Bruce Sunpie Barnes.

Roger told my parents, "Hey, our tuba player in the Dirty Dozen could use a place to live." And that was Julius McKee—Jap. Jap comes and lives in the apartment, but I didn't pay too much attention to it. I had closed myself off to a lot of what was going on. My main form of entertainment was X-Box. But then more people started moving in. I really don't know how Revert "Peanut" Andrews ended up living next door with Jap.

Benny: Peanut is a great trombone player. He was on my first CD, *I Got a Big Fat Woman*. His family is in Mississippi somewhere and when he came into town he was looking for a place to rest his head. By him and Julius being friends, I guess he got a chance to be over there and practice with him and they got gigs together.

Will: We had a bunch of people over at my house. Jap says, "Yeah, I have this cousin Dwayne." Dwayne knows how to do renovation work, started fixing up the apartment, and living over there. Eventually, they get it all fixed and then Eleanor, Dwayne's wife, moves in, too. Sometimes you'd have like six or seven people living in one tiny apartment.

Benny: You had just about a whole band. You had the opportunity to have the older guys help you.

Will: It ended up being really important because halfway through sixth-grade year, I got put out of Ridgewood for fighting. Someone threw a can at me. It was really dumb, but they were antagonizing me. My parents had to home school me the rest of the year. I had my clarinet, but no teacher. Peanut showed me different songs like Paul Barbarin's *Second Line* and *It Ain't My Fault* that people would play in a brass band. Jap kept to himself more, but when he'd hear me practicing, he'd come over and explain the music theory side of the songs.

A few times, Jap also brought other bands over to the house. He was playing with some steel drum players. I remember this very specifically because when you hear the steal drums, it is that real Caribbean-type beat. Jap starts playing the tuba. Peanut is on trombone. Dwayne and Eleanor are making fried chicken in the house.

Benny: You hear it through the wall and you have to go see what is happening.

Will: You could hear it—and smell it—leaking into the house. I was playing video games and I went over there and it was awesome.

Solo

Jap told my mom, "If he's playing clarinet, you should get him more involved in brass band music." She looked around and found out about Sunpie's program on Saturdays. I started meeting other kids like John Michael who were also really open—just okay with being with all kinds of people. At first, I was scared to even get on stage.

Benny: I remember when you started out, you were shy. You were very, very shy. But you really came a long ways.

Will: The teachers in Music for All Ages were always encouraging you, "Take a solo, take a solo!" If you didn't try, they would sit there and let the chorus go around a couple times and it would be the most awkward feeling. I remember thinking, "Eh, what do I do? Do I make noise? I should make noise!"

Benny: They might tell you to take one chorus, then, when you do a second chorus, you feel some notes. It is called expressing yourself. The second time going around you are going to feel some notes. You might want to go another. Always believe in yourself.

Will: And hearing clarinet players in the program like Ricky Paulin, Joe Torregano, and Bruce Brackman play, it was like "Wow! Yeah, now I wanna play!"

Benny: How did you learn how to solo?

Will: I'm still learning how to take a solo! I think it had to do with deciding to go down a different path. After I was in the MFAA program for awhile, I decided to go back to school for my seventh grade year. Instead of going back to the private school, I enrolled in a really crappy public school called Riverdale Middle School. And, honestly, dealing with the people over there was ten times more enjoyable than dealing with those pricks at any of the private schools I went to. Some of my classmates were dirt poor and dealing with horrible situations in their lives, but they weren't judging people for being different. They're just like, "Whatever. Everyone's different." I was a lot better off in public school. Even though it was a worse education, I made a lot of friends with people who were minorities. I had Spanish friends, black friends, Asian friends, and it wasn't an issue.

I also had a really great band director named Mr. Desmond Veneable. He was a student of the St. Augustine Marching Band and a member of the Pinstripe Brass Band. He always used to tell us how, at our age, he was out there playing music for a living. Everything started coming together. Mr. Desmond could explain the music theory and playing by ear. And I would go over to your program and I would have the same kind of experience.

When I'd go back to band class during the week, I started asking Mr. Desmond, "Hey, when are we going to start doing brass band music? When are we going to start doing jazz band?" After about a year of asking, he finally started to do the jazz band thing in the summer. He taught us how to use licks and blues scales when we were soloing. I picked up some stuff in recordings, too. It all falls into place once you start playing.

Benny: What are some of the favorite traditional jazz musicians you've listened to?

Will: I've been listening to a lot of Sidney Bechet.

Benny: You ever listen to Alphonse Picou?

Will: Everybody knows him, man! *High Society*. A while ago, there was a lick I liked on a solo that I heard on a Nicholas Payton album. When I did some research,

Left: Band director Desmond Veneable giving instructions to his students. *Right:* Riverdale Marching Band in a Mardi Gras parade. Photographs courtesy of the Hightower family.

Charlie Gabriel (*right*) playing chess at his cousin Donald's house on North Miro Street in the Seventh Ward. Photograph by Bruce Sunpie Barnes.

I found it really goes back to Alphonse Picou's solo of *High Society* on a King Oliver album!

I've also been listening to George Lewis. A lot of the early jazz clarinet players used the Albert system, which is tuned differently than we do now. Picking up stuff from out-of-tune recordings is really hard. It's really, really hard. George Lewis was more in tune than most, but he still sounds flat.

Benny: He's related to Uncle Lionel, George Lewis.

Will: Somebody told me that Uncle Lionel used to work at a morgue!

Benny: He used to work at the funeral parlor right there on Rampart by the Jazz Fest office.

Will: One of the clarinet players that I really like now that I'm starting to go listen to is Charlie Gabriel who plays with the Preservation Hall Jazz Band. He travels a lot, but sometimes when he's in town, I'll go hear him.

Benny: He is a great player. He can play tenor, alto, soprano saxophone, too.

Will: You can tell he is not confined just to do that one thing. It is ridiculous. At first, I really didn't know him so it was kind of that awkward thing. You kind of go up and go, "Hi, I'm a clarinet player." Even still now, it is weird, but I love to go hear him.

Benny: He lives in Metairie, too.

Developing a Community

Benny: How have you developed a group of friends around the music?

Will: By eighth grade, I was really into music. At my school, you started to see where kids were gonna end up being if they didn't have a passion. My best friend in band and I had a dispute. He was going down one path and I'm going down another. I wanted to start doing music more seriously and he wanted to start doing drugs. Some people can balance it, but he wanted to sell. He's in jail, and we're the same age.

I've been playing in music programs like MFAA and the New Orleans Jazz Institute's Project Prodigy for years now, so most of my friends now are musicians. I have other friends who aren't musicians but most of them just want to do the normal teenage things like going to house parties.

It is like, "Okay, I do that, but it doesn't eat up my life."

I like to have this culture in my life. I don't just want to waste away doing stupid stuff. But not too many girls are playing music. It is weird.

Benny: In my day, there were a few ladies, but they played music like in the church. The piano. They ain't playing that brass band music. There ain't too many women playing music on the street. But they could sing all them songs. My wife could sing any song you can name because she was surrounded. I told her, "Girl, why don't you come in the band?" She said, "No." She was kind of shy.

Who are your biggest musical influences?

Will: It is most of the brass band people I've interacted with like you, Jap, Roger, Uncle Lionel. You set this example that you can play music, make money, have fun, and live happily. Jap and Peanut really helped me get ready for my audition at the New Orleans Center for Creative Arts (NOCCA). They grilled me on my scales and told me how to act during an audition.

Since I've been at the arts high school, some of my friends mix the traditional roots thing with modern music. It's different than what some of the younger brass bands play, but it still has a New Orleans feel to it. It still that freedom of expression with a modern jazz, but has the fun factor that New Orleans has. What's your opinion on that?

Benny: Depends on the kind of crowd you can get. Some people prefer to play it straight ahead. Ain't nothing wrong with that, but there's a market for brass bands and traditional music. You've got a market for blues. If you can get a crowd for bebop music, they love that—hey, that's your thing—go with it.

Will: I've been trying to do that. My second year at NOCCA, John Michael Bradford told me about the Tipitina Foundation's Internship Program. It's Tipitina's way of having a youth band they can use for publicity. And it works really well. We get to do really cool stuff and it helps them raise money.

In the three years that I spent with Donald Harrison, Jr., he got so much of my stuff together and made me want to be a professional musician. He just has so much knowledge. It's ridiculous. The most recent thing he's been telling me is, "It's time to grow up. You're about to go to college. It's time for you to start doing this for yourself." And when I listen to what he and Terence Blanchard did with Art Blakey and the Jazz Messengers when they were in their early 20s, I'm like, "Wow!"

Will dressed up for Uncle Lionel Batiste's funeral. Photograph by Bruce Sunpie Barnes.

Opening Up

Benny: What is one of your biggest struggles with music?

Will: As a kid, all I could play was soft. I couldn't open up, and it was a problem when I first started playing parades. The Black Men of Labor parade was hard. The first year I sat down at the second stop at the Candlelight Lounge, and did not move for a good 15 minutes. I actually had to run to catch up with the parade under the overpass on North Claiborne.

Being in the woodwinds section, you're walking next to all these killer cats and it's just like, "Oh, man! What can I pick up while I'm out here?" And you really don't pick up anything in the moment. It's definitely sensory overload. You have to tell yourself, "I just need

to focus on breathing, playing, and not falling over!" Jap came up and checked on me a lot. He would just come outta nowhere and ask, "Yo! You doing okay?" I was like, "Oh! Jap cares!"

After the parade was finished, I realized I did pick up a lot. I picked up, "Hey, I need to bring up my sound more. I need to do some more research on what the clarinet sounds like in a parade." It creates this like, "Yeah, I didn't do it this time. But I'm gonna come back and do it." But then the problem was that I wasn't balancing it right. I was only playing loud so that was detrimental to my playing, too. But now that I've gotten to this point where I can play both ways.

Benny: The best way to keep learning is to keep on making the gigs. And when you get to my age, don't stop. Keep on playing because I ain't stop! I

Musicians gather before Uncle Lionel Batiste's funeral. *Left:* Kenneth Ferdinand, Leroy Jones, and Herlin Riley. *Middle:* Frank Oxley, the leader of the Eureka Brass Band, and trumpet player Wendell Brunious. *Right:* Michael Duffy, who now plays bass drum in the Tremé Brass Band with Al "Carnival Time" Johnson in between Gregg Stafford (*bass*) and Shannon Powell (*snare*). Photographs by Bruce Sunpie Barnes.

ain't thinking about a nine-to-five job! I'm going to continue playing music. Mr. Charlie Gabriel's older than me and he is still playing. That is what he loves. That's what keeps him busy. All that keep an old man living. An instrument.

Will: I thought about that with Uncle Lionel. Everyone knew he was really playing into his old age. He had been sick, but when he died it was still sad because he was someone who represented such a concrete image of what jazz is in New Orleans. For a couple of weeks, there was a parade every day leading up to his funeral at the Mahalia Jackson Theater for the Performing Arts.

It was pouring down rain so the musicians paraded, but they didn't bring out his body. Then we all gathered a few days later at Charbonnet-Labat Funeral Home. That was massive.

There were musicians there that you would never usually see doing a second line. A lot of stage musicians. I had never seen that many people united just for one particular person. You'd have different musicians show up for different funerals, but this was like everyone was there. It was really, really unorganized. You had to figure out where you wanted to be in the procession, and I decided to walk next to Bruce Brackman and Evan Christopher. They were the people I knew the best. Walking with so many musicians, I kept thinking, "Who's gonna take that place now as an icon?" You are a huge icon, too.

Benny: I never worry about sticking out. I'm the quietest one in the band. Everybody make noise but me. When I get off the bandstand, I greet people. It is never about me. It is about all of us.

Will: I got a scholarship to go to Berklee School of Music. I'm really excited to get up there and be on that scene— to be around all the people that are really diligent. I've heard there's no room for slackers. But I'm also interested to see how people up there will interpret New Orleans' influence on jazz. What I've learned growing up here is it's hard to get it right if you don't have the right mindset. If you go in thinking that it's just a piece of music, you are going to miss it because it's an entire cultural entity on its own.

111

Roger Lewis at BMOL's gala in 2012.
Photograph by Bruce Sunpie Barnes.

ROGER LEWIS
LONG TONES, FRIENDSHIPS OVER TIME

Roger: *When we met, you were about six years old, and my daughter was four. Matter of fact, you weren't playing anything. Probably video games.*

Will: *Yeah!*

Roger: *Your parents and I became friends. Later on, I was on the road, and when I came back, you were playing clarinet. Before I knew it, you had a saxophone—a soprano saxophone, and now you've got a tenor. You want to be "Tenor playing Will!" Right now you're hungry—you really want it bad. You want to get out on the bandstand and blow hard into your horn: brrrrrrr! But you got to take your time, man. I've been playing baritone for 40 some years and I'm still trying to learn this instrument. And playing music is also about relationships— your associations with other musicians.*

Benny and I have been playing music together for almost 40 years. Reporters look at the front man of a band and think that's it—they don't really know the mechanics of how everything works, and how it came about. They only know visually

what they see, but that's not necessarily what it is. The Dirty Dozen was created by Benny. After he left, people used to ask, "Who the leader of the band?" Well, everybody had something they did with the band. It's always been like a collective.

Benny and I stayed connected. When he had the Chosen Few, I was a member. When we started the Tremé, it was basically some of the same members as the Dirty Dozen. Benny is responsible for a whole bunch of young musicians playing music. He has always had been a training ground. Just about everybody who plays brass band music in the city's been through him. Benny is a straight-up hustler. That boy got some skills. And one of the nicest dudes you would ever meet. All the young cats, he'd give them a gig. That man has a lot of patience and compassion.

Let me tell you a story. When I first met Benny, we'd been gigging but I didn't know him too well. My oldest son was 22 years old. He had just come out of the Marine Corps and was going to UNO when he developed a muscle cancer that only attacks young people. The doctors gave him two weeks to live.

We wanted second opinions, and I told Benny I was going to fly with my son to Indiana. You never know who your friends are. I didn't know how tight we were. Benny said, "Hold on, take my car and drive up there. Keep it as long as you need it." That's as real as you can get.

A Man at 15

I've been hustling this music a long time. You don't wait for the phone to ring. You're young, but you're a different kind of young. When I was your age, I was playing in barrooms. I got a saxophone when I was ten years old, and by the time I was 12 years old, I was walking on the bar, kicking over drinks. I was a man when I was 15 years old. I went to school year-round. During the regular school season, if somebody offered me a gig, I wanted to make some money, so I made my classes up in summer school. I got married when I was 19. By the time I was 24 years old, I had four kids, man.

Will: *My dad was telling me about the R&B bands you were playing with.*

Roger: *Growing up, Frederick Kemp was my best friend. He played saxophone. Back in the 1950s, when we were teenagers, we played at a club called Mary's Tavern on Magazine Street. Kemp was an acrobat. I was playing on top of the bar. People were throwing money, and I'm feeling all good—cocky. All of a sudden: Bam! Kemp did a backflip while playing his horn. All of the people came from the bar because they saw it, too. I said, "I know I didn't see what I seen." "Yeah, you seen it." I said, "Do it again!" Bam! I tell you no lie. When we went down the street to a little sweetshop on LaSalle, I had 47 dollars. Now, bear in mind, school teachers weren't making more than 200 dollars a month at time, so that was a lot of money.*

I started playing with rhythm and blues musicians like Irma Thomas, Deacon John and the Ivories, Oliver "Who Shot the La La" Morgan, Big Joe Turner, Chuck Berry, Wilson Pickett, and Johnny Adams. Every time Kemp or I got into something, we pulled the other one up. As years went by, Kemp got the gig with Fats Domino, and I joined too.

Early on, we went out on the road, we were riding six deep in a station wagon with stuff on top! Talk about the life style of a musician, you've got to know what you are doing before you step into this world because it is unforgiving. I was playing with Eddie Bo, and we were running the chitlin circuit. We got to a gig a half an hour late. All the people had left. The club owner gave us 50 cents a piece—two quarters—and a ham sandwich, with no mayonaise on it, to get to the next stop.

People don't really have no clue what you go through before you even get to the bandstand. If you decide you want to step off into this world, you have to be strong. You have to be a soldier. Especially if you want to be a road musician. Or you can bury yourself in the school system, which is cool, teaching other people how to play music.

Will: *I don't think I, honestly, want to teach.*

Roger: *You want to perform. You want to be a soldier! You want to get on the bandstand and spar notes at people. The youngsters be saying they piping at each other. Piping?! This ain't basketball! This ain't a competition! They used to talk about cutting heads. I played with Deacon John and the Ivories back in the 1950s. Man, we were young kids. We probably had the best young band in the city. We used to go ask the people if we could go sit in on their break. We would sit in, and you see, next week? They didn't have their gig no more. But that was survival.*

You might not know it, but you did the right thing starting off playing clarinet because it is the mother of all reed instruments. If you start with it, it's going to make you faster. Clarinet players play faster phrases.

Will: *I was looking at Victor Goines' hands and I could tell he started off playing the clarinet because his fingers are right on top of the instrument.*

Roger: *Now you've got to get the sound, because some clarinet players pick up the saxophone, their sound is really not right. You got to develop long tones. The best way to build up tone is to stand out on that levee and try to fill up all that space around you. Your sound will be big. When I joined Fats' band he had five tenors, man, and me on bari. I had to find me an open field and play long tones so I could kind of play above the tenors, or fill in.*

One thing that's important is that you already got the street in you. You got it in your playing. When you are playing a solo, check out how people dance. I play off their rhythms. I will get inside your body. So if you are moving one way, you don't know I've got you moving like that. That becomes part of your musical experience. You'll find you have more to say than what they teach you in school. Because some of the music schools, those kids come out and all of them sound the same. It sounds like they read the same book. What I'm talking about, I don't think you can write it, but you can feel it.

JOSE
BRAVO
BESSELMAN

&

ANTHONY
BENNETT

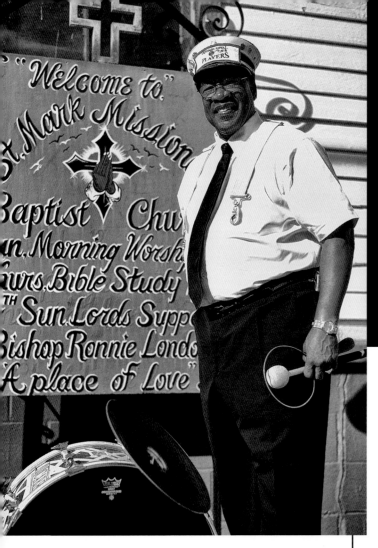

Anthony Bennett in front of St. Mark's Missionary Baptist Church's Welcome sign. When he was growing up, the church was located in Economy Hall, which was built by the Societé Economie et d'Assistance Mutuelle in 1856. The group consistently came out against slavery during the Antebellum era and the Citizens Committee, who came together to protest de jure segregation and file the case that became *Plessy v. Ferguson* after Reconstruction, met at their Hall. In the early 1900s, it was rented out to other benevolent associations who hosted *soirees dansantes* that ran from eight in the evening to four in the morning. Louis Armstrong, Kid Ory, Sidney Bechet, Buddy Petit, and Alphonse Picou all played there.George "Pops" Foster compared the opportunity akin to playing at Carnegie Hall. In the mid-20th century, it was also where they had the first black union for musicians before St. Mark's took over. Photograph by Bruce Sunpie Barnes.

Economy Hall. Photograph by Ralston Crawford, courtesy of the Hogan Jazz Archive.

ANTHONY BENNETT

Bruce: *Anthony Bennett is a bass drummer and the leader of the Original Royal Players Brass Band who also works for the Charbonnet-Labat Funeral Home. What I noticed about him from the beginning is that he has a very solid understanding of human nature. He was very sincere in dealing with the students in the program and took his time to make them comfortable. Many times he stopped, took a piece of music and had the students work on it in small sections before bringing them back together as an ensemble.*

Anthony is a good example of someone who had been around the music all his life. His father was a drummer who played with Alfred "Uganda" Roberts and Harry Nance. Anthony played music for fun and in school, so he had it in his ear. He followed drummers in the Olympia Brass Band like Nowell "Papa" Glass and Nowell's father, Booker T. Glass, but wasn't playing professionally. For years, he had traveled the country working with racehorses. He handles the animals the same gentle way as he handles people. I've seen him driving everything from a pony to an eight-horse team, which takes a lot of understanding.

Midway through his life, Anthony felt a need and a drive to commit himself to music, and Kirk Joseph, virtuoso sousaphone player who played with the Dirty Dozen for a long time, took him under his wing. Kirk likes to find the humor in situations but is also sensitive and passionate about life. He plays bass lines that everybody would want to reach for. He has a very big round smooth tone because his technique is so good. He's been very humble about it, but he's changed the playing field for what you can do with a sousaphone. One of the first cats to take a microphone and just drop it down the bell of the sousaphone, and play it through a bass amp like a bass guitar. He is always challenging himself to play new styles, and encouraged Anthony to get serious about music.

Introduction: A Creole Neighborhood

Anthony: The Sixth Ward/Tremé was a lived-in neighborhood. It's so strange to go around there now and see it so quiet. When I was the president of the PTA at Craig Elementary, there were 50 children on Dumaine Street alone! I was born November 27, 1952. We lived with my mother's mother, Elenor DeLarose, at 911 North Villere, and that is the address on my birth certificate because where we lived there wasn't an address. I wouldn't even call it a slave quarter because it was just a room with a kitchen behind her cottage.

My mother raised me Catholic but when I was growing up, I went to St. Mark's Missionary Baptist Church across the street from my house. There were always activities for children in the neighborhood. Reverend Alexander's church was located in the world-famous Economy Hall. My cousin, Rosemary Holland, was a crossing guard, and she ran a program there called the Junior Police Band. I played bass drum because it was the closest to how my dad, Ernest Bennett, Jr. had shown me how to beat with my hands. He was a percussionist and played bongos and congas. He was immersed in Latin music, and hung out with a lot of Cubans.

The connections to the Caribbean in the neighborhood and my family wasn't something I thought a lot about. There were Jamaicans, Haitians, and Hondurans but, to be honest, I didn't know that they were from a different place. I just knew that they spoke with a different kind of accent, and I guess that wasn't a big deal because it was true for my family who was raised in New Orleans as well. My grandmother Na Na spoke patois. Half the time you couldn't understand what she was saying. She would say, "Look," but in Creole, "*Garde cá.*" She sang little Creole songs to you, too. Uncle Lionel Batiste used to call her "Talk of the Town." She was a tall woman and very outspoken. She told me about when the police chief of New Orleans, David Hennesy, was killed in 1890. People were running around the city yelling, "They killa da chief! They killa da chief!" They started rounding up Sicilians. Her uncle could have easily been confused for one. They had to put him in the vegetable cart to sneak him out of the neighborhood. It was hard to tell the difference between a lot of Sicilians and blacks back then.

My dad was a product of a Creole woman named Alma Carter and a Jamaican merchant marine who ended up here in New Orleans working on the Mississippi. My dad didn't have his father very long. He was a longshoreman, and he died in the river. His body was never recovered. When I was young, my grandmother Alma was quiet. They called her Yut-Yut. She was the mother of a Spiritual church she ran from her house in the Seventh Ward. She wore white and was real strict. My father said one time he started reading something out of one of the books he found in her house and felt this strange spirit. It unnerved him.

On Sundays, I would be sent to church at St. Peter Claver but I never went. I'd sit on the steps around the corner, and when people would come out of church, I'd walk alongside them like I'd been inside. I didn't really get into my own spirituality until I was older. Because of St. Mark's, church was mostly fun to me. On other Sundays, the Junior Police Band would go on the radio station WBOK and play our only song—*The Saints*. We also participated in little community parades. We wore black and white and had the little seven star hats. It was ragged, but we did our best. I have the one memory of the bass drum being much bigger than I was. I remember me trying to play it while somebody walked in front holding it up! It wasn't a really serious thing at that time. It was just being involved. That was the most important thing to me.

Early drum influences. *Top:* A band gathering in front of St. Mark's Missionary Baptist Church, by William Russell, courtesy of The Historic New Orleans Collection. Acquisition made possible by the Clarisse Claiborne Grima Fund, 92-48-L.158. *Bottom:* Anthony's father, Ernest Bennett, Jr. Photograph courtesy of the Bennett family.

Part of a Society

After church, it was a tradition to dress. You would come home, change, put on another set of clothing and come out to the bar. If you had a green suit on, you would have green shoes and a hat. All of your accessories matched and your tie pin. Cufflinks. There were tailor shops all along South Rampart Street like Harry Heiman's and Murphy's Tailors where you would go to choose the material you wanted. They would measure you for your suit. My mother, Miriam Martin, was a seamstress for what she used to call "the factory" at this place up on Julia and Baronne. All the suits for the different tailors were sewn there.

Her mother's brother Louis, my Uncle Doc, was known as one of the sharp dressers of the Sixth Ward and was in a club called the Tremé Sports. I had another uncle, James Irving, who they called Tampin Light—after his light way of walking. He was one of the well-known grand marshals in second line parades. As a kid, I got a spanking for following the second lines, or told not to go, but I loved to listen to the band. People were dancing, and I walked alongside, watching and paying attention to the syncopation between the bass drum and the snare drum. Like with you, Jose, when you came to get lessons, I played the old music, let you play along with it, and told you where to accent. You remember that? Or I would tell you, "Don't listen to that. As a bass drummer, what you have to remember is you're 'one.' No matter where they go, they have to go back to you." I figured that out myself following the bands.

There was a man in Tremé we used to call "Good Time Totsy." He had this big cigar sticking out of the side of his mouth. He wore his pants pulled up high above his waist. Totsy was a member of the Square Deal Boys. When he would parade, he would ask me, "Want to carry my basket?" Every time I wanted to go, my mama said no and Totsy would say, "Mimi, leave that boy

The Sudan Social and Pleasure Club emerged from the Bucketmen. They are known for keeping a traditional second line style that developed in the Sixth and Seventh Wards. Each year, they wear suspenders and streamers, and usually carry elaborately decorated baskets. Photograph by Bruce Sunpie Barnes.

alone. He can come with me." I followed Totsy. Before you knew it, we were in front of the parade, and all the focus was on me. It felt good. I think Totsy and my uncles all motivated me to join Tremé Sports and be a part of a society. Parades suited me. I was an introvert, but never stable. I was quiet, but was that person who was cutting here and there. Never in one place.

"Urban Renewal" in Tremé

In 1960, the city started tearing down houses around us, and moving folk out as part of the city's urban renewal project to build a "cultural complex" that became Louis Armstrong Park. Bulldozers coming in. Cranes. Wrecking and knocking down buildings. It was like a friend being taken away. That is what actually happened. You saw family leave. People started going to different places. They ended up across the Mississippi River in the Fischer public housing development. You had people who were in there that ended up down in the Ninth Ward, or that went further Uptown. After the houses were torn down, I got a job

sitting on a bucket, knocking the mortar off bricks for a nickel, in the rubble of someone's house. But even when those people were moved out to different areas, with the live oak trees on the neutral ground of Claiborne, you could still see people. They were going to come through Claiborne. After the trees were taken away and they put up the highway, there was no place to congregate.

In junior high, I walked across Claiborne every day to go to Andrew J. Bell. The middle school I would have gone to—McDonogh 41 in Tremé—had been torn down. It was a big thing to be in the band. If you didn't know anything about music, by the time the band director, Donald Richardson, got done with you, you knew something. He was strict, but he was fair. He let you know, "If I don't do anything else, you are going to learn this." He was one of the first teachers I had who involved your parents. But then he also had this mallet that he would swat you with. His favorite expression was, "Let me chop it."

The remaining neutral ground of North Claiborne Avenue, between St. Bernard and Elysian Fields, gives a glimpse into what the whole corridor would have looked like before the Interstate-10 overpass was built. Photograph by Bruce Sunpie Barnes.

Top: Building Interstate-10 on North Claiborne. Photographs by William Russell, courtesy of The Historic New Orleans Collection. Acquisition made possible by the Clarisse Claiborne Grima Fund, 92-48-L.46 *Middle:* The Tremé Sports, courtesy of the Hogan Jazz Archives. *Bottom:* Anthony Bennett at a parade, courtesy of the Bennett family.

Partly because all of the people in the band were friends, there was that camaraderie. When Joe Torregano joined the band, I think he already knew he wanted to be a music teacher. He was serious about it, but I had a fever for horses I developed from going to the racetrack religiously with my dad. We also had family members who were into horseracing. My Uncle Herman's son, Herman Jr., was traveling as a groom. It was always intriguing to me, "Where's Herman?" "Oh, he's in New York." And I was like, "I want to see all these places." I grew up in such a close-knit family, I wanted to be missed for awhile.

During my last year of junior high, I used to walk horses at the Fair Grounds early in the morning and on weekends. I didn't care about pay. I just wanted to be around the animals. My cousin's husband, Gilbert Edwards, took me under his wing. The first time he gave me a horse to walk, he stopped to get a drink. When I pulled the horse's head out, he threw it up and the water went dripping from his mouth. I got scared, "Ahhh!" I thought he was having a seizure. Gilbert said, "Look, let me show you. If you take care of these animals, they will take care of you." I learned that horses are just like people. They have their own spirit. You can't treat two the same. You have to treat them as individuals because they do different things.

In the summer, I started going up North with Gilbert to Chicago and Detroit. When it was time to go back to school, I would come back to New Orleans. But to show you where my heart was at the time, when my class graduated, I was in Detroit! I think that the experiences I had leaving New Orleans helped me a lot. When I was away from here, I was allowed to be whoever and whatever I wanted to be.

Getting Organized

At home, I was friends with a lot of the guys who ended up getting involved with the Dirty Dozen. I remember one year I was back in town, and Tambourine and Fan sponsored an event called Super Sunday that brought out all the Mardi Gras Indians with the children who participated in the youth programs. I'd always admired Jerome's activism. He's like our New Orleans own Malcolm X. I know he's one of my heroes. He's always been about the children.

A group of us were collecting money for the event. Benny Jones had this big truck—a 1949 something—that we were going to use to travel around. Jenell "Chi-lite" Marshall said, "Here," and handed me a trombone. The two of us grew up in the neighborhood doing all kinds of silly things together like swinging from the pipes all along the ceilings of Craig Elementary. I don't know where Chi-lite got the trombone, but I took it. Of course, Anthony "Tuba Fats" Lacen, being the musician that he was, started organizing, saying, "Look, we are going to do this."

I'll never forget, we were in front of the Superdome collecting the money, muddling through *Lord, Lord, Lord* and Chi-lite said, "Take a solo!" Solo?!? I just got the horn! All I'm doing here is making noise. Alfred "Dut" Luzard had a clarinet. He was a character now. Oh, Lord, he was a character. He was younger than my mother, but he was older than me. We met in the streets, and hit it off. I lived two blocks from Clark High School, and Dut would start yelling my name as he got to the school. You could hear him blocks away, "Anthony!!" My mother would say, "Dut, why you making that noise?" He said, "Because Anthony say I'm embarrassing to him, that's why."

Dut was a family man, especially involved in things with children. Dut would walk down the street with his wife's pink houseshoes on, and if you told him about it, he'd say, "Well, if it was against the law, I'd be in jail."

On the truck, every now and then Dut would get in front of us with the clarinet and go, "Toot!" It was this big joke, but the people thought we were an actual band and were clapping along and donating money. When I was back on the road with the horses, they started getting serious. Dut called me and said "The Dirty Dozen are getting gigs! They are getting real gigs!" He became the grand marshal for the band.

On the road, I was trying to do some organizing in my work, too. I was at Arlington Park, which is in a mostly white suburb outside of Chicago. During that period, there were a lot of Hispanics coming to the racetrack as opposed to a lot of blacks on the backside. We were working almost 24 hours a day, seven days a week. We were going at five in the morning to get the horses out for their training, and expected to stay through the racing at night and be at work the next morning. But people were afraid to say anything because there were more people who wanted to work than jobs.

A friend and I said, "There's gonna be no racing on Labor Day." We figured that would be the time. We're going to boycott the racetrack, rent some buses, and have a big picnic. Later on that day, the chaplain came and got me. He brought me to his office, and I saw the security. They started asking me questions. Then they made me pack my stuff and brought me out to the highway.

They asked me, "Where do you live?" I said, "New Orleans." They went, "Good luck."

The same thing happened at Louisiana Downs. I started preaching, and they gave me the same thing. Brought me out to the highway. I got all upset. "I'm gonna take this a step further!" I called the NAACP but they didn't think I had a case. They said, "You know you are on private property."

Those experiences made me aware that unless I had some money, or the backing of an organization, I wasn't going anywhere. The next thing people would be saying about me was, "He's crazy." You know when you pass on Canal and you see the guy with the bullhorn pacing up and down the street preaching? People are going to be saying, "That man crazy." And really, they aren't even listening to the message—it's the delivery.

I decided I wanted to get more control over my life. I lived in Detroit for awhile on Woodward Avenue. Right around the corner, the Nation of Islam had a restaurant, and I used to go in there all the time and eat. They were black people who had businesses. They spoke of the resources that they had—the fish came from their own factories. The bean pies were good, too. That was attractive to me. In other cities we traveled to, I started noticing them more, and decided to join. I maintained my prayers while I was traveling, and finally settled in California where I worked my way up from a hotwalker to a trainer.

Self-Preservation

The one thing I promised myself when I got my horse trainer's license was that I wouldn't just have horses to say I got a stable—I would have horses that I could compete with. In 1987, I had a bunch of garbage. I really did. All I was doing was making bills. I was paying the feed man and the blacksmith. If I had money in my pocket, it was because I didn't pay one of my bills. I was really miserable.

The owners included an ex-football player, a used car salesman, and a guy who had a record store. They were always bickering about, "Did you pay your part?" One guy would come to tell me what another trainer was doing at their barn. I'm like, "You know what, you like what they are doing? Take your horse over there."

"Oh no!"

"Well, stop telling me what they are doing. They are not doing better than I'm doing. They can't beat me." The thing was, I had been away from home so long. I left New York and was in California for eight years. In New Orleans, my friends were parading and playing. And then the Dirty Dozen came to LA for the Hollywood Bowl, and were on *The Tonight Show*. I was like, "Hmm, I need to be home. I'm missing all this." I got back to California and just started getting rid of stuff. I had enough for somebody who maybe had 20 or 30 horses. I had two cars and a motorcycle and can't tell you where any of it went. That's how bad I wanted to be away from there.

Back in New Orleans, I started working for the coroner, Frank Minyard, doing autopsies. It was at the height of the crack epidemic in the city, and we were having to deal with an increasingly high murder rate.

Now that I was more settled, I wanted to get more involved with the Nation of Islam, and my friend Randy Mitchell, who I grew up with in Tremé, introduced me to Minister Harold Mohammed. The NOI was meeting at the offices of Endesha Juakali, an activist and lawyer who grew up in the St. Bernard project. Through the study sessions, I realized that the teachings didn't come from the Koran. More than religion, their beliefs were based in economics and politics that came from the United States. They were teaching about self-preservation. About loving yourself as a black person, and not trusting the white man.

Some brothers came from Washington and wanted to clean up the St. Bernard project: "We are going to do what we did in Washington D.C." They wanted to go in, beat up brothers who were selling drugs, and tell them to get out.

I'm like, "Well, you know, Brother, this is a different animal here. You can't come here and think you can do what you did other places."

"Oh, Brother, we're going to." The drug dealers ended up shooting Endesha in the leg. Next thing I know, the Brothers from out of town were leaving.

The final straw for me was when Louis Farakhaan when came here in 1990 for his "Stop the Killing" speech at the Municipal Auditorium. I usually helped them prepare statistics about the city through my job with the coroner. This time I collected information about the murders in the city, and gave it to them to use. The place was full. He told the audience, "I have a hundred dollars and I'm going to give it. And I want all of you to follow in suit." After the speech and everything was over, they went back to the hotel. Money was piled up on the bed. A sheetful of money. Randy

asked, "Well, how much of that money is going to stay here in New Orleans?" They looked at him.

I said, "That's it. This is not right. This is a hustle." It had been less than a year, and I decided to leave. I started searching for a place in Catholic and Baptist churches around the city, trying to feel my way.

Grand Marshalling

When Benny started the Tremé Brass Band, Dut used to grand marshal for him until he got sick with kidney disease. Benny needed a grand marshal for a gig at a hotel, and asked me if I was available to work. I said, "Okay," but I was anxious about it. I was like, "I don't know if I want to be in front of people like that." I not only had to be the grand marshal but I had to be the preacher because the corporation used the format of a jazz funeral to "bury" a problem they were having with the company. I had to read a eulogy and I really got into it. I tapped into what I saw my uncles doing a long time ago. I moved the way I saw them move and acted the way I saw them acting. It fit me.

One of the other things that Benny and I always connected around was horses. He used to go out riding on Sundays, and the director of the Charbonnet-Labat Funeral Home, Louis Charbonnet, got intrigued and

bought a horse named Joe Dancer. He thought, "This could be part of my business." I grew up next door to Louis, so he knew my history with the animals. He started asking me questions.

He bought another horse and got a carriage. We would ride around City Park on the weekends to see if we could hustle a ride from people out picnicking. As he started getting more into it, he bought horses to pull a hearse for funerals and asked me to train them. Getting to work with horses again helped me bridge different parts of my life. People would see me all over. I would take them out to get them used to moving in traffic.

Riding on the hearse, I remembered the jazz funerals when I was young—just to hear that sound or to watch the grace—the way that the musicians moved along with the way that they played. The bands marched in unison. Everyone on the left foot; everybody in a sway. On the carriage, I had to maintain that grace, too, because I'm carrying the deceased. Sometimes I'm driving the horse and there is no music. I have to maintain my focus. Maintain the animals. It is a lot like being the grand marshal.

You hear people all the time saying, "The horses are dancing." They hear the music. They hear it and I'm thinking they feel it. I always say this—there is a rhythm to life and everything in it. Once you get those animals used to doing something, they'll pick up that rhythm. It begins to be a part of what they are, and they will move in unison.

I was involved in parades, but I didn't know quite how to break into the music itself. Kirk Joseph, who was the tuba player for the Dirty Dozen, kept saying, "Well, look, I'm playing for this parade tomorrow. Come on."

And then Kirk's like, "See. I know you want to do this. I know."

Anthony driving the hearse with a jazz funeral procession, courtesy of the Bennett family.

Kirk Joseph and Anthony Bennett. Photographs by Bruce Sunpie Barnes.

KIRK JOSEPH
THE BASS SOUND

Kirk: *When the Dirty Dozen would be playing a second line, you used to aggravate the band. You'd be behind us at parades yelling,* Blackbird Special. *I'd say, "Dude, stop!!" We had just played it, and you wanted to hear it again.*

Anthony: *That tune brought energy whenever y'all played it. The other songs were kind of dull.*

Kirk: *That was the first song that we had recorded that was different from what the older bands were doing. Then you said you wanted to play bass drum. One day, I was playing a gig on Louisiana Avenue, and I told you, "Get behind me, and put your left hand on my shoulder, put your right hand on my right side, and beat on me while you are walking. Let me feel where you're at." You did all right.*

Anthony: *You know, I had played the bass drum since I was about eight years.*

Kirk: *That's the thing. I was fortunate enough to have parents with musical backgrounds, but for a lot of kids, their parents didn't understand practice.*

Anthony: *Then I went to your house, remember?*

Kirk: *Yeah, I grew up in that house on Elysian Fields and North Dorgenois, which is the backside of the Seventh Ward. You came by and we went through bass drum patterns on different songs. I wanted you to understand that when you knock off the first four beats, that's the time signature you stay at throughout the song. That's where you are supposed to stay!*

Anthony: *At your house, I would talk with your daddy, Waldren "Frog" Joseph, and he had a way of saying things. If I asked him, "How you doing?" He'd say, "That's not your business."*

Kirk: *Or he may say, "I'm outchere."*

Anthony: *"How you feeling?" He'd say, "With my hands."*

Kirk: *I never heard him say it. That's funny. I didn't know what he did for a long time. He was always gone, but my mother would play his recordings, and say, "That's your dad playing trombone." He also played piano and upright bass. As a child, I thought he was in the music box. Listening to the recordings of them today, a lot of bands are still trying to capture their sound. The thing about it, the people who are trying will never get it until they give love to each other. That's what those people had. They had love.*

I remember when my dad would be on the road, Brother Cornbread knew that my mom had all these kids and she didn't drive. He would come by the house and ask, "You need anything from the store?" That's love. And that's about music. Music is love for each other and family.

My dad played with Paul Barbarin, and he was someone who was close to me. When he died, it was the first time I ever experienced a jazz funeral. It started right there at Sacred Heart on St. Bernard by Claiborne. This was before the I-10 overpass was finished, and it was a sea of people. Because my dad had polio when he was young, he couldn't parade. He always wanted his kids to do it. He didn't force that on us. He let us make that decision on our own. From that moment on, I watched the parades, and felt what was going on in them. The first one didn't hit me when I was there. I hit me that night when I was going to take a bath. He was a guy who was always cheerful, always whistling. That's one of the reasons that I always whistle, between him and my dad. I thought about that—I wouldn't get to hear him whistle anymore.

In junior high, I decided to go to Andrew J. Bell to join their band. Whenever I saw them marching in their blue and white, they always sounded great. In the seventh grade, I went to Mr.

Donald Richardson and said I wanted to play drums. He said, "I have 500 drummers. I don't need no drummers."

Anthony: You know, I was playing clarinet at Bell. He told me, "Your lips too big to play clarinet." He put me on trumpet. I found out later he needed trumpet players!

Kirk: In my eighth grade, I was a heavier kid so Mr. Richardson said, "You would be a good sousaphone player." They had the horns on the back of the stage. I turned around to look at them and said, "Whoa, that's pretty big!" I went home and told my dad. He leaned back with a cigar in his mouth and said, "Yeah, you know something? Do that. You could make you some money while you're in school."

The lights went off in my head! My own money?! I don't have to clean windows around the house and garden!? Well, I learned I still had to do that, too, but that's how I started playing the sousaphone. I got into the program and Mr. Richardson taught us pop tunes and concert pieces.

The first week that I was in the band, Mr. Jeremy Green, an upright bass player, gave my dad one of his extra horns for me to use. One Saturday morning, I was at home looking at cartoons, chilling, and I get this call from my brother. Charles is right before me, but seven years older. There weren't any cell phones back then. He called the house phone: "Put on black and white, I'm coming to get you."

Now this is the brother who didn't want anything to do with me. He figured if I'd go with him, I was gonna rat him out. I thought, "This is a plan to get rid of me. He's going to get rid of me today!" I said to my mom, "Charles said to put on black and white and he's coming to get me!"

But my mom knew what he meant. He was going to take me on a gig with the Majestic Brass Band. She got out the ironing board and started ironing the clothes. I thought, "This is serious, what's about to go on?"

It was a funeral right there by Ruth's Cozy Corner. I saw everybody around me crying. I was like, "Whoa, how should I pay respect here? Should I be crying too?" So I did. I cried. I didn't make myself cry, but I did when I saw everyone around me really distraught. I'm a baby, you know.

Anthony: We were in Finland, and Harold Dejan died. We started playing, and you started crying!

Kirk: That's me! To this day, I still do that.

Anthony: You know who else, too? Chi-lite. He will cry at the drop of a hat.

Kirk: When I was on the road with the Dirty Dozen, and we got word that somebody's passed on, whether it was a family member or a musician, we played a dirge. No matter who we were playing for, or how big the stage was, we let the people know why we were doing it.

A Place to Practice

Kirk: My dad built a den for him and his friends as a place to hang, but by the time he was able to do it, most of his friends were gone. He got to enjoy it, but probably not as much as he wanted to.

It was getting to the end of his era, and we were just getting started. Charles was playing with the Hurricane Brass Band, and I caught the tail end of that in my teens, because Tuba Fat had gone with the Olympia and Big Al Carson was busy with the Tuxedo Brass Band so they needed a sousaphone player. After the Hurricane broke up, the second coming of Dirty Dozen started formulating, and my dad told us we could use his den for practices—just make sure we clean it up. We're like, "Really?! Okay!" That's somebody who had a vision of what could be and knew they had the means to allow it to happen. That's love, too.

Anthony: I've never seen anyone practice as much as you.

Kirk: Oh, I need to practice more. That's what it's all about.

Front Row: Waldren "Frog" Joseph, Alvin Alcorn, and Louis Cottrell, Jr. *Back Row:* Placide Adam, Chester Jones, and Walter Lewis. Photograph courtesy of the Louisiana State Museum. The Adam family was known as a family of musicians. Placide explained: *My mom, Dolly Doudreaux Adam, was an all-around piano player. She used to play behind silent movies at the Lyric Theater when she was 12 years old. She would put us to sleep at night playing* Poor and Pleasant—*that's nine pages long and she memorized it. Her uncle, Manuel Manetta, had a music studio in Algiers that catered to black and white and nobody ever bothered him about it. Music came down the line, and we all had to get at that piano. I played piano and then trombone, and drums. I just started playing bass in 1959. My ankle got all messed up in the army. I got the GI bill and went to school to learn the bass. Well, I didn't have to learn it, I already knew it, but I started to play professionally. Paul Barbarin hired me when Dixieland Hall opened in 1961.*

Anthony: *You practice constantly, even when we're on a gig.*

Kirk: *Yeah, that's me. I have to keep making the wheels turn. I don't want to shut myself off. That's one of the things about the newer bands—they only caught the funky side of the Dirty Dozen. They didn't realize that we had roots in the traditional bands.*

For the bass sound, it's the voice first, then the sousaphone where it's air flowing through an instrument. The upright bass and your electric bass are percussive, meaning it is a sound made by striking an instrument. But they are all rhythm.

Growing up, I listened to upright bass players like Frank Fields and Placide Adam, so I learned a lot about the more intricate chord changes that are a part of trad jazz. Although Placide was playing the upright bass, and I'm playing the sousaphone, if you want to play a song, you have to portray that part. You have to figure it out. When you listen to what an upright bass player is doing, you may be able to take it and put it into another song you have to play on sousaphone. You never know. You may discover some things of your own. And in terms of getting a sousaphone to sound like an upright bass, one of my main influences was Anthony "Tuba Fats" Lacen. He developed an R&B sound, and I listened to that and turned it towards the funk in the Dirty Dozen.

In the early 1980s, my dad hooked us up with George Wein, who helped establish the New Orleans Jazz and Heritage Festival. We were playing a school function that Walter Payton, the music teacher at McDonogh 15, got us to play, and George Wein came out to see us, and he launched us nationally.

When I would see bands like the Onward travel with a grand marshal, I didn't really understand what the point was until we got on the road with the Dirty Dozen. We used to ask Alfred "Dut" Lazard to do it, but sometimes we couldn't afford to bring him. Then you realize how important that grand marshal is because the average person has no clue to the music from New Orleans or what kind of dancing they should do. If no one is there to show them, they might just sit there.

I parted ways with the Dozen in the early 1990s and came back to New Orleans. I used to practice with the Soul Rebels by Milton Batiste's house back there on St. Anthony, I was playing at Snug Harbor every week with my band Kirk Joseph and Friends, and I used to do brass band gigs.

Playing the sousaphone on stage with the Dirty Dozen so long, I wanted to let more musicians know, you don't have to always have a bass guitar, it could be a sousaphone. In New York, there is a group called Gravity, which is made up of all tuba players. I thought it was cool. I thought we should have something like that in New Orleans, too.

A musician, Ken Ferdinand, used to be involved with the French Market, and I worked with him to organize a gig and parade of all tuba players in honor of Tuba Fats, and other great tuba players like Walter Payton and Kerwin James who have died. It's a respect thing. Some musicians will get in a competitive mode, but that ain't me. Now if you need that energy, okay fine. Keep that inside you. I don't want to see it.

It's hard to pull together so many sousaphone players because they are so busy here, but we did it the day after Thanksgiving when most people were home so we had 30 or 40 tubas and five or six drums. When you think about cities famous for tubas, you got to think about New Orleans. This is one place that hasn't forgotten about it.

Anthony: *On bass drum, I have more interaction with you then I do with the snare drummer. I can feed off of what you do, because your playing is so rhythmic.*

Kirk: *The bass and the sousaphone have to be locked, other than that it's going to be a train wreck.*

Anthony: *I could just ignore the snare drum because he's playing on the 2/4.*

Kirk: *The snare drum is more like the horns—they are playing a whole lot of stuff on top, but we are the foundation playing on the 1/3. The bass drum is the bottom in terms of*

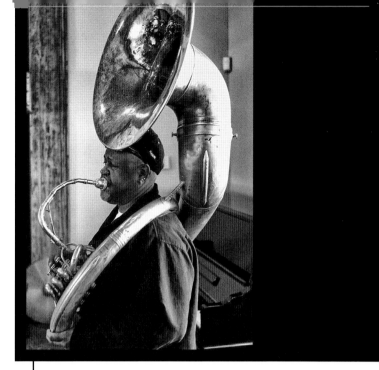

Kirk at the MFAA program. Photograph by Bruce Sunpie Barnes.

rhythm and the sousaphone is the bottom in terms of chord changes. I'm the root chord. When I make chord changes, that lets all the other horns know, "Okay, it's time to change." At the same time, I'm playing rhythm, too. I'm the bridge between the top and the bottom.

Anthony: *The reason why I enjoy playing with you so much is that there are a lot of times when you play what they call ghost, or grace, notes. I play those notes. I play them because you are.*

Kirk: *It's good if somebody is paying attention. The whole thing about the ghost notes, I try to make them reality notes. It's an emphasis so the music is going to move.*

Anthony: *I was playing with another sousaphone player, Julius "Jap" Mckee, one night and he said, "Man, you play the ghost note, I enjoy playing with somebody who listens."*

Kirk: *I'm a listener of the world. I'm not above anyone. We all have something to offer, and if we could understand that musically it could be more beautiful, but in life it could be, too.*

Portait of Darryl Adams at Preservation Hall, by Bruce Sunpie Barnes.

The Royal Players

Anthony: After working with Kirk and getting to play with different brass bands, in 1991 I went to Finland with Darryl Adam's Tornado Brass Band. Something happened with Darryl's passport and he wasn't able to get to the airport. The rest of the band was having a discussion, "Are we going to make this trip?" I said, "Well, the only way we are going to get paid is if we go."

We got on the plane and arrived in Finland. We were told that when we got there we would get a portion of our money. That night and the next day we played. Days go past. The other guys start grumbling because there is no talk of money. I asked, "Is it all right if I speak for the band?" Whenever I was doing something that I could consider activism, I always thought, "How would Jerome Smith handle this?" I remembered how he told me about moving the screen that said "For Colored Only" on the streetcar and was told by an older black lady, "Don't ever stop doing what you're doing."

After six days in Finland, I'm sitting having dinner and the manager came over, "Look, we need to go." I said, "We are not going anywhere until I find out who is going to pay us, and how much. If not, we have our tickets. You can take us back to the airport. We'll sleep there till it is time for us to leave." He went, "Oh, wait a minute."

It turns out there was mismanagement of money. Someone said that they had paid us but they hadn't. The producer asked me, "What is the name of your band?"

I said, "Tornado Brass Band." He said, "No, *your* band." Just right off the top of my head I said, "The Original Royal Players."

"Here, write down who is in your band. I'm going to give you a deposit for next year, so you can pay this band. Next year," he said, "when you come back, you'll get your money." I was skeptical because I was thinking, "If I take this money, and pay this band, then when I come back he's going to be saying, 'Well, you owe me.'" He gave me the money to pay that band, and when Darryl finally got there, he gave Darryl a contract as well.

Back in New Orleans, I could begin to see where I was headed with music. The Original Royal Players could be a band. But it's hard work. A lot of times you hear musicians griping about what other bandleaders are doing. From my experience working with the horses, I realize that you can't make people work for you. They have to want to work for you. And if they really want to work for you, they're gonna do just that—they're gonna give you their all. As a bandleader, even when you're feeling really vulnerable, you have to suck it up. My Uncle Doc used to say dress so that you could be broke and people would never know it. It's the image that you project and you have to keep up that image no matter what's going on. But I couldn't have done it it without people like Joe and Kirk.

More Than the Five O'Clock Band

The children in Tremé are raised up in music. Their five o'clock bands—taking to the streets of the neighborhood—are iconic. After growing up there, and spending my life both craving the music and wanting to have other experiences, I decided I wanted to help children be involved in learning it in a serious way, as well as helping to show them other possibilities in their life as well. In the mid-1990s, I decided to adopt Craig Elementary. I was always doing stuff like an Easter Egg Hunt or going out in the French Market and making apple candies for their parties.

The mothers in the PTA drafted me to get involved, "Why don't you come to our meetings?" At the time, Craig had a real bad problem with rodents. I was in the cafeteria one morning while the children were eating breakfast, and rodents were running in and out of the walls. I'm scared to death of rats. At the coroner's office, I've seen what they can do to you. They'll eat you alive. When the PTA tried to talk to the school board, the response was basically, "Well, you're getting a free education, you shouldn't complain."

My thing was this: There's no such thing as a free education. My tax dollars are paying for this, and I want the very best. I met with a group of mothers at the Tremé Center, and I wanted them to assert themselves. I told them, "Look, you need to do something." They kept telling me, "Well, you need to speak."

I went on TV with the news and said exactly what I thought. "You're gonna close the school and these children are not coming back until the problem is eradicated." After my public statement, the school board didn't want to talk to me anymore. The ladies were the ones who stood up and said, "Well, if you don't want to talk to him, you don't want to talk to us." We closed the school, and when the problem was fixed, the PTA drafted me to become their president. The principal, Mr. Norris, asked me, "Do you have children yet?" And I was like, "They're all my children." And he said, "I'm excited." I implemented a grandparents' program and a reading program with Craig alumni and other public figures.

One day, this little girl was passing when I was coming out of my house. She said, "Today is my birthday." I said, "Well, happy birthday, baby." She said, "My mom was gonna buy me a birthday cake but she doesn't have any money right now." That bothered me all morning.

I went to McKenzie Bakery and got one of those sheet cakes, put "Happy Birthday" on it, and went by the school. I didn't even know the child's name. I said, "This is for all the children's whose birthday is this month." Afterwards, every month, I would bring a cake.

Harmony

What I try to do now—especially with people like you, Jose—is try to get them involved. It is like, "Don't do what I did! Get yourself in this when you are young and it will pay off in the end. It will really be important to you, if you involve yourself with the music." To the point that it affects the way you live, and the way that you deal with people. To say it simply, it creates a harmony in you. This peace. It comes in colors. It creates this peaceful harmony with the universe.

I don't know if I told you about Craig Klein. I had him doing a funeral with me at my family's old church, St. Peter Claver's. Some guys were sitting out in front of a corner store, drinking beer. One guy said, "I see you got a white boy in your band." I said, "What?" He said, "You got that white boy in your band."

I said, "Who?" I said, "Oh, he ain't white, he's a musician. He came out here to play the trombone, he didn't come out here to hear that foolishness from you." I'm sure those people don't care what color he is. They are concerned with what comes out of his horn. Now, if that didn't sound right, then they might have a problem with it.

Two years ago, after years of looking for a spiritual home, I joined the Sunni sect of Islam. Its beliefs in serving mankind, no matter what your color, are in line with what I've learned from a life in music. Being a Sunni is about doing good deeds, and trying to change things that way, as opposed to saying. "She's white, so she's no good." Malcolm X became Sunni, too. The values come from my spiritual self, and those are things I like to incorporate in all aspects of my life. I want it to reflect who I am, not what I am.

Craig Klein at MFAA. Photograph by Bruce Sunpie Barnes.

Jose at the Music for All Ages Program.
Photograph by Bruce Sunpie Barnes.

Jose and his mother, Pat, at his drum teacher Johnny
Vidacovich's house in Midcity. Photograph by Bruce
Sunpie Barnes.

JOSE BRAVO BESSELMAN

Bruce: *It's hard not to be friends with Jose because he's such a nice, cool dude. Originally from Colombia, he has been raised by his adopted parents in a suburb of New Orleans along the Mississippi River called River Ridge. Throughout his life, Jose has had many serious surgeries to correct a double cleft palate, and has been able to use music as a medium to move through the pain. Since he first started coming to the program with his mom, Pat, he has been deep into percussion. He began on the snare drum, but moved onto the bass. He can really channel Uncle Lionel Batiste's style and has studied with Anthony Bennett for a long time as well. In Jose's interview with Anthony and Pat, they also talk about how Jose's love of traditional brass band music has given his family a chance to get to the know the city in new ways.*

One of their weekly excursions is to the home of his other drum teacher, Johnny Vidacovich, in Midcity. Johnny is one of the best drummers in New Orleans. He can synthesize all the rhythms you hear in the city, and wherever else he focuses his attention. He's played funk with George Porter and R&B with Earl King. He played with pianists ranging from boogie woogie and calypso with Professor Longhair to modern jazz with Ed Frank. His longtime Astral Project gig was often celebrated for incorporating Mardi Gras Indian music and marching band rhythms from the St. Augustine High School band into modern jazz. When it comes to percussion, a lot of people can play but they can't tell you what they are doing. Johnny can articulate and teach what he is doing. Everyone from Stanton Moore to Brian Blade has sought him out as a teacher. He encourages his students to be musicians, not just drummers.

Along the Guapi River and the Pacific Coast of Colombia, there are many Afro-Colombian villages and townships. Most of the people who live there come from maroon villages created when people escaped slavery. In opposition to the Colombian state that sanctioned bondage, they had to build communities without any assistance. Photograph courtesy of the Besselman family.

Introduction: Afro-Colombia

Anthony: Where did you come from?

Jose: I came from South America, Guapi.

Pat: It is a jungle village on the Guapi River on the Pacific side of Colombia. In fact, it is like 10 miles from the Pacific. The only way you can get there is by a little one-engine airplane. They have a road that you can land on. Or you take a two-day trip by boat.

Anthony: What was it like there? Do you have any memories?

Jose: No.

Anthony: You were very young when you left. How old?

Pat: Six months. We found Jose through Operation Smile, which is an organization that does reconstructive surgery on children who have cleft palates. My husband, Jim, went to Holy Cross High School with Dr. Tom Cray. One time, I met Tom in the shopping center and he had just come back from an Operation Smile mission. He said he wanted to start a Louisiana chapter, and knew I did a lot of charity work for Ladies of Leukemia League and various other organizations. Jim was in Rotary. He asked if we could help him, so we did. We raised funds and the first mission was Colombia, and that is where Jose was found.

On the flight over, the doctor for Operation Smile and a Christian missionary happened to be seatmates. The missionary told the doctor, "Well, we have a six-month-old who you might be able to help." The doctor said, "Bring him to the mission in Manizales, and we'll look at him and see what we can do." The doctor saw him, and realized Jose's anomalies were too severe.

He said, "Well, get him to the United States." They pulled off a miracle. The mission was in October and on January 12th he came into the country. New Orleans was the host chapter for that mission, so he was brought here. They got permission from the United States Embassy because it was a very well-known organization and the missionaries had their way of doing things, too.

Anthony: Over the years, I've seen these programs on *The Learning Channel* where they'd have the children come in from different countries.

Pat: With their parents.

Anthony: Yeah.

Pat: But his mother didn't want to come. We were supposed to keep Jose for a week. I was going to take him through pre-op and then the doctor's nurse was going to take him after the surgery, but her mother had a heart attack so she couldn't do that.

Jim and I have six biological children, and, at the time Jose came to us, the youngest was 16. The rest were out of the house—going to school, or married and building their own families. My husband and I thought we would just relax after the last one was out of the house and travel. But it didn't work out that way. God had other plans for us. And no regrets about that, either.

After Jose's surgery, he developed spinal meningitis and was in ICU for two and a half months. Here was this little 17-month-old child who was in severe pain, and didn't know anybody. I'd go down there every day, rock him and try to feed him lunch. On the weekends, Jim would come with me. Then I found out the son-of-a-gun was sneaking down there in the daytime, too, to play with him! And the nurse said, "Mrs. Besselman, Jose watches that door from the time you leave until the time you get back." Of course, he didn't have

 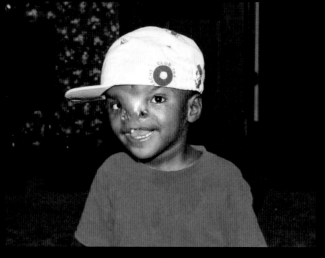

Left: Pat with Jose as a toddler. ***Right:*** Jose growing up in River Ridge, a suburb along the Mississippi River. Photographs courtesy of the Besselman family.

insurance. He was a charity case, so they wanted him out as soon as possible. When he got out of ICU, he had tubes coming out of his head. My husband and I had to learn how to give him intravenous antibiotics. He survived that. Then we found out he wasn't going back to his family. He was going to an orphanage.

Anthony: Do you think there was some sort of fear on the part of his family?

Pat: Oh, absolutely. People called him the Devil's Child because of his anomalies. We heard that the grandmother stood at the door of the hut with a baseball bat to protect him. People in Guapi are so poor, it would have been very difficult to afford what it would have taken to raise him.

Anthony: I'm just still curious about his family. Are they staying in contact? Are they writing?

Pat: Well, through the missionaries, because they speak Spanish and we don't speak or write in Spanish. We send pictures.We knew he was going to have many surgeries ahead of him, so we said we'd become his

guardians. About three months after that, Jim gave me a glass of wine and said, "Let's go sit out on the patio." I said, "What is up?" He said, "What are we going to do about this child?" I said, "I don't know, but I don't want him to leave."

"I don't either, so we are going to adopt him." Isn't that something?

Anthony: I take it you like this kid.

Pat: Oh yeah! It was a point when we first started with the adoption that I thought I would have to go live in Colombia with him. Most adoptions, you go to the country where the child is. And at the time, the drug cartels in the area were extremely dangerous. I said, "Well, the only way I'll go is if they put me in a convent." But I found a different way because he was already in the country.

Anthony: So did that make it easier?

Pat: In a way, yes, and in a way no, because we went through five lawyers in Colombia, trying to get them

to get the signatures they needed. None of them wanted to go to the village. I had always envisioned, perhaps, when he got older and finished with his surgeries, that we would go to Colombia and have the mother and grandmother come up the Guapi River and have a reunion for them. But I'm trying to wait until it's done, and for the political situation there to become better.

Anthony: All the time I've been meaning to ask you that, but I wasn't sure if it was my business. I wasn't sure if it was the proper thing to ask.

Pat: I don't mind sharing his story at all. I mean, this kid has so much courage. He is getting ready to have his 32nd surgery, primarily on his face. When he'd have surgeries, his youngest sister helped me. She would have him come sleep in her bed—to give him solace, relief. He's come a long, long way.

Starting Music

Anthony: In his development as a musician, it is that same way. He has come so far. He is good at what he does and he does it so humbly. And that is another question. Your interest in music. Do you know where that came from? Was there anything else that you were interested in before?

Pat: Guapi has a reputation as having the best drummers and dancers in the area. I said he came by his drumming honestly. They say that babies, while they are still in a mama's body, can hear. So maybe you heard a lot of drumming.

Anthony: I always say that is the first thing you hear is the heartbeat and that is a deep resonating sound. You didn't know where that propensity for drumming came from, but it was born in you.

Johnny Vidacovich and Jose during one of their drum lessons. Photographs by Bruce Sunpie Barnes.

Jose: Yes.

Pat: Music started for him when he was seven years old. He came home and said he wanted to play the violin. I looked at him and said, "Well, if I buy a violin, you better play it!" I bought it from one of the instructors of a music camp. He would go to Europe and buy violins. I told him I wanted to get an old violin because supposedly they have a better quality sound. He showed me one that went back to the mid-1800s. He had been offered $1,000 for it and didn't sell it. He sold it to me for $500. He said, "I want Jose to know you can be scarred and dented, but you can still play good music."

Anthony: I always liked the sound of the violin—wanted to play it but every time I've ever put my hands on one, I just make noise.

Pat: We started a group at Jose's school called Violins Not Violence. Some of the students couldn't afford to buy violins, so I went to Rotary and various organiza-

tions, and we bought violins for them. It was based on the Suzuki Method. You don't learn how to read music—you play through memorization and sound—until you've gone into two or three books of music. They say Jose has a good ear.

Anthony: He does. When you would come to the house, I'm telling you, he's got it. It was almost as if he anticipated the next bass progression even if he never heard the song. He went to where it was supposed to go.

Pat: He started playing the drums in middle school. He wanted to join the band and he couldn't play one of the wind or brass instruments so it was left to the drums.

Anthony: Jose, who should I ask is your biggest influence musically?

Jose: Johnny Vidacovich.

Pat: Johnny Vidacovich is his instructor on the drum set.

Anthony: He's real funky. He is a good drummer. He's been your biggest influence. Why is that?

Pat: He has been taking lessons from him for about six years. You know how Tipitina's has that program on Sunday where professional musicians play? The kids come up on the stage and help them put a tune together. By the end of the hour and a half, they are able to play that song.

Until Jose got into the music, I didn't know much about any of the musicians so all I really know about Johnny is that he is one of the best drummers in the city. After one of the Sunday sessions I asked him if he'd give us lessons. He said, "Absolutely. I've got plans for Jose." Sometimes I have to pull him out. It is supposed to be an hour lesson. They can go an hour and a half to two hours.

Jose: He taught me to have fun. He makes me laugh.

Johnny Vidacovich and Jose at Johnny's home in Midcity.
Photograph by Bruce Sunpie Barnes.

JOHNNY VIDACOVICH
MELODIC DRUMMING

Johnny: *How many years, Jose? Has it been six? Seven? Five? Eight? After Katrina, we started hanging out playing music at Tip's on Sundays.*

I've been doing this Sunday gig since the 1970s. Nothing's really changed over the years. It's still the same idea, with different funding. Back then, I was playing with Professor Longhair and James Booker, and involved in projects all over town. The National Endowment of the Arts realized all the

money was going to the West Coast, and New York. They said "Hey, you gotta send some people down South, teach them how to fill out grants so they can get some money, too." The National Endowment for Humanities threw a bunch of money at Tipitina's to teach kids how to play jazz. Richard Payne, a bass player; Phil Parnell on piano; and I had the gig. Trumpet players like Wynton Marsalis and Nicholas Payton would come in when they were teenagers, and we'd say, "What song do you want to play?"

Your job in the rhythm section is to create a safety net. A lot of guys, as they're learning their horns, depend on the rhythm section to hold them. We are gonna lock up so tight that anything that guy in the front plays is going to sound good. As you grow as a musician, you learn not to be so consumed with thinking of your next note in your own world. You're up in the bigger world looking down at yourself playing something that's part of a whole, and that's two different places.

Modern Applications

I started out in a traditional band. I was very young. I grew up right here in Midcity, and by the time I was 12, I was playing in a band of all young kids, slightly older than me, in Dunk's Honky Tonks. We dressed in derby hats and red-and-white striped shirts, and went to play little gigs at places like the Lighthouse of the Blind and the Home for the Incurables. I remember playing for the tuberculosis people a lot, because they had to wear masks. Yeah, they would wheel them all out in the courtyard at the Veterans Hospital, and we would play this traditional repertoire for them like The Saints *and* Way Down Yonder in New Orleans.

The importance of traditional brass band music comes up over and over again. A number of years ago, I was part of the New Orleans Drumming *video projects. It was broken up into three parts. The first one was on funk and studio playing with Earl Palmer and Herman Ernest; the second was* Ragtime and Beyond *with Herman Riley; and the third video was called* John Vidacovich Street Beats/Modern Applications. *The producers were very interested in the music I played*

with Professor Longhair, more than the jazz, but they quickly saw that it was all one thing. It's really not the style of music. It's a concept in the head—an approach that comes in playing music in the city.

We finished recording, but the thing was that the company that was doing this project didn't want any white boys in it. For nine months, Kerry Brown, who's a drummer from here, had to talk with them. He said, "Listen, you New York boys, y'all not gonna get it right if you don't put Vidacovich in there, cause he's the guy that turned it into modern stuff, that kept it growing." He argued with this. "No white people in here." And Kerry's black. He's telling them, "Look, if you're gonna do it, do it right."

The people who do the packaging want to put you in categories and determine who can be in or out of it. That experience was very odd to me because once you get to the music, the race thing is broken down. It magically breaks down this living illusion that we are a part of.

It seems to me having too clear-cut of a picture of what you want to do can be bad. I think the safest bet is to play the music with love. You can play with people you hate. Cats may really hate each other—won't stay in the same hotel or ride the same bus. "I ain't eating breakfast with him!" But they can play good music together. It's just a weird experience, but I've experienced it more than once. It breaks down ego.

I think, energy-wise, music becomes something bigger and more powerful than either one of us as individuals. Playing music together, we can only attain this higher feeling of energy and beauty in the molecules and atoms and sound waves. Neither one of us, as individuals, can achieve this, but being musically sensitive to each other, we can achieve this beautiful thing, which makes us feel good, and hopefully makes people listen and feel good. That's a very important part of the equation. Musician plus an audience equals the music. It's not just a musician playing music. You know, that's kinda ineffectual. That process is bigger than any one part. For me, that's probably the attraction, the feeling of excitement, which

Johnny and his wife, Deborah Vidacovich, run the Tipitina Foundation's Sunday music program, and he takes one-on-one students at their home. Photographs by Bruce Sunpie Barnes.

is immediate with the audience. Teaching is different. The way you feel good teaching, you have to wait for that. You have to be patient. The results of sharing this music you will see ten years from now: "Oh, gosh, he's a really a great musician, or a great human being."

Formally speaking, I think you would be a good teacher, because you have patience and a cool about you. You have a cool that a lot of teachers don't have. They think something's gotta happen and they have to see results on it. I don't think that way, and you don't think that way either. You're very much a person who lets things happen. And you don't make a mess when things happen. When stuff's going on in front of you, man, it's easy to make a mess. I know.

Learning drums is one thing, but then you have to learn how to play music on drums. And you don't have notes. That's one thing you don't have that everybody else has so you have to imply. I have to set out into the abstract and still make you think that it's music. You have to stop playing boom-boom-crash-crash *and start thinking in terms of the music you're playing and, "How do I play this on drums?"*

We talk about internalizing the melodies of songs and playing on the rhythms of those melodies. When we start out we use simple songs like Happy Birthday. *We start shadowing the rhythm of the melodies as a way to communicate without notes. It's up to me to keep the listener's ear and hold onto the rhythm. I very much think it's like playing a basketball game. There's a lot of improvising going on, but you have to keep dribbling to keep the ball in play.*

We work a lot on phrasing—the tension between the harmony and the melody. You have a lead on the pack because you already play the violin well. You lose yourself in the music. It's not about what you play. It's not about how good you are. It's about this music that we're playing right now, for these people right now. I'm not gonna make it happen. I'm not that great. You have to give yourself up to the music, and just let it go through you. You're just strictly a temporary passageway for the music, that's so abstract, that people think they're creating and composing, when really all you have to do is just allow yourself to be open.

All the notes that Charlie Parker, Dizzy Gillespie, Miles Davis, John Coltrane, and Murray Horowitz played—all

of those notes are still ringing in our universe because our world is made up of sound waves and atoms. They are bouncing around in the science of our stratosphere. These vibrations are still ringing.

You don't really have to create anything—all you have to really do is be an open channel, and it's going to keep going through you. When it happens, I feel buoyancy. I don't know if that's a word or not. I just made it up. But I can feel myself being lighter. Do you feel that lightness?

Jose: *Yes.*

Johnny: *You are the most lyrical drummer I've worked with in this front room. Some people have a specific plan for their talent. Some people you just kind of wait and see what happens. I would say with you, Jose, what's gonna happen, you're gonna play music, and people are gonna look at you, and say, "Hmm, what's he doing?" What I would like and hope is that music gives you a kiss. You know? That's what I hope for every night when I go out to play. I just look in the mirror and say, "Man, I just hope I have a rendezvous with music tonight."*

Left: Jose playing with Kirk Joseph. **Right:** Anthony Bennett at the MFAA program. Photographs by Bruce Sunpie Barnes.

Music for All Ages

Pat: When Jose started at the Jazz Park, he was playing snare drum. I told Doyle Cooper's mother, Leslie, "Maybe he should have bass drum lessons because you see a lot of snare drummers but you don't see many bass drummers."

Anthony: Because it's heavy, and we don't get much attention!

Pat: Leslie said, "Well, Anthony Bennett would be a good one for you to get lessons from for Jose."

Anthony: I've had kids follow me and listen to what I'm doing at parades, but Jose is my first steady student. You came to me and asked me and of course I wanted to do it. You kept asking me, "How much?" and I kept saying nothing. We finally agreed $20 was

enough. I just wanted to have somebody else come along that was going to do this. Especially the bass drum. Everybody wants to play the trumpet or snare drum. Nobody wants to play the bass drum, even though that is the driving force behind the band.

On top of a simple beat, you accent—but then you accent where you want to. It all depends on the person. I always tell Jose, "You are one. You just stay on the one. Then whatever they are playing, you just stay where you are at." They are going to find their way back by listening to you. Duke Ellington said, "Dancing is very important to people who play music with a beat. I think that people who don't dance, or who never did dance, don't really understand the beat...I know musicians who don't and never did dance, and they have difficulty communicating."

In traditional brass band music, you dance to the bass

drum. When I'm playing, I might tap out something that I think I would sound out if I were dancing. If somebody's dancing, I'll watch them dance, and I'm playing what I think their feet are doing. And vice versa. Or sometimes I'll grand marshal for someone, and I'll dance to whatever the bass drummer is playing.

Pat: Jose sat in and this guy came up to him and and said, "Jose, you must have been channeling Uncle Lionel."

Anthony: Jose plays the traditional beats. He plays, in other words, the beats he's familiar with, but sometimes when I'm playing the melody, and I'm humming the song to myself, I'll hear Jose accent at different intervals—where most people wouldn't, he will. It doesn't really shift it, but it actually enhances it. He'll add something just a little bit different or take away something, and it's like, "Oh, I hear you over there."

Anthony: Does your music experience help you cross racial boundaries?

Pat: We live in River Ridge. Although we would come into the city for the shows and dinner—entertainment—most of our dealings were out in Jefferson Parish. Now, when my husband and I were dating, we went to the Saenger Theater on Canal Street.

Anthony: Do you think that you are going places that you never would've gone before?

Pat: Oh, absolutely. It's a brand-new experience, and I honestly feel it's keeping us young, because we are going to be 70 this year. People our age are sitting around the house watching TV, and I can still do a second line. In fact, Jose marched in a Black Men of Labor parade last year, and I marched along with it. We are experiencing what we didn't experience with our children. They were sports kids, and now we have a musician, and that's a totally different world. I didn't

Dancing to the Tremé Brass Band at the Candelight Lounge. Photograph by Bruce Sunpie Barnes.

go to these places—I'd go to a lot of football games, but I didn't go to these clubs, so it's amusing.

Anthony: There are a lot of places that you probably didn't know existed.

Pat: Absolutely, like the Candlelight Lounge and places like that, I didn't know that existed.

Anthony: And this fellow got you going all over the city.

Pat: Mm-hmm.

Anthony: I guess in other places it would be known as the back alleys. Because that's the way a lot of people treat Tremé. It's like, "Oh, don't go over there," or "I wouldn't go over there."

Pat: I wouldn't go there by myself.

Anthony: I know. I understand that. I'm saying, once you get there, you find out that it is not any different than going to a football game, except that they're not playing football.

Pat: Right, they're playing music.

Anthony: Yeah. But if you listen to other people, you probably wouldn't go. If it weren't for him, you probably wouldn't go.

Pat: Yeah. I don't think I'd have the energy to go. I mean, he kind of inspires me. If it wasn't for Jose, I'd be home on the sofa reading a book.

Anthony: But your longtime friends, they wouldn't necessarily know a thing about the Candlelight, would they?

Pat: No. No.

Anthony: To them, it would probably be some culture shock to transition to that.

Pat: Yeah, I guess so. I was introduced to it incrementally, whereas for them to just show up...although they would appreciate the music, I'm sure.

Anthony: But you know what I'm saying. Like, you're in the Candlelight, and all of a sudden all these people just start jumping and dancing. I've been there, and sometimes groups of people will come in and they'll sit down, right? And then when the music starts and all of these regulars—and I'm not just saying the black people, but I'm talking about some of the white kids that come on a regular basis—start dancing, and the people just sitting there will go, "Damn!"

Pat: Right.

Anthony: Sometimes when I'm over there, I just watch the people.

Pat: I like to people watch.

Anthony: Yeah, and their reactions to what's going on. Some people expect that. Some people don't know what to expect.

Left: Jose playing the bass drum with the Red Hot Brass Band as it leads a wedding up Decatur Street past Cafe du Mondé. Photograph courtesy of the Cooper family. *Right:* The Red Hot Brass Band takes a small convention through the streets of New Orleans. Jose plays the bass drum while Pat (*up front*) walks with the second line. Photograph by Rachel Breunlin.

Pat: Different experiences. There's a lot of people I wouldn't have met. I mean, there would've been no reason for me to meet you.

Anthony: There would've been no reason for that, because I would've been going to Candlelight [*laughter*] and following second lines, and you would've been going to the Saenger Theater. The only contact you probably would've had with me is if I was in a band playing over there.

Pat: Some of the music world is a step back in time for me. I was the head drum majorette for West Jefferson High School. I used to twirl two fire batons at one time. My boyfriend in high school was the head drummer. And actually, after that, I started a marching group across the River for six through eight-year-old girls. It was callled the Westbank Strutters, because I'm from the Westbank. I taught them how to twirl the baton and march and drill.

Anthony: Yeah?

Pat: Mm-hmm. I don't even know if Jose knew that.

Anthony: He didn't know that!

Pat: When my husband was in his senior year at Tulane, we were married. I worked as an auditor for the Louisiana Rating and Fire Prevention Bureau. Because I had this talent and because we needed money, I started the Westbank Strutters. It paid more than my five-day-a-week job. I instructed the girls as a marching unit, and they participated in parades and things like that.

Now I drive Jose to a lot of the Red Hot Brass Band's gigs, and some times walk along with the parades.

Anthony: What have been your biggest struggles with music?

Jose: [*Shakes his head*]

Pat: When I get frustrated, when I can't find what it is that he needs to have, I just say, "God, he's your child. I just told you I would take care of him. Now you do it." And it has always come through. Everything. Not my schedule, but His schedule.

137

JEREMY
JEANJACQUES

&

JOSEPH
TORREGANO

Joe Torregano in front of Andrew J. Bell Junior High on Uruslines Street and North Galvez in the Sixth Ward, where he studied the clarinet under Donald Richardson, and did his student teaching for music education. Bell was originally an all-white, girls Catholic boarding school called St. Joseph Academy and Convent before the Sisters of St. Joseph moved closer to Lake Pontchartrain on Mirabeau Street. Orlean Parish School Board bought the building from the nuns and turned it into a black middle school. Donald Richardson was charged with starting the music program, and worked with many students who became professional musicians including Frank Oxley, Big Al Carson, Anthony Bennett, and Emile Hall. After Hurricane Katrina, Bell did not reopen, and it is being turned into artists' lofts. Photograph by Bruce Sunpie Barnes.

The Bell band. Photograph courtesy of Joseph Torregano.

JOSEPH TORREGANO

Bruce: *Joe Torregano is a clarinet and saxophone player who has played with legendary brass bands like the Fairview, the Olympia, and the Young Tuxedo, as well as running his own jazz bands. He also plays regularly with the Original Royal Players. He was a high school music teacher and special events police officer for more than 30 years, so very few people are as well organized about their daily life. Ask him a name, place, date, time—if he was there, he knows. He can tell you who was standing on the corner, who was selling the cotton candy, and who their family is. That's his gift. His gift for music is the same way. Joe might seem no-nonsense, because he is, but if he's connected with you, he's going to follow you throughout your life.*

Joe brought his organizational skills to the MFAA program. He knew that most of the kids were in school music programs as well and would give them sheet music to practice with their music teachers. When they came back, he'd say, "Okay, let's see about the assignment you had." A few years into the program, he got diagnosed with cancer and had

to go through chemotherapy. I'd tell him, "Joe, you don't have to push it." He always said, "No, man, this is what is keeping me here. Being able to work with these kids." I know a lot of days, honestly, he didn't know if he would ever be there again. He was very serious about his commitment to his health and to music, and came out the other side.

Joe met Al Kennedy when Al was the public information officer for the Orleans Parish School Board. Al had developed a love for the stories of the band directors who devoted themselves to the music programs. He decided he was going to document what was going on and started writing about music educators in the city. When he interviews people, he has a very good knack for getting to the center of what is important to them and elevates these parts of their lives in his books. When Al wrote Chord Changes on a Chalkboard, *Joe shared his life in music in and out of the classroom, and they have continued to invest in music education around the city together.*

Alphonse Picou's jazz funeral going down St. Claude (now Henriette Delille Street) past St. Augustine Catholic Church on February 9, 1961. Photograph by Howard "Cole" Coleman from the Thelma Hecht Coleman Memorial Collection, courtesy of the Southeastern Architectural Archive, Special Collections Division, Tulane University Libraries. Picou was born in 1879 and played with the Onward Brass Band when it was under the direction of Manuel Perez. He tells the story of how his solo for the song *High Society* became famous: *We had to play at a hall where they had all the Creole meetings. At that time they didn't allow a dark man to come in. If you were dark you had to stay out. I was there, and Manuel Perez liked the way I played* High Society *and he says, "Come on in"..and they let me play that solo by myself. I made a wonderful hit—Lord! They played* High Society *all night.*

Joe: The inquiries I get about who I am are unbelievable. If people try to guess, Spanish is probably number one, and then it ranges. Anything from Filipino to Pakistani could be possible. It usually begins with, "Do you mind if I ask you a personal question?" If I say, "No." They will ask, "What is your ethnic background?" I tell them, "African-American." It confuses them. If I add, "I'm from New Orleans," they might get it.

To my knowledge, the Torreganos in Louisina originated from southern Italy and mixed with the Creole culture here. There was a very ugly split in the family because some of my father's family crossed the color line and passed for white. My father, Louis Anthony Torregano, Sr., was a tad darker than me. He could pass for Spanish, but he was always proud of who we were. I was named after my grandfather, Joseph Torregano, who was a trumpet player in both the Excelsior and Original Tuxedo Brass Bands. In 1910, two months after my father was born, he died at the age of 36. I never saw a picture of him, and my father didn't have any stories to pass on, but his godfather, Adolf Alexander, was a brass band musician so he knew a lot

of musicians. On the weekends, I'd be following them at the funerals. I was just attracted to it.

In 1961, when I was nine years old, I got to hear the Young Tuexdo play along with the Eureka and Olympia Brass Bands when the jazz funeral for Alphonse Picou, the clarinet player who made the solo on *High Society* famous, went by Craig Elementary. It was during Mardi Gras, and the principal had made an announcement to close the windows and for the kids to not lose their focus. About a month later, she called my kindergarten teacher, Ms. Ross: "Go see Ms. Dedeaux in the office." She had a package with a magazine. She opened it and said, "Could you explain this to me?" It was a picture of us peeking through the front door of the school as the funeral passed. Fortunately, it was a free music education. I could relate to, "I would like to do this one day." You know, I played for Ms. Ross's funeral. She requested it.

I started playing the clarinet at Bell Junior High and I'm sure you heard stories about the experience with the band director, Donald Richardson. The man built a program from nothing. For the 1963-64 school year, he started with 28 drummers and 15 trumpet players, and formed a bugle corps. Two years later, he had a full concert band. Despite seeing so many brass bands growing up, black schools couldn't have marching band. We weren't allowed to march in Carnival parades because of the color of our skin. Mr. Satcherie was his band director at Booker T. Washington, and he would have the Booker T. band come over and play for us in the gym. Those guys gave me goosebumps.

Watching Donald Richardson, and other educators, I realized teaching was like becoming a priest. You had to prepare for a life of service. In junior high, I decided to dedicate myself to a life of music—in and out of the classroom. In many respects, as an educator, I emulated the passion of my mother, Anna Torregano.

The Rex parade going down Canal Street on Mardi Gras Day in 1963, courtesy of The Historic New Orleans Collection, 1974.25.19.426

An Art Degree

My mother was from Convent, Louisiana in St. James Parish. When she met my dad after World War II, she had a sixth grade education. My father had quit school in eighth grade to help support his family. While I was growing up, he was a truck driver for the old Delta Drayage Company, and belonged to the Teamsters Union. My mother worked as a domestic, then she opened her own business and did laundry for fraternities at Tulane University. After I was born, she went to school at night at Booker T. to get her GED.

She was studying, and making sure that her children would be well-prepared for school. By the time I was four, I was pretty much reading at a third-grade level.

I can remember watching the integration of the Little Rock school system on TV, and her telling me, "By the time you get to high school, you are going to go to the high school right around the corner." At the time, John McDonogh Senior High was an all-white school. But she was right, that's what happened.

When my youngest brother was born in 1959, my mother decided she was going to go to college to study art education at Southern University of New Orleans, which had just opened up. She waited until Michael was two. There were very few daycares for blacks in this area so she carried him to school with her every day for two years. Other students would watch him while she was in class. The last two years, she had to go to Baton Rouge to finish the art degree, so she

finally found a daycare and my brother and I would pick Michael up in the evenings. My mother graduated when she was 50 years old, and worked as an art and special education teacher in Orleans Parish for almost two decades.

My mom was the kind of teacher who, if a kid got in trouble, she'd get him out of jail. She'd make them come over to the house on Saturdays and wash windows or cut the grass. When she died, one of her old students who was in the Marine Corps in San Diego happened to be in town visiting. He came by the house and said, "There are six of us who your mother taught who are stationed in San Diego and we will all be here in dress blues for your mom." She had gotten them all out of trouble at one point.

Integration, 1967

In 1967, St. Augustine's band, the Marching 100, integrated the Rex parade. It was the first year time that a black marching band played in a Mardi Gras parade. You can imagine, it was a very big deal in this community. My father made sure we were along the parade routes on St. Charles Avenue, upfront, to see them. We got lucky. The parade stopped, and the band was in front of us for ten minutes before they moved on. Watching those kids perform, I never would have thought that their band director, Ed Hampton, would be one of my competitors as an adult. Years later, when I was a band director at East St. John Parish, he told me, "Well, Joe, you've come a long way, but you know eventually you are going to have to face me some time on the football field." I said, "Yeah, I'll tell you one thing, Ed, the only thing I can do is have my kids watch and learn, because nobody can beat you marching." Best marching band I ever saw.

1967 was the same year that I walked into John McDonogh Senior High. Having grown up in an

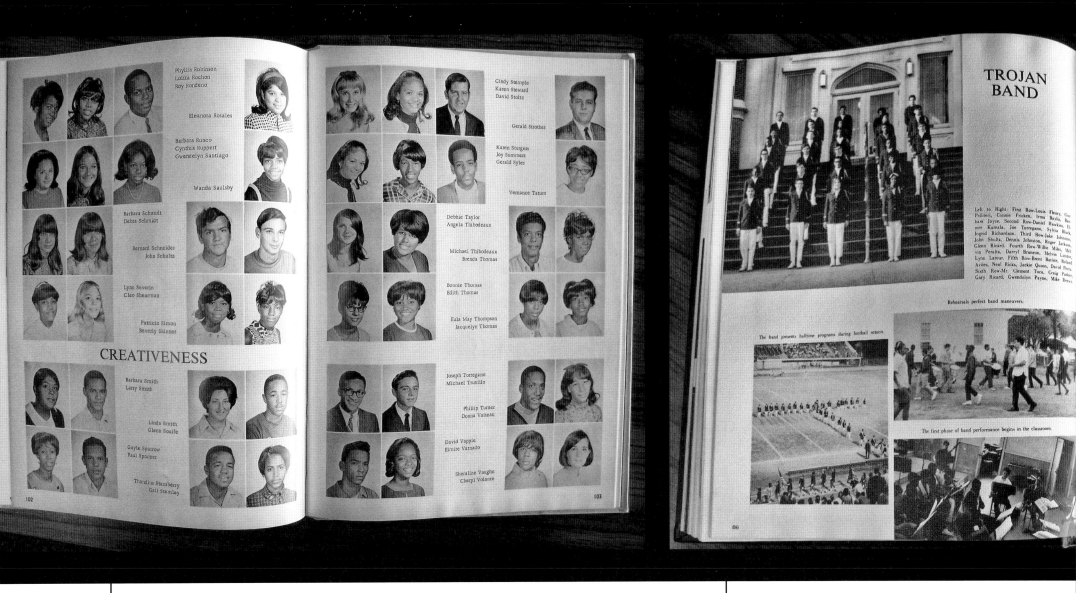

Left: High school yearbook pages for Joe Torregano at John McDonogh Senior High show the diversity of students who came from the surrounding Sixth and Seventh Ward neighborhoods in the late 1960s. *Right:* The Trojan band's yearbook picture and candid shots of practices and a football game.

integrated neighborhood, it didn't bother me as much as it might have others. The first day of school, my principal, Joseph Abrahams, was in the gym. He said, "This is something new for all of us. We are going to do our best to make it work, and if you have any problems come see me. Have a good day." That was it. Only discussion we ever had about this massive change, and it never did stabilize.

When I joined the band, we had to play at the East Jefferson Stadium for a football game against Archbishop Rummel. One of the white kids from the opposing team looked at one of our white kids and said, "How can you hang with all niggers like that?" And our student politely put his tuba down and punched him in the face. He said, "Don't ever fuck with me like that again!"

Integration didn't last long. The school board opened Abramson High School in New Orleans East, and John F. Kennedy on Bayou St. John, and all the white kids started moving to these schools. There were so many students at Abramson that they were on a platoon system. The whites in my neighborhood around John Mac started heading to the suburbs, and we started getting kids from the St. Bernard project area. By my

senior year, we had only two white kids left in the band. Our band director had left as well, and Mr. Sanders took over.

My senior year, we marched in St. Bernard Parish where the racism was still very intense. There were quite a few black bands in the parade—St. Augustine, Xavier Prep, St. Mary's—and they ended up dropping out because of the taunts from the crowd. Finally, we had an incident where we were harassed by a white motorcycle gang. Mr. Sanders had his umbrella, and 80 kids behind him who were willing to do what we needed to do if the gang had hit him, so fortunately it was just an exchange of words.

Clarinet Players

During high school, I had no social life outside of music. I decided I wanted to be a clarinet player, and I studied privately at a small studio on Aubrey and Rocheblave in the Seventh Ward called Crescent City Music School. You got a half hour lesson for $3.50. You could take any instrument. Carey Levigne was a teacher in the school system, and stressed the importance of the technical side of music. He got Mr. Willie Humphrey to show me more about the clarinet. Mr. Humphrey played in the Navy Band during WWII, and he'd tell tell me, "You got to play the Sousa marches and the Filmore marches. It will allow you to do what you want with your horn because it will allow you to control your instrument." He also transcribed some Benny Goodman solos from his records in the 1930s that he let me read and work on.

They encouraged me to teach myself off of records. Got to have an ear. Got to be able to hear it. And don't just listen to one clarinet player, but listen to as many as you could and find out what you like so you can develop your own sound, your own style. I would sit on the sofa and my dad would sit in his chair, and just listen. In those days, when school was out, I could

Left: Sheet music showing the Piron Orchestra, with Louis Cottrell, Jr.'s father playing bass drummer, courtesy of the Hogan Jazz Archive. Louis Cottrell, Sr. learned to play the drum from a German boy, John Kornfeld, who was taking drum lessons and would come home and teach him. Louis Cottrell, Jr. said the two boys were inseperable, and maintained a lifelong friendship: *The things happening now, they happened way back then. It's just that they have certain laws that tried to curtail these things. But even with the laws, it didn't because as for the real segregation, they didn't have that as a whole. There was always mixture in the neighborhoods.*

Top right: Louis Cottrell Jr. playing the clarinet. His father was in the Piorn Orchestra with Lorenzo Tio, Jr., and Cottrell Jr. learned to play the clarinet from taking lessons from him. *Tio's uncle and father were both*

clarinetists from Mexico. They were some of the finest musicians who ever came to New Orleans. My training started with solfege. Like you learn the alphabet before you learn the words, it's learning music before you get the instrument. It's singing the music. You're learning the division of music at times, and learning how to count. You get ear training with it. **Bottom right:** Barney Bigard took lessons from Tio as well before going on to play with Louis Armstrong. When Tio went up to New York to play with the Piron Orchestra, he sent Louis Cottrell, Jr. to him. Cottrell recalled: *There are plenty of things I hear Bigard do that I can remember hearing Tio do. And that's the same way with all his students. One of the things was his liquid style of playing—more of a flow rather than staccato.* Photographs courtesy of the Louisiana State Museum.

144

Pete Fountain with his Half Fast Walking Club on St. Charles Avenue on Carnival Day in 1963. He started playing the clarinet for the same reason as Joe—he had weak lungs. He played in Warren Easton's band when it was an all-white school for boys in the 1940s before he dropping out because he was working late at strip clubs on Bourbon Street, eventually playing with the Dukes of Dixieland and Al Hirt. More than a street musician, he called himself, "a saloon player" who traced his musical inspiration to white clarinet players like Benny Goodman and Irving Fazola: *It's best to have two, or possibly three, that you like. You can mix those two styles together and have a pretty good chance of coming out with your own style. I tried to combine Faz's fat mellow sound together with Goodman's drive and technique.* Every year, he hired the Onward Brass Band for his Carnival parade, and played the E-flat clarinet in Paul Barbarin's jazz funeral. *I really respected him. You know, not just as a musician, but as a gentleman.* Photograph by Jack Hurley, courtesy of the Hogan Jazz Archive.

literally do that for eight or ten hours a day. Every day. Serious about that end of it. I listened to Benny Goodman, Louis Cottrell, Barney Bigard, Matty Matlock, Irving Fazola, Cornbread Thomas, Albert Burbank, George Lewis, and Pete Fountain.

When I was 18, I met Pete Fountain. He had national exposure on Lawrence Welk's television, but people didn't really treat him like a celebrity. It was, "Hey Pete, how you doing?" This is the guy whose dad drove a beer truck for Dixie Beer. He used to work with him in the summers. What did he do on his dad's last day? He showed up and rode the truck route with him. Brought his clarinet and played like when he was a kid. This time, he was making a personal appearance at D.H. Holmes in the record department on Saturday afternoon. He autographed, "To Joe. Your friend, Pete Fountain."

Well, there used to be a concert series called New Orleans Summer Pops, and Pete Fountain's band did one of them. I walked backstage, and nobody questioned it. Pete said, "We've met before, haven't we?"
I said, "Yes, we have."
We talked much longer than we should have. He finally said, "It is getting late, I have to go."
"Yeah, me too."
"You got your car?"
"No, I'm going to catch the bus."
"No, come on, I'll give you a ride home. Where do you live?"
"2623 Governor Nicholls. You know where it is?"
"Yeah, it is my old neighborhood."

He grew up on St. Ann Street. We got to my house and he gave me a box of clarinet reeds that he used. He told me, "It is nice to have a young clarinet player coming up. Come by any time you want. Catch the show. Just call me in the back and you are good." I said, "Okay, I appreciate it." That following week, I got a package from him with an autographed album. A lot of

his recordings were quartet style where he was playing the lead. I'm a very melodic clarinet player because of listening to that.

Music Education On and Off the Street

1970. Southern University of New Orleans was not known for music majors. Most music majors at that time either went to Loyola—if you were white—or Xavier, if you were black, but Mr. Levigne at Crescent City Music worked with the band director at SUNO, Mr. Ernest Chacheré, and they got me a scholarship. It was a small department with a long curriculum. I had 185 hours on my transcript, which is a lot. You have to courses in strings, brass, woodwinds, percussion. Then arranging, theory, harmony, sight singing, and piano.

A trumpet player named Archie Robeson and I put together a little band for the homecoming festivities. He was the third trumpet player in Doc Paulin's Number One Band. They had a good job coming up on a Sunday afternoon at the old St. James Church for the Zulu Ladies New Auxiliary. He told Doc, "Well, I got a friend who wants to be looking for a chance to play. Can he come and sit in?"
"Yeah, tell him to come on."
I show up, but Archie, for some reason, did not. Doc said, "Well, I guess you are going to get paid today."
I said, "Well, you don't have to. I just came because I want to learn."

On the gig, I saw Joseph "Cornbread" Thomas, who played with the Oscar "Papa" Celestin's Band and Albert "Papa" French. Excellent clarinet player, but had the most unusual habit. He had complete dentures—upper and bottom. He took them out when he played clarinet, which is almost impossible. His tone quality with no teeth was just as good as anybody's tone quality with teeth. His gums had just hardened enough over the years. I came up to him and said, "Man, I got some of your records at my house."

He said, "That's nice."
"I like your playing."
"Where you come from?"
"This is my first job."
"Well, it ain't going to be your last." It meant something.

I worked with Doc's band for about maybe ten months. He paid eight dollars for two hours, so four dollars an hour when normal wage in the United States was $1.60 an hour. Do the math and you say, "Boy, I want to be a musician!" I was making about as much as my daddy was making as a Teamster, and that was one of the best unions in the country.

If you want to talk about getting credit for taking young musicians in, Doc Paulin's band was similar to what the Fairview Band became later on. In fact, many of the older musicians in the Fairview like Gregg Stafford and Tuba Fats got their early training with him. He didn't teach you anything directly. It was on-the-job training—you had to hear it. If you didn't pick it up that day, you better go find a record and listen to it during the week. Fortunately, I had heard enough records, I didn't have a hard time keeping up.

Who Controls the Music

In 1971, Gregg and I were both at SUNO. He was more of a risk taker than I was. I tend to be a little bit more conservative on some things. He was playing with Danny Barker's Fairview Baptist Church Band, and invited me on Monday nights to rehearsals in Leroy Jones' garage at 1316 St. Denis Street. Gregg, Tuba, and I helped introduce songs we'd played on the street into the band. Afterwards, we'd leave rehearsal with Danny and ride the bus down to Preservation Hall to listen to music. If you were down there on the weekend, they'd let us sit in on the last number of the set. Then we'd go to Maison Bourbon and stand out on the corner to listen cause we were too young to get in.

Left: Members of the Hurricane Brass Band, from left to right: Michael Johnson, Joe Torregano, Leroy Jones, and Gregg Stafford. *Right:* Joe Torregano playing with Gerald Joseph (*trombone*) and Milton Batiste (*trumpet*) with George "Kid Sheik" Colar in the back. Photographs courtesy of Joe Torregano.

We knew Bourbon Street was strictly union-controlled, as were most of the hotel and convention gigs. There was a certain level of pride and professionalism that was obvious with some union bands. They'd be in uniform. Percy Humphrey, the leader of the Eureka, would inspect you from head to toe. You couldn't get by on your ability to play by ear because when they were playing funeral dirges—*Fallen Heroes*, *Westlawn*, the *Medley of Hymns*—they would hand you the sheet music with the titles cut off. You couldn't glance at the title and know the melody, you had to be able to read all the notes.

When the Fairview Band was asked to play a convention gig at the Fairmont Hotel with the most famous union bands—the Onward, Eureka, and Olympia, and Young Tuxedo—we were excited. I remember it was a long night. We got there around seven and didn't get up to one in the morning to play. Afterwards, some of the older guys complained to Louis Cottrell. The common rule of the day was if you want to be a musician, join the union. Turn your contracts

in, build your pension. But some of the kids in the Fairview were very young. What does a 13 year old know of a being in a union? At the time, I was 19 and my dad had been a Teamster so I had more of an understanding. I was the first one that crossed his line and joined. I knew I was good enough to play with the union bands. I had sat in with enough of them to know that I could do that.

The Olympia Brass Band

The alleged mafia had a lot of control of Bourbon Street. There weren't hardly any that had jazz that were not Italian-controlled. Fortunately, my last name is Italian! I heard stories where clubs on Bourbon would make musicians take the trash out. I think by being raised in a mixed neighborhood there was a slight advantage of knowing how to get along with people of different races socially. The older musicians would know I was studying them. If they wanted a night off, they would call me and say, "Look, I'm tired of seeing you out there, listening outside of the club, stealing my stuff. Come make some money." It got me my first regular club gig at the Famous Door on Bourbon Street.

Harold Dejan, the leader of the Olympia Brass Band, called me and said, "I need you to come into the band because Emmanuel Paul's working so much with Kid Thomas." I said, "Okay." He gave me two jobs right away.

The first night here I was on the bandstand with Edmond Foucher, George "Kid Sheik," Colar Milton Batiste in the trumpet section. Harold Dejan on alto, and William Brown on sousaphone. Fats Houston was the grand marshal. Legendary grand marshal— there will never be another one like that. Nowell "Papa" Glass, son of Booker T. Glass, on bass drum, Andrew Jefferson on snare drum and this little wide eyed 20-year-old kid on clarinet.

I ended up playing with the Olympia for eight years. The assistant band director, Milton Batiste, wanted me to learn Emmanuel's baritone horn lines on the tenor saxophone. I can play his lines, but I tell you what, his solos on this album I've been trying since the 1970s. I ain't got them yet. There is just something about his phrasing, his dynamics, the tone quality. They are not complicated. They are not Charlie Parker, but there is something about him I just haven't been able to grasp. When he plays the saxophone solo dirge in *Westlawn Dirge*, it will send you. It comes right up your spine.

When I'd play with Emmanuel, I'd add his bit of vibrato, and he'd tell me, "Don't play like me, develop your own style." He really didn't want me to learn his way of playing, so I couldn't do it around him, but when he wasn't there, I could do it. It got me a job in another brass band because they liked that style so much. I tell people that is the smartest thing he never told me because it is tradition that needs to be preserved.

When you played with the Olympia in those days, it was like reaching Carnegie Hall or the Apollo. You knew you had made it. This band was literally working five nights a week. You could make $35,000 or $40,000 a year doing that as a side man, which was very good money for that time period. Traveled all over the world. The James Bond movie, *Live and Let Die*, did the recordings. TV shows. We did the *Bob Hope Show* one time.

In 1972, Harold Dejan called and said, "Can you go to Europe with me?" I said, "Excuse me?" He said, "Well can you make arrangements to get out of school? Start working on it today and call me and let me know what they said." I went on a two-week trip, five-country tour. I made another trip with him to Berlin in 1974 before they tore the Iron Curtain down. I got to stand at Check Point Charlie and look over at the Russian side and look at the land behind. But then we'd be playing in some hotel ballroom in New Orleans and Andrew Jefferson would poke me in the back with a drumstick and say, "Joe, stay in school. Finish and get your degree. Start teaching like you want to do. You don't want to be around people like this." I said, "Okay, I got it."

When the "right to work" laws came in, that was the beginning of the end for the union. In fact, when I look back on the law now, they even made it so that the leader of the band couldn't pay pension contributions on himself. My total contribution for my retirement is so low it's not even worth drawing. It's less than $5,000. Still, I've never broken my membership with the union. In fact, I ran for president of the union one time, but Deacon John beat me by six votes.

Teacher Training at Bell

When we did student teaching from SUNO, you did it every day like a full-time job. If you had classes to take, you had to take them at night. I did my student

teaching at Andrew J. Bell. It was really like going home. It had the same principal and a lot of the teachers were still there. I worked under Donald Richardson. He taught me: Number one, the discipline that it took. Number two, the organization. Number three, the need for strong fundamentals with the kids. And number four, the strength. As a teacher, you could not let your fire burn up—you really didn't have any consistent assistance.

His fourth period class was advanced brass and concert band drums. There were about 25 kids. On time, he turned toward the chalkboard and somebody balled up a piece of paper and hit him in the back of the head. And who the hell did that? Nobody would tell, so he called out the big three: the shop, English, and French teachers. I think the entire class got at least one or two licks.

The class still would not tell. For a whole week, he made them stand in a straight line out in the hot sun during lunch while the whole school was watching. He sat in front of them in a chair with his umbrella drinking an iced cold Coke. And to this day, no one has ever broke and told who did it. The unity was amazing.

When I was interviewed for my first teaching job, I was asked who inspired me. I said, "Well, my junior high director, Donald Richardson. If I could be half the band director that he is, I would be satisfied." He was competitive with an arrogance that rubbed off in me. He had a certain degree of cockiness because he knew he was good, but he also wanted to continue to learn. He reached out to the other band directors around the city. When I started teaching, he'd call me at home, "We're playing this piece with the concert band and they got trill fingering in there that the clarinet players need to know."

I told him, "I'll be over there tomorrow and show them how to do it."

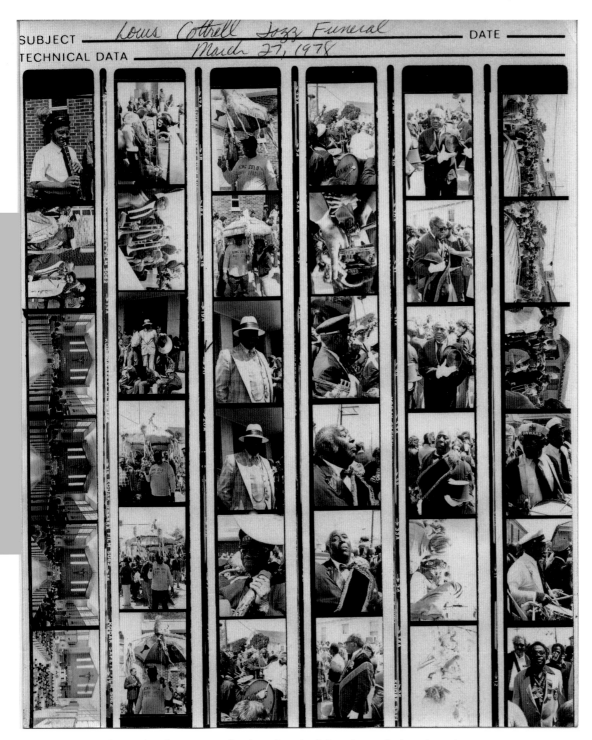

Contact sheet for Louis Cottrell, Jr.'s jazz funeral includes a photograph of Joe playing the clarinet on the top left corner. Photograph courtesy of the Louisiana State Museum.

It was a shame he died young. He had been in and out of the hospital. When Gregg Stafford took over the Young Tuxedo Brass Band, I went on trip to Portugal with them and Mr. Richardson said, "Do me a favor? Bring me back a set of coasters." When I came back to give them to him, I could tell his health was deteriorating. I asked him if he would consider retiring—he didn't have anything left to prove. He said, "I know what you are saying but the principal is about to retire."

They had been at war. As good as his programs were, something happened with her and she stopped giving him support. He said, "I think I can outlast her, and the new principal and I can get the program back the way I want it." But he didn't last the year.

Eulogies for the Living

I became a much more successful teacher than I ever thought I would be. I didn't come to be nobody's servant. My dedication was to the kids and their parents. I rolled my sleeves up every day. When I was at Gregory Junior High, I had the only marching, concert, and jazz band ensemble at the middle school level in the city. There was a $33,000 profit for the band every year. I had an accounting system, and I kept financial records equal to, if not better than, what the office did because we controlled the concession stands for school. We were self-sufficient. I did a $27,000 lease purchase on instruments for five years and I paid it off in three. We got connected with Yoshio Toyama and the Foundation from Japan. They donated instruments.

It wasn't easy to be a professional musician and a teacher, and I haven't even touched on being a police officer.

During Mardi Gras, I've been a police officer, a band director, and a jazz musician all in one day. Trust me, I've done it all. I can play a brunch, work a parade, and march a parade with my students. I can get up the next

148

Left: The Gregory Marching Band, courtesy of Joe Torregano. At Gregory Junior High in Gentilly, Joe helped mentor a new generation of musicians by bringing in professional musicians to work with his students. He also created award ceremonies honor jazz musicians who were important in the city like Harold Dejan. ***Right:*** Portrait of Harold Dejan, the leader of the Olympia Brass Band, in 1993. Photograph by John McCusker, courtesy of *The Times Picayune.* Harold was born in 1909 and grew up in the Sixth Ward at St. Ann and North Miro. His grandparents spoke Creole, and he took clarinet lessons from both Lorenzo Tio, Jr. and Louis Cottrell, Jr. Joe recalls: *From the time I was 20 to the time he died when I was in my 50s, I never saw Harold Dejan refuse anyone to sit in on the Olympia. I never saw him turn anybody away.*

morning and do two of the others again and then on Monday, back in the classroom teaching again.

A lot of times as a professional, you can get spoiled because, after all of your own practicing, you can play so easy. But as a teacher, you need to remember, for some kids, it's very difficult to get what you just did. You have to be able to articulate how to do it. In the public school system, very few people can afford to have their kids have private lessons. Very few own their own instruments. A lot of them won't take the instrument home and practice. They aren't focused enough to understand what 30 minutes a day can do.

After recognizing many of the musicians who had been important to me by playing in their jazz funerals, I also saw the need to honor a lot of people who influenced me as a musician while they were still alive. I started a lifetime achievement award with a nice plaque. The first year, I had all the Gregory Band directors who went here, my college band director, and Harold Dejan from Olympia Brass Band. The last year I did it, Pete Fountain was one of the recipients. He called me on Sunday morning and said, "I got your letter of invitation." I said, "Can you be there?" He said, "I wouldn't miss it for the world." He was the only one who was a professional musician who ever made it to the ceremony.

Years later, when Harold Dejan died, I wrote a card to his family and told them playing with his band felt like being a rookie on the 1927 New York Yankees walking into the locker room with Babe Ruth and Lou Gehrig. The day before his funeral I had to fly to Finland to play. Dodie Smith Simmons called me after I got back. She said, "Do you have a copy of that eulogy that you wrote?" I said, "I didn't write a eulogy." She said, "Well, they read that card that you wrote at the funeral as part of the eulogy. The way you phrased that was the most beautiful thing." I said, "No, it came right off the top of my head. That is the way I write. That was right from the heart."

Al Kennedy as a pallbearer at Lionel Ferbos' funeral.
Photographs of the procession by Rachel Breunlin.

AL KENNEDY
ARRANGEMENTS FOR MUSICIANS

Joe: I turned on my iPad on Sunday morning and saw that the trumpet player Lionel Ferbos had passed.

Al: He had his 103rd birthday at the Palm Court Cafe, and he really wanted to be there. A few weeks ago, I brought my grandson, who is three, over to his house when he was in town. The funeral is going to be at Corpus Christi. Charbonnet-Labat is doing the arrangements.

Joe: I guess when we first met it was at a funeral for Donald Harrison, the Big Chief of the Guardians of the Flame Mardi Gras Indian tribe. I was teaching at Gregory and had Donald's grandson, Christian Scott, in the band.

Al: I had probably some awareness of you as a musician before I knew you were a teacher. Christian was living with Donald while I was doing interviews with the Big Chief. I wasn't aware that Christian was one of your students.

Joe: Anything you said that Christian didn't know, he'd take out a pencil and paper. One time I talked about trading four—you play four measures, I play four, he plays four and then we go out. And he's like, "Okay, let me write it down."

In his seventh-grade year, the concert band did Close To You by the Carpenters. It called for a trumpet to play the first 16 measures and I gave it to him. He said, "Can I jazz it up?" I told him to go for it, and he did a good job. I remember at his grandfather's funeral we came out of St. Augustine Church. I don't know if that's when I gave you my card or not.

Al: Probably when I stapled it to my folder. I've brought you back all the pictures I've collected. In 1977, I got a new job as the public information officer with the New Orleans Public Schools. Orleans Parish was trying to do all they could to generate more publicity for the schools. I had latitude in my job to go from school to school, and I started seeing these people I'd paid the night before to go hear play in the clubs in the classroom. I'd hear about Sam Henry being at Allen Toussaint's studio, or Clyde Kerr, Jr. performing. I really saw this closeness between the classroom and the world. As I began putting two and two together, I started seeing newspaper articles about musicians around the city, and I'd throw them into folders in my office never knowing it would grow into anything.

Joe: From there we kept running into each other. The relationship grew into a friendship, and we've done quite a few projects together. You started your book project about band directors and I worked on it with you.

Al: Last spring, I developed a course at the University of New Orleans called the History of New Orleans Public Schools. I felt there were so many people coming in to the area that, through no fault of their own, did not know the history. And you were one of the people who I asked to come speak about the role of band directors in the schools. If you listen to people's experiences—yourself included—in the schools before Katrina, you begin to hear a chorus. I remember going to a show and hearing you perform, and then overhearing you talk with your brother Michael about your high school bands, musical arrangements, and how to get money for the school year.

Joe: Mardi Gras was coming up. Insurance.

Al: I've seen you perform many times after that, and over

The "first line" of Lionel Ferbos' funeral went down St. Bernard Avenue with a horse-drawn carriage led by the Charbonnet-Labat funeral home.

and above how much I enjoy you playing, I'm impressed that part of your mind has been allocating space to make sure that the kids have insurance to get on the bus and be able to go some place. You can't underestimate that. It put you in a bigger context—not just seeing you on the bandstand, but seeing you in the classroom, or at the events that you would sponsor. You were always involved in honoring the older guys. It's not that other people didn't do that, but no one did it as much as you.

Joe: And it's the way that we did it. We did educators and musicians.

Al: In terms of music history, when you look at interviews with the musicians, it's always: "What neighborhood did you grow up in?" "What bands did you play with?" "Who did you hear?" Rarely did I hear people ask, "What school did you attend?" Once you open that door, it unlocks a lot of answers.

Around 1982, I told Dr. Connie Atkinson, who ran Wavelength, about all the music I was seeing in the schools and she said, "Why don't you write an article about it?" For the piece, I followed up with Pete Fountain's experiences at Warren Easton High School, and tracked down his teacher, Anthony Valentino.

Joe: His brother, Rudolph Valentino, was the first band director at Gregory.

Al: Once I started talking to band directors, they would talk about their former students who were performing, and I started to see this wonderful network that stretched all across New Orleans. Many people pointed me in the direction of Yvonne Busch. All of these guys with more gray hair than I have now—and that's a lot—talking about how this woman changed their life. What was the arena for that? A band room.

Ms. Busch was an everything player. She made her mark by winning a student competition in Little Rock performing a complicated trombone concerto. She also went to Piney Woods Country Life School in Mississippi, and toured the country playing music with their band when she was 12 years old. Early in her teaching career she was at Clark and McDonogh 41. She ended her career at Carver.

When I called her, she had been retired for a few years. She said, "Oh, there's better people than me to talk to. I'd rather not." I gave it a year and called her back, explaining, "So many people keep mentioning you, I'd really love just to talk with you." It wasn't that she was really shy, she just didn't care about publicity. I don't think she fully understood...

Joe: The impact that she had on her students.

Al: *After Katrina, it was too much to rebuild. They tore down her house, and she moved close to her family in Arlington, Texas. I had a daughter in Austin, so my wife and I used to drive out of our way to Dallas so we could see her. And then she came back to live in Westwego. Once word got out she was there, you always had people dropping in. I remember Herlin Riley brought his trumpet to play for her birthday. She said, "Let me see that trumpet." She inspected it like a teacher, looking it up and down. The roles never change.*

At her funeral, every time I looked up at the church you had more and more musicians playing for her. And then when the procession walked around the church, we went by where her house used to be and the band had swelled.

Joe: *Even though so many people have passed on, you never really get used to it because every time, a certain part of my life dies at the same time. I spoke at Donald Richardson's funeral, but I liked to evoke his memory in other ways, too. When I was at Gregory, we played a game against Bell at the Pan American Stadium. A bunch of band directors from around the city came and sat on my side to see my band play against my alma mater. I said, "I'm going to do what Donald Richardson used to do to me when I was at John Mac."*

During Mardi Gras, he would march his band from Bell all the way to my school and play under the band room window. He was telling us, "Yeah, we're here. What you going to do about it?!" Gregory had a very large contingent of marching units. From the first person with the banner to the back, you probably had 170 kids involved. I said, "I want everyone to march in in a single file line go straight to their side of the field, and go all the way around the side line. I want them to be sick of looking at us." Which they did.

After Katrina, everybody in Orleans Parish was fired. I had been gone two years so I didn't have to go through that nightmare, but so many of the teachers relocated—mostly in Atlanta and Houston.

Al: *Even after working in the school system for so many years, I still don't fully understand the new landscape. It keeps changing. I don't want to defend what was wrong prior to Katrina. Heaven knows any institution needs to be shaped up. But afterwards, you wonder how you hold the new systems accountable when you have the schools broken up into so many divisions. Not that a clearinghouse is the answer, but I don't know if it's possible to even say how many schools have band programs, or how big they are. Now they are expected to raise*

a lot of their own money, and have to compete against each other for the grant funding.

Joe: *When I talk to teachers, I hear horror stories. There is no security in education anymore. The teachers union is broken. At East St. John, we had one teacher who was from the Teach for America program, and she had no classroom control. She finally told us, "In our training sessions, Teach for America told us not to partner with the experienced teachers."*

I said, "My whole thing is, you are not the Peace Corps. You are not here to do missionary work. You are here to teach, and you cannot teach if you do not have control of your classroom." It's the same thing I teach my students, if you don't control that instrument, that instrument will control you.

Left: Joe Torregano, who played the funeral with the Tremé Brass Band, talked with a young cornet player. **Middle:** Louis Charbonnet, the director of the Charbonnet-Labat funeral home, was responsible for connecting the family, the band, and Black Men of Labor as the grand marshals of the parade. **Right:** Lionel's family walked with his portrait down St. Bernard Avenue.

Since Danny Barker's funeral, BMOL has often been asked to grand marshal traditional jazz funerals. At Lionel Ferbos' funeral, Tyrone Casby opened his arms to recieve the moment as other BMOL members brought his body down. Todd Higgins held the BMOL banner.

Jeremy Jeanjacques standing on the corner of Henriette Delille (formerly St. Claude) and Ursulines with St. Augustine Church in the background. Jeremy moved to Tremé in elementary school, and got to know other musicians through practicing his horn outside. Photograph by Bruce Sunpie Barnes.

Jeremy playing the trombone with the New Orleans Young Traditional and Tremé Brass Bands at a BMOL parade. Photograph by Eric Waters, courtesy of the BMOL archive.

JEREMY JEANJACQUES

Bruce: *Jeremey Jeanjaques was one of the young people in the program who would walk over from his neighborhood. His house in Tremé is exactly one block away from trombonist Jim Robinson's home on St. Philip. Despite growing up in a neighborhood known for jazz, I could tell Jeremy was more influenced by high school marching bands. He knew a lot of their horn lines, and would entertain the French Quarter on his way over to the program because he'd be warming up, playing his horn as he was walking in.*

One of the things I noticed about him early on is that he thinks like a very mature old man. He used to sit beside Eddie King with the Tremé Brass Band and Craig Klein with the Storyville Stompers, and started playing the blues scales. It changed his playing style. Blues phrasing puts you into conversation with other musicians because they are set up to have a give and take between the instruments. That's where improvisation comes in—when you can listen to what other musicians are doing and being able to give something back.

In this interview, Jeremy and Joe Torregano compare experiences in marching bands in New Orleans, and discuss how they are different from jazz bands. Joe wanted Jeremy to know the different trombone players who have shaped the sound of jazz in the city. At the program, Jeremy worked with trombonist Charles Joseph, whose father was Waldren "Frog" Joseph. Frog was a contemporary of Jim Robinson and played trombone with Joe Robichaux and the Onward Brass Bands. He made his entrance into the music scene during the Jazz Revival period and raised some wonderful musicians in his household. Reading Frog Joseph's interview about his early career, Jeremy can see that the creative struggles the bands he's been involved with, the Baby Boyz and 21st Century Brass Bands, are ongoing dynamics each generation confronts.

Around Jeremy's house in Tremé, the Backstreet Cultural Museum's annual All Saints' Day parade brings the community out to honor people who have passed throughout the year. *Left:* A horse drawn carriage holds a picture of Big Chief Cyril "Ironhorse" Green of the Black Seminoles Mardi Gras Indian tribe. *Middle:* The parade stops in front of Little People's Place, a small barroom in the neighborhood that hosted live music for many years until new neighbors launched a campaign against it. The memorial T-shirt is for Vanessa Quint, whose family owns the bar. *Right:* Kim and Louis Charbonnet at the parade to honor Ike, a white horse who worked for their funeral. Photographs by Bruce Sunpie Barnes.

Joe: Jeremy, nice Thursday morning. Sun shining. Good breeze. How are you feeling today?

Jeremy: I'm feeling wonderful. I woke up on the right side of the bed this morning.

Joe: That is good. Tell us where your family is from.

Jeremy: Well, I only know of my mother's side of the family. My real father's side, I didn't have nothing to do with those people. My mom is from New Orleans. Way back down the line, my family was Haitians. They settled in New Orleans. My family was free black people in New Orleans at the time. My grandfather taught in Catholic school pretty much all his life.

Joe: Now, were there any musicians in your family? That is usually a part of the New Orleans tradition. There is always one or two, or a Mardi Gras Indian or a social aid and pleasure club.

Jeremy: Well, musician-wise my mother played drums, and marched for St. Mary's. My stepdaddy marched for your brother at Warren Easton. He played drums and the trumpet.

Joe: What neighborhood in New Orleans did you grow up in?

Jeremy: I grew up in two different neighborhoods. At the beginning of my life, I grew up in the Seventh Ward on Rocheblave a block away from where the Musicians Union is.

Joe: I grew up at 2623 Governor Nicholls between North Broad and North Dorgenois.

Jeremy: Right down the street! I moved to Tremé when I was seven. 1124 Ursulines is where I stay at now. I really never took any initiative to get out and learn about my neighborhood until I started playing music. That is when it became the best place around because I had musicians everywhere. I had people when they first heard me play my horn outside, just walk up and say, "Here, listen to this."

They gave me CDs. I had Trombone Shorty's, Rebirth, Danny Barker, Louis Armstrong. Everybody was very accepting with the fact that I play this instrument. It actually made me take more pride into it.

What happened with me was, I was a sports person when I was younger. I used to do nothing but the sport. I never really thought I would become a musician, but I ended up getting hurt after the storm. I was playing football in Texas.

They gave all the children who had evacuated from New Orleans a test. I was supposed to be in the seventh grade, but I tested into the ninth grade, so they moved me to MacArthur High. I was on their ninth-grade football team, but I was small. I played defensive tackle in the little championship game. We had beaucoup people come out. I caught an interception and the other team's quarterback ran me down! He hit me and broke my leg. I wheelchaired it for a little while. When I came back to New Orleans, I was part of the first seventh grade class at McDonogh 35.

Joe: They put you back from the ninth grade to seventh grade?

Jeremy: Yeah, if I'd have stayed in Texas I probably would have finished two years earlier.

Joe: If you tested and upgraded, it seems like the upgrade should have stayed.

The McDonogh 35 Marching Band, courtesy of the McDonogh 35. Before the storm, 35 was one of Orleans Parish Public School's citywide "magnet" schools. It was one of the few schools that Orleans Parish was allowed to keep when the state took over all the "low performing" schools in 2006. At a time when most schools did not reopen, 35 expanded its enrollment to take middle school students as well.

Jeremy: When I went and talked to the football coach at 35, it was like, "You are not going to be able to play until you hit high school." I was like, "I'm not about to sit on no team, go to practice for no two years and never get to see the field no time soon!" The band director, David Jefferson, Sr. stopped and asked me, "Would you like to come be in the band?" Of course, me, I was like, "No."

He was like, "Just come by and check it out." My older cousin graduated from 35 in 2002, and she was trombone section leader. She was like, "If you are going to do it, let's do it." She gave me my own trombone with a mouthpiece, and I got in the band.

It was pretty crazy because I had to settle in to a whole different type of schooling. I had been in Catholic school my entire life I really didn't get into the public school feel until I got to 35. I had to adapt to being in a public school and doing this easy work that they gave me. But being in the band program, and learning a brand new instrument, was pretty tough for me. I'm going to be real. I had a hard time learning how to play that trombone.

It wasn't because I couldn't play it. It was the fact that I didn't have any wind power. When I would play my loudest, it would still be pretty low so nobody ever heard me. I had to work out to build my diaphram. From there, I had to learn my tones. For what I had to do in a month's time, I actually was kind of proud of myself because I got it done. I was able to play every song that they asked me to play when it was time to step out for parade season. Mardi Gras was extra short, but I marched. We end up getting a good band out there.

Joe: Let me ask you personally. Did you think that was a fair demand to put on the band programs to hustle like that? Give them a month to organize?

Jeremy: No, I really didn't think it was fair. I did my history on Orleans Parish and how they felt about the band programs. They don't give the band programs nothing. Every year we march 30 to 40 conventions to pay for the expenses. Do you know how hard it is to put a complete band together, put them out on the street within a month with no money?

Joe: You must have forgot who you are talking to!

Jeremy: Well, I know! We had practice, long practices.

Joe: I'm going to tell you a story. As we sit here, this is true. I was at John McDonogh as a sophomore in 1967. We had the Reading Enrichment and Writing Program, which is a summer program. That was the last time funds were used by the Orleans Parish School Board to purchase instruments—1967. When I came back to John McDonogh in 1987, to be band director,

we were still holding onto some of those 20 year old instruments that had been re-padded again and again.

Trombone Shorty was in ninth grade at Gregory with me. A parade happened to stop right where the superintendent of Orleans Parish School District was standing with his family. He said, "You band director?" I said, "Yeah." He said, "Have you got Trombone Shorty in your band? I want to meet that kid. I've heard a lot about him." I said, "He's right there, I'll introduce you to him." I said, "Now you need to do me a favor. We need to have an appointment to sit and talk because bands have been mistreated and abused in this system for too long." I explained the instrument situation. He told me, "Put together a committee. Draw up a plan. Call my secretary." I got ten local people, and ten band people. We met in the band room at Gregory. We told him the need to have a strong Supervisor of Music and how they needed to contribute for uniforms and everything down the line.

Low and behold, typical New Orleans school politics, the position for Supervisor of Music was filled without interviews. No one was ever notified about it. A lot of people thought I had a shot of getting it. About 2003, they did make a minimal effort to buy some instruments.

My program at Gregory stood on its own two feet. They never gave me anything. My brother at Easton? Never gave him anything. All of the sudden here comes the hurricane. Many of the band directors who were certified never came back. It hurt to watch their replacements come in off the street with one or two years of college, no degree, no certification, and reap all the benefits that we should have reaped. They gave them uniforms but they didn't buy our uniforms.

Jeremy: Speaking as a person who just graduated from high school, a lot of people don't take pride in the music programs no more like they used to. When you see bands go out now you only see about—in the max—about 60 people. My seventh grade year I had the liberty of being the only crab in the band!

Joe: I never had the hazing process in my band program. My brother didn't allow it, either. It is like half the band directors did and half didn't. As you see, it got out of hand. There is the case of Southern where the whole French horn section went to jail for sending two new band members to the hospital after they were beaten with a 2X4.

Jeremy: I went to Southern Band Camp for a week and that was the time that they went to arrest the entire French horn section. Dr. Jackson came in with the police. Stopped the whole practice. Pointed at each one of them, "There you go, right there." They arrested them and took them away. I was like, "Wow." Back to practice.

Joe: One thing that's true is a marching band is basically like the military. You have to have discipline. If you don't have discipline, it will not come out correctly. That first year is spent putting discipline inside the person so the rest of the years, when the people come behind them, they have the discipline to put the discipline in others.

Jeremy: My first year of being in 35's band, they put the discipline factor in me. Anything they told me to do, I did it. If they told me to sit there and look straight, and I looked to the side, they told me to get down and do push-ups. I got down and did them. I knew they told me to look straight and I didn't look straight. It was serious. I had to duck walk. Run laps.

Joe: Talking about push-ups? My band from East St. John was on the Orleans Avenue parade route. One of my trombone players did something and I just pointed to the ground. He put his horn down and started doing push-ups. A sergeant named Tony Canatello came

Lois Andrews and her son, Troy "Trombone Shorty" Andrews, watch the Young Tuxedo Brass Band play at David Lastie's funeral (*Joe Torregano on clarinet*). Photograph by Michael P. Smith © The Historic New Orleans Collection, 2007.0103.4.389.

along and said, "Excuse me, how did you get him to do that?" I said, "Sergeant, it is a privilege, it is not a right. You put on my uniform, you coming here and representing me. I don't tolerate foolishness."

Jeremy: My band always had a problem with field shows. We would do the most excellent job in the stands, but when it was time to do a field show for some reason nobody just couldn't get it right. We end up messing up the St. Augustine field and that is a cardinal sin. Mr. Jeff got mad because when we meet St. Aug, which is known for having this amazing band, everything got to go right.

The fact that we messed up, we had a Saturday practice. I never forget this because I still feel that heat. We had to stand in the heat for three hours in marching

position with my trombone up. One leg up. Couldn't move. You move—you going to do push-ups and then you go right back to standing there.

With no discipline, you are not going to have nothing. To me, that is what is going on in this brass band world. All these different people talking about, "Okay, yeah, let's start a brass band." But how you going to start a brass band and you don't know the fundamentals of music? I'm going to be honest, I've been doing music for years now. I still feel like I don't know the fundamentals of music yet. I think in the next seven years I still won't know. All you can do is learn. Now it is like, "I will go find people to play tuba, snare, bass, trumpet, and I got me a brass band now." It doesn't work like that.

Young Traditionals

Then right after parade season, my band director told me about Music for All Ages. He was like, "You should try other arenas." I asked him, "What other arenas are there?" At the time, all I knew of was the marching band and concert. He was like, "Try jazz." I was like, "Okay." I was the only person in 35's band that went to MFAA. It was right down the street from my house in the French Quater so it wasn't nothing for me to wake up on a Saturday and come down to the program. The first two Saturdays I just listened. That third Saturday I came and played right in with the band.

Becoming one of the Young Traditionalists helped my playing so much. It took my experience to a whole new level. By me learning to play jazz music, it gave me my own form. My own feeling. Everything was just mine. When I got to marching band camp, my band director and the section leaders started saying that I had done improved dramatically. For that, I kind of feel like if I didn't go to this jazz program I really would not be the trombone player I am today.

When I first got in the marching band, all I thought about was, "Okay, I got to get loud. I got to be loud." That is a problem that a lot of people have, but being in MFAA helped me start understanding the true meaning of band—play as one. When I became section leader at 35, it took me a long time to be able to get the other trombone players to get that. I had four dudes on my line who were excellent players. If I was like, "Play this whole entire line," they are going to take the whole line up. But the problem with them was, all they thought about was showtime. "When I'm out here it is my time to shine, not the band."

We watched some of the videos from our football games and all you heard was my section over the whole entire band. They were all happy, "We loud!" I set them down and had a real serious meeting with them. I'm like, "To be honest, that does not sound good to me. It doesn't not sound good at all to swallow the whole entire band." At the end of this meeting, I asked Mr. Jeff to give his opinion on it. He gave the same point I had. No way in the world they should be blowing as hard as they were.

I started introducing them to solos. I wrote four parts and I taught it to each one of them. The first time they played, it was a mess. It was uneven. Everybody tried to blow it. I said, "Do you hear how you all sound?"

They was like, "Yeah, why does it keep sounding like that?"

I said, "You are going to have to learn to play together." Once they learned, everything worked out smooth. I think the same thing happens in brass bands these days.

Trombone Players

Joe: Let me ask you this. You spoke about the people in your neighborhood contributing CDs and advice. I was in Colorado Springs for the Earl Klugh Weekend Jazz at the Broadmoor Hotel. The headlining act was Trombone Shorty. When I saw him listed I said, "I'm not going to tell him I'm here." They do an artist question-and-answer session in the afternoon so the people in attendance can get to know the artist. A lot of people were curious about him because, to them, he was a new discovery.

It was a surprise to him that I was there in the audience. I said, "I'm going to ask you to explain to these people about your street education." When I was actively playing parades and funerals, Shorty was four or five years old. The horn was bigger than him. He could barely get to fourth position on the slide. He would always come out with his horn and follow behind the Tuxedo and the Olympia Brass Bands playing the real traditional music through the neighborhood.

Nicholas Payton was another one because his dad, Walter, was our tuba player in the Tuxedo Brass Band. I have a picture at home with Nicholas on stage with us at Jazz Fest with a little toy slide trumpet trying to get into what we were doing. Were there

Top: Jim Robinson. Photograph by Ralston Crawford, courtesy of the Hogan Jazz Archive. *Middle:* Louis Nelson. *Bottom:* Edward "Kid" Ory. Photographs courtesy of the Louisiana State Museum.

any particular musicians that stand out as being that kind of inspiration to you?

Jeremy: I have a little story! About a week after I first picked up my trombone, I was walking home from practice and one of the neighbors stopped me because I had my trombone on my back. The neighbor asked did I know who Trombone Shorty was. I was like, "I never heard of him before."

I had got home and asked my mom, "Mom, who is Trombone Shorty?" She was like, "Trombone Shorty is a famous trombonist." I was like, "Ma, they say he stayed around here."

She was like, "He did. He stood around here."

I was like, "I want to meet him."

"Well, you got to get better."

I'm like, "Really?"

"Yeah, you got to get better."

I practiced my long tones outside. Mom would not allow that inside! Oh no!

Two weeks later, we didn't have practice. I came home with my horn case, and I ran into him, but I didn't know who he was. He stopped me and was like, "You know how to play that?"

"No, I just started, but I know the scale." He was like, "Play me the scale."

I played him the B flat scale. He said, "Can you play the E flat scale?" I was like, "Yeah, I just learned it." I played the E flat scale for him. He was like, "You sound good. Keep practicing."

He ended up walking me home. When I got to the house he was like, "Look, I need you to do me a favor.

I need you to listen to this." He gave me his first CD. I look and was like, "You are Trombone Shorty!?"

He said, "Yeah, I'm Trombone Shorty." I was like, "Pleased to meet you."

For about three weeks straight after practice, I would go sit with him, and then he moved out of the Tremé. He actually put the love of the horn inside of me. At first, I was just doing it because my band director had asked me to. And I always have been the type of person to always be a part of something. I can't be no normal person—not dealing with anything. I have to be a part of something. But hanging with Shorty put the love of the horn in me. Like, there being times I would come home at ten at night, put some head-phones on, listen to a song, and try to play along. See how I sound with it.

My mom would come outside, "Why are you blowing this horn so late at night? What is wrong with you?" But right across the street from my house they have a little bench. My neighbors used to sit outside and listen to me play. That encouraged me.

Joe: Everybody in your band should listen to four or five people who play their instrument. You borrow something that you like from each one of them and that is how you develop yourself and your own style. Remember when you interviewed me I talked about how I wore the paint off the pole standing on Bourbon Street studying clarinet players when I was young? That is how I did it. I listened to records. There is nothing like going back. If you go back being a clarinet player, for me my favorite clarinet player was Omer

Simeon, from Jelly Roll Morton's Red Hot Peppers. His tone quality is immaculate. Very creative. Very fluid clarinet player. Now, let me quiz you right quick.

Jeremy: Ooh – quizzes!

Joe: That's what teachers do. Tell me if you have ever heard of these people: Jim Robinson.

Jeremy: No.

Joe: What about Louis Nelson?

Jeremy: No.

Joe: There were two Louis Nelsons. The other one was a clarinet player. Louis Nelson will teach you how to play soft. Listen to how soft he plays, but he is very smooth. What about Kid Ory?

Jeremy: Yeah.

Joe: Edward Kid Ory was from LaPlace, where I live now. He is considered the father of the tailgate. You know what tailgate trombone was?

Jeremy: In a traditional brass band, the trumpets play the melody, the clarinet plays around the melody, and the tailgate would be the trombone to fill in the spots where there is no music being played.

Joe: Okay, who told you that?

Jeremy: I actually had to find that out on my own; I really did. I did a second line and we played traditionals, but I was playing the same parts that the trumpets were playing. One of the trombone players was like, "You don't have to play the melody all the time. It is not about the melody. Just relax and fill in where you need to fill in at." He showed me how to tailgate.

Joe: Everyone wants to play melody, but you have to learn the parts each instrument plays in a brass band. Tailgating got its name during the early days of jazz, when bands would advertise an event. Say there was going to be a picnic at Shakespeare Park and they were going to have a jazz band play. They'd get on a horse drawn wagon, and let the tailgate down so the trombone players had room to move the slide. That is how the expression "tailgate trombone" came out. What about Wendell Eugene?

Jeremy: No.

Joe: That's a shame. Freddie Lonzo.

Jeremy: I've heard of him.

Joe: Waldren "Frog" Joseph.

Jeremy: I've heard of him, too.

Joe: He's the father of Charles and Kirk Joseph, who were founding members of the Dirty Dozen Brass Band. I also play with them in the Royal Players.

WALDREN "FROG" JOSEPH
SITTING DOWN TO READ

Waldren "Frog" Joseph and Blanche Thomas.
Photograph courtesy of the Louisiana State Museum.

Frog: I was born September the 12th, 1918. My mother's name was Anatasia Asnnor. My father, Arthur Joseph, was a longshoreman and played three string bass. You know, the majority of those people played music mostly for their self. You hear them play at banquets and parades and all that. My dad used to rent the bass out so much. Mr. Alcide "Slow Drag" Pavageau used to come by and get it.

Sometimes I use it as a joke, when people ask, "Well, how long you been playing music?" I say, "When I was born." My daddy's daddy was a musician, then my brothers were, too. My brother Ferdinand sang with Papa Celestin, my other brother Arthur played with Kid Rena's band, and William was a very legit drummer with Harold Dejan and them—he was a very good reader with drum music. So I found it.

They had music by the house all the time. If you had a piano, you always had some musicians who were going to want to rehearse. We had a pianola. I didn't know that was help for me. When I was 22 months old, I had infantile paralysis, which is polio. I really wanted to be a drummer, too, but I wasn't able because I had braces all along my leg, and the pinola helped me exercise. My wife's name is Adele Bijou. She learned piano the right way. And when we fell in love, she stopped playing the piano because I played better than her.

Adele, Frog's wife: That's right.

Frog: That's a little joke. I didn't think I was no good piano player. No, indeed. If I had a band, I wouldn't hire nobody to play piano like that. My daddy loved the trombone. Man, I had so much private lesson on the trombone, it was pitiful. My first teacher for the horn was a man they called Eugene Ware. He was working on a boat with my brother, and was staying

right around the corner from me. They used to rehearse by my house. He showed me all the alto positions.

I tell you something, a lot of foreign people learning about jazz think that black musicians can't read music. The way they put it in the books, it's like, "Nobody knew how to read music; nobody do this." If you know how to do that, they say, "Oh, he's too legit." Don't that hurt you, though. Yeah, they're hitting you right on the head that you are dumb.

During my time, if you didn't know how to read some kind of music, you was in bad shape because the communication of music with the popular tune coming out was stocks. Now, I'm gonna tell you something else. This the God's truth. I knew some musicians who didn't know how to read and write, but would read all that damn music you got.

A lot of the musicians from here used to play on the boats, but you had to know how to sit down and read. And then you had to play that stock music if you played all them Mardi Gras balls to keep up with the popular tunes. It wasn't like now—the kids listen at their tapes.

Some of my friends and I always had a little band, but the only thing was I couldn't parade with them because of my legs. Austin "Boot" Young was the one that really had helped me out a lot. Boots used to like to gamble on Rampart Street. At a taxi dance, they played stock music, and then they play their own thing. Boot knew I knew how to read, so he used to send for me, and I played a couple of hours for him, and he'd go gamble. See, I just read the alto part.

I got the name Frog when I was working in Joe Robichaux's band. Joe played the piano, and was a good man. Nice fella, and everybody liked him. He had made a whole lot of piano rolls. He had a small band, but at that time, the big band was coming up. You got a big band, you got to rehearse them. You might rehearse a brass section. Then they used to rehearse the saxophone. Then they all get together with the rhythm.

Radio was a big thing then and they broadcasted by the Rhythm Club at Derbigny and Jackson. Joe had a theme song, and my teacher, Gene Ware, was the writer for the band. He say to me, "Well look, I ain't gonna write you anything for this thing because it ain't gonna last long." The name of the song had Frog in it. When it was time for the band to start, Gene Ware said, "Frog!" And I said, "Boom, boom." Then the rest of the band said, "Da-da-dee-da-dee-da-dee-doo-boom-boom." That's how my name Frog come. I stayed with Robichaux for a long time.

Adele: When his first child was born, he was in Cuba.

Frog: Yeah, we had a big show in Cuba. It must've got about 1937. Earl Palmer's mama was the head of the chorus girls. I think we stayed two and a half weeks.

With Joe's band, we played for white audiences or just black audiences. You play according to your audience, man. You've been doing it long enough, you'll know what to do. You'll go on a gig, after you play about a half an hour, you dig what's going on. And you can tell what they want.

Listen. I think the greatest trombone player they got is Jack Teegarden. That's just what I think, now. He used to come here all the time. I been in his company many times. In my career, I made quite a few records. I went to Carnegie Hall twice with Al Hirt's show, once with Ronnie Cole's show. And I played for a long time with the Onward Brass Band. I knew Paul Barbarin since I was a little boy. That's all family friends there right there. He was a damn good writer, good composer. In fact, he told me, "You'd be surprised, boy, me and sister had

to eat." He said, "I sold a whole lot of tunes, so we could eat." During the Depression time, he was in New York. See, a lot of people don't being knowing some things musicians go through, know? [Turns to Adele] That girl know how to squeeze a dollar. She know what to do.

During the War, bands went small. Most of my friends went into the service, but I couldn't go because of my legs. I played the piano and worked on my horn. Paul came back home. "To hell with New York." That's what he said. "New York ain't where it's at." He was beautiful. Yes, indeed, man.

Adele: He was very easy. He liked our boys, and the boys liked him.

Frog: He knew I couldn't do no marching or nothing. You know I can't do that, no, but he didn't leave me on any of the other gigs. And that's the way he wanted to die. Playing music. He went like that in a parade.

Adele: That's the way he wanted.

Frog: I never did want to be no leader, now, I tell you that. When Paul died, Old Louis Cottrell kept the Onward going. Then come Placide Adam. Now, ain't nobody left but just Placide and me. People died, and I'm still there.

I always tell my boys, "Man: learn to play around the melody. If you learn melody, you got it made." I don't care what instrument you play. I'm gonna tell you something. I'm not criticizing—now remember I'm saying, please remember now—all them way-out flatted fifths, they ain't nothing but playing chromatics. You don't hear no melody. If you a musician, I mean, all right. But if you're just an ordinary person, you want to know what the band's playing. You got to have a little melody in there somewhere for the customer.

Paul Barbarin playing with the Onward Brass Band. Photograph courtesy of the Jules Cahn Collection at The Historic New Orleans Collection, 2000.78.1.106.

This edited transcript comes from an oral history with Barry Martyn conducted in New Orleans on April 9, 1999 for the New Orleans Jazz National Historical Park and the New Orleans Jazz Commission. It is archived at the Hogan Jazz Archive.

Jeremy playing the trombone at Nine Times' annual second line parade in November of 2013 with the 21st Century Brass Band. Photograph by Bruce Sunpie Barnes.

Jeremy: In the modern brass bands, we are listening to the popular songs of the day and turning them into brass band music. One of the main things we listen for is melody. Take for example, my brass band, 21st Century, just started playing the pop song, *Love on Top*. In the song, Beyonce modulates—changes key—six times. We modulate all six times.

Joe: You are crazy.

Jeremy: Exactly. The song starts off in B flat. We modulate from B flat to D flat, E flat, F, G flat, G and then we go back to B flat. It is chromatic half steps. If I was to give a brand new trombone player a copy of this song and tell him, "Listen to it and learn it," I highly doubt he is going to pick up on six different modulations.

Joe: You are not going to hear too many marching band playing that song.

Jeremy: You won't. I've actually wanted to upgrade my music. This is what happened. We had practice on Tuesday. I ended up running into Kenny Terry. He asked how many traditionals we know as a brass band.

We could only play two for him.

I got so mad. He knew that I knew a lot of traditional songs because, of course, Kenny was one of the people that taught them to me at the MFAA program. But, as a band—and this is what is going on with newer brass bands that are coming out—all we know are these hip songs or the songs that they hear other brass bands play. The younger brass bands aren't listening to the traditional brass bands. So the other day we had a whole practice dedicated to learning traditional style music.

KENNETH
TERRY

&

JOHN MICHAEL
BRADFORD

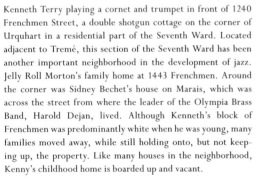

Kenneth Terry playing a cornet and trumpet in front of 1240 Frenchmen Street, a double shotgun cottage on the corner of Urquhart in a residential part of the Seventh Ward. Located adjacent to Tremé, this section of the Seventh Ward has been another important neighborhood in the development of jazz. Jelly Roll Morton's family home at 1443 Frenchmen. Around the corner was Sidney Bechet's house on Marais, which was across the street from where the leader of the Olympia Brass Band, Harold Dejan, lived. Although Kenneth's block of Frenchmen was predominantly white when he was young, many families moved away, while still holding onto, but not keeping up, the property. Like many houses in the neighborhood, Kenny's childhood home is boarded up and vacant.

Kenneth playing on Frenchmen Street, where the Junior Olympia used to practice. The neighborhood has been renamed by historic preservationists as the New Marigny. Photographs by Bruce Sunpie Barnes.

KENNETH TERRY

Bruce: Kenny Terry is a trumpet and cornet player who has pure, raw talent. High notes, low growls, and screams—he can make that horn sing the blues. He's got a voice that sounds like a concrete mixing truck full of gravel, but he sings in key and makes it do everything he wants to do. He has a tremendous ear, and is a great ear trainer. Kenny came up masking with the Yellow Pocahontas and learning music with Tambourine and Fan. He was a member of the Bucketmen Brass Band and the Junior Olympia before going on to play with the New Birth and Rebirth Brass Bands. He has an incredible memory for traditional brass band music, and played for many years with the Tremé Brass Band. In the program, he taught the trumpet players how to play the lead parts, as well as the second trumpet's role in harmony. He was one of the main people who forced the kids to take a solo: "Come on, man, you can do this! Put your heart into it. Don't be scared! If you put something in the horn into it, you'll get something out." He was also happy to work with them and encouraged them to come by his house or Jackson Square and get some extra lessons because this is the way he was raised.

Kenny learned to play from Milton Batiste, the trumpet player in the Olympia Brass Band. Milton loved to listen to the music that was coming out of the streets of the city. You don't see kids hanging out in the volume they used to, but there used to be 30 or 40 kids on a corner on any afternoon beating on buckets. That kind of thing was hilarious to Milton. He'd come over close to it, and pick up what they were doing and see who had talent. That's how he was with the Junior Olympia as well. He loved to teach young people how to organize music. He didn't mind investing time and money into getting them to do something. He felt like the investment was worth it. He had a group called the Magnificent 5s and the Magnificent 7s, which he based off of Louis Armstrong's Hot 5 and Hot 7s. And oh, could he talk. He could talk anybody out of anything and into anything, which is how Kenny got his start pretty early on.

Introduction: Your Sound

Kenny: I've played with musicians from other cities, and they are like, "Where did you get that sound from? What kind of style that is?"

"Man, New Orleans."

The difference between New Orleans and a bunch of other places is that here, a lot of these musicians don't just play music. They live it. They actually live it. This is every day for us. This is our life, and it's not taught strictly out the book. To me, it don't take a scientist to run up and down scales all day. Anybody can do that. Try doing what Louis Armstrong was doing, and make it sound like something. Seriously. It is really hard. He made it look easy, but it is hard.

This is what you learn as a musician in New Orleans. You have to read the audience. It is hard for me to explain, but it is about taking control. You see how I get out there? I might be sitting down for one second. I go to standing up. I go to moving around in the audience. You know what I am doing? I'm getting the crowd's attention to focus on the music and the band. Once I have them with the energy, they ain't never leaving.

You know what I have to think about when I do all this? I'm thinking about what songs I'm going to play. I'm watching the audience to see how they respond. My eyes are wide open everywhere. If I see you got a frown on your face, I know not to do that the next time.Go do something else.

Tambourine and Fan

I got to be constantly learning. My mother, Elaine Simmons, was a school teacher at Holy Redeemer High School. She was a city woman who grew up on St. Claude Avenue, right outside of the French Quarter in the Seventh Ward. I was born and raised

at 1240 Frenchmen Street. My mom was actually the first black lady to move in that block between Marais and Urquhart. It was pre-integration, and, during that time, it was mainly Caucasian. The block voted to see if you could meet their standards to be around Caucasian people.

Here's the interesting thing about "race." My dad, Clarence, grew up a country boy in Napoleonville, Louisiana, and part of his family there is actually Caucasian. A lot of people don't know that. On the other side, my mom's dad was the darkest child in the family. They used to call him Midnight. Yes. And my mom inherited her skin tone from him. My parents connected and were together for 46 years. The 1200 block of Frenchmen voted about them, and, as a family, we passed.

My dad opened up a body and fender shop, and I helped him sand cars at the shop from really young. But I was mostly raised up in Tambourine and Fan. I got involved through my mom. She was a secretary for the organization and worked at "the Building" just a few blocks away from our house on North Robertson. I used to sit up in the office and answer the phones. In time, they wound up moving to St. Bernard and Claiborne. Hunter's Field is where Jerome Smith brought everybody together. Still today if he says, "Come here," I will stop in a heartbeat.

Tambourine and Fan ran programming through the New Orleans Recreational Department. Three hours after school to go hang out—sports, Mardi Gras Indians, and also parading with the second lines. The coaches taught us the ropes about how to become a man. You got in trouble, you got the paddle. I know today some people call it cruel punishment, but it actually saved a lot of our lives. To get to Hunter's Field from where I was living on Frenchmen, I had to pass through a drug-infested area over on the corner of Pauger and North Villere. I'm around people who were being beat up, shot, and stabbed. Everything.

Tambourine and Fan collage shows its holistic approach to child development: reading, music, parades, sports, and a critical conscience. Image courtesy of Jerome Smith.

Buying drugs. I kept myself away from it by going to football practice.

Through the summer programs, all we did was learn black history. We used to sing a lot of spiritual tunes to help learn our history, and how to resist the pressures of the street. One chant we used to have to sing was,

What is dope?
Dope is poison death!
What is dope?
Dope is poison death!
Who uses dope?

A dead man!
Who is a man that use it?
A dead man!

Who is Dr. King?
A black man trying to make things better for the black people!
Who was Malcolm X?
Malcolm X was a freedom fighter!
Why do Hunters have to study?
That is to build control. Reading, math and science!

A lot of the people in Tambourine and Fan were related to the Yellow Pocahontas. We're all the same people. The older guys who were masking Indian had kids playing football. I started masking when I was really young. My mom sewed four suits by herself for my dad, my brother, and me, and then later on my baby sister. It took her about a year. The kids used to set up trays with the needles, and the adults would say, "Hold up, we need some blue beads." You find out what color blue they need and set them out. We had to wrap feathers. Sometimes we traced patterns. Then my mom said, "Come here. Let me show you how to do this. You are going to sew this by yourself." The first time, it took me a week to sew one little bitty piece on cardboard. She said, "Boy, that ain't tight enough. You got to tie it down tight." She was teaching me how to whip stitch, coming up one side, and going down

the other, and then having to tie it off at the bottom. When Mardi Gras was over, she tore those suits down and started a new one.

At one point, the Yellow Pochahontas was one of the biggest tribes in New Orleans. One of the baddest. Also, one of the prettiest. On Mardi Gras day, the gang used to stretch from Orleans and Claiborne all the way to St. Bernard Avenue. We had Spyboys. Flagboys. Trail Chiefs. Second Chiefs. Third Chief before Tootie Montana. Just the kids would fill up a few blocks. They had Wild Man Russell in the front of the kids to protect them. He ran all around them kids.

We were kids. We were having fun. It was more serious than what we really thought. It was about our culture, and giving appreciation to the Indians for hiding the slaves through slavery time.

My first position was just an Indian—no title. After I became an Indian, we had a meeting at practice and Tootie Montana said, "You are going to be a Flagboy." You have to work your way up the ropes. You don't just come jump into it. When I was masking, guys older than me never stepped up. They never got promoted to another position. That is where the Chief wants you at, that is where you stay at. Nowadays they got people that just want to jump in and say, "Hey, I'm going to be

a Big Chief this year." It doesn't go like that. I masked with Yellow Pocahontas until I graduated from high school. The last couple of years I masked, I said, "Ma, you going to help me?" She said, "No, I can't see them little bitty beads no more." It wears your eyes out trying to put those beads on the needles.

At Hunter's Field, Fred Johnson and Jerome Smith used to teach us how to dance to the Olympia Brass Band. You'd have 40 boys and 40 girls learning to second line. Danny Barker had just left the Fairview Baptist Church Band, and he taught the Roots of Jazz at Hunter's Field, too. After football practice, I sat out there and listened. I'd see these guys coming with old beat-up instruments. Danny came with a little banjo. I thought, "Fine. I play my sports, I ain't worried about it."

That summer, a friend of mine wound up getting killed. He was no more than ten years old. Little LaBaron Bernard. A guy wanted to ride his moped. He told him no. Guy went inside and got a bat. Hit him in his neck and killed him. Found him in the gutter. The Olympia Brass Band came for his funeral. Harold Dejan called the shots. He was the leader. Milton Batiste was the assistant leader. On Claiborne, I'm watching Milton play trumpet with one hand. I said, "Ma, I want to play like him." She said, "Oh boy, here we go. All right."

Milton Batiste. Photograph courtesy of the Jules Cahn Collection at The Historic New Orleans Collection, 2000.78.1.482.

MILTON BATISTE
BRINGING IN NEW SONGS

Milton: I was born September 5, 1934. Growing up, I lived on the 1500 block of North Claiborne, and went to Corpus Christi. In the Catholic school, we had very few black teachers. At Corpus Christi, we were being taught by Sisters of Blessed Sacrament. We didn't get black history. We sang opera. We had a lot of hand-me-down books from the white schools. But if you educate yourself with a good book or a bad book, if you read it, you'll get something out of it.

My mother had twelve children, and I am the first. My mother had one of those good, old Creole names—Feliciana Mary Golivette. On her side, we can go as far back as my grandmother, who was a part of the Blackfoot tribe. She was a slave in Breaux Bridge on the Edwards Plantation, and that probably is the reason why her maiden name was Virginia Edwards. All the slaves took on the names of the slaveowners. She married my grandfather, Joseph Charles Golivette, who was French-African. He came to America, and interpreted French to English for the generals in World War I.

When I was on Corpus Christi's Altar Boys Baseball Team, a baseball hit me in the side of my head, causing a tumor and sebaceous cyst. It was extracted, analyzed, and found out to be cancer. I was put in Charity Hospital, and the doctor, Michael DeBakey, explained to my mother that this tumor was of a very new and detrimental disease. People didn't know very much about cancer then in those days. He got her to agree to do an experimental operation on me. He gave me treatment with this ultraviolet light that was just being invented. That ultraviolet light today is chemotherapy. They put me in a room, and wrapped me up in a blanket of lead. They used this leather and leaded shield contraption so that the light shined on only a little part of my head. I had that treatment done to me three times a week for nine months. Afterwards, I developed an inferiority complex because of the scar on my head. I always wanted to wear a hat to hide it, or try to comb my hair that it would come over the top of it. For a long time, even to a young man of 20-some-odd years old, the inferiority complex followed me about being in public and people staring at me. Some of my childhood friends still call me "Half a Head."

Playing the Trumpet

When I was about 11 years old, I saw a movie at the Circle Theater. It was a little colored boy laying on top of a doghouse, playing the trumpet. That is the image that is still in my mind 50 years later. I decided, "Hey, if he could do it, I could."

My mother wanted my father to sign a credit note from Werlein's to buy me a horn. My dad said no. "We go get in all that trouble, he probably going to take that horn put it in the closet and leave it there, just like all the rest of them."

My father didn't play an instrument beyond tinkling on a piano, but I was told that his father, who was from Jamaica, was a bass violin player. My father only had a second or third-grade education. He worked from sun-up to sundown, sometimes seven days a week as a riverfront worker hauling bananas and trucking rubber. He worked for the Coca-Cola Bottling Company. He did stevedoring at night. And when the World War II broke out, he became a Pullman porter on the train, hauling the troops all around. By the time I was in high school, he worked as the first maintenance man at St. Augustine High School.

I told my dad, "Oh, Dad, I want to play that horn, I want to play. I'm gon go out and buy my own then. I'm gon buy my own." I used to deliver newspapers. I saved up ten dollars and went to the J&M Pawn Shop on Rampart Street. They had this $35 trumpet there. Well, I put it in a layaway. I don't exactly know how long it took me to pay the other $25 because it took me awful damn long time to get the ten, but that was my beginning.

My junior year of high school at Clark High School, I joined the Musicians union to play with Professor Longhair. Throughout the 1950s, I was in and out of his band. We played a black nightclub in the Sixth Ward called the High Hat that had female impersonator shows and people dancing with snakes and fire. Professor Longhair was popular at all these little nightclubs along the river, too. At one time, the name of the band was "Professor Longhair and the Shuffling Hungarians." It was not the name of a nation known to many black people. They didn't know what he was talking about but that was his way of getting over that we had rhythm, and we were the best.

I learned a lot from Fess. When he played, he wiggled his right foot. He called that the "Ism." If you didn't have that Ism, you couldn't be in Professor Longhair's band. His feeling of music had African, Jamaican rhythms to it. And reggae, too. In those days, reggae was not even recognized in our culture of music, but it's there! In 1988, the Olympia took a tour of Africa and visited Gorée Island off of Dakar in Senegal. The last Spanish slave house had sent slaves out to three different parts of the United States—some landed in Jamaica. Some went to North Carolina. And the rest came to Louisiana. We've got that feeling. And those styles.

On the Road

I didn't start going on the road until the middle 1950s. I played with Smiley Lewis and Papa Lightfoot. We'd go on the road with different people. I'm not ashamed to say now, but a lot of them were fakes. We had a fake Shirley and Lee. We had a fake Ray Charles. They were just imitators who sang just like them. Remember now, there's no television in these days. Nobody knew exactly how they looked.

We traveled all over the South and played the clubs on the other side of the tracks while the Civil Rights Movement was going on. I witnessed some of the first sit ins going on with Dr. King and other people marching in different places. In Jacksonville, Florida, I took pictures from the balcony of a hotel where we were staying—right down upon a big, blue bus where people were being hit in the head and crammed into buses, because they were sitting at a counter trying to get something to eat.

Another thing I witnessed was we went to a play a job with Joe "Google Eyes" August. He took a five-piece band to the University of Alabama on the south part of campus to play a fraternity party. At the same time, on the north side of the campus, state troopers and the governor were standing in front of the university, so a black child, Autherine Lucy, could not come in to get an education.

We arrived in time to play the job, and the state troopers just opened up, and let us through. The kids came out and picked us up—each individually—and put us on their shoulders, stuffed whiskey in our pockets and money in our hands, and brought us into the fraternity house. You know, "Let's have a good time!" That said to me that they wanted us to entertain, but they didn't want us to be smart. You can't come here and get an education at the University of Alabama. But you can come here and entertain us. And we'll pay. It seems that that's the most fearful thing of the white community, or the white man, was to have an educated black. And it's still happening, we still got the problem today.

I came back to New Orleans, and my father said, "What you oughta do is go around that French Quarters and play that jazz. That's the music!" I decided to take up on his advice, and took this gig during Mardi Gras from George Williams' Brass Band for the Jefferson City Buzzards. It started Uptown at seven o'clock in the morning—went to Audubon Park, down to Canal Street, and then back up. I finally got back home about nine o'clock that night. I had blisters on my feet so bad, I couldn't walk for the next three days! And it was "Damn, my daddy sent me down here, what the heck am I into now?"

I'll never forget, Teddy Riley gave me my first encouragement and lessons about playing a parade. I shouldn't tell them young guys that, but I'll tell them anyhow. What makes you sound nice and loud out there in the street is that you have to bounce your music off the buildings and the houses. You just turn to the side—left or right—and bounce it off. It comes back to the band, and you loud as hell. Blow straight ahead, and it's just gone. It's gone. Teddy Riley gave me that.

In 1959, Ernie Cagnolatti had to have his leg amputated. Harold Dejan wanted me because Cag couldn't walk anymore. First gig I played was a practice parade for the Lions Club in the Uptown area. And I said, "Now, practice what?" It was practicing how to walk, drink, and play at the same time! You go to each of the barrooms in the local area that you gonna be doing at Mardi Gras morning.

The era of 1959 to 1965 became a transition era of rhythm-and-blues songs being turned into traditional brass band songs. It was met with a lot of opposition. They don't want that rhythm-and-blues on the street. As I introduced R&B to Olympia, the Young Tuxedo Brass Band recorded the Shirley and Lee song, Come on, Baby, Let the Good Times Roll on Atlantic, so this was a help for us.

To the young musician, you're bringing in new songs, because you got new people walking and parading. What's traditional to me was not traditional to Kid Thomas. He came up around music by people who made songs from the late 1800s, and he changed them around. Kid Howard was the most progressive trumpet player of his era. These guys were ahead of their time in music because some of the licks they play right now are just the same notes played faster.

As I got more involved in the Olympia, I became an employee of WSMB radio. I worked there for 18 years. I started off by cleaning the wastepaper baskets, sweeping the floors, dusting the place, and making the coffee. And I started collecting and distributing the commercials that went on the radio station. We had to go to different advertising agencies, and pick up tapes.

I met a lot of public relations people. And naturally, when I went there, I told them I was a musician. I started getting calls from them for a band. I worked there so long it became like family to me. They would always let me off to go play a job, and eventually it got to be I was playing more jobs that I was working there. In 1978, I turned the job over to another person.

There came a time when I saw it was necessary to record and document people who may never get a chance to. They got musicians who sat in the studio, and did all the recording. You understand, they were a recording band. And then there's the side musicians who have played all the gigs, but never recorded. The majority of people don't know about a lot of things that happened and went on with younger musicians. And some of the older guys have never been recorded. Duke Bat Publishings is Duke: Dejan and Bat: Me. My label is Olympia Label. And we have another label called Rose that I dedicated to Harold's wife, who's passed away, and we record gospel like the Zion Harmonizers on it.

I remember when I first started playing rhythm-and-blues on the street, my Aunt Felicia was a staunch gospel singer. She organized the choir at the Sixth Union Baptist Church, and told me, "You oughta look into gospel." She said, "That's all right, wait until you get older, you're gonna find out." And she was right because jazz and the gospel are so closely related. You can't do one without the other.

This edited interview is from an oral history with Milton Batiste conducted by Tad Jones on February 5, 2002, and housed in the Hogan Jazz Archive's oral history collection.

Left: The Bucketmen Brass Band, courtesy of Jerome Smith. *Right:* The cover of the Junior Olympia album produced by Milton Batiste. Image courtesy of Cayetano Hingle.

The Bucketmen Band and the Junior Olympia

Kenny: At Hunter's Field, my home away from home, Jerome Smith came up to me and said, "Kenny, you and Fat Man (that's Kerry Hunter) come here. Where that horn at? Go get that horn." I go and get my little school horn. Little ratty thing. You should have seen it. We go to the locker room where we used to practice and are just making a bunch of noise. Up comes Milton Batiste. I'm like, "I know you." He said, "Yeah, I remember. You are the one that said you wanted to play. Listen, sit right here."

First traditional jazz tune I ever learned was *Down by the Riverside*. I couldn't play it. He said, "Man, look. You are going to learn this song." I said, "All right." I get that song. I'm like, "I'm digging this." He told me, "You can play one song, it will never come out the same way." And it is actually true.

My mom gave me a gospel book with all the hymns in it. I called Milton. "Mr. Batiste, *Just a Closer Walk with Thee* is a jazz tune?" He said, "Yeah." Before you know it, *Amazing Grace*. I said, "Hold up. Let's go to the church." I was raised Catholic—an altar boy and everything—and we didn't have this kind of music. I had to go into the neighborhood. We had a little hole in the wall Baptist church on our block. It used to be a barroom. They had the doors open and I would listen to all the people singing. I'm liking this. I used that. I put that into the music. I started playing the way one of the ladies is singing. When you read music in a book, you don't have pick up notes. No grace notes. No trios. They don't show you all that.

Before you know it, we had other guys come in. They want to join the band. We said, "Hold up, man. We the Bucketmen Brass Band." We actually wrote a song. We played the renaming of London Avenue after A.P. Tureaud, the Civil Rights leader who fought for the integration of New Orleans public schools with the NAACP. But after eight months, we wound up leaving. Under Tambourine and Fan, we weren't allowed to play on the street. We was like, "Maybe in the French Quarters, we can do all this." We was on our own. We didn't have no name. We were just little kids running wild.

One day, I got a phone call. Milton Batiste said, "Kenny, get them boys together. Meet me on the field. I'm going to take you up by my house."

I said, "Oh Lord, here we go again." I called all the band members together. We met at Hunter's Field, and went by his house at 5335 St. Anthony Avenue. We go back in his yard in the shade. We are amazed. He collected trains. Toys. Statues. We were like, "What?!" Milton said, "Kenny, you are going to be the leader. You all going to be the first Junior Olympia Brass Band." Our first practice wasn't actually blowing

The question is always asked, "Who will, or are there any youth who will take the place of elderly jazz men?" Back in 1883, the first Olympia Band was started. Many jazz men have emerged from the ranks of this organization.

The young men on this recording have set a goal in life: To take over the New Orleans music tradition.

They enjoy working hard at their work.

At this time, they are ready to play short concerts, parades, jazz funerals, etc. Their ages are from 14 years to 16 years old and attend Joseph S. Clark Senior High and Colton Junior High Schools.

Six of them play in their school's band. The bass drummer is very likely to excel in other things like sports, basketball and football. In tutoring them about the music, I always let them use most of their own ideas and correct them if they are wrong. The arrangements on here are of their own thoughts. They rehearse at least 3 days a week. These young men are very serious about their music. The sale of this record is to help provide a place for all youngsters who wish to preserve a knowledge of their heritage in music, dance, etc.

The place will be called The Music Wood Shed, located across the street from Armstrong Park, named after one of the band's top musical heros, Louis Armstrong. He, like them, started at a very young age. So the profits from this record will go to buy instruments, restore the house, practice and to give small performances.

We dedicate this album to Mrs. Rose Dejan (1909-1986) who once danced the many stages of New Orleans. Special thanks to the Fan Tamborine Club. They gave these young men guidance to go forward in the right direction.

Here comes the next generation of New Orleans Music Makers. We hope they too will keep going another 103 years.

Jazzly Yours,
Milton Batiste, Jr.
Band Director

Milton Batiste's liner notes for the Junior Olympia album, courtesy of Cayetano Hingle.

horns. It was mainly listening. Can you imagine listening to one song about 100 times a day? I mean, it just get in your head. "Now play it."

We were practicing twice a week on Tuesdays and Thursdays. Milton picked us up in the van at my house on Frenchmen Street after school. He rode straight up Elysian Fields, stopped at Popeye's to get chicken and cold drinks, and took us back to his house. We learned how to read music, too. Got to read the music. You get a new song Tuesday, Thursday you better know it.

After awhile Milton said, "Come on, I got a gig for you all. Everybody need black pants." Come out in black pants on. Gave us hats, shirts. Went to the Monteleone Hotel and the Olympia Brass Band called us up for one or two songs. We used to go to Preservation Hall when they played on Sunday nights to listen to that band play. These old cats, we don't even know half of their last names. At the time, we were one of three young brass bands. The other two were the All Stars Brass Band and Rebirth. Rebirth had started playing traditional music, branched off, and started going in the direction of the Dirty Dozen in writing their own songs. We couldn't play that. Milton would put you out.

The Junior Olympia played in Jackson Square, but you had to get there early. Whoever got the spot first could play there all day. Actually, they still do that today. They'll be there at six in the morning waiting on their spot. The Junior Olympia took one side, the All Star Brass Band took the other, and Tuba Fats' band was right in the middle. Everybody loved Tuba. When he arrived, it was like the Square was his stage—he owned it. He invited other musicians to come sit in, and we learned songs from him, too.

We started getting used to making money. There was a parade on Canal Street called the Louis Louis parade. Ten different marching bands were supposed to play the song, *Louis Louis, Oh Louis*. Milton booked us in and we had to learn the song. We learned it, but then, keep in mind we was kids. We were like, "You going to pay us for that?" When there wasn't any money, nobody showed up, and Milton said, "All right. Junior Olympia is no longer." It wasn't ever no bad blood. He still was teaching us music, but he wasn't booking no gigs for Junior Olympia.

Some of the members of the Olympia were getting old and dying out. Harold Dejan told Milton, "Bring them boys by my house. Bring they instruments." That is when it started getting serious. I'm like, "Uh-oh, Mr. Dejan wants us to come by. What does he want?" We normally deal with Milton. Dejan come out there with his saxophone with the little red mouthpiece on it, and starts calling all these old tunes: "Let's go. *Saints Go Marching In*." Before you know it, "*Struttin with BBQ.*" We're playing them, but we're nervous. What the hell is going on? Batiste is just sitting there. He said, "The old man want you to play them." Finally Dejan said, "All right, kids. All right." Went in his closet. Come back with a box. Olympia Brass Band shirts. They didn't have "Junior" written on it. It used to have "Dejan's Junior Olympia Brass Band." Now it said, "Olympia Brass Band."

One day Milton went out of town and I had to take his place on a gig. Tuba Fats was like, "Kenny, come here Lil Milton." He tied a tambourine on my side just like Milton did to keep the time. I'm doing the whole gig like this here, and they are saying, "You better hold it like your Pops." I held the trumpet with the one hand, just like he did. And I still do it.

Kerry "Fat Man" Hunter (*snare*) and Cayetano "Tanio" Hingle (*bass*) playing with the PresHall Brass Band. Along with Kenny, Kerry and Cayetano have been playing music together since they were in elementary school. Photographs by Bruce Sunpie Barnes.

Cayetano Hingle: *When we were growing up, Tambourine and Fan ran two day camps at Marie C. Couvent Elementary School in the Seventh Ward and Joseph A. Craig in the Sixth Ward. In the summer, you could say Jerome was the principal of those schools. Early in the morning, you'd go have breakfast, and everybody would run around and have their little fun.*

But when the bass drum started beating, every kid in the camp knew one thing, you need to line up and get into "Congo Square." Everyone wanted to play the bass drum, and look like it was Kerry and me who were the first ones to the drums, every time. We were playing the special beat:

The tambourine was born down in New Orleans,
In the little field they called Congo Square.
The tambourine was heard by Louis and Celestin,
My sister Mahalia, the world's gospel queen.
We honor the day of Martin Luther King
And if it wasn't for the struggle, the tambourine wouldn't ring.

Then Jerome Smith made his announcement, "Let's get ready to learn!" And we'd get ready to go to class. During the day, we had second line practice. The Olympia Brass Band would show up and Jerome and Fred Johnson would call two classes down. The girls would get on one side, the boys on another.

We would line up like a Soul Train line. The Olympia would start playing, and we'd start dancing.

One day Jerome Smith came from his head, and had Milton Batiste and the Olympia Brass Band to start teaching us how to play the music. Kenny became the leader of the Junior Olympia. He was the front man. What Milton played, Kenny played. Oh it was his, it was all Kenny. Believe me. It was all Kenny! We were living in his house every night. Kenny's mama, Ms. Elaine, had our clothes ironed at all times before the gigs. Starched. Red pants with the yellow stripes—just like the Olympia.

Then we look up and Da dah! Da dah! We got Milton Batiste, Harold Dejan, Nowell "Papa" Glass, Boogie—we got the whole Olympia Band—picking us up. We're looking like them, and they're teaching us the tradition. I learned from Papa. His style was traditional all the time. He had that four. His daddy, Booker T. Glass, was one of the best bass drummers. From there, I listened to Benny Jones, Uncle Lionel, and Keith Frazier. Mix it all together, I don't think you can go wrong.

If we could teach the same things that Milton and Harold did, it would be different in the world—music-wise. Kenny is one of the people who can do it. I know he can. Ain't nobody can

take that front like Kenny. He handled it with New Birth, too. That's Kenny's also.

He's real educated. Believe me. He might say one word that you don't want to hear. It might not be the best word at the time, but he'll call you the next day, "Hey baby how you doing? You all right?"

"Kenny did you hear what you told me last night?"
"Oh, man, that wasn't me." You got to laugh it off.

Kerry and I have been in the back at all time—from the Junior Olympia to New Birth to what we're doing now with PresHall Brass. He's a brother. We talk to each other. If he plays "pop," I say, "boom." Now, he can go off beat, and I can go off beat, but by the time we look at each other— bam—we're back on.

Kerry keeps the band moving. The snare drum keeps that steady, steady drag and roll to keep everybody fired up and hyped. Then I come at you and I'll be feeling beats in different places—just laid back. I'll be thinking about Tambourine and Fan, and that Congo Square beat. It's a drop beat. Instead of playing straight ahead, I'd rather keep it dropping. I want to keep it funky, and Kerry always makes it easy for me.

Left: Members of New Birth Brass Band: Kerry "Fatman" Hunter, Derrick Shezbie, James Andrews, Cayetano Hingle, and Kerwin James. *Right:* Kenny playing trumpet with New Birth at Donna's Bar and Grill on North Rampart Street. For many years it was known as the "Brass Band Headquarters." Photographs courtesy of Cayetano Hingle.

Kerwin James

In the early 1980s, I was fortunate to win an award in high school for *Who's Who in Music.* I had a scholarship to go to the Berklee College of Music, but I told them, "No. I want to play New Orleans music." My mom said, "Boy, it is your decision." I'm 17 years old. I went to Southern University of New Orleans with Kidd Jordan, and I used to give him a run for his money, too, because he was teaching straight ahead jazz. "Mr. Terry, when you coming to class?" I would brush it off, "Man, I be at practice in a little while. I got a gig."

Kerwin James and I started a band called New Birth. He was the brother of Phillip Frazier and Keith Frazier with the Rebirth Brass Band. One of the best guys you want to meet. We did everything together. We used to have little rivalries with other groups—who can do this and who can do that. I'd say, "Man, I bet y'all can't mess with Fat." Kerwin had amazing talent—his concepts, how he wanted things to be performed. So many small things. He taught me a lot just being in his presence. We took half of the All Star Brass Band, half of the Junior Olympia Brass Band, and we would take

whatever jobs that the Rebirth couldn't make. It was a branch off of Olympia and Rebirth mixed. We rolling now. It is the best thing I could have ever done.

On the road, Kerwin was my roommate. It was almost like a marriage, and he was even in my wedding. Even after I got married, we still went everywhere together. I used to tell my wife, "I'm going over there by Fat."

"You are always going over there by Kerwin."

We just was together all day, every day. It was like a family outside of a family. Just like Tambourine and Fan was a family outside of a family. New Birth wound up losing three band members—Glenn Andrews, Stafford Agee, and Derrick "Kabuki" Shezbie—to Rebirth, but picked up Reginald Stewart and Revert "Peanut" Andrews. Then I went to Rebirth for 12 or 13 years while still playing with New Birth and Pinstripe. After I left Rebirth, I went back with New Birth. I was playing with five or six different bands at one time. I was never home. I was always playing gigs. Constantly working.

Dangerous

I loved it, but playing in the city could be dangerous. I remember I had just turned 18 and was playing music on Royal Street. It started off well. The conductor of the band on the Lawrence Welk show put a few bucks in our tip box. We left from out there and went to Bourbon Street by the Famous Door until their band started up and we moved to the middle of the block. A white police lady with a long pony tail said, "Where your permit at?" I said, "We don't need no permit to play music." She said, "You need a permit. You all go home." We were young—we went around the corner. She left, and we come back and play. Soon as I blew the note, the beginning of *The Saints*, I'll never forget it, the lady said, "Put your hands behind your head. You are going to jail."

"What?"

She said, "You don't have no permit."

I was handcuffed walking down Bourbon Street to Conti to the station right there. Show you how people love what you do, a white man—never met him, a tourist—said, "Let that boy go. How much is a permit?" She said, "It is $75." Man went in his pocket and said, "Here is his money. Let him go." She didn't take it. She put me in the police car. The band members had to call my mom.

I wasn't going to juvie. I was going to Central Lock Up. I was scared to death. But I had a cousin who was a politician. Here comes the call over the radio, "You have Kenny Terry in that car?" The officer said, "Yeah. We transporting him now." The voice said, "I advise you to let him go right now." If the call hadn't come through I'd have gone to the big jail. You get different calls for street brass. For block parties, they don't want Tremé Brass Band to play, they want Hot 8. They want the Rebirth. They want the New Birth. That style of music. Being a musician, only thing you should worry about is, "I got this gig. These people hired me to play. I'm going to make these people happy." I shouldn't have to come on no job and worry about safety, but you just never know. A shooting can happen when anybody is playing. It happened at Mardi Gras parades. It can happen.

I did a gig out on America Street in New Orleans East. We played a repasse. They hired a band to play two hours. We played for two hours. We finished, and were ready to collect our money so we could leave. They said, "You all ain't going nowhere. Play some more." We asked, "What you mean?" They said, "Play some more." I said, "Man, you got to pay us our money."

What you think they did? Pulled guns out. Seriously. At a repasse. What you think the band going to do? Got to play. That was one of my scariest moments in my life. Two hours turned into like four hours. I told my wife, "I'm never going back there again."

Now when someone dies, people all over the city want brass band music more than just at the funeral. We'd get a call out the St. Bernard or Desire public housing project, and they'd say, "Man, our boy got killed. We want the band." The same day! The man's body wasn't cold yet. They called for the band. We would go play. "Say, brah, we need you back out tomorrow." We'd play tomorrow. "What day the funeral is?"

"The funeral ain't til Saturday." We'd be out there the whole week. Before you know it, the whole city caught on to it.

If a younger musician dies, we automatically know it is going to be a long week. We're going to play until they put him in the ground. Every day, all day. When Kerwin died, we did it for Kerwin. Go around for Fat. The police tried to shut it down in the Tremé, but we kept playing. Kerwin's passing, it still haunts me.

Top: Kenny singing with the Tremé Brass Band at the Candlelight Lounge. *Bottom:* Kenny also plays in Jackson Square on a regular basis. Photographs by Bruce Sunpie Barnes.

Despite issues with disinvestment and violence, Kenny's mom stayed in the Seventh Ward her entire life. She passed away a number of years ago, but Kenny's great aunt, Doris Gould, still lives on Frenchmen Street. She remembers the block being full of music as Kenny and his friends grew up and formed bands that have now traveled the world. She keeps a copy of the Junior Olympia's album at her house. Photographs by Bruce Sunpie Barnes.

John Michael Bradford in Jackson Square. Built as the public square of the original French city, it is located next to the Mississippi River and is surrounded by St. Louis Cathedral and important governmental buildings from the colonial era. The square remained a local gathering space while there was still a large residential population in the French Quarter, and became known for an important artist colony in the mid 1900s. In the 1960s, it was designated a National Historical Landmark. As the Quarter became the central tourist zone of the city, the Square became one of the main attractions and is now home to tarot card readers, artists, and musicians who have struggled against City Council noise ordinances. Photograph by Bruce Sunpie Barnes.

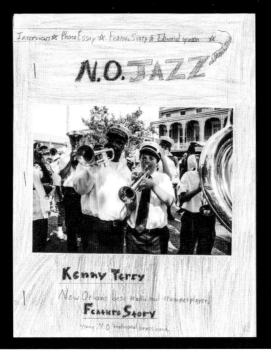

The cover of a book that John Michael made for school in 2008 about the MFAA program and his friendship with Kenny Terry. Image courtesy of the Bradford family.

JOHN MICHAEL BRADFORD

Bruce: *When John Michael Bradford started in the program, I knew he didn't know what end of the trumpet was which, but when he put lips up to the horn, a big, huge sound came out right away. For most kids, it takes a lot of effort to get a horn to do anything when they are first playing. It didn't look like John Michael was breathing at all. I said, "Man, this dude has a tremendous diaphragm." It caught everyone's attention. He had a great ear, and could quickly play the lead parts. Kenny Terry would toss him more lines, and he'd play it right back. In their interview together, the same kind of banter goes on. In John Michael, Kenny found a protégé, but also someone who was going to be on a continual journey with music.*

Coming in from Metairie, John Michael started practicing at Jackson Square after the program, and then started seeking out other music programs around the city. He joined Donald

Harrison, Jr.'s mentorship program at Tipitina's when he was very young and began to learn modern jazz. Donald's own journey into music was featured on the HBO series, Treme. *A world-renown saxophonist, his father, Donald Harrison, Sr., was the Big Chief of a number of Mardi Gras Indian gangs. Donald Jr. always appreciated the street culture he came up around while pursuing a musical education through the Berklee School of Music and band leaders like Art Blakey and Eddie Palmieri. He understands the art and value in giving back. The Tipitina's program has become very popular strictly from the results of the students. Donald has taught them what they need to do to get to a world-class level in modern jazz, and helped put a new generation of musicians from New Orleans on the map.*

Left and middle: John Michael playing at Jackson Square with Mark Smith and Thaddeaus Ramsey; Kenny Terry and John Michael playing in the Square. Photographs courtesy of Angie Bradford. *Right:* A trumpet call after a morning rainshower. Photograph by Bruce Sunpie Barnes.

Introduction: Keys Over the Phone

Kenny: Where are you from?

John Michael: My mom, Angela Kimble Bradford, grew up on the Atchafalaya River. She lived there for most of her childhood and then later moved to Port Sulfur, Louisiana. My dad, Michael Bradford, is from upstate Louisiana. He worked for Ochsner in Metairie, so we moved there when I was still a baby.

There was always music in my family. My mom wanted to sing. That didn't end up happening professionally, but she was always involved in music. My sister Christin is 12 years older than me, and knew Big Sam Williams through their connection to NOCCA. My sister was best friends with his girlfriend, Shanika. When Katrina happened, we evacuated to the ABC Missionary Camp in Eunice, Louisiana and invited Big Sam, Shanika, and her brother to come with us. We stayed in these little dorms that were used for the camp. I went in Sam's room, and he was playing music. I was like, "Well, who is this?" It was his band, Big Sam's Funky Nation, and that was the first moment that I discovered that I loved this music.

When it was clear we couldn't come home right away, we all went to San Antonio for a few months. Nine people plus two dogs. Sam was always practicing his trombone. I memorized every solo on his songs and would walk around making the sound of a horn with my mouth. I wanted to play trombone, but my parents didn't think I was serious. But for Christmas, my grandfather gave me his brass trumpet to use. It was a beginner trumpet. It was like 30 years old. It had mold on it.

My mom saw the ad in the newspaper about the MFAA program. The first time I went to the program, I was about to turn ten. When the Tremé Brass Band started playing in the workshops, I didn't even really know what I was doing.

Kenny: My first time meeting y'all, Benny and I were shocked. I said, "Oh Lord." I said, "All right, Benny. We got to work with them. We going to start showing them songs."

John Michael: When I met you, I was scared.

Kenny: You ran from me! But you and the others caught on so fast, which is good. I told your mother, "Bring him by the house." My wife said, "Boy, watch what you wish for. You know what happened the last time." Pre-Katrina, when we were staying in the Ninth Ward, I used work with kids by my house and give them music. I said, "Yeah, the little kids were driving me crazy." I said, "Babe, he actually can play."

I used to call your house, "Man, where is John Michael, is he practicing?" Your mom was like, "Yeah, John get your horn. Play this for Kenny."

See, we used to do that for the Olympia. We get a show out of town and you had to learn certain songs. They gave you the key over the phone. Play in F. Learn that song.

Remember when I moved to Kenner past the airport? That was a big switch for me. I'm a city person. At that time, they had a lot of violence going on and I was trying to keep my family safe, but man, it is like the country. It is boring.

John Michael: Exactly.

Kenny: They used to throw *The Kenner Tribune* papers out there, and I would look up the music section. Where can I go to play music? I said, "Baby, I'm going

Mark Smith started with the Doc Paulin Brass Band and then joined the Pinstrip Brass Band. He plays regularly in Jackson Square. Photograph by Bruce Sunpie Barnes.

downtown." I go to my jeep, get on the freeway back to New Orleans. Play music. I told her, "Baby, this ain't working. We got to move back in the city."

People down here, they appreciate you coming from out of Metairie and playing music. It don't make no difference where you from or where you at. You can do it. You have a lot of people in this city, they love you. As far as musicians, that is what type of love there is in this city. Nobody knew you when I brought you around. I was kind of hard on you because you was so shy. I thought, "I don't know if this boy going to try to blow me up or something!"

Jackson Square

John Michael: Going to the program in New Orleans, I would get the hour of learning the music and then I'd be like, "I want to play more." I decided I don't want to go home and be bored playing video games. Mark Smith invited me to Jackson Square with you and him. "Come out to the Square."

Kenny: Yeah! The Jackson Square All Star Band.

John Michael: I'd take the songs that I learned in the program and work on them with you. I did that for so many years—just going out every weekend and then in the summer time, every day from in the morning til like seven in the evening when the Square would be closed and we couldn't play there anymore. Getting the experience was awesome. I learned all the songs and the tricks. I was forced to play and sing even though I was scared.

Kenny: Yeah! I wasn't going to do all the work!

John Michael: Later on, I realized learning the lyrics is how you truly know the song. You don't just play the melody, but you know the story behind it. Through going to the Square with you and Mark, I told my mother, "I want to be just like Kenny and them."

Kenny: John Michael, we did you the same thing they did to me and many other musicians.

John Michael: Mark was very nice and kind to me. He took care of everybody in the Square. He's like a guardian for a lot of people. The homeless people really depended on him and he would help them out a lot. He'd buy them food; he'd buy them drinks. Sometimes he would get annoyed with them because after awhile they just expected him to do things. And he helped me out a lot—he stood up for me when some of the other musicians didn't want me out there, being

this young white kid playing in black New Orleans traditional music. Music that they grew up with throughout this whole time and then just me coming out there expecting to play and get paid. Mark stood by me and said, "No, he's gonna stay here and learn and I'm gonna teach him and I want him here."

Kenny: Sometimes you used to tell your mom, "I want to go home." What you didn't realize is that the things I was being hard on you about, it actually helped. Now you aren't afraid to play. Now you can't stop you from playing. I be like, "Man, shut up. Take a break or something." You are singing more. You know how to work the crowd. All that come from, what? Somebody helping you what? Push you out there.

John Michael: It took me awhile to actually start getting paid at the Square with y'all because I had to learn the music to get the money. When I started getting paid, I was like, "I need to get a new horn." I saw the trumpet in a music store by my house. Big shiny Bach. People at the store said, "It is a great, professional horn." I saw the price tag, and the guy said he would give me a deal for $2,300.

I played it with the mouthpiece. It sounded great. My mom said she couldn't afford to pay for it, but would put it on a credit card and said I could pay every month for it. A lot of the times at the Square, I played on my old trumpet because I didn't want to mess up the new one, but I made enough money in seven months to pay it off.

Kenny: How do you feel about the colored people, with your music?

John Michael: My mom is a youth minister. In church, there were some black people, but I wasn't around a large group of black people until I started getting involved in the music.

When I started, color was never a big deal to me. I loved you guys. I didn't care about that. But there were a lot of situations where a lot of black guys were like, "What is this white boy doing playing this music?" I'd be scared being the only white kid so young with all these other black people. It is kind of like all these people are looking at me. I'm like the odd man out. But then once people know you, everything is cool.

Kenny: They just had to get to know you. I think that is a lot of life. People are curious, but they are afraid to introduce themselves. I got a friend of mine who plays music, and said, "Man, I'm not going to play with them white boys."

John Michael, Thaddeaus Ramsey *(bass)*, and Sam Jackson *(wearing band hat)*, and Marshan Bowden *(tuba)* with other members and supporters of the Young Fellaz Brass Band at the Porch Seventh Ward Cultural Organization's office on Urquhart Street. Photographs courtesy of Angie Bradford.

"Hold up, man. I don't talk racial. Never did. If you are going to play music, you are going to play music."

John Michael: Thaddeaus Ramsey was in the MFAA program, too, and he'd come down to the Square to play. We formed the Young Fellaz Brass Band with your son, Sam.

We didn't play traditional music. It was Rebirth music, New Birth—all those bands that you were in. We learned the New Orleans street music. We would listen to records and you know Mark and them knew a few of those songs. We would go play with To Be Continued Brass Band, and they would make their own arrangements of pop tunes that were on the radio, or older, like *Casanova* or *Lovely Day.*

We would just all be together all the time. I was way too young, so my mom drove me around, and then when we started getting gigs, she started driving everyone. The guys in the band called her their second mom. She was a youth minister at a church in Kenner, and some of the guys asked about coming to church with us. I thought it was a good thing because a lot of the guys who hung around the band were dying because of all the things that was going on in their life. My mom

tried to look out for them and help them become better people—not get in that lifestyle of going to jail; to accept God in their life or really committing to purity in life and that they didn't need those things. She would take them to church, and other people in the congregation didn't want them there, but she didn't think it was right to exclude them.

The band had expanded, and we had a few new members. The Porch Seventh Ward Cultural Organization was our place to practice, and it became almost like a program because the director, Ed Buckner, wanted to adopt us to be the official brass band of his social and pleasure club, the Big Seven. We went up to Boston with them, and played their second line on Mother's Day.

I'd played the Black Men of Labor parade with you and the other Young Traditionals in the Tremé Brass Band, which was pretty much like playing with our mentors. But when we played the Big Seven, the Young Fellaz led the band and controlled the songs. We just did our own thing. It was cool. I got to bring all those years of experience in the Square, of learning how to be a trumpet player and singer, into this band that I helped form.

I was the only white person in the band. The main thing I heard in the parades was, "Look at that white boy play the trumpet!" It wasn't like anything bad. If I would have sucked then it would have been like, "Oh this white kid playing our music," but through the mentoring and all the years of practice and learning the songs I was paying my dues. Of course, there's many more to pay, but during that time I was doing the things I needed to do to be respected in this music.

Kenny: Do you know where jazz come from?

John Michael: Yeah.

Kenny: Where?

John Michael: Congo Square.

Kenny: That's right. That goes back to what I was telling you, jazz comes from the gospel. From Congo Square. It was created right here in New Orleans.

John Michael: Playing music, I learned a lot about the history of African-Americans, which wasn't really taught in school that much. In school they mostly teach about slavery and things. Just like the basic generic

African-American history. It is not very thorough. But I've learned a lot being with all the people who did the music—all the history they know, their ancestors and all they bring out in the music.

Ear Training

Kenny: What are some of your biggest troubles?

John Michael: What do you mean?

Kenny: With the music.

John Michael: When I first started, I was just starting to learn the notes and scales. I didn't really understand what was going on. A lot of the time, I would be looking at your valves. Then you'd cover it away so I could hear it, instead of relying on looking at it.

Kenny: That was ear training. The way I learned it from was Tuba Fat. I used to listen when I was playing with Olympia. Tuba say, "Come here, boy. Let me show you this song." He hummed the melody to me but he wouldn't show me the notes. Then he started playing a bass line. Tuba Fat had huge fingers, man. He'd be playing, "Hold up, I can't see the notes!"

"I'm training your ear." When I caught it, he opened his hand up and placed it, "There you go." That is what I was doing to you. Just pass it down. Even today, I still do that. I still look at people's valves when they play. I look at your valves when you play. Trombone slides, I look at them, but I can transpose trombone to trumpet, too. I can't play sax.

John Michael: I think it is like a mental thing…

Kenny: It is a tone for each note—do, re, mi, fa, so, la, ti, do.

John Michael: If I hear something when I'm walking around, I can sing the notes in my mind. I don't even have to practice it because I know what it is just by knowing what the valves are. The scales, then being able to hear the melody.

Kenny: Somebody taught you right, man!

John Michael: That was one of my strengths—to be able to hear everything—but learning to read music was harder because I don't really want to sit down and take the time to read. I have to do it every day to keep it up. And the theory of jazz—the more technical side of knowing rather than just playing.

Kenny: There is a million books out there to show you this and show you that, but always keep in mind that is the interpretation of it. That is their story. You have to put your story up.

John Michael: If I'm hearing a song I'm trying to learn, and I don't have time to pull out my horn, if I move my fingers, I can hear the note. That is just crazy. I can just hear what note it is going to be.

Kenny: I do the same thing—just listen to it. Even in the car, I can hear something going on. Just now we listened to *Old Rockin Chair*.

John Michael: I listen to that LP with Louis Armstrongs and His All Stars all the time. Everything was on that.

Kenny: It was amazing to listen to Louis Armstrong because a lot of the tunes he did he was doing them in minor keys. I was like, "You serious?" That steps off of the major works. Until today people are still listening to it. Back in the days, a lot of funeral parade songs were in the key of A flat. Today, most of the bands play everything in the key of B flat. F, G. We rarely play C. We play it in E flat. You don't do too many tunes in D. Louis Armstrong was doing stuff in

John Michael Bradford and the Vibe publicity shot, courtesy of Angie Bradford.

C sharp, D. F major. F minor. G flat. Come on. He was the total package.

John Michael: He changed the key to how he could sing it. The trumpet is like a vocal. A lot of his voice reflected in his playing because he sang through his horn and then he put that through his vocals. That is why he is such a great singer. When I play, I play like I'm singing through the trumpet.

Kenny: You have to sing.

John Michael: Without it, you are not going to have as much soul—as much heart than if you were just playing randomly.

Kenny: That is why the lead instrument in most brass bands is the trumpet. You are the trumpet player, but you are singing the song.

What I was taught through Milton was to not worry about what they are playing—find the roots. The root will bring you to the chords. From the chords, you go to the melody. You can play anything throughout that chord. Before you know it, you got that song. Talk about my tricks!

John Michael: When I learned *West End Blues*, the trumpet call was hard.

Kenny: It took me a week and a half to learn that. I was taking it note for note. Play a note—stop and think.

John Michael: That is what I had to do. I had to keep stopping.

Kenny: Go back. That is why I used to like the albums. You pull the needle off and put it back on. With the CD player, I got a remote in this hand, a trumpet in that hand. Then when you see it on paper, you say, "Man, did I actually play that?" It is amazing.

Straight Ahead

Kenny: Let me ask you this. What is the difference as far as playing through the streets and what you do in NOCCA?

John Michael: At NOCCA, it's jazz studies. Because there are four levels and I was placed in three because of what all the jazz I played before I got there. At school, we played a few traditional songs, but it is more like the history of jazz like Charlie Parker, John Coltrane, Miles Davis. What they did. Their songs. Theory. Musicianship.

Kenny: You say they teach you who? Charlie Parker. They teach you who? Miles Davis. They teach you Dizzy Gillespie. Teach you all that? Why they don't teach you Buddy Bolden? Bunk Johnson? Louis Armstrong? Keep in mind, it is New Orleans Center for Creative Arts. There is nothing wrong with learning all those other things. Learn this first.

John Michael: I would say I'm one of the only people at NOCCA who really experienced New Orleans traditional jazz. I guess it is hard to explain

Nicholas Payton (*right*) listening to Doc Cheatham play the trumpet at the Palm Court Cafe, a jazz club dedicated to traditional jazz, in 1995. Doc became good friends with Nicholas when he visited New Orleans, and they recorded an album together that won an Emmy. Photograph by Michael P. Smith © The Historic New Orleans Collection, 2011.0307.21

to them because they haven't experienced any of it. They don't really know. A lot of my friends will say, "I saw you in the Square." It is different from where they are coming from. They are coming from regular school then go to jazz class.

Kenny: When I was watching you perform with the guys on Frenchmen, I know you are playing more straight ahead—what I call New York style—bebop and all that. I'm looking at the people, and they are just sitting up there with their heads in their hands. That is one of the reasons why I don't play that kind of music. There is nothing wrong with it, but I like to interact with the crowd. Like Miles Davis. Miles was a real good trumpet player, but I don't understand why you got to play with your back turned to the crowd. I would never pay to go see that. Seriously. I love his playing, but if he made me sit up there with my horn and turn my back to the crowd, and hold my head down, why? Even Stevie Wonder. He is blind, but his

head is always up like he is watching what is going on. He can feel it.

John Michael: I feel like no matter what kind of jazz I'm playing, I always have a good time. A lot of times you see people playing modern jazz and they stand there like they are mad or bored, but I think it's because a lot of people who get involved in it are kind of shy. They want to keep to themselves and play. With New Orleans jazz, it is more open. In my band, John Michael Bradford and the Vibe, we play a mixture of New Orleans music with funk and modern jazz. We are starting to write some songs and I want to get people dancing. We are calling the band a mixture of all black American music mixing all the different styles—funk, jazz, R&B, hip hop.

Kenny: That is what I was telling you as far as interpretation. Just like the alphabet, who created that? Who decided that was gong to be an A? You are taking

Left: John Michael before playing at Jazz Fest with Donald Harrison, Jr. **Right:** Fred Wesley, of the JB Horns, playing with John Michael and Donald in 2013. Fred is credited as the inventor of the funk trombone, and is the main soloist on *We're Going to Have a Funky Good Time.* Photographs courtesy of Angie Bradford.

the spirit from out of the tradition and putting it into the straight-ahead. That is what makes you stand out. That is that makes me stand out is putting the gospel music to the traditional jazz music. I wasn't going to give you my secret! But that is what I do.

John Michael: I've been inspired by the way Nicholas Payton talks about mixture.

Kenny: I'm glad you brought his name up.

John Michael: He is one of the musicians who has both sides, too, because he really sounds like a New Orleans player. His dad, Walter Payton, was with Preservation Hall.

Kenny: He's another rare talent. Nicholas Payton used to play with the Junior Olympia and the All Stars. His dad was also the band director at McDonogh 15 in the French Quarter. He used to have to beg his parents to let him come out and play music. His mama said, "You can't go nowhere til you had your piano lesson." "You got piano lesson? Go ahead."

We'd be mad, but we waited. We could have been making $300 in the Square, but we waiting.

One time I got a book of sheet music, and asked, "Nicholas, you can read that?" "Yeah, I can read it." Guess what he asked me, "You want me to play it backwards?" He played it backwards! I said, "Nicholas, stop!"

John Michael: Donald Harrison, Jr. is another major influence on me. I started working with him at the mentorship program at the Tipitina's Foundation when I was in sixth grade. Donald is one of the greatest saxophone players to play the horn, and he didn't start until he was in high school. He took it really serious. Before I got into the program, he'd mentored musicians like Khris Royal, Jonathan Batiste, Trombone Shorty, and Edward Lee. When I came in, there was another group from NOCCA who was much older than me. Donald asked me if I could play my major scales, and I played everything he asked me to play and he just like, "All right, I'm gonna work with you, let's do it."

When I first came in, I was scared because most of the kids talked about how he was mean. I wasn't sure what that meant, but then I would watch how some of the kids wouldn't learn their assignment, and then would come back the next week just making an excuse. I learned not to do that. I would come back and know it. Donald looked out for me, and helping me. He was never mean to me. He might be hard on

me because he wanted to push me. He would make jokes in class saying I could do stuff that some of the older kids weren't doing. He's like, "Cause he actually practices."

I really paid close attention to what he taught—not just about my instrument because he focused a lot on the rhythm section a lot. He'd worked with Ron Carter a lot, and knew a lot about the bass. I wouldn't just learn horn parts or scales, I would learn how to play bass lines on my trumpet. And there was a lot of times where I just sat there and watch him work with the drummers, which was a great experience to see. Donald can actually play the drums. He would talk about watching Art Blakey and Roy Haynes play the drums. He asked them what they were doing, and they would show him. Things that would take other people a lifetime to figure out, he was given. And then he's giving it to us. That's the amazing thing about his program.

Kenny: It takes time, man. Nothing comes over night. Only thing you got to do now is just keep it up. Can't teach you everything. Some things you have to learn on your own, just like some things I have to learn on my own.

Left: Portrait of Donald by Bruce Sunpie Barnes. Right: Portait courtesy of Donald Harrison, Jr.

DONALD HARRISON, JR.
SWINGING

Donald: *You can come through a system and build on top of it, or you can create a new system. I chose to go through it. I had choices to make money, but I always chose the music. I said, "You might be able to make some money later on, but you won't get this opportunity to learn." I got that from my father: "Stay on your path." If somebody said, "You can play with the double-bassist Ron Carter or you can lead this mega-group," I would feel like I was going to learn more from Ron Carter. We started a trio together with Billy Cobham. It's through these experiences that I know I made the right choices. I wanted to truly understand.*

I grew up in the Sixth and Ninth Wards. I can remember always hearing drumming and singing at home. My mother tells me I was beating on the crib. I can remember all those

drum rhythms that can't be quantified with the Western system of music. It's stayed with me.

At the age of two, I began masking as the Little Chief of the Creole Wild West. At the time, my father was the Chief of that tribe. I was around Robert "Robbie" Lee, who masked under Brother Tilman, and Lawrence Fletcher. That's the line I know. I mean, I can't help but know it. Those guys were nattily attired, and gentlemen with strong spirits. In my estimation, that's how you should be as a human being. They respected you if you did your work. They kept alive things that were older. You had to work on telling the stories. I'd say they are the ones who had meticulous articulation of our language.

I started sewing around ten years old. I got an understand-

ing of traditional music of New Orleans like Louis Armstrong and Sidney Bechet, but also big band swing music like Duke Ellington, West Coast jazz like Jerry Mulligan and Chet Baker, and then New York jazz where bebop started. My father intellectualized everything. He'd tell me about trading fours, blue forms, the 32-bar form, AABA. He'd play classical, soul and R&B, and ethnic music from all over the world, and throughout my career, I've taken all of these styles seriously.

Bebop took the innovation of Baby Dodds' swing beat and said, "Anything can happen. If you know what a pulse is, now you are free to go in any direction." Guys like Charlie Parker, Max Roach, and Art Blakey opened up to any possibility. They ventured in the area of technical facility being a hallmark of what they are doing as well—being able to double up, triple up, quadruple up notes. They opened up every note. Instead of saying what you can't do, say you can do anything.

When I was in elementary school, my father bought me a saxophone, but I didn't want to play it. I picked it up in high school, and split my day between Nichols and NOCCA. A trumpet player at NOCCA said, "I'm playing with the brass bands, you should come with us." I said, "I would love to." He introduced me to Doc Paulin, and Doc would call me and say, "I got a little to-do for you, Harrison."

I'd be like, "I'm there."

I started in his Number Three Band, but whenever Dr. Michael White was in the Number One Band, I'd sneak up there to listen to him. I didn't care if I got fired! As Louis Armstrong was under the wing of King Oliver, I used to stick with Dr. Michael White and try to steal everything he was playing. He had the right spirit, the right notes, and the dedication. And I loved Harold Dejan, too. Those were my two guys. Harold had changed the saxophone in the Olympia into his own thing. He was like the Maceo Parker of second line music for me. He was soulful and funky.

Charlie Parker, New York City, New York in 1949.
Photograph © Herman Leonard Photography LLC/
www.hermanleonard.com

You'll Know Something

At home, my father put the Charlie Parker records on, and said, "If you can learn this, then you'll know something." He had a way of saying little short things that got you to understand. I started trying to practice Charlie Parker and realized it was so difficult. Even to this day, the more I play music, the more I realize how brilliant and how special Charlie Parker was, and the dues you have to pay in order to get through that portal to internalizing what he did. At a young age, I decided I really wanted to understand that.

I remember when I told Doc Paulin I was going to the East Coast to go to Berklee College of Music, he said, "Why you want to do that? You got everything you want right here. You got red beans and rice and pretty girls." I'm back, Doc, and Mary is my beautiful New Orleans wife.

You go to New York, there is a jazz community but modern jazz is not the culture of New York like traditional jazz is the culture of New Orleans. Berklee is a great school because the teachers actually play in New York, so they become a resource to get connected to that community.

When I was 19, I went to New York to hear Roy Haynes, a great drummer who played with Charlie Parker. In between his sets there was a jam session. Ray was checking me out. He called me over and started talking to me. Maybe I shouldn't be saying this but he told me, "You've been born again, brother." I think he could feel that I was already committed. He took me under his wing, He was able to tell me, "This is the way we did it with Bird. This is what Bird was thinking." It deepened my understanding of what I had to do to learn it.

Modern jazz is like doing calculus at a blinding speed, but doing it together. These musicians on the bandstand have done so much work, they can do make it look natural. As the drummer is making his moves, I'm calculating instantaneously. When you get to a certain place, you just know. In my program, my students will be looking chord scales and all these hard passages, and I tell them, "If you have to think about it, you can't play it." It has to become something in your subconscious that you can just pull up. You have to know this hard music—100s of thousands of combinations of each instrument. Then we can talk. We can discuss this hard music on the bandstand.

When I was young, I played in Harlem and some older women came over to me and said, "Baby, you know how to lindy hop?" I always liked to dance. My mother used to make us dance as little kids. They took me on the side and taught me. They said, "This will help you, baby," and they were right on point. They gave me another understanding of what bebop and jazz was. I started realizing how to play from a dancer's perspective. But if you don't understand how to dance to it then that's not part of your consciousness. The way you look at the totality of the music you are playing. Back when bebop was first starting, they had a dance like the lindy hop that informed the music. People used to dance the lindy hop to Charlie Parker.

I stayed with Roy Haynes for 15 years. Ten years into it, he told me, "You're my brother now." I guess I was around 30, and I was so taken aback because I had worked so hard, I must have looked like I was crying. He said, "Don't you cry on me, man." I didn't cry, but I was overcome. I was just so happy that someone as great as him was saying you're my brother. But I felt at the time and I still do that I have a lot of work to do because music is infinite.

Indian Blues

For years, I lived between two worlds, New Orleans and New York. In 1982, I joined Art Blakey's Jazz Messengers. My teacher at Berklee, Bill Pierce, was playing tenor saxophone with them, and recommended me to him. Then I would come back to New Orleans to go out with my father on Mardi Gras. One year, he was singing Shallow Water, and all of a sudden, I'm hearing, "Oh, Art Blakey goes on this. That's swinging." I heard these different drums together, and I decided to make a record called Indian Blues in 1991 that incorporated modern jazz and Mardi Gras Indian music.

I went to RCA Studio in New York with my working band and my father. It was probably perfect for him because he said his style of singing came out of using elements of Miles Davis in his vocalizing, which you can hear in his phrasing. And now this guy who used jazz in Afro-New Orleans music was coming to New York to play with modern jazz musicians. So many great jazz records have come out of RCA. I felt like we were in the right place, but they were looking at me like, "Is this guy crazy?" I don't think it would have happened without my drummer, Carl Allen. He understood me. I said, "I need some funky bass drum and a swing beat on top." We put some of the tambourine stuff on the snare drum. We got together and played all the percussion while my father did the chants, and the other musicians sang background. I think it's some of my father's best singing.

From there, I recorded Spirits of Congo Square and Nouveu Swing in 1995, which had a concept of putting a swing beat together with modern dance styles. I got a lot of flak for

Left: Art Blakey in Paris in 1958. Photograph © Herman Leonard Photography LLC/www.hermanleonard.com
Right: Donald Harrison, Jr. as Big Chief of the Congo Nation. Photograph by Bruce Sunpie Barnes.

all those records because, at the time, nobody was thinking like that. I guess when you do something first you've got to be the fall guy. I took the hits, but all of this is cross-connected. Baby Dodds says his family were drummers in Congo Square. Sidney Bechet says everything I'm doing comes from Congo Square, and then we know that, most likely, Jelly Roll Morton was a Spyboy, so you know, it's still the same. It's just a modern perspective on what those guys did back then.

When I was thinking about getting married, my father said, "It's you and your wife against the world. Just stick together." After a long time in New York, my wife said she wanted to raise her daughter in New Orleans. I said, "That's cool." I followed them. It has been a very rewarding in a number of ways. I feel reconnected to my roots. I guess I was in New York so long my roots are now New Orleans and New York. I still go between them. Here in New Orleans,

I started running a music mentorship program on Monday nights with the Tipitina's Foundation. The word has gotten through the music community that I listen, and a lot of the older musicians are trying to teach me what they are doing and their concept of music, so that I can be a person that can give it to younger musicians.

What I try to do with my program at Tipitina's is to give you an understanding of what I know so that you have the ability to make a choice. I'm doing something similar to what my father did with me. If you know something, you can choose, "Oh, this is what I want to do." You don't have to use it, but if you don't know it, you are only stuck with what you can do. The program helps them understand what it takes to get a music scholarship. Initially, I didn't have the right stuff when I left here, but when I got to Berklee, I understood what it took, and then I had a full scholarship. I want to pass that stuff on. I've been fortunate enough to play with so many

people I can specifically tell someone this is what this guy is looking for, so if you learn it, you can have a good chance of being in that band. Like Bill Pierce did for me with the Messengers. You can lead them in the right direction.

One of the things I also teach them, too, is to take things lightly. I have seen some musicians take it too seriously. A critic may not like you, but you got to keep going. If they don't get you in the beginning, they might get you later on. As long as you get you! I want them to know that playing music can be a rollercoaster. Even if the audience loves you, you may have 10,000 people cheering for you one moment, and then the next you are in a hotel room by yourself. The emotions can be extreme. I've seen so many musicians who can't stay steady throughout it. It's an important aspect of what I'm trying to pass on. Stay steady.

John Michael: I met Jesse McBride at the Don Jamison School of Music. Harold Batiste is his mentor. Jesse loves him, and Harold passed on the Next Generation to him. It's a band that has been compared to Art Blakey's Jazz Messengers in terms of mentoring. Jesse takes them from high school to college with him, and then as they go on their own path, he's got new people to kind of like fill in those gaps.

It took time to build a relationship with Jesse. One time, he made me cry. Class hadn't started yet, and I was listening to Shamarr Allen's *Can You Feel It?* on my new iPod. It was my favorite song. I was obsessed with Shamarr—he's like my hero—and I was singing the solo. Jesse looked at me, and he was just shaking his head. He's like, "No, what are you doing? Are you serious?" He kicked me out. I was crying and so mad, but as we've gotten to know each other, he has become one of my best friends and mentors.

Right: Pianist Jesse McBride hosting the Next Generation concert series at the Prime Example on North Broad in the Seventh Ward in 2014. Jesse is a product of University of New Orleans' jazz studies program started by Harold Batiste and Ellis Marsalis, and teaches jazz studies at Tulane University. *Below:* John Michael reading the chart to a composition in *The Silver Book*, a collection of AFO Records modern jazz songs that Harold Batiste put together with the New Orleans Jazz Commission, a steering committee for the New Orleans Jazz National Historical Park. Photographs on both pages by Bruce Sunpie Barnes.

Throughout the years, he invited me to play with the Next Generation with musicians like Andrew Baham, Rex Gregory, Joe Dyson, and Max Moran. I'd sit in and work on standards like *Bye, Bye Blackbird*. I'd learned the song from Mark Smith in the Square, and then studied Miles Davis' version as well. Jesse liked the way I blended the styles together and made me play it all the time.

When I first started with the Next Generation, I learned all these tunes by ear that were in *The Silver Book*—Harold Batiste, James Black, and Ellis Marsalis tunes. If I had looked at the sheet music back then, all of the chord changes would have looked so foreign to me. I still wasn't developed enough to know the theory, but over time I learned to read them, too. And Harold Batiste comes to our gigs now, and it's such an honor to be able to play in front of a master and then him tell you he loved the way you played on his music—like you made it come alive. That really meant a lot to me.

Left: Melissa Savage sings while John Michael answers her on the trumpet. ***Top right:*** John Michael with Jasen Weaver (*bass*) and Miles Labat (*drums*). ***Bottom right:*** New Orleans music icon Harold Batiste listens closely to the latest version of his long-standing modern jazz student development program. Batiste is president of perhaps the first black-owned jazz record label in the United States: AFO Records. He formed the label with Ellis Marsalis, Alvin Batiste, and others. Harold was the musical director of the television show *Sonny and Cher*, and also helped launch the careers of musicial stars as Barbara George, Tammy Lynn, Dr. John, and Sam Cook. Photographs by Bruce Sunpie Barnes.

WOODY
PENOUILH

&

DOYLE
COOPER

Woody in front of the New Orleans Free School at 3601 Camp Street in Uptown New Orleans, where he taught middle school and ran a brass band for many years. The school began in 1971 with a group of radical educators, and became part of Orleans Parish Public School system in 1973. Over the years, the principal, Bob Ferris, struggled against the rigidity of the centralized structure. At one point he wrote that the Free School wanted to: *Give the student a chance to breathe, to stand, to fall, to explore, to experience, to conquer, to win, to lose, to question, to think.* Photograph by Bruce Sunpie Barnes.

NEW ORLEANS FREE SCHOOL
SPRING FESTIVAL
Sat. April 16 - noon till...$1.
3601 Camp, 899-0452
★ BROWNSVILLE ★ DAVID TORKANOWSKY ★ DUKA PADUKA & B-B ★ PFISTER SISTERS ★
★ EARL TURBINTON ★ ERNIE K-DOE ★ JAMES SINGLETON ★ SED SEDLAK ★
★ JOHNNY VIDACOVICH ★ KEN "SNAKE BITE " JACOBS ★ STORYVILLE STOMPERS ★
★ AARON NEVILLE ★ MARCHING BANDS AND OTHER SURPRISE GUESTS!!
Parade: Noon, Napoleon and Magazine.

One of the posters advertising the annual music festival at the school, courtesy of Woody Penouilh. In 1972, the New Orleans Free School had its first music festival with Professor Longhair. Over the years, the event showcased blues, R&B, jazz, and brass band music to raise money for the school.

WOODY PENOUILH

Bruce: *Woody is a sousaphone player and leader of the Storyville Stompers, a traditional brass band that was mentored by the Olympia Brass Band. Woody is an educator as well. Music and teaching weren't the first things he did, but once he zeroed in on what he wanted to do, he's given a lot. He brings joie de vivre to the music and plays in a very fluid style.*

When the Young Traditional Brass Band was going out to play, I always liked to put one adult with them, and Woody was the perfect musician to send them out with. He is a very cool, gentle spirit, and kept things together for them—calling a song out if they didn't know what to play, and getting them in the right key. As a sousaphone player, Woody's very good on the turnaround. Say you are playing three chord changes: C (1), F (3), and G (5). When you come out of the five chord to go back to one, the song is going back to the beginning of the pattern. In that turnaround, there is going to be some kind of

extra riff, or motif. Woody showed them how to be creative and to stick together in those transitions.

The same thing could be said for his tenure with the Storyville Stompers. Woody's kept many of the same band members for 30 years. One of his main running partners is Wesley Schmidt, who is the grand marshal for the Stompers and the manager at Snug Harbor. Wesley's a rascal, but a good rascal. You don't get to see that many grand marshals outside of the black community who can really do it in a traditional way, but Wesley learned the art of grand marshalling from one of the best, the Olympia Brass Band's King Richard Matthews. He has his own style. I'd call him a tipper. He's light on his feet, and strides and tips along. Woody and Wesley hold together two ends of the band, as well as a lot of amazing memories of the streets of New Orleans.

Introduction: A Free School

Woody: The New Orleans Free School was Uptown on Camp Street. The best way to describe it initially was a hippie school. It was inspired by schools like Summerhill in England that were based on the belief that if you give young people enough things to do to learn, they'll find something they are good at—it is just finding what it is and focusing on it.

In the early days of the Free School, the parents were teaching. Eventually, it caught on, and Orleans Parish took it over. Every year, the school had this giant music festival. One time, the Storyville Stompers played for it, and we did a little parade around the neighborhood. I had just gotten my degree in education, and the first grade teacher who had done most of the bookings for the festival said, "We have an opening here if you want to come."

I said, "This is cool. I think I'm gonna go here." I've always had that mentality that the Free School had, although that wasn't the background I'd been raised up in. When I started teaching at the Free School, I got real comfortable in my beliefs on education.

St. Ann's in the Sixth Ward

I grew up Catholic during segregation. Even when I was a kid, I questioned why there had to be separation. I went to school with white people. The street I lived on, Esplanade Avenue, was almost all white. A lot of the side streets were black.

My mother lived on Esplanade Avenue for most of her life. She was raised by her grandmother on the corner of Esplanade and North Liberty. Her grandfather was a doctor who had a buggy that served Storyville, the redlight district of New Orleans in the early 20th century. My mother learned French from her grand-

Left: Woody's class picture in front St. Ann's shrine on Ursulines Street. *Right:* Woody with his parents and grandmother. Photographs courtesy of the Penouilh family.

mother, and went to an all-white girls high school on Ursulines that later became Andrew J. Bell.

My daddy was from Matthews on Bayou Lafourche. During the Depression, his family moved to New Orleans to look for work. I don't think he got to finish third grade. He spoke Cajun French. The way my parents talked to each other in French was a little different, but they understood each other. When I grew up, they didn't speak it to me, but we commonly used a lot of French words, like "banquette." We didn't say sidewalk.

My parents never owned a house. Until I was about 20, we lived in old houses on Esplanade divided into a bunch of apartments. In them, we had a neglected piano we must have inherited. I used to sit on that thing and play until the neighbors called and told me to shut up.

Our life centered around being Catholic. We had the crucifixes and the pictures hanging on the walls. Every once in a while, a house in the neighborhood would have a miracle—usually a shadow shaped as a cross. Everyone would line up to look at it.

I never knew the history of our church, St. Ann. I didn't know it was the white counterpart, and St. Peter Claver was the black, of a congregation that used to be together. St. Ann was known for its novena. It was nine days long, and if you needed a prayer answered, it was supposed to be really powerful. I went to St. Ann's Elementary School, and an early mass on Sundays for children. It was all in Latin so I couldn't understand anything, but I remember if you tried to leave early, the priest would change to English, and say right the middle of the mass, "Where you going? Mass isn't over."

As a teenager, I worked at Smith's pharmacy nearby on St. Philip and Galvez. The doctor was white, the pharmacist was white, but the patients who came in were mostly black. It was always crowded. Visits were two dollars and sometimes when people took numbers it would go up to the 60s and 70s. My job was to work behind the counter, and say, "Can I help you with your prescription?" when the patients exited the doctor's office.

Mount Zion Baptist Church was nearby, and members used to come in after church because we had a soda fountain. I used to see them in the neighborhood, passing on the banquettes. And I thought about them when the city first desegregated the buses. It used to hurt me so much to see the way white people were treating black people. There was so much trouble in the schools then—to feel like a person should be shunned for the color of their skin. It was terrible back then.

Not Studying Much

For middle and high school I went to St. Aloysius, an all-white boys Catholic school. It was tough. They paddled you if you misbehaved. You didn't misbehave too much, because it hurt. To get out of going to school you pretty much had to have a fever. When I'd stay home I'd have the radio on all day—WTIX and all the local radio stations. New Orleans music was dominated by rhythm and blues musicians like Ernie K-Doe, Fats Domino, Bennie Spellman, Lloyd Price, Shirley and Lee, and Eddie Bo. It had such a different music scene from other parts of the country. My parents would say, "Turn that stuff down," which made me like it even more.

During Carnival season, I remember going to a lot of neighborhood king cake parties and dancing in people's living rooms. Whoever got the baby hidden in the cake had to give the party the next week. The Christian Youth Organizations and high school dances had live bands. In those days, you used to cut in. I was shy and afraid of girls. I used to wait until the end of the song and cut in, so I'd only have to dance for about three minutes.

I was an honor student all through high school, and was used to getting through high school without studying much. I graduated in 1961. My mother had told me that if it wouldn't have been University of New Orleans, I wouldn't have gone to college because they could not afford the private schools like Tulane. LSU-NO was unbelievably cheap, I'd guess like $150 a semester. Everything was in barracks because it was an old military base. When I first started there, they didn't have a graduating class yet. I was going to school with girls for the first time since elementary school. I partied so much I didn't even go to class. I didn't waste any time. I flunked out my first semester.

I went back, but started totally screwing off again. I guess I was lost at that time. Talking with a friend of mine one night, we said, "Well, let's go join the Army tomorrow." I went and he didn't. I was enlisted in the infantry, and was sent to a little bitty village in Korea for about eleven months. Somehow or another, I got assigned doing communications. The clerk typist was going back to the United States and I jumped on that. I said, "I know how to type!" I wound up being a clerk the rest of my time in the military.

I moved back to the States and was stationed in Texas for a year and a half. I was tired of the regimentation of the military, and wanted to get out so I reenrolled at UNO. When I got accepted to a college, I was given an early release because I wasn't considered essential.

I was more serious in the 1970s. I kept up an A average and got a master's degree in economics. On the side, I bartended nearby at this very big pizza parlor called Luigi's. Wesley Schmidt was one of the managers. Back in those days, he was as wild as all of us.

The music scene in New Orleans was just beginning to change. The local R&B was tailing off because the British invasion was on the rise. Weekends were kind of schizophrenic. On Friday night, you could go to a dance at F&M Patio, and the deal would be they would have a house band, Tommy Ridgley and the Untouchables, and then they'd bring a guest on, which could have been Bennie Spellman, and he would do whatever his hit was. The second set would be the house band again with Irma Thomas. Saturday night, you could go to Labor Union Hall and it would be a fraternity dance held by some Tulane or Loyola organization with British cover bands with names like Cellar Door and Basement Wall. I don't think they were architectural.

WESLEY SCHMIDT
CRISSCROSSING THROUGH MUSIC

Wesley: I'm from Gentilly, off Elysian Fields. The area was built on reclaimed swampland. It was nice because you were still in New Orleans, but it had the trappings of the suburbs. There was off-street parking. Most of the houses, even if they were doubles, had access to large yards as opposed to the house I live in now in Midcity, which is a typical shotgun that butts right up to the next house.

My mom was a school teacher. My dad worked for the Treasury Department. My mother likes to say she was from the Irish Channel, but she must've been on the good side of the Irish Channel. She had a big-ass house on General Pershing Street and my dad came from failed aristocracy. The surname Schmidt is German for "Smith," but my father always considered himself to be French because he was raised closer to his mother's family. She was a Bagneris and they owned the stockyard in Arabi and had plenty of money. It all went bad during the Depression, and they became what we referred to fashionably as handicappers. They were bookies. He had this beautiful family home on…what is the street that Ray Lambert lives on?

Woody: Angela.

Wesley: Angela. Really beautiful house. I went to public grammar school and Catholic high school. Cor Jesu; it became Brother Martin.

Woody: When the Brothers of the Sacred Heart merged it with St. Aloysius, where I went to school.

Wesley: There is something very peculiar about going through puberty and being taught by guys who wear black dresses and claim not to have sex. I remember my first coed class at University of Louisiana-Lafayette, or I should say my first coed exam. It was a history exam. A girl with a v-neck fuzzy sweater on leaned over to look at the answers on my test paper, and I leaned over to look down her fuzzy sweater. And I want to tell you, at 18 years old, it was the first time in my life I was ever motivated to study. I wanted that girl to look on my test paper again.

My friends who played music were in in blue-eyed soul bands, and by the late 1960s they were in power trios doing Beatles or Cream covers. Many of them went out to California to do acid and be whatever that mecca was about. They were there for a while, they freaked out, and came home having discovered that the music that they left was the music that started everything that was going on in California. But by then, there weren't many places to play in New Orleans. If you wanted to do something, you had to invent it yourself.

Parallel Worlds

In our immediate case, Jim, the owner of Luigi's, had lately discovered folk music. It's like 1972 and he hired this duet, Smokey and Helt, to play for 100 dollars on a Wednesday night. Nobody showed up. Jim was tight with money. I talked him into taking an ad out of UNO's weekly newspaper, The Driftwood. To get the best rate, you had to buy six weeks, so we wrote an ad that said, "Live Music, No Cover Charge, Wednesday night." As it would happen, Smokey and Helt broke up before the next gig.

Left: Wesley with saxophone at a tumble, circa late 1970s. Photographs courtesy of Wesley Schmidt. **Right:** King Richard Matthews as grand marshal of the Olympia Brass Band, circa 1990. Photograph by Ed Newman.

I talked to some of the guys who were in a band that would become Rhapsodizers—the precursor to the Radiators. I said, "Look man, I can't pay you any more than 100 dollars. If that's worth moving your equipment to Luigi's, you can rehearse here." They didn't know if they had two sets of material. I said "It doesn't matter. If you got three songs, that's enough. Just play them over and over." This became live entertainment for UNO every Wednesday for 15 years.

Woody: *I used to bartend Wednesday nights and it was so packed. A lot of the faculty from UNO hung out there.*

Wesley: *It was so slammed. It was like there was a lot of serendipity involved, but there was a lot of rolling your own to make it happen. At the time, I was hanging out at a bar called Bacchus, and met King Richard Matthews because were both madly in love with the same barmaid. I don't think either of us got anywhere with the barmaid, but we became famous friends.*

Woody: *Richard was Milton Batiste's stepson, and the grand marshal for the Olympia Brass Band. Now we are godparents of King Richard's first daughter.*

Wesley: *Yes indeed, we were the godfathers. My knowledge of brass band music was pretty limited. I think the second LP I ever bought was a Dukes of Dixieland record because that's what I thought traditional jazz was. Pete Fountain was selling in my world. That's what was being marketed to me. I didn't frequent Preservation Hall a lot. Being fair to us, that music had been really overexposed. If you're trying to get laid, that's not what you're doing. But even if you're not going to hear Sweet Emma Barrett, how do you not get touched by it in some way? It's like a goddamn heat.*

Woody: *That was brass band music, too.*

Wesley: *What was great about knowing Richard was— well, there were plenty of things—but in musical terms was he took me places that to hear and see things in which I*

became a very comfortable casual observer that I would not have been introduced to. Even things like going to Eddie's in the Seventh Ward.

Woody: *Yeah, run by the Baquets.*

Wesley: *He would just take us to really nice places—*

Woody: *That were different for us.*

Wesley: *There were plenty of different worlds going on. Sometimes you run parallel and sometimes you get to criss-cross, and we got to crisscross in a really good way. Richard and I were friends for a while before I met Milton Batiste in a social way. I had gone to gigs, but Milton was a scary looking dude, man. I can remember being terrified of him. He was this big black guy with a steel plate in his head. But he was such a gentle, wonderful, kind guy to us once we got to know him—once we got to that place.*

Woody: *Milton took care of business. That Olympia band really took off, man.*

Wesley: *Oh, did it!! It was like an escalator. If you talk about brass bands in New Orleans, there was only one brass band according to the world and that was Olympia.*

Instruments in Attics

Wesley: *I'd been saying I wanted to play saxophone for a long time, so as a birthday present my friends bought me one. I should've kept that horn, man. The problem was, it was in the key of C and I was reading all the charts in B flat. I got the sax on Sunday, and by Thursday I was the leader of two bands. I can't read a note, I can't play a note. I don't care, I'm bulletproof. Sick Dick and the Volkswagen was a parody band.*

Woody: *I was in it, too.*

Wesley: *Ed Volker named the band from a Thomas Pynchon novel,* Crying of Lot 49. *In the story, a guy was locked in a car while a tape loop played continuously and the band was so bad he gnawed through his wrist. It was my philosophy that our band was so bad that that you shouldn't have to listen to it unless you were in it. We used to play the Rhapsadizer's breaks, which meant we jumped up and used their instruments. I had this big box of instruments full of cowbells and things that made noise, and I would hand them out to the audience.*

Woody: *That's how I found my tuba when we were looking for cowbells and noisemakers and the lady was about to make a planter out of it.*

Wesley: *From the stage, I would direct: "Everybody play," or "Shut up." And if I pointed at you, that meant, "You gotta solo." If you knew how to play an instrument, we would make you play a different one, just to even the playing field. That philosophy kind of moved over into the Pair-a-Dice Tumblers. The quality of the music was not paramount. It was the fact that it was this rolling party and it just went wherever. The basic assumption was that if you're a marching band, you only need two songs because the audience stays put. They won't know that you only know two songs once you get started.*

The band was populated by people who had played for six weeks in junior high and quit and still had an instrument in their attic. One guy who could play was Morris. Morris and I would go in the back room of my house with sheet music that had a voice line at the top for the singer, which is one note, and he would say, "Well, that first note is a C." I would look on the fingering chart on the side and then he would say, "This is D flat." And then I'd go teach it to the band. Now think about this as an arrangement methodology. If we did it all correctly, we're all playing one note at the same time. At its best, it was gonna be absolutely awful.

Woody: *In 1979, the first time the Pair-of-Dice Tumblers marched in the Quarter, the city cancelled Mardi Gras because there was a police strike and they had no policemen. The National Guard didn't mess with us because they were overwhelmed keeping order. We were a moving party, full of color, just like a second line. We wore shiny and loud clothes. People jumped in and followed us. It was just wonderful playing music, whether it was good or not. You felt like you were just king of the world.*

Wesley: *After that, we used to jump into other people's parades on a regular basis.*

Luigi's Pair-A-Dice Tumblers 'marching music therapists'

by karen ford

In a city famous for Mardi Gras, parades, marching clubs and the like, the Pair-A-Dice Tumblers just has to be the most outrageous and the most fun of any marching club around.

With virtually no provocation at all the Tumblers will turn out en masse for a stroll through the quarters, making music, cutting up, and dancing in the streets to shouts of "Roll on Tumblers! Roll on!"

"We're just a bunch of amateurs," says Mike "Bear" Lemoine, unofficial spokesman for the group. "Some people really know how to read music, others just improvise." Lemoine joined the Tumblers about a year ago and, like many other members, is a UNO student. He explains that their goal is to learn a new song each month until their repertoire is large enough to

According to Johnny McGuinness, UNO student, and bartender at Luigi's, the real impetus of the group is Wes Schmitt, Luigi's bar manager. "It all started back a few years ago," recalls McGuinness, "when some of Wes' friends got together and put up $10 or $12 apiece to get him a sax. He had been saying he wanted to learn to play the sax and that's sort of where it all got started." Today there are more than twenty regular

members who "get together to get drunk and blow music notes" at band practice each Tuesday at Schmidt's place.

Schmidt reigns supreme over the hodgepodge of musicians and

[...] and when they get enough money together, blow it on a trip to the Kentucky Derby.

merrymakers, not only [...] their efforts, but [...] suggestions and [...] agement as well.

Band practice is fun. [...] nothing compared to the [...] "The topper is running [...] the quarter. It's the bon[...] treat — the dessert [...] McGuinness. "Walking [...] Sloppy Jimmy's and [...] 'Gimme twenty bucks [...] draft.' It's being able to [...] public — my chance [...] obnoxious."

When the Tumblers tu[...] parade, the Poodles, [...] described by Janet Bl[...] group of "females purs[...] freedom to display bad [...] public," are not far [...] Although they aren't m[...] they are part of the fe[...]

dancing with the old men [...] streets, and having a grea[...]

The Tumblers have attra[...] much attention with their [...] that Charles Zewe, Chan[...] news director, took a film [...] out and taped them parad[...] was subsequently included [...] Journal show about how [...] Orleanians party.

McGuinnes did speak [...] whole group when he said [...] social club – I'll quit the fir[...] it becomes a thing with [...] ture. It is the very lack of [...] ture that makes the Tu[...] what they are – marchin[...]

Midsummer Mardi Gras

Shelby

Second Line in the Summertime

— JULY 12 —
5305 ST. ANThony Ave.
The OLympia BRASS BAnd
The PAIR-A-DICE TUmblers MARChing Ban[...]
SWImmINg - BEER - BAnd[...]

Woody: *One time the Tumblers met at Luigi's, and a Mardi Gras parade was passing by. We hid in the bushes, jumped into the parade.*

Wesley: *We got to the reviewing stand and we're not in the sequence. They announced: "And now we have the St. James Major All-Girls High School High-Steppers!" And there's 20 drunks from down the block.*

The Most Genuine Thing

The Pair-A-Dice Tumblers was a bucket of fun, except by

this time, Richard and I were friends and I was terrified, absolutely terrified, that he would think I was making fun of music that he held dear and embraced. I mean, it really was something I was concerned about, but Richard didn't feel that way at all. He would come over to the house and he wouldn't say it was bad, he would say, "Well, what you gotta do is this." He'd take a tambourine and show us, and I would be like, "Okay, Richard, go away. I don't want you to see this. This is embarrassing."

This went on for several years until I got to be friends with Harold Dejan and Milton and the rest of them and found out

that that's the way many of these bands started anyway. It wasn't like everyone said, "I think I'm gonna start a band and we're gonna wear white shirts and black ties and make money." To a certain degree that was true for guys who were reading musicians, but I can remember when the Dirty Dozen was a kazoo band and they were dressing up in women's clothes. They were coming from a similar place. And that thing I was so embarrassed about was probably the most genuine thing I've ever done in my life. I was just looking for a party and the band was the inroad to that, but because Richard was so unabashed about his affection for us, we started to take ourselves more seriously.

Woody: They took us under their wing. I remember Leroy "Boogie" Breaux called me. He was at a bar that's the Candlelight now, and said, "You wanna play a funeral?" I said, "Well I don't know. I don't know if I can." He said, "Come on, you can do it."

Wesley: Another case of serendipity was that this buddy of ours, Dan Johnson, lived a few doors down from Milton and his wife Ruby on St. Anthony Street. Once a summer, he would throw a block party. He had a real in-ground swimming pool and went to an ice house, got this big block of ice and threw it in the pool. All the neighborhood kids tried to climb up on it while Anthony "Tuba Fats" Lacen was sitting in the pool with his feet up in the air playing sousaphone half underwater. It's like, "Are you worried about the valves rusting?" Nah.

Woody: The neighborhood was well mixed, which is what I like. In a nice big neutral ground there, they would set up a stage, block off the street, and the Olympia and Pair-A-Dice Tumblers would play.

Trial and Error

Wesley: One time, someone tried to hire Pair-A-Dice Tumblers for a gig, and that was about as good idea as having a Hell's Angels be the security guards at Altamont. It was a release party for a guy who did a book on streetcars.

Woody: Our bass drummer had done all the drafting.

Wesley: It was a very Uptown kind of gig, but you got to remember the Tumblers was not a band. The Tumblers was a call to a party. You could get five people; you could get 50 people. The word went around, and there must've been 30 people who showed up, banging on shit. They ate all the food, they drank all the booze. It was just like a penultimately wrong idea, but it somehow worked. And what was happening at the same time was that ex-working musicians who through

life circumstances were forced to get real jobs—they got married and had kids, their wife didn't want them to work at night, something like that—started hanging out with the Tumblers because it was fun. And they could actually play.

One of those guys was Larry Talerico. He was a trumpet player who played with Jackie Wilson, and he was at this fiasco. He realized that people would buy the Tumblers, but you had to eliminate the wheat from the chaff. He hand-selected a group of people who essentially became the Storyville Stompers. I was such a good saxophone player they took it away and gave me an umbrella. They said that if I didn't sing or try to play a musical instrument I could still hang out with the band.

My audition gig as grand marshal was at the Rivergate. It was a Seed and Feed convention for guys who bred bulls. A feed guy hired us to march around and then stop by his kiosk and garner some attention. Nobody told us that there were real bulls—like big animals tied down to the floor—so we show up in red shirts playing brass band music. We got about one-third around the room, and these bulls start kicking down the stalls. The partitions are falling down, and I'm just totally oblivious, trying to fake my way through this thing. The cops stopped us and said, "You're creating this disaster." I survived both the bulls and the cops.

Woody: We used to do the St. Patrick's Day parade in the Irish Channel with politicians in convertibles. If you were behind one of them, they'd stop and shake hands, and then drive off three blocks to meet the rest of the parade and leave you behind. We always had to run to catch up. One time, we kept going straight and the parade had turned.

Wesley: We took 400 white guys into the St. Thomas project. The people in the projects, they didn't know what to do because clearly we weren't supposed to be there, but after a little minute it was all cool. Everyone went back to drinking and playing. But that's something about grand marshalling:

Wesley and Richard as grand marshals at Harold Dejan's funeral in 2002 with Tuba Fats in the background. Photograph by Bruce Sunpie Barnes.

Know the route before you leave. What happens with all groups, when you get together, the collective IQ drops. There's that old joke, "What's three miles long, green and white, has 1,000 legs and an IQ of 12?" The St. Patrick's Day parade. I learned by trial and error until I started hanging with Richard when he was grand marshalling, and learned your role is a lot about logistics. You're not there to pose and get your picture taken. That is not your job. Your job is to clear the way. When there are no barriers between you and the crowd, your job is to make sure there is enough space for the band. If someone butts into their space, and hits their instrument, it can do real damage. In the case of funerals, getting a funeral director like Louis Charbonnet to tell you beforehand which side of the altar to sit on, and where he wants you to go as you bring the body out.

You Can Get Work

Woody: The tuba players in the Olympia were inspiring to me. I remember one time the band was parading and I was right by Allan Jaffe. The minute I heard the sound of his tuba, I thought, "That just really anchors this." Once I got a sousaphone, Tuba Fats said, "If you learn how to play that thing, you can get work."

I was staying at Larry Talerico's house, and he began to show me how to play it. There were other tuba players in the Tumblers who really knew how to play, but Rico said, "I'm gonna teach you how to play the right notes. I like the feel you play them in. We just gotta get the right ones."

One of our stops on the Tumbles was Molly's at the Market, which was, and still is, one of the most eclectic clubs in the Quarter. When Jim Monaghan started it, that neighborhood was real rough. The French Market hadn't really been remodeled as nicely as it is now. It was a seaport full of sailors. His bar was one of the anchors that helped develop that lower part of Decatur Street. When the Storyville Stompers became its own band, Jim hired us regularly at Molly's. You know, part of keeping a band together is having a place to play.

We'd only been together a year or so when Jim took us to Washington, D.C. for Louisiana Mardi Gras. It's a krewe whose membership includes most of the well-to-do, well-heeled people in Louisiana. They get together and throw a big party to lobby for the state. They rent out almost a whole hotel to have a complete Louisiana experience with zydeco and brass bands, and all the best food—oysters, shrimp—to show people in Washington about Louisiana culture.

The Olympia was the regular paid brass band there. They played in the beginning, and then had to wait in the green room before marching in the flaming desserts. They invited us to join them. Tuba Fats was

Larry Talerico at Vaughn's Lounge in the Bywater in 2014. Photograph by Bruce Sunpie Barnes.

laughing because I had just got my tuba, and chained it to my bed in the hotel. I was so proud of that sousaphone. I didn't want anybody stealing it!

It was through our time in Washington, D.C. Milton decided they'd produce our records on the Olympia label. It made us feel accepted being part of the people who were making the music. After a few years, Rico got promoted at Latter and Blum to one of the managers so he didn't have time to deal with the band. He said, "Why don't you take it over?" It was right around the World's Fair in New Orleans in 1984. I remember the first three jobs I booked, I was a nervous wreck. I still get nervous that everybody is going to show up, but we always do. Being a bandleader isn't the fun part—I'd rather just play—but it keeps us together. I've been the band leader for 30 years, and there are still a lot of original members, too.

Bad Notes Go Away

I started hanging in the Sixth and Seventh Ward—the side streets off of Esplanade that I grew up around. As a child, especially during segregation, I'd hear white people say, "Oh, you gotta stay out of that neighborhood. You're gonna get in trouble if you go in that neighborhood." Benny Jones, who was a real inspiration and supporter of us, would invite us to come in that neighborhood, and say, "Nothing's gonna happen to you. We'll take care of you."

I soon realized these places weren't dangerous. You walk into a place where there are people who are different than you, and you're always a little nervous, but then you realize that these people are out here having fun, too. They frowned on humbug. It opened up a whole new understanding of people for me, too. I

Left: The Storyville Stompers with Wesley Schmidt as grand marshal in the 1980s, courtesy of Woody Penouilh. *Right:* Woody, Benny, Joe Lastie, and Craig Klein at a jam session, courtesy of Benny Jones, Sr.

think when you hang on a social level you get to know them better than in a work context.

When Benny started the Tremé Brass Band it gave me a lot of chances to play with musicians from other bands. They used to have a jam session on St. Bernard at Sidney's Saloon. They would say, "Come on, that is the only way you can learn, go out there and take your hits! Make the mistakes and get them out." Benny said, "The bad notes just go away."

I started learning more songs because I thought, "If I want to go to Sidney's and jam, I gotta learn these two songs that I heard last week." When other bands started calling me to play with them, I used to be a nervous wreck, but it was a sign I was improving.

Sign Up

For six years, I worked as an economist at the Chamber of Commerce, and was starting to feel restless.

On the weekends, if I wasn't playing music, I used to love going to the little festivals all over Louisiana. They used to have a zydeco festival in Plaisance on Labor Day weekend, Festival Acadiens in Lafayette in October and a Frog Festival in Rayne in November. They had the Islenos festivals down in St. Bernard Parish, the Rice Festival in Crowley, and the Strawberry Festival in Ponchatoula. I went to one in Lockport on Bayou Lafourche. It was on school grounds, and the bathrooms and everything were in the school. I remember going in that school, and I said, "This would be a great place to work." I mean, all those drawings on the wall—just kids' stuff all over and old books. It put the bug in my ear to go back to school to get certified to teach.

It was hard at the beginning. I started teaching math and science in a public middle school, and it was so different than where I went to school. But the Free School was different from most public schools as well. The teachers and students were on a first name

basis. Just like Bob was the principal, they called me Woody. It was about 80 percent African American. It wasn't a neighborhood school, but we were near the St. Thomas and Magnolia public housing projects, and a lot of kids came from there.

If anybody asked me the secret of your first year is, "Give them more work than they can possibly do. It's the ones that finish early that get you!" Your first year of teaching, you want to be liked by the kids, but that shouldn't be your priority. They could tell I was green. I never thought kids wouldn't listen that much, but the other teachers were really supportive. They had a math teacher named Jeanette there who was fantastic, but she wasn't certified yet, so they had to have a certified teacher in the room with her when she taught. That was a beautiful learning experience for me. I'd go around and help the kids, and she taught me how to run a classroom.

In the morning, we would teach the core subjects and then, in the afternoon, the kids got to pick two hours of electives—what we called "Sign Up." The teachers would offer art or ballet or painting and they would rotate it every week. One of my first years teaching the granddaughter of Big Chief Ferdinand Bigard of the Cheyenne Hunters was in my class. He volunteered to do one of the Sign Up classes to teach the kids beading. That's one way of showing the value of the art that comes out of New Orleans neighborhoods because some people are not as exposed to Mardi Gras Indians as other people are.

I was inspired to get a grant from the Jazz & Heritage Foundation to promote traditional brass band music. During the summer, I went to pawn shops and bought 100 to 250 dollar horns. Didn't have any tubas, so I had one baritone horn, a bunch of trumpets, trombones, and drums. A lot of times, it was the first time the kids had ever been introduced to music. When you're trying to learn how to play music, familiarity is important. When we first started, they wanted to play what the high school bands were playing, which was not really jazz. I used traditional songs that they knew—maybe hymns from church or songs like *Second Line* to make a connection. They would go for it. It was a way to get to them through the back door. I showed them the fingering and gave them each parts to get them used to playing music and working together. Nothing real complicated. The technique would have to come later. Some of them went on and played in bands like St. Augustine's.

The Free School's enrollment went from 100 to 300. We started to have to conform more and more, more and more, and more to get along with the school system administration. Bob kept us abreast of all the cutting edge literature, but the state pushed testing as a solution to improve the quality of public education. Curriculum started being geared towards the tests, and we had to cut out one of the Sign Up classes.

The Free School's Brass Band, courtesy of Woody Penouilh.

Day-to-day was not easy, but it all came together at the end of the year. We used to take the kids camping for three days. We'd get them out in the woods and there would be no fights. The only problem was keeping the girls and the guys separated! But the school system administration, in their infinite wisdom, said we couldn't do it anymore because it wasn't instructional. You know what instruction happens the last three days of school? There is no instruction. We are babysitting! Nobody comes. Everybody used to want to go on this camping trip.

Orleans Parish School Board tried to close us down so many times. There would be such a big commotion at the school board meetings that they'd always change their mind. The building that we were in was falling apart. The summer before Katrina, we moved to the old Daneel School building closer to Audubon Park. I'd just come off of sabbatical, so I was getting used to teaching again. We were open for seven days, and then the storm came.

This school had a lot of community backing and support, but was still one of the many schools that didn't reopen. Another charter school opened in our old building under the name of New Orleans Free School Academy, but it wasn't the same principal or the same faculty. They were kicked out after a year because the building was condemned. It should have been condemned a long time before that.

I had to retire after Katrina because there weren't any jobs. There were no schools open, so I sat out my mandatory year, and then went across the river to Algiers Charter Schools. I was there for one year, then another three years part time before retiring again. I see kids I taught all the time. When we see each other in life, they come up and say, "Hey." I ran

into Ferdinand Bigard's granddaughter not too long ago. She told me that I was the best teacher she ever had. Made me feel good. My old faculty from the Free School still hang around together. During Saints season, some of the old teachers from the school watch football together. It was a family school.

It's interesting, after Katrina, I joined a committee at St. Anna's Episcopal Church that was organized by Father Bill Terry and Bethany Bultman from the Musician's Clinic to support musicians coming back

to the city. There was nothing similar for teachers. Father Terry is always doing unique things. He keeps a public list of people who were murdered. At one time, he had bones all over the place to raise awareness of the lives of people who have been lost. The Storyville Stompers plays their Palm Sunday parade every year. Like the Society of St. Anne parade on Carnival day, it is part of our yearly calendar. I get to parade through the streets of my childhood, playing my favorite music—traditional jazz.

The Society of St. Anne convenes in the Bywater early on Carnival morning and then marches through the Faubourg Marigny and French Quarter up to see the Rex parade on Canal Street. After the parades passes, St. Anne continues on to the river where members to pay homage to friends who have passed away during the year. Photograph by Jeff Day.

Left: Reverend William Terry leads St. Anna's Episcopal Church's Palm Sunday parade with the Storyville Stompers. *Right:* Palms to be handed out. Photographs by Jennifer Zdon, courtesy of *The Times Picayune.*

Doyle in the Music for All Ages program, by Bruce Sunpie Barnes.

Doyle Cooper at the Musicians Union Hall rehearsal space at 2401 Esplanade Avenue. Photograph by Bruce Sunpie Barnes. The American Federation of Musicians' New Orleans branch began with Local 174, which only accepted white members. Black musicians working on excursion boats had to file their contracts in Mobile. In 1926, Papa Celestin and other musicians filed to have their own union, which gave rise to Local 496. If white musicians wanted to play in black union bands, they would have to join the black union, which is exactly what a number of European musicians like Barry Martyn, Joe "Kid" Simmons, and Clive Wilson did in the 1960s. In 1969, the two unions merged despite serious concerns about equity. Barry Martyn, representing the black union, said there were fears that *when they merge it won't be 496-174, but will always be 174-496.* In 1974, Louisiana passed a "right to work" law that prohibited agreements between labor unions and employers that required employees to join the union as one of the stipulations for being hired, which greatly weakened the power of the newly integrated Local 174-496.

DOYLE COOPER

Bruce: *Doyle Cooper's family is originally from Mississippi, but his family moved him to New Orleans when he was very young so he could come up around jazz. When he first came to the program we called him Trumpet Red, but he has grown into sousaphone player, the bandleader of the Red Hot Brass Band, and a music educator. Doyle was a little older than the other students, and quickly found the value of being a custodian of the teachable moments. He had played music in school, and was happy to show the younger musicians the technical part of music, like embouchure and fingering.*

After a while, he also decided that he wanted to have his hands in organizing, not just playing, the music. As he was getting his band going, I hired the Red Hot to play with the younger kids in the program at festivals in the French Quarter, and they did a residency with the program itself. Although he will do student teaching for his music education program

in college, he has gained a lot of knowledge about teaching music from playing music with teachers like Woody Penouilh. During this interview, they talk about the benefits of formal and informal training.

Doyle's mom, Leslie Cooper, was a supermom when it came to supporting the program. She was a singer in her family's trad jazz band for many years, and was at the program every Saturday to help out. Like a lot of the parents who got involved, she branched out to other parts of the music community. She helps Doyle run his band and puts together a successful traditional jazz camp for adults each year. In Doyle's chapter, she talks with Joe Torregano about the politics of race in the traditional jazz scene.

Introduction: Moving From Mississippi

Woody: Okay, true or false, where is your family from?

Doyle: True! My dad was born in Electric, Texas, and grew up in Vidalia, Louisiana.

Woody: Vidalia is by Natchez?

Doyle: Yeah, right across the river from Natchez. It is a really weird landscape. It goes from really low to where they have to have a levee on the Louisiana side. The Mississippi side has a 200-foot bluff.

Woody: On the Natchez side, there is a town on the bottom.

Doyle: Yeah, by the river. My mother grew up between Jackson, Mississippi and a small town about 30 miles outside of it called Pelahatchie. One red light, two cop cars and 42 Baptist churches!

Woody: Where did you grow up?

Doyle: My parents moved here when I was one. They had been living in Natchez. My dad did period woodworking on antebellum homes in the area. My mom was studying to be a nurse. They'd been coming down to New Orleans for Jazz Fest for a while. I have a half sister and a half brother older than me, and my parents wanted to live here where there was a better school system. Better mentality growing up. More cultural. Better music.

Woody: What kind of experience did you have with music in your family?

Doyle: My mom grew up as a vocalist with her stepfather, Woody Coats, who had his own band and played clarinet and saxophone. She knew Pete Fountain well enough to call him Uncle Pete. My mother said her father tried teaching her how to play clarinet, but her hands were too small to reach all the keys. Instead, he put on records of all these female jazz vocalists and would say, "Listen to this person." He'd leave out and once the record was done he'd come back in. "Listen to this." She was in a room by herself just being mesmerized by great music.

I didn't hear a lot of that music around the house when I was young. My dad was a hippie, and I grew up with classic rock like Led Zeppelin and Kiss. He played guitar before he had an accident while he was working, and took the top of his bone out of this finger with a saw. He stopped playing music, but he'd come into the Under the Hill Saloon in Natchez to listen to my mom's band. He knew all the songs that she was singing and he would be like, "Oh, I love that Bessie Smith song." They got to know each other through music.

Woody: That is interesting because after the storm they moved one of the river boats up to Natchez. We went up there to play the Hot Air Balloon Race. We were hanging out at the Under the Hill bar on our days off.

Doyle: My family goes back to Natchez every year for the Balloon Festival. They'll tether the balloons down and at night they'll flame them. They light up this dark bluff. You've got the Mississippi River flowing right below you. And then you had live music and carnival rides going while thirty of these enormous balloons are glowing.

Woody: Where did you grow up in New Orleans?

Doyle: We moved around in the city. I started out in Lakeview on Harrison Boulevard. My sister and brother both were in private schools. I was just about to go into kindergarden when my mom felt something like a grain of sand on my dad's arm. About a month

Grappling with the legacy of segregation in Natchez, Mississippi. *Top:* A black pharmacy in the 1930s. Photograph by Ben Shahn, courtesy of the Library of Congress, Prints and Photographs Division, Farm Security Administration, Office of War Information Collection. *Middle*: Leslie Cooper performing with her stepfather Woody Coats at the Under the Hill Saloon. Photograph courtesy of the Cooper family. *Bottom:* The Longwood Plantation in 1936. The Moorish revival mansion is now owned and operated as a house museum by the Pilgrimage Garden Club. Photograph by James Butters, courtesy of the Historic American Buildings Survey, Library of Congress, Prints & Photographs Division, HABS MISS,1-NATCH.V,3-1.

later, it was the size of like a small walnut. They went to the hospital and the doctors didn't know what it was. A med student was like "God, I remember that from school." He flipped to a page in a textbook, and he's like, "That's what it is." A sarcoma.Usually the cancer is between the muscle and the bone so you don't see it. His happened to be on the top of the muscle so they were able to catch it.

There was no waiting. I remember my uncle coming to stay at the house while my mom took my dad to M.D. Anderson Cancer Center in Houston. They had to take out a pretty good chunk of muscle and he wasn't able to close his fist or move a couple of fingers for awhile, so he had to retire from woodworking.

My mom was still nursing, but when my dad stopped working, they needed all their saved up money they had been using for private school. My brother and sister ended up graduating from Grace King, and they put me into Hynes Elementary in Lakeview. I don't really remember much about this time. Apparently, it was pretty rough.

Can You Play That Horn?

Woody: Why did you choose to play trumpet?

Doyle: The first time I remember playing a trumpet was at my mom's friend's house who was babysitting me during Jazz Fest. Her house was on Mystery Street right near the entrance to the festival. I didn't have any toys to play with, so she gave me her trumpet from high school. Here was this shiny thing in a case. I was like, "How do you even hold it?" I went outside and started to try to play *Second Line*. I didn't know the fingerings, but I went "Ha, ha, ha." My mom said I came back inside with 40 dollars in my pockets. People on their way to Jazz Fest had been giving me money. I brought out the case and ended up making enough to buy tickets for both of us. She was just like, "Huh?

Whoa. We got something here."

I was never a timid child. When my dad's cancer was in full remission, we moved into an old house on Music Street in the Gentilly Terrace, and my dad got a job as a part-time bartender in the neighborhood. I remember my mom leaving me to go get change at a Washateria near his job. She came back in and everybody knew her life story because, apparently, I was a very talkative.

In fifth grade, I started playing in the band at Jean Gordon. My mom took me to the Satchmo Summer Festival's second line parade. Right off Esplanade, Kenneth Ferdinand saw me with my trumpet. He came up to me and said, "Can you play that horn, boy?" I played it.

He said, "No, I said can you play that horn, boy?" I played a note, and it cracked really badly. He looked up at mom, and said, "Mom, we have him." He took me into the parade and the hand that he didn't use to play, he had it on my shoulder and was showing me fingerings. He was teaching me. I came back and I was freaking out,"Dad, Dad, look! This is a G! This is an A!" That was a big moment for me.

Woody: That is the sense of music here. At its best, musicians in New Orleans won't look at each other as competition. They look at is as just friends joining together to make a good sound. Everybody shares their knowledge.

Doyle: In sixth grade, I started attending NOCCA Academy, and was part of Clyde Kerr, Jr.'s big band. I'd get home and drive my parents crazy listening to Al Hirt. He was my idol.

Woody: Where did you get the red trumpet?

Doyle: That was after the storm. We evacuated to

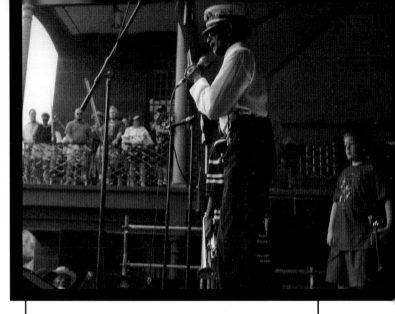

Doyle watching Uncle Lionel Batiste sing during the Satchmo Summer Fest's "Trumpet Summit" where he was invited to perform in when he was young. Photograph courtesy of the Cooper family.

Vidalia, Louisiana for a little bit, and a store owner in Natchez said, "I have the perfect trumpet for you. The Musicians Union gave me some money to help Katrina evacuees." My mom had already signed me up in the Musicians Union in New Orleans. For awhile, I was the youngest member. They gave me some money, and I bought the red trumpet.

I attended seventh grade at Vidalia Middle, but played second trumpet in the high school band. My mom wasn't happy there—she said she wanted to get out of rural Mississippi as fast as she could. The music education was not like New Orleans. Luckily, our house didn't flood. The area around Gentilly Ridge runs along the former banks of Bayou Gentilly, so it is on higher ground. We were able to return home the day after Christmas 2005. I recorded a song with a musician in my neighborhood, Jonno Frishberg, called *Gentilly Terrace*, where the catch line is that high ground in New Orleans is really just "less low."

Woody: What led you to get involved with MFAA?

Doyle: My mom doesn't push me to do anything, but she gave me opportunities to learn. I noticed that because she would bring me to musical events and programs all the time. If I didn't want to do it, then I didn't have to do it. She said if there was a program that would teach me traditional jazz I would learn from the actual bands that are performing—you guys who were doing it for a living.

I like music that you can tap your foot to—that makes you want to get up and move around. In college, I've read studies on how music affects the body, and I really like how influential music can be on in the development of the brain. It's pretty astonishing. There's a video of a 90-year-old man who was sitting in the nursing home, and he didn't talk to anybody. He didn't react to anybody. They put headphones on with one of his favorite songs, and he started moving. He started tapping his foot, singing along with it. That's the power of music.

I'm a little too big of a person to be just dancing willy-nilly. I've got size 15 feet. I trip over everything. But I like to play music for other people to dance. And I think what drew me to the trumpet was that you get to be in charge of a lot of the band as the instrument out front.

Woody: What did the older musicians do to help you learn to play?

Doyle: Most of the traditional jazz is written down and archived, but there is very few pieces of paper going around like *Down by the Riverside*, or *Old Rugged Cross*. You can go into a hymnal and find *A Closer Walk With Thee*. But most of what we think of in terms of those songs is improvised. When you learn it orally, you don't have to have that image of that piece of paper in your head. When you do learn it on the streets, it is more embedded in you. It sticks with you a lot longer. You see how they teach and then it helps you teach other people how to do it.

Woody: I know when I get kids, I make them all learn the scale and then we learn a song in that scale. A scale and a song—to know what the notes look like.

Music Education

Doyle: At the MFAA program, I started being able to show the younger people. I realized that I liked teaching—the idea of keeping it going. If nobody tries to perpetuate it, it'll get stale, no one will like it, and it'll be a thing of records, and I like the music too much to let that happen. I decided to go into music education at Loyola University in New Orleans. I plan on having a band program at an elementary school. With little kids, you could go on for days on the proper start to a musical instrument. Make sure they have good posture and play with the horn up and not down or off to the side of their mouth because down the line, those things set you back. I explain to my students, "You have to learn your C scale, your chromatic scales, your arpeggios, your lip slurs." It's literally lifting weights with whatever muscle you use to play your instrument. It's the same thing as doing reps in a gym. The orbicularis oris muscle is just like any other muscle. If you don't exercise it, it's not going to be as strong.

Woody: One thing that made me click after not having any real formal reading training is when I learned how to construct a chord. From there you understand how to move into a minor or a seventh chord, and it helped the music make more sense. That is where I could see the formal stuff is really helpful.

Doyle: I've learned from both.

Woody: You are lucky that you've learned both.

Doyle: I'm studying classical trumpet at Loyola. I really liked working with Dr. Joseph Hebert, who used to play with the New York Philharmonic Orchestra.

Doyle working with young trumpet players at the Music for All Ages program at the French Quarter Festival. Photograph courtesy of the Cooper family.

Woody Penouilh practicing with the Red Hot Brass Band at the Musicians Union Hall while Leslie Cooper and Pat Besselman watch. Photographs by Bruce Sunpie Barnes.

Being around him showed me that anyone can do it if you put yourself to it. A little Cajun boy down South gets to play with one of the most premier orchestras in the United States. I mean, hundreds of people audition for one spot. It's pretty phenomenal. Then I've learned the oral music from—I wouldn't call you old, I'd call you more seasoned musicians!

Woody: Who are your biggest influences?

Doyle: Seeing people like Leroy Jones and Mark Braud play definitely had a profound impact, but I don't just listen to trumpet players; I listen to everything. I'm still a big fan of Al Hirt and Pete Fountain. I listen to a lot of Sidney Bechet.

Woody: What is one of your favorite experiences with traditional jazz?

Doyle: I'd been in love with Louis Armstrong for

years, and the Park Service started sponsoring the "Seeking Satch" competition. My junior year, I won the high school division, and then right after I graduated, I entered the competition again. It was really hot outside, and we were in the air conditioning inside the Jazz Park at Dutch Alley in the French Quarter. Each trumpet player had to come up, play two songs, and then the judges, Delfeayo Marsalis and Wendell Brunious, asked us to play a song of their choice. First place was an all-expense-paid trip to Germany.

You could tell some of the kids were nervous. Everybody was in the competitive mindset, and most were keeping to themselves. I was sitting up in front, smiling at everybody, just trying to keep the mood from getting weird. If you start getting stink eyes, it's just no fun for anybody.

Jason Marsalis was accompanying us on drums. When it was my turn, I got up and played the cadenza in *West*

End Blues, and then I did Louis Armstrong's beginning to *Struttin' With Some BBQ* from his Hot Five record—the one in A-flat. Delfeayo Marsalis said, "Play *Tin Roof Blues* or *Whooping Blues*, which ever one you want." It was a trick. They are the same song. He wanted to see how much I knew. When I found out I won, I was like, "Yeah, I went out of high school with a bang!"

The trip to Germany took place my freshman year of college at Loyola. I went to Berlin with a group of musicians from New Orleans. Along with some German musicians, it was Delfeayo, Big Chief Smiley Ricks, the vocalist Robin Williams. Some African dancers performed with the percussionist Alexey Marti. And then we had me showcased on traditional jazz doing some of Delfeayo's arrangements.

One of my family friends, Michael MacAndrew, met me there. We got my plane ticket pushed back, and I was able to see more of Europe. We went to Paris and

Orleans. We called it "The Last Train to Orleans." It seemed like a song title.

Woody: Can you give some examples of times you were allowed to cross racial boundaries with your music?

Doyle: I'm not that old, but my parents made sure I never grew up in a segregated place. Math and Science, where I went to high school most of my years, was predominately a black school.

Woody: You were lucky not to have to go through segregation. All that tension. It is possible for people to learn from each other and nowadays a lot of the schools, they are not officially segregated but could still be all-white or all-black. Either way, people are missing something when they don't get to be around each other. I know I missed it when I went to an all white high school. That is all they had then.

Doyle: You can definitely see a separation at the schools like during lunchtime—different races will sit together. I really never was into that.

Woody: You miss so much when you don't embrace other cultures. What do you think your generation is doing with New Orleans music that is different?

Doyle: I formed my band, the Red Hot Brass Band, right before my 14th birthday. After going through the MFAA program, I saw bands like yours or the Tremé Brass Band playing the traditional music, but there was a lull in the younger people playing trad jazz. Even today, if you go to Frenchmen, you see more of string bands with the traditional jazz, and then brass bands playing modern music. They are more into taking music that is more popular with our generation right now and mixing it with brass.

Woody: I'm interested in what happens when there is a fusion between two types of music. Like in Central

Texas and Mexico, they got accordions in the bands and those are instruments that weren't part of their culture until the Germans moved into that hill country of Texas, and brought them. Now a lot of the musicians use accordions. What are your biggest struggles with music?

Doyle: Finding practice time. My mom uses a quote, "Busier than a one-armed wallpaper hanger." Especially with school. You definitely need to give your instrument enough time to mature.

As a bandleader, you realize that sousaphone players are scarce in New Orleans—they are always working. Some times we would play gigs without the bass and I didn't like it at all. You don't realize how much a sousaphone does for you in an ensemble until it's gone. I've done plenty of gigs without a bass drum, because that sousaphone can take over its job. But on the gigs without the sousaphone, I found myself playing its parts on my trumpet, and it was exhausting.

I decided I needed to learn how to play it. Everybody and their mama plays trumpet in New Orleans. You could find another trumpet player, so I could fill in for a sousaphone if need be. It's a B-flat horn, just like trumpet. It has three valves, one mouthpiece, one bell—it's basically the same thing, but shaped differently. It takes a little bit more oxygen and a little bit less playing. I still catch myself playing tuba like I'm trying to play it like a trumpet, and I'm like, "I gotta back off a little bit. This is getting too busy."

Woody: What parts of New Orleans have you gotten to know because of music that you might not have gotten to know about?

Doyle The Tremé. Certain parts of the Ninth Ward. The French Quarter, the Marigny, Bywater. I know more about the CBD than I want to. Hotels, and parties at warehouses and museums, back corners of hotel

Doyle leading the New Orleans Traditional Jazz Camp's annual second line through the French Quarter. Photograph courtesy of the Cooper family.

ballrooms, and all kinds of odd places that I've been put with our band. I've lost count of how many second lines I've done from St. Louis Cathedral to Jax's Brewery.

I've also learned a lot about the Quarter from working my mom's jazz camp that she started five years ago. I remember during MFAA, when Bruce would be getting us to line up and teach us how to do the proper marching thing—how hectic it was just trying to get ten musicians to do the same thing. Now I lead a second line every summer with my mom's jazz camp that has a 100 musicians in it. You think getting 10 musicians is hard? Get 100 musicians to do the same thing!

LESLIE COOPER & JOE TORREGANO
WHO PLAYS TRAD JAZZ?

Leslie: At the New Orleans Traditional Jazz Camp, our mission is to perpetuate jazz. Not just preserve it because preserve is putting it in a jar and sticking it on the shelf. Perpetuating it is taking it off the shelf, unscrewing the lid, and sharing it with everybody. We get as many charts to teach the music as it was written. To try to bring it back. I know you were given it through Fairview Baptist Church Band.

I learned the songs from my stepdad, Woody Coats. Right out of high school, he enrolled in music education but he got the opportunity to play in a big band that was on the Air Force base circuit. He traveled all over the world. He had an established band when he married my mom, and she became the vocalist. Mom would tell Woody I should be able to sing, too: "She's got pitch, she knows the meter, and she's cute as a button. Why aren't you letting her perform?" But he had a hard, steadfast rule: Do not get on stage with children or animals because they will upstage you every time.

When Mom left the band to go to nursing school, I finally got a chance to sing with the band. I played big band swing and

trad jazz with them for the next five or six years. Five nights a week. He taught me, "As a female singer, the band is going to follow you, but you have to know where the hell you are taking them. You are going to learn to call keys, how to front the band, network, and socialize."

On Sunday nights, we played at the Under the Hill Saloon in Natchez. Natchez proper is up on a 400-foot bluff overlooking the river. In many respects, it's locked in the 1850s. People say the town is run by the ladies in the Pilgrimage Garden Club—the blue-haired mafia—and its economy survives on the tourism generated by their antebellum homes.

Down under the bluff, "Under the Hill," there used to be six or more streets that developed alongside all the boat trade—the steamboats and paddle wheelers. Cotton was sent down to New Orleans, and out into the world, or up north into the textile factories. But over less than a hundred years, the river has eaten away all but one of those streets, and the only one that is left is Silver Street. They have since tried to shore it up.

You can't stop the river. It will eventually take it, but there are still a few buildings left from the late 1700 and early 1800s and one of them is the Under the Hill Saloon. It reminds me so much of New Orleans. It was where you went to hear music in Natchez if you were of any color. Bikers were sitting at a table with a guy with a three-piece suit. My dad actually had quite a biker following for being a trad jazz band. I always loved that music brought people from all walks of life together.

By the time I was 18, I was managing his jazz band. I continued to sing with other bands even after he quit. I started doing more rhythm and blues, but my two older kids needed me a lot more. It's one thing to sing to two in the morning, but it's really hard to get up a few hours later to help your kids get to school. I decided to put it on the back burner and said, "One day."

I was going back and forth to New Orleans with my dad to hear music and the music scene in Natchez seemed to be at a standstill. The population was 60 percent black, 40 white.

There were two sides of town, two high schools. Being around musicians in my dad's life, I had been insulated from some of those divides. But I had stopped playing professionally, and right before Doyle was born, Natchez got a new police chief who was black. He began to stir things up by pointing out the injustices, and it created a big backlash with the white community. There comes a time when you realize you can't fix something on your own, when you have to put it down, and it has to become someone else's issue. I wasn't going to have every third word out of my kid's mouth be the n-word. My husband and I decided it was time to move to a place where people got along better. I remember the third day after we moved here I got that bumper sticker that said, Eracism. I must have gone through eight of them over the years.

Jazz Scenes

After the MFAA program, the boys wanted to play in Jackson Square, but Bruce talked with the owner of the Tisket a Tasket bookstore near the Jazz Park's visitor's center and asked the owner if they could play outside of his store. One day, Otis Fennell, who owns Faubourg Marigny Art and Books on the corner of Chartres and Frenchmen, told me, "I'm having a book fair next week, if the kids want, they are welcome to play out in front."

I grabbed a few of the kids from the MFAA program who had been playing in front of Tisket a Tasket, and had them wear black and whites. Nobody had a hat yet. I had a piece of poster board that still said "Garage Sale" on one side and "Red Hot Brass Band" on the other.

We were passing by Ray's Boom Boom Room, and the owner, Ray Holmes, said, "Hold up, hold up! Let me hear y'all play something." They played, and he went upstairs and came back with a tiny E-flat sousaphone. He started playing with them. A woman came up and said, "My sister is getting married in two weeks and she's been looking for a brass band. I just think it would be so special to have these kids." I said, "Okay. Here's my phone number."

The Old New Orleans Lil Big Vaudeville Variety Show tailgating through the French Quarter. Photograph by Bruce Sunpie Barnes. The Variety Show often featured Mischya Lake, a singer who grew up in South Dakota and traveled the country performing with the Know Nothing Family Zirkus Zideshow and End of the World Circus. Mischya Lake explained her initial reaction to New Orleans: *I looked around and noticed the gas lamps and the classic, Old World feel, just this feeling of timelessness. And I eventually learned that it's a very nurturing place to things that are different. They're supported. They're celebrated. And I knew immediately that this was where I belonged.* She began singing with a traditional jazz band called the Loose Marbles on Royal Street before starting the Little Big Horns Jazz Band.

And then Ray said, "I got Monday nights open and I can give these boys 200 dollars. Would they be interested in coming in and opening for Bob French?" I figured it was a one time thing. Bob French came in and stared at them for awhile. He looked at Ray and said, "I want these kids here every week." Some people say, "Oh, they didn't pay their dues." Well, for nine months they played every week for Bob French.

Leslie: One night he had Doyle stay over and play with his band. A man from California came in, and said, "I want to bring Doyle to my camp out here in San Francisco." He's flown him out every year, and now he's a mentor in that camp.

Doyle also got a scholarship to attend the Traditional Jazz Camp in Sacramento, California. A lot of the kids from that camp have grown up and moved to New Orleans to play music. They are mostly young bands. They are part of predominantly white scene that includes bands like the Gypsy Jazz, the Smokin Jazz Club, the Loose Marbles, Tuba Skinny, and the Viper Man Trio. They have built relationships and networks that are largely outside of the trad jazz scene, so there also becomes a dividing line around race. I remember Doyle looked at me when he was about 15 and wanted to know how he could become like Bruce Brackman—the white guy who seemed to play easily with all the black bands in the city. Doyle would have so much passion in his voice when he'd say, "I just care about the music."

I even asked Bruce Barnes one time at the MFAA program, "Do you have a problem with me taking these young men and turning this into something that Doyle can lead?" Bruce told me I had to be careful. He said, "Straight up, taking a bunch of white kids..." And I said, "But they aren't all white!" He said, "It's as much of a turf as anything else and you are going to be careful."

Joe: It's partially true. You still have a good bit of black musicians who will tell you white boys can't play jazz. But then you have the other side, too. The Original Dixieland Jazz Band did the first jazz recording because Freddie Keppard turned it down—he didn't want anyone to imitate his

sound. But Nick LaRocca turned around and was so bold as to say, "This is not a black music." He flat out refused to recognize Buddy Bolden, Jelly Roll, or Louis Armstrong. To make things worse, state law in Louisiana prevented blacks and whites from playing together. Louis Armstrong was denied playing here in New Orleans because he had an integrated band. He couldn't play at Tulane University. He said, "I'll never come back here again." And he never did.

Leslie: You still see people's expectations about what is authentic. A movie was filmed in the area, and Doyle's band was asked to play for the red carpet. About three o'clock in the afternoon someone called me and said, "I'm sorry we can't have you play, but we are still going to pay you." We were still invited to the event, but I pushed for the reason the band couldn't play. The reason was because it was not an all-black brass band.

Joe: I've got one to beat that. They filmed this King Bolden movie. Delfeayo Marsalis called me for some of the soundtrack recording, and I played on that. Then they wanted to cast the guys in the Royal Players to do the brass band scene. The casting director met me and the next day I got a phone call, "I'm sorry we can't use you. You are too light-skinned." She said, "We want it to be authentic and Bolden's band was not Creole musicians."

Leslie: I remember a friend of my father's, Bill Davis, was a trombone player with Cab Calloway. When I was a little girl, he would pick me up, put me on his shoulder and play his horn around me. He was about the same color as me. I thought he was white. One afternoon, he said, "Y'all come over to the house for a barbeque." When we arrived there were lots of black people there. I asked Bill, "Where's your family?" He said, "This is my family." I remember thinking, "That's cool. Family doesn't all have to be the same color."

Joe: I have a question. As someone who is a leader in this realm of antiquity and deeply committed to it, it bothers me that you won't see the Onward or the Young Tuxedo Brass Band back on the street playing strictly traditional brass band

The Red Hot Brass Band with Joe Torregano on clarinet goes up Royal Street. Photograph by Rachel Breunlin.

music. Do you think you will ever see young black musicians wanting to come back to the music of Jelly Roll Morton and Louis Armstrong rather than the Dirty Dozen and Rebirth Brass Band? I don't see it. I have a hard time seeing it.

Leslie: To be honest, I'm just glad they are playing music, but I've also been trying to provide some opportunities for young people to connect with the traditional music. The first year we did the jazz camp, we had 68 adults. The vast majority of them were white and the average age was 69 and up. We had a drummer who was turning 86 that year, and he is now 91. He's been all five years. A lot of our campers are weekend warriors. They played in high school or college but their parents told them you got to become a doctor or a lawyer. Put down that horn and get serious. Now they've retired and can pull it back out.

It is not uncommon for conventions to distribute white hankerchiefs to use during a second line parade, and to keep as a momento. Here members of the Red Hot Brass Band hold up the ones that will be used in a parade they are leading. Leslie Cooper then shows the participants how to hold them up in the air to commune with the moment. Photographs by Rachel Breunlin.

One of the women who went to the camp wrote a really nice letter about how wonderful it was, but they wanted to see more young people. We said, "Well, we would like to also, but we don't have the money to do that." A week and a half later there was a check for $500. I said, "Maybe we can do this. Let's bring in one kid for each instrument, and not segregate them in a kids' band, but put them out there with the adult campers." This year I had 18 kids from New Orleans, and it is a very mixed group.

Now I've been pulling some kids from the jazz camp into the Red Hot. Halfway down the street I realized they were playing Margie, *and I was like "Yes! Yes!" During the jazz camp, I was on a balcony at the corner of Bourbon and Orleans, and I heard,* The song has ended but the melody lingers on… *I looked down and it was Kyle Gancayco from the New Creations Brass Band, who was enrolled in the camp. He was trying to teach it to another horn player in his band. And there was this moment where I was like, "This is what I'm*

talking about." When the band's break was over, they started playing the street brass again.

The Red Hot Brass Band, to my knowledge right now, is the only young brass band that is dedicated to tradition. Now, do they play Grazing in the Grass? *Yeah. Do they bridge from* Little Liza Jane *to* Funky Liza? *Yeah. But they are going to start with some of the earliest ones, and they do a little chronological thing and they may end with Rebirth's* Do Whatcha Wanna.

I know one thing, Doyle's world be so much different if it wasn't for guys like you, Woody Penouih, Mr. Benny Jones, Uncle Lionel Batiste, Will Smith, Oscar Washington and all the guys that have helped to "raise" him musically through the MFAA program.

Joe: *Tell Doyle to call me when he needs a clarinet player.*

Leslie: *What are you doing Wednesday night?*

Joe: *Nothing. What you got?*

Leslie: *Are you feeling good enough to handle the streets?*

Joe: *How far do we have to go?*

Leslie: *Six blocks from the Ritz-Carlton down Bourbon Street, up Royal to the Acme Oyster House.*

Joe: *I can do it.*

Leslie: *Sweet! Excellent! I think Woody is going to make it. I need a sousaphone player.*

Joe: *Well, if Woody can make it, I can. He's eight or nine years older than me.*

RAY
LAMBERT

&

XAVIER
MICHEL

Ray Lambert on the 500 block of Frenchmen Street in the Faubourg Marigny, where he first encountered the Pair-A-Dice Tumblers. Frenchmen was named after five Creoles who were executed there in 1766 after leading an uprising against the Spanish crown, who had come in and outlawed French wine. A commerical corridor, music venues opened there in the late 1970s with The Faubourg/Snug Harbor at 632 Frenchmen catering to modern and experimental jazz, and the Dream Palace becoming the homebase of the Pair-A-Dice Tumblers. When Cafe Brazil opened on the other side of the block, music began to spill into the streets. Some now worry Frenchmen may become "Bourbon Street South," but, if so, it is still more like Bourbon during the 1950s, when jazz clubs brought tourists and locals together. Photograph by Bruce Sunpie Barnes.

pair - a - dice
tumblers
marching music therapists

information   282-9210

A business card for the Pair-A-Dice Tumblers, courtesy of Woody Penouilh.

RAY LAMBERT

Bruce: *Ray is a snare drummer who plays with the Storyville Stompers. He came into music later in life after working in construction, and is self-taught. An artist as well, he paints his snare and bass drums with the most colorful* veves *from the Haitian vodou religion—hearts for Erzulie Fréda, snakes for Damballah.*

During the MFAA, what I loved about Ray was how pumped up he was to make it to the program. He was the first one there. The program started at eleven, and Ray would be there at 9:30 dressed out in black and white, his band hat on, ready to give his whole self. He brought his painted drums, and an instrument he created called the rugalator, which intrigued everybody. I think he felt like he was making up for lost time, and drew a lot from his own experiences learning music in how he taught the students. I used to hear him explaining to them, "You are going to get your feelings hurt if you play it that way. It's not going to work out so well for you."

One of Ray's best friends in the world was a baritone saxophone player named Hart McNee—a triple threat street philosopher, musician, and artist. You could often find them on Frenchmen Street holding very sophisticated metaphysical conversations. It was hard not to be infected by Hart's outlook on life. He had a funny grin that would tap into the core part of yourself. When you left you'd feel like, "Yeah, I've just been in contact with Hart McNee." Both Ray and Hart felt the stirrings of the universe in their music, and shared it in their paintings. Through their friendship I think Ray found someone who affirmed his path in life, and in the program, the students got a chance to benefit from it.

Introduction: The Defining Moment

Ray: There was the defining point in my life, April Fools' Day, 1979. I could almost tell you the time. Best thing that ever happened to me, but it happened quite by accident.

When I was 29, I was a heavy equipment operator doing construction work, and just broke up with a girl. I was really feeling bad. I was into photography a little bit, and came down to the French Quarter to take some pictures. I was driving around trying to find a parking place. There was none to be had. I wound up driving down Frenchmen Street and I passed up a club. It used to be the Dream Palace—now it's the Blue Nile. There was this big, tall, tall brunette girl. Gretchen Zibilich. Good looking as anything. She had a big silly hat on and she was playing clarinet. I said, "Whoa, I got to check this out."

I hurry up and find a parking place and I come almost running back with my camera and lenses. At that point, there is about 15 people on the street all dressed in some form of Mardi Gras costume, blaring instruments and banging on drums. It is real noise. You could see they were having a great time. I decided, "I'm going to follow this thing. This looks like a group having a good time. I'll shoot some shots."

About three hours later, I'm still mixed in the middle. We parade through the French Quarter blocking traffic, stopping at barrooms having drinks. I decide this is way too much fun. I got to find out more information. I start asking questions. They called themselves the Pair-a-Dice Tumblers.

After my first tumble, I was pumped up from this whole thing. I had played guitar in high school, but I know I'm not going to be able to drag it out on the street. I stopped off at my mom and dad's house in Chalmette and asked my brother, "You stopped taking drum lessons, right?"

"Yeah."

"What are you going to do with the drum?"

"Nothing."

"I'm taking it."

I took the drum. That next Tuesday, I went over to a practice at Wesley Schmidt's house. Wes is a generator. He's got concepts and ideas. At his house, I knew nothing that was going on. Woody just stopped playing on the drums and had picked up the sousaphone. He said, "I'll help you out. Are you right or left handed?" I said, "I'm left-handed."

He said, "Good, you hit it once with this hand and twice with that hand."

That was my first music lesson. I'm trying to keep up with what they are doing and it sounded real awful, but everybody was having a good time. It turns out about once a month they would march to the French Quarter doing exactly what I saw them do the first time. I started playing with them, and I wound up getting a real job. I was trying to tell the band leader Larry Talerico, "I don't know how to play this drum."

He said, "That's okay. I have enough drummers, I just need more people and I want you in."

He didn't have another drummer. He was lying to me. I get on this job and I'm the only drummer. Now I'm nervous. I don't think I'm going to be able to hold up my end. It is a hairdressers' convention. There are all these women. It is supposed to be a two-hour job. We only played about a half an hour. We were just busy jumping around, cutting up, having a good time. At the end of the night, the bartender hands me a bottle of rum. Two girls have stuck their phone numbers in one of my pockets, and then Rico comes up and shoves $40 cash in the other. At that point, I threw my arm around his shoulder and said, "If you get any more work like this, don't hesitate to call me!"

You get these defining moments in your life. Ten seconds either way, it wouldn't have happened. That is mine. It was my association with people from that area of the city that things started to open up for me. I actually had a chance to start playing music. I caught on late in life to a lot of things because I had lived a pretty sheltered life. It has paid off a lot.

A Nicer One

When I was growing up, New Orleans was overwhelmingly Roman Catholic. As a matter of fact, if you knew someone who wasn't Catholic, you looked at them kind of strange. My mother, Betty, was a semi-orphan. Her mother died when she was five-years-old. Her father worked for the railroad and didn't seem to have much concern for the family. She was pretty much raised in a convent on the downtown side of Elysian Fields between St. Claude and Claiborne. She stayed with her sister in the convent dormitory during the school week, and then they would get on the streetcar to go stay with her aunts Uptown for the weekend.

My dad, Raymond, was raised in the Uptown area. I always heard him talk about St. Henry's around Napoleon and Magazine. He was the oldest out of four boys. His father was a cop, and I think my grandfather was too. From what I gathered, they both had problems with alcohol. My father was a pretty good football player. His big dream was he wanted to play in the NFL, but he had to drop out his first year of high school to support the family. His father wasn't bringing home enough money.

When he was 17, he wanted to join the Navy. His mother wouldn't sign for him, but she agreed he could join the Merchant Marines. Her brother was a seaman and they could ship out together. At 18, he got his draft notice, and was stationed in the Army in Europe. My mom was working at the telephone company and when he got back, they started going out and got married in 1948.

My earliest memory of where I lived was on Marengo Street, right off of Magazine, in a double camelback. My grandparents lived on one side, and my mom and dad were living on the other. Once he got married and had children, my father was focused on the family. He put in his eight-hour day at work with Boh Brothers. Back then, the only work Boh didn't get was work he didn't want. The city was dumping all kinds of work his way. Every new subdivision coming up in the suburbs or in New Orleans East, Boh got. My father was in the pipe gang—putting the drainage and sewerage in. When he got off work, he came home. No stopping at the bar for a couple of drinks. His focus was working on our house. He always wanted to get a nicer one. The first house my father bought was on North Prieur in the St. Roch neighborhood. We stayed there for four years while he worked on it. In 1960, he sold it to buy a house in one of the first subdivisions out in Metairie. We stayed out there until my mom wanted to be back by her family who raised her.

Music Lessons

We moved back Uptown around Camp and Jena. My mother's aunts had a piano in their house and somebody could play it to some degree or another. Before TV, you had to entertain yourself. You had a radio and you had a piano. My mother was determined that we would all play piano, which is not what I wanted. She got us signed up to take lessons from Ms. Cross. This lady had hardening of the arteries or she was just out of it. But kind of weird. We kept trying to tell her that something wasn't right, but she wouldn't believe us until she got a call from Ms. Cross reminding her we had lessons the next day. Not only did we not have lessons the next day but it was three o'clock in the morning. It finally hit home for my mom.

She found a nun. Nuns continued to play a big part in my mother's life. Every year one of the Christmas presents I get for her is a calendar "Nuns Having Fun." And she loves them. She finds a nun at Good Counsel on Louisiana to take lessons from. She had a big steel ruler and she'd crack me across the knuckles if I didn't have my hand arched right. I like to tell people I developed a real good vibrato from that! I'm kidding. I wasn't comfortable with it. I didn't see myself really achieving anything.

I started middle school at St. Stephen's. The church played an important part in everybody's life in your younger years. In addition to going to Catholic school, it was a social outlet. Once you reached a certain age, they had the Catholic Youth Organization (CYO) dances put on by different parishes. This particular Saturday night, it might be at St. Stephen's and the following Saturday night it would be at St. Henry's. Hearing the bands like the Contours, Deacon John and the Ivories, Irma Thomas, and Benny Spellman and seeing the interaction between the musicians and the crowd put the bug in me to where I wanted to be a musician.

I really wanted to play guitar. That didn't sit well with my mother, but I was finally able to convince her to let me quit piano. I took over things myself. After I started working a little summer job at a snoball stand, I bought my first guitar from a hawk shop off Rampart Street. This real piece of trash. You had to use a pair of vice grips to make a chord. I found Werlein's—a famous music store in New Orleans on Canal Street. They had a big sheet music selection. They sold musical instruments. They had lessons. A repair facility. It was a mecca. If you were in music in some way, shape, or form you ended up at Werlein's for something. I took group lessons there and private lessons with a guy who played with one of these R&B bands on the CYO circuit. He kept a metal tuning fork. If you didn't' have your hand just right—bang!—across the knuckles. I guess corporal punishment was a big part of growing up in New Orleans.

A drawing of Werlein's at 600 Canal Street. The music store opened in 1905. In 1932, it sponsored a music contest at Loyola Stadium, which was recognized as the largest school music event in the country. Inspired by its success, the state of Louisiana decided to develop a band program for the public schools. Image from a detail of a New Orleans Jazz Club's *The Second Line* cover.

Integrating Catholic Schools

I started high school at De La Salle in 1963. It was right after the Catholic high schools were integrated by Archbishop Joseph Rummel. Obviously, it was a big thing to do. How was all of this going to play out? Growing up in an all-white household, I didn't really have a lot of connections with black people. It was frightening in a way it shouldn't have been. It was a concern.

I'll give you a story that showed me how screwed the whole thing really was. My father was up in arms about it. I thought he was not going to let me go to De La Salle, which I really wanted to do, because of the integration thing. I became very upset. It wasn't too long after that we stepped outside to go somewhere, and this black man comes walking by the house. My dad says, "Hey so-and-so, how are you doing?" And the man said, "How are you doing?" And keeps walking. I said, "Who was that?" My dad told me the man's name. It was like, "What is your connection?" He said, "We used to play together as kids."

It turns out integration became a non-event for me. We had one black guy in the class. His name was Richie Cezanne. I had no contact with the guy whatsoever. He was in advanced classes and I was down at the bottom. But today my heart really goes out to this guy for what he had to deal with for four years. He was pretty much ostracized. Years later, I talked with Kenneth Ferdinand about how he was one of the first black students to go to Ben Franklin. He said he lasted about a year, and transferred to St. Augustine. Listening to him put a lot of that in perspective for me.

I don't know if it is a good thing or a bad thing that I was in the generation where all this started to change.

I look back on it today and think of the things I could have done and should have done, but social pressure keeps you from doing it—you didn't want to step out and do something your peers were going to judge you by. That is how ludicrous the whole thing really was. Then to see the situation with my father. He grew up playing with black people. So why was this thing such a big deal?

Just sitting here now trying to go over it, the only thing I can see is the fact that you were being told you had to. I'm kind of concerned by the look on your face—it is a lot to deal with. This is really getting to be…it is touching a nerve in a lot of ways. It is good because it is forcing me to deal with it. I'm sitting here telling you this whole thing. It eats at me, but I am not going to get over it unless I talk about it. Your high school years are tough. You're changing, you're maturing. All the stuff you have to deal with in those four years, multiplied by what he had to deal with. No support whatsoever. No friends. How did he deal with that, man?

Like a Machine

During that whole time frame, I wasn't too happy of a camper. In a way…how's the best way to word it? It's possible that I realized that what I thought I wanted out of life was not what was preordained. I think I was getting a few inklings that what this is going to lead me to is not really what I want, but I wasn't exactly sure.

During Mardi Gras, my parents loved to take us to the parades on St. Charles Avenue, not far away from our house. When those high school bands would pass by—the drum and bugle corps—I wanted to be in it something awful. The American Legion posts would sponsor them, and it was all brass horns and different drums. There was the Metairie Rebels. There was Star Duster. They had the hats with cavaliers with the one

side up and the big plume. Every single one of them had sunglasses on even at night. The horns would rest between songs, but those drums didn't stop. You could just feel the pressure. It was like a machine throwing something at you. It got your blood boiling.

I went to the band director at De La Salle and expressed my interest about wanting to join the band. Brother Eugene was a real old gruff guy. He asked, "What do you want to play?"
"I'd like to play drums."
"Okay, sign this form." I reached for the pen. He said, "Wait a minute. You're left handed." I said, "Yes." He shook his head. "No way."
I looked at him. "I'm not adding a left-handed drummer in my drum line."

Back then, you wore a sling with the drum resting on your leg, and that's where the traditional grip comes into play that they teach kids because you had to learn how to play off to one side. It is a very awkward feel. If I joined, all the drummers would have been hanging their drum off to one side, and mine would have been on the other. It didn't make any difference in playing style because, in my mind, I just had to flip things around. But he didn't want it messing up the way his drum line looked. He was so negative I just wanted to get away from the guy, but it may have worked to my favor. If I had started drums back then, by the time I had gotten through college, I probably would have been burned out and wanted nothing to do with it. Everything happens for a reason.

Deferrment

In the late 1960s, my family went through a lot of changes. I graduated from high school, and our house had been broken into a couple of times. My mom's aunts starting dying out, her other family members began to move away, and my dad came down with an aggressive form of colon cancer. We did surgery that was somewhat successful, and the doctor said, "We're rolling the dice here, we'll see what happens." It was during the Vietnam War and my friends were being drafted.

I'm not going to say I was for the Vietnam War, but I was buying what they were selling at the time: "We were there for a reason." The anti-war movement wasn't that big of a thing in New Orleans like it was in other parts of the country. It might have had to do with how the local economy was tied to the war effort. The whole Port of Embarkation was on Poland Avenue, and Avondale was where all the boats were built. As a matter of fact, there is an old Ford truck plant down here on River Road. They used to build trucks between World War II and Vietnam and ship them to Central and South America.

I remember seeing the protests on the news and thinking, "Why are these people doing this type of thing? I don't understand this at all." My friends' older brothers had been drafted for the Korean War in the 1950s. Vietnam seemed a natural progression of things. After high school, I wanted to go into the Army and fly helicopters. My father and I had a knock-down, drag-out fight over the issue, because he wanted me to go to college. He knew what the Army was and what was going on at that time. A lot more than I realized. Finally, I made a plan. I thought, "Great, I'll start college at the University of New Orleans, I'll flunk out, they'll take me in the Army." There will be no more arguing over this thing.

When I was in college at UNO, they kept sending me my 2S college deferment, but I wasn't carrying enough hours to keep it. I almost went to down to the Draft Board to demand my 1A so they would draft me. This was in 1968—you know where my behind would have wounded up.

I was adamant about wanting to go into the military until the whole My Lai massacre came to light. On March 16, 1968, a U.S. Army unit under Second Lieutenant William Calley wiped out a village suspected of harboring Viet Cong guerillas. Between 300 and 500 unarmed civilians, including children, women, and the elderly, were killed. It was a helicopter pilot, Hugh Thompson, Jr., who saw what was going on, and tried to protect the civilians. He then reported what he saw. The more I learned about it, the more it sounded like something I didn't want any part of, that's for damn sure. That's when I changed my whole mind about going to the service. And that's when I was sent my 1A.

Now I have a 1A and I'm twenty years old. They decided they were going to come up with the lottery where they picked birthdays. They picked my number 353. There was no way I was going to the service at that point. I had ridden the thing out. I didn't dodge the draft, the draft dodged me. And that's the best thing that ever happened to me. My father was obviously totally right to try to keep me out.

St. Bernard Parish

In 1970, we wound up in the Chalmette area of St. Bernard Parish. Boh Brothers had a lot of work going on there, and my parents decided to build a house from scratch. It could have been anywhere, but that is where roots finally took for us. I've been out there ever since.

White people who lived in the Ninth Ward area had moved out to Chalmette. That migration started after World War II with the G.I. Bill and FHA loans that went towards new construction and not refurbishing old houses, but it really built up during the 1960s. There are a number of reasons why white people left to the suburbs, but number one was the integration thing. They were scared and didn't want to deal with it, but with that migration, they missed what this city is really about. I'm willing to bet most white people

aren't aware of how important the black community has been to this city from the get-go.

The house in Chalmette was far away from UNO and I needed a car. But I also wanted a nicer guitar. I busted my butt one summer getting together enough money, but it didn't sit well with my father that I had become a bedroom guitarist, trying to play Beatles and Jerry and the Pacemakers music. It was causing tension at home, so I told my parents I'd take a year off school and work with my dad to save up enough money to buy a car. I never went back. I had some self-imposed pressure to keep working because my dad was sick and I thought I may have to become head of the household.

You don't want to hear all the stories of what they used to do to you on the job. You pee on your own time. Get your ass back out there. You better not pull out anything to eat before 12 o'clock either. There's a water barrel over there if you are thirsty, that's it. It started to change in the 1970s when federal law mandated that you've got to take breaks every few hours. But back then, they could run you ragged. Every so often my dad would get really sick again and have to go in for operations. But by the time I was 26 years old, I finally realized he's not going anywhere any time soon, but it's time for me to move out. I stayed nearby because I still had that mindset that I needed to be around. While I was waiting for him to go, he hung in there for 30 years.

To this day, I admire the living hell out of my father. There are a lot of things that we didn't agree on obviously, but that man would outwork me until real late in the situation. He was really driven. I worked for Boh Brothers for 10 years. The only time I didn't work was when it rained. I was off every weekend, but Monday through Friday, my ass was out there. No vacations. My dad wasn't getting any vacation. It just didn't register with me to do it. When I finally took off a week, I was like, "What am I doing? Am I going to lose my

An excerpt from a letter that a soldier, Ron Ridenhour, wrote to members of Congress after collecting accounts of the My Lai massacre from other soldiers. Ridenhour went on to become a journalist in New Orleans. Other American soldiers attempted to stop the massacre, including a helicopter pilot, Hugh Thompson, Jr., who evacuated some civilians and later reported what he had witnessed. Image courtesy of the Nation Institue.

job?" Real insecure about the whole thing. In a way, they had you brainwashed that if you couldn't work for them, you couldn't work for anybody. You were going to starve to death.

Storyville Stompers

When I first started playing music I didn't think I would ever do it full-time. The Tumblers was a lot of fun, but I didn't start to get serious until we officially became the Storyville Stompers in October of 1981. We were on a job and somebody come up and said, "You all are pretty good." We weren't!
"Who are you?" I started to say, "We are the Pair-A-Dice…" and that is as far as I got. Rico said, "No, we are the Storyville Stompers Brass Band."
I said, "Oh! We got a name!"
That is when we became the Storyville Stompers. I didn't like the name for a long time, but history and geography were my favorite subjects in college. You start thinking about the the old songs and how the lyrics all came about in a particular time frame. Why these catch phrases? You start making connections.

Take *Basin Street Blues*:
Now won't you come along with me
To the Mississippi?
We'll take a trip to the land of dreams
Blowing down the river, down to New Orleans

The band is there to meet us
Old friends to greet us
That's where the light and the dark folks meet
A heaven on earth, they call it Basin Street

Basin Street was on the edge of Storyville, which was the redlight district in New Orleans where a lot of early jazz musicians played, and its what our band is named after.

When I started to play real gigs, I realized I better start studying and learn what the hell my part really is in this thing. I got a hold of Brenda Catillo's telephone number. She lived out in Chalmette and taught in the Catholic schools around town. Her area of interest was percussion. I started out studying movement with her, which is the basic starting point with

drums. It is like learning how to play scales on horns. As a matter of fact, she is still the music director at St. Mary's Dominican.

At the same time, the Stompers were playing at Molly's. It was a watering hole for the press and regular Quarter residents. If you're not looking for it, you'll walk right past it, except on Halloween night and Friday before St. Patrick's Day you will definitely know where it's at because of the huge crowds. The guy who owned Molly's, Jim Monaghan, was from Zanesville, Ohio. He was just one of those people that got the whole idea of what the culture of the French Quarter was about. He celebrated the whole thing, and we called him the Unofficial Mayor of Decatur Street. He got involved in politics and was backing some political candidates. That's where he started using us. We'd played for rallies, and then he said, "Look, every year I take an entourage of people up to Washington, D.C. for the Krewe of Louisiana. I'm having a good time with you guys. How about I take you?" Hell yeah! I'd never been there in my life. He stuck eight people into two rooms.

The Krewe of Louisiana was the Olympia Brass Band's gig. To a certain degree, we were infringing on their turf, but we really weren't there to do much of anything but play after-hours parties—wherever Jim wanted to turn us loose. But I also got to sneak in and watch Olympia doing their thing. They had a very, very distinctive uniform—red pants with stripes, a military cut jacket, hats, the whole deal. I'm sure I'd seen them elsewhere, but now I was focused on this type of music. It was a natural transition from the whole drum and bugle corps desires that I had when I was younger. But now, all of a sudden, here it is in a different form. It's possible this time. The Olympia had a green room and invited us to come in and hang out with them. That was another education right there—just to hear them telling stories about all the traveling they did. It was definitely my rumination. This is all I wanted.

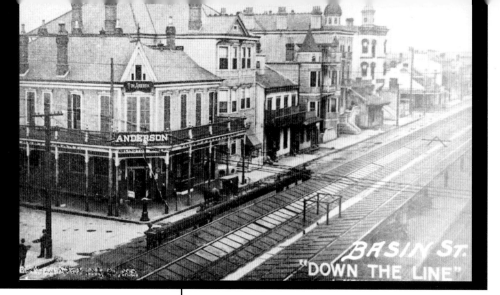

A photograph of Basin Street in New Orleans, courtesy of the Hogan Jazz Archive. Sidney Bechet worked in Storyville as a young man. In his autobiography he argued that the place where musicians played shouldn't be confused with the essence of the music: *You know, you take a woman. Say she's got a light dress on; maybe it's summer—if you look through her dress and see she's a woman, it's not her fault. That's your mind putting something on something very natural; that's a fact and shouldn't be made out of shape. And that's Jazz too...the [blues that really enter your heart], they're about sad things—about loving someone and it turns out bad, or wanting and not knowing what you're wanting. Something sincere, like loving a woman, there's nothing dirty in that.* Both black and white musicians worked in Storyville, but it was designated as a redlight district where the clientele was exclusively white. The neighborhood was torn down in the late 1930s to build a segregated white public housing development called Iberville. After integration, it experienced its own white flight and became a black neighborhood. Despite protests from residents, the majority of the buildings were torn down for redevelopment in 2014.

Traditional jazz gave me the opportunity to play. If I had forced myself to stay with rock and roll and the guitar, I'd still be banging on chords in the bedroom. At the same time, I was exposed to a different culture than what I grew up with. A lot of people considered trad jazz music a black domain. Does it mean white people can't play it? Maybe a little different. It's something to be appreciated. What is the best way to put it? If you wanted to learn the music, you had to learn about black culture—that is where you went. You start talking with the guys in Olympia. You begin to realize there is a whole part of New Orleans you never really are exposed to as a white person living in the suburbs just coming into the city every once in a while. There was a whole lot more you were missing. The faster you can throw off that separation of black and white, the faster you start to learn a whole lot of things.

Sitting down talking to people, barriers start to fall. You realize you are two human beings. I started growing as a person from doing this. I don't know if anybody could sit around and stand to talk to me if I was still on the other career path I was on. Do you ever run across people who could tell you how many years, months, weeks, days, hours, and seconds until they retire? Do you ever find these people interesting to talk to? It's a whole negative outlook on life.

I decided to leave Boh Brothers and work in the plants along the River. I worked "turnarounds" where you work 12 hours a day for months at a time, and then the plant shuts down and you have a long period off. There were times when I was completely available to play music, and others where I couldn't play at all. I realized if I stuck with that schedule, I'd probably lose my place with the Stompers. Keep turning down enough gigs, they are going to move on to someone else purely out of necessity. I sat down one day and crunched the numbers to see how much I was actually making playing music versus doing construction—it turned out to be right about the same amount. I thought, "Well, then I'm going to go with the thing that really makes me happy."

My family was all blue-collar workers, and that was expected of me. It was ultimately not what I chose. I think there are some things I did that my family was not too happy about. I don't regret it, even though my family doesn't understand what this really is. Doors started opening up for me. I had a chance to travel. I've been to China. I've been to Japan. I've been to Italy. That wasn't going to happen doing construction work and doing grunt jobs around town.

I still fight the mind of "the sure thing." That will play with me big time. Big time. As work is coming in, I'm usually pretty happy-go-lucky, but when we go for a week or two without a job, I start thinking I wish I could have set a steady day thing that gave some stability to everything and then still have the time to play music. Even though you work a normal day job, it can be what defines who you really are. You pay the bills with this thing, but you really are a musician at heart.

Culture Shock

One thing I learned early on about brass band music is you're either going to get into it and have a good time, or you're gonna get way from the situation real quick. I'll give you a real instance of the culture shock of the whole thing. We get hired to go do an Indian casino up in Kenosha, Wisconsin. We're gonna do what we normally do: We're gonna start out at point A, march around the facility, and stop a couple different places to play.

We get set up and all these curious people are looking at us: "What's all of this?" The minute we start moving through that casino, people were running to get out of the way. It's like we're invading this place. They're used to, "We're this, you're that." And the band is saying, "We're all this now." Some people have a tough time coming to grips with it, but most, by the second set, are coming a little bit closer to the whole deal. By the second night, they're all on top of you.

At the Convention Center in New Orleans, usually we're left to our own devices. We walk around and play for people trying to conduct business at booths. I love watching the expressions on their faces as we parade by. Some people are like, "Get the hell away from me. I'm trying to make the sale." Other people drop everything they're doing, and start dancing and shooting pictures. We stop and play for these people. This year, one convention sent a map to us of the route we could walk. We had this loop we had to keep making. It was like a Nascar race. They didn't want you veering off. No matter how much that guy four booths down cut up, hoping for us to come by, we couldn't do it.

At these tradeshows, people are often more concerned about their own little world, the business types—"We want you here, but we really don't want you here" approach. "You just stand back in that corner there, make a little noise. Don't get too loud." You know you're not a little string quartet in the background, but you back down on the volume, have fun amongst one another, and make the paycheck. If they aren't paying attention, you can use the time to stretch rehearsal tunes. You might ask why we practice when we've been playing the songs for so long. How many times can you

The Storyville Stompers in front of Molly's on the Market at 1107 Decatur in the French Quarter, circa 1980s. Photograph courtesy of Woody Penouilh.

play old standards like the *Saints* or *Down by the Riverside*, and not want to put a gun to your head? But that's the beauty of the music. You don't have to play it the same way. If you have a real creative horn player up there like Will Smith and he starts goofing this thing, the old song all of a sudden becomes real fun to play. Right now when we play the *Saints,* I throw my snare off and play a rumba beat. We've dressed it up again.

Rugalator

One year we were up in Washington, D.C. and the guys came back to the hotel. Some music store was going out of business and they bought a whole box of those little plastic egg shakers. It came to me that everything is on one pitch. It would sound better if they had different pitches. I decided I was going to make one. Bigger. To condense the story, I came up with the idea to use a coconut. When I had a coconut with a bunch of bbs in there, I thought, "I'll paint it."

One day I was painting and listening to the organ player Jimmy Smith's version of *I Got My Mojo Working.* I heard this line, "I got my rugalator working." He says it five times. It must have been the power of suggestion. I thought, "Rugalator? What the hell is rugalator?" Then I looked at the shaker in my hand and thought, "That's what this is!" I wound up with the nickname Rugalator Ray from a bunch of people. A lot of people know me by that.

I wound up with a whole box of acrylic paints and way too much free time on my hands. One rugalator became 50. It was one of those deals. If somebody really liked it, "Well, here is one for you." People started saying, "You've got to sell these things." Well, how are you going to put a price tag on them?

I can't. How long does it take to make one of these things? How do I shorten up the time frame? It is too much to worry about. If somebody does something

Both pages: In 2014, the Phunny Phorty Phellows hired the Storyville Stompers to accompany them on their ride down St. Charles Avenue. The band then rejoined the group of revelers for a set at Vaughn's in the Ninth Ward. In these photographs taken in the reflection of the streetcar, Bruce Brackman and Steve Burke; Ray Lambert, and Woody wait to usher in the official beginning of the Carnvial season. Photographs by Bruce Sunpie Barnes.

nice for me, some people bake cookies. This is something I figured I'd do for other people.

Around this time, my wife was in the Army Reserves, and I brought her uniforms over to the Bywater Cleaners. The lady there asked me what I did. I said I was a musician. She said, "Oh yeah, a musician from San Francisco just moved across the street over there." It was Hart McNee, a bari sax and bass flute player. Two very interesting instruments for a little short guy to be playing.

Somehow we crossed paths on a job. I'd wind up picking him up because he didn't have a car. He didn't mind leaving early like I like to do. We got to be really good friends. The more you talked to Hart, the more profound things you learned about him. Hart could not lie. Be careful asking him anything because you are going to hear his honest to God truth. If you said, "Hart, we recorded something. How does this sound?"

"This sucks, man. You are capable of doing something better than this."

One day, we were talking about saxophones, and I said, "I didn't have much interest in saxophones until I heard this guy John Klemmer." He said, "Oh, yeah. I used to play with him in Chicago. We used to jam in his basement." Hart played with Alvin Bishop, Boz Skaggs, Steve Miller. And as he put it, none of these guys would be anywhere today if he hadn't played with them because they really got big right after he quit the band. He would leave the band and these guys would catch fire.

He had a phobia about flying. He was supposed to go on tour one time and he was sitting on a plane. He said he had an epiphany: "This thing is nothing but a whole bunch of fuel, I'm sitting in a tube, and it could go off at any minute and I'm dead." He panicked, and he couldn't get back on a plane after that. That's one of the reasons why he stopped playing with people because he didn't want to fly.

It was Hart who told me about the vodou shop that opened up on Piety Street. We walked over there and I met Sallie Ann Glassman. She was a girl from Maine that became a vodou priestess. There has got to be a story there! I became pretty intrigued with the whole thing. You want to really see vodou? Go to a Roman Catholic high mass. There's some vodou right there, Jack. I got interested in the cultural ties between Haiti and the city, and the art involved in the religion. I got Sallie's book, *Voodoo Visions*, and studied the *veves*… they're pretty hip. Let's see if I can do something with that. I started painting the rugalators.

After Katrina, my house in St.Bernard Parish was gone, but I found out the Stompers are actually getting work. What the hell am I going to do? I'm stuck up in Atlanta at my sister's house. I don't have any place to live. I get in touch with Hart. He had contracted cancer, and couldn't come back home because of the chemo treatments. He said, "Oh, yeah, move into my house. My ex-wife, Kate, has the key."

"Hart," I said, "I got three cats I've got to deal with."

"That's all right. Bring them there."

I stayed in the house and he came back home. I slept in the front room; he had the back bedroom. We started hanging out a whole bunch then, and I started finding out more stories about Hart that were totally amazing.

Two rugalators that Ray made for Hart and Kate.
Photographs by Bruce Sunpie Barnes.

Portrait of Hart Mcnee, by Wylie Maerklein, courtesy of Kate McNee.

HART MCNEE
ROOT MELODIES

Hart: I grew up in Chicago on the Near Northside in an area that's really kind of tony now, it wasn't so tony then, called Lincoln Park West. At 13, some friend of my mother gave me a radio because I was a teenager, which I didn't want to be. I wanted to be a kid, but there it was—what could you do? I don't want to be 63 either, but here I am.

They gave me this radio and I really hated what the teenagers of the day were listening to. I turned it to the right side of the dial where the little cheap stations were, and there were three black stations in Chicago. They were playing Otis Rush and all these blues records.

Really, it's true: When I heard that, I got a chill. The blues they were playing then was really raw and new. It was the time when a lot of working class black people were listening to blues in Chicago and white people hadn't discovered it yet. I was amazed. They'd have black preachers that would be talking like this and a half an hour later they'd be singing.

I listened to that and the first thing is, not only do you want to play that music, but you want to be those people. I wanted to be Otis Rush. I subsequently made a record with Otis Rush 20 years later. Wow, man!

My mother bought me a tenor sax. It was Cahn with a split B and a B flat. It was a really good horn. I started honking on it, but I was a very, very lazy kid. I really regret how lazy I was as a young kid. Some friends and I started playing in my basement. We thought it was cool. In the old days, when you saw those Saturday night horror movies, they show some guy going, "Heaaaa! Now we're going to…" and he would always be out of some basement. I learned a lot of blues and I learned harmony from the guitarist. He taught me how chords move and the relationships and the keys. The chords are really complicated. It's like a puzzle. Then I went to a music teacher,

Lillian Pangish, who was a classical clarinet player, and she taught me to read. I was very lazy. But you can't talk to kids, they won't listen to you. Especially if you are 63.

All My Secrets

After high school, I got drafted. I tried to get out of it as a conscientious objector. Though my father was in the Second World War, we are peace and love and all that stuff and I don't believe in war. Although I do believe it happens, I don't believe it's a good idea. But they wouldn't go for that—they were drafting everybody. They needed so many bodies. I had my parents drop me off at the place where you do the physical and I went to a friend's house and hid out for two months. I thought about, "Do I want to go to jail?" No. "Do I really want to live in Canada?"

I've since found out that parts of Canada are really nice, but I didn't know that at the time so I went back and they drafted me. I had a list of all the drugs I took. It was about 20 drugs, including DMT—that stuff will knock you out, it's like instant LSD. It's like when you are watching a presidential debate and it's on all the channels. You go from Channel 6 to Channel 4 and it's the same, but it's different. That's what it was like: Boom! "Oh my God! I'm not on the same channel as everybody else."

I gave the draft board this long list of drugs, and they said, "That's okay." Which I, subsequently, added other items to that list after I got out of the Army. Taking heroin, I wouldn't recommend it. Heroin users are pretty nice people. The problem is, if you misjudge the dosage, you die. You're thinking, "How stupid am I to be doing this?" I got Hepititis C and I regret that. I regret my drinking because my behavior was bad when I drank and I drank a lot, a lot, a lot. Now I smoke weed—that's it. Oh, what am I saying, I'm strung out on morphine as we speak! I forgot about that! I'm taking morphine because I got cancer.

In the Army, I went into guided missles. I got a confidential clearance because they could put nuclear warheads on these things. They are supposed to be secret. We'll talk about that later. I guess all my secrets are obsolete now. At the place that they trained me at, they had this big sign that said, "We train the free nations of the world." At the time, they were training India and Pakistan, and they trained a number of Arab nations and Israel all in the same building, but not the one I was in.

They threw a guy out of my unit because he had a grandparent in Yugoslavia at the time Tito was still there. My father used to do cartoons for the Socialist Labor newspaper. The bad guy would look like the guy from a Monopoly set with the top hat—the Industrialist. There would be a guy who would be the worker. And then there would be some lame joke. Anyway, he published in these radical things. My mother had joined the Communist Party in the 1930s. I figured, "This is it, man, they are going to take me out of the missile unit and put me in some frontline infantry," but they never did find out.

I hated the basic training. They basically scream at you all the time and make you feel like an idiot in front of everybody. They make you feel like a fool so you want to disappear. That was difficult. In fact, they are still training for World War I. At nighttime, they have these series of trenches and holes and a trench on the other side about 300 hundred yards away. There is mud and barbed wire, and bombs exploding. They have machine guns firing live rounds with tracer bullets so you can see them, and the machine gun is on a bar so it can't depress low enough to hit you unless you stand up and jump around like a fool. I was so tired of people yelling at me that I crawled out in the middle of the night. We got like 400 guys going through this thing, and I got halfway through and I laid there for about 20 minutes and went, "Ahhh" because nobody could scream at you.

Another bad thing I did in basic training was the sargeant

Left: Hart playing bari sax with the Society of St.Cecilia. Named after the patron saint of music, the group organizes a parade that begins in the Bywater on Carnival day. Photograph by Jenny Bagert. *Right:* Hart with Kate McNee and their daughter Lily at St. Cecilia, courtesy of Kate McNee.

said, "Go in the gas chamber" and I said, "I'm not doing it." I was terrified. I'm claustrophobic and the phobia is really strong. The saregent gets an officer because only an officer can give you an order. They bring over a lieutenant, and I said "I do know you can put me in jail. I just know one thing: I'm not going in there." That's how the fear was. I basically put everything on the line and they said, "Oh, to hell with it." They ignored me.

You Can't Get Out

Finding out I had cancer was the worst moment in my life. And cancer—in my case, it had moved. One guy said I had six to 18 months to live. Man, I just sat there and cried like a baby. Like a little baby. I was living a very healthy life. I hadn't had a drink in 18 years. I never had a drink in New Orleans. I was running three miles every other day, lifting weights. It's like claustrophobia—the same fear of not being able to get out.

At first you feel like, "Oh my God, why me? Why me?" And then you go around like a zombie, and you are just numb. And then you get to a point where you are like, "Okay, my children love me. Even my ex-wife loves me. All my ex-girlfriends love me." I went out and made a CD of music that I wanted to do. They are tunes I was playing with Soul. We were doing a bunch of Thelonious Monk tunes, there are a couple of tunes

that I wrote, and then there were a couple of orisha songs that I think are very beautiful.

Root Melodies

A friend of mine, Michael Skinkus, learned to play bata drums, which are the sacred drums of Cuba. They play very complicated interlocking rhythms that are in 6/8 and 4/4 at the same time. It's all memorized—you aren't jamming. There are points when you kind of do, but it's all very meticulous because the idea is that it's religious drumming and if you do it wrong, the orisha—that spirit—will not appear. Michael taught me how to do the okonkolo on the smallest drum, which is the simplest drum. I learned when I was in my late 50s, and I thought it was great to learn a whole new aspect of music that late. It was hard to learn, but man, when I learned, my playing is much more accurate rhythmically.

In Santeria, they don't want to change the songs. Of course, they will eventually change because they aren't written down, but they will change very slowly because it's like a formula: you have to sing this song, do this dance, and play this rhythm, and then the spirit will possess someone. What you have are melodies that are very ancient. The Yoruba religion predates Christianity. It's very much like Greek mythology. All of the Greek ones have counterpoints in the vodou and

Left: *Milagros* [miracles] on the wall of Kate McNee's house in the Bywater. **Right:** Kate McKnee at home. Photographs by Bruce Sunpie Barnes.

Santeria religions. They are like root melodies. They are very simple but they are very eerie. They sound like Chinese or the old Irish melodies with the flutes and Gaelic. I find that these melodies are real essential. It must be something that comes out of the human spirit.

Once I had the CD, I said, "Well, I'm ready. I can die." And then the doctors said, "Maybe we can keep you going for awhile." So then I had to get out of that mode, and go into the fighting mode, which is tough because it involves a lot of unpleasant medical things that they do to you. Now they give me four years, which I don't know...is that a lot or a little?

More Than a Physical Product

I'm supposedly an atheist. My parents were atheists. I mocked religion as a young man, but later it didn't bother me that much. A friend of mine died very young. He asked me, "Do you believe that music is more than the notes and the sounds that you play? It's more than that physical product you create that moves molecules that move in the air? You have played music for so long for so little money, for so little reward. You basically chose a life of poverty. Of course, everybody accepts that there is an emotional response to music. Is it more than that?"

I said, "I think there is. In a way, it's like my religion. I believe that there is something spiritually there."

He said, "Then you believe in God in a sense." I think I must believe that there is something more. Now, if I thought that it healed, I would be playing music every day, man, trying to heal myself. I think positive emotional experiences are good for you, but I do believe that music is more than that. I do think that it—I don't know how to say it. One thing, if you could say it, you wouldn't have to play it. Words are a different thing. Music is a different thing. The answer is really a sound.

What happens after you die? I'm afraid. I really am afraid. I've sat next to both of my parents at the moment of their death and the second they died, they looked different. It changes from my father to a body. I'm having to face my death, and I don't know how I'm going to do with it because I don't believe in an afterlife. I find that highly improbable.

I do believe in the soul. I don't believe that the soul lasts forever or stays the same. I think the soul is like a verb. I think our language screws us up. If you say "soul" then that's a noun, the soul is an action, it's a movement, it's a process. And it's not a thing at all. It's something holding together, events in your life. Something that you are. But it's not a noun; it doesn't go anywhere. It never was anywhere.

This excerpt was provided courtesy of StoryCorps, a national nonprofit whose mission is to provide people of all backgrounds and beliefs with the opportunity to record, share, and preserve the stories of our lives. Hart McNee and Henry Griffin recorded with StoryCorps in New Orleans in 2006. For more information see: storycorps.org.

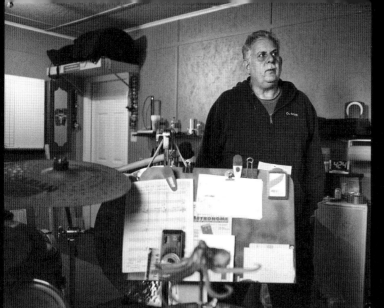

Left: Ray in his studio at home in Old Arabi. ***Right:*** Ray's studio with one of Hart's paintings next to the door. Photographs by Bruce Sunpie Barnes.

Ray: After Katrina, we started going to the house of Hart's ex-wife, Kate McNee's for movies on Monday night. She's a really beautiful person. Everybody would throw a little food together. We spent the first hour bitching and moaning about things, and then we'd put the movie on. It was therapy, entertainment, and dinner all rolled into one.

Kate came up with these really interesting films. And then I noticed that she had a big old thick book with almost every movie that's ever been made. What's her big interest in film? Her father is Jim Clark, a film editor who won an Academy Award for his work on *The Killing Fields*. It's a film about the U.S.'s involvement in Cambodia during the Vietnam Era, and the discovery of Pol Pot's mass execution of more than two million Cambodians. One of these moments like when Ron Ridenhour wrote a letter to Congress about the My Lai massacre.

One night Kate surprised us, and who is sitting in her living room but her father. And in his honor she went out and rented *Day of the Locust*, which Jim worked on with film director John Schlesinger. It's a film based on a Nathanael West novel about a strange group of people who gravitated to Hollywood's movie industry. We all sat around watching it with her father—our own group having gravitated to Kate.

One Sunday, we were sitting around at the Feelings Cafe for breakfast while Kate was working there. I looked around. It's all the people who were in the Movie Night Club or were soon to become, and I quickly realized I was the only person born in New Orleans. Every single other person was born somewhere else. I said, "I got something to ask y'all. I'm from here. I'm born and raised down here. I know exactly why I'm back. None of you are born and raised here. Why did you all bother to come back?" They all looked at me like I was crazy.

Their response was, "Because this is home and this is going to continue to be our home." It was so profound. To me, many people who are transplants who moved down here make better New Orleanians than people whose family is from here but live in the suburbs. They've chosen to be here for this.

At that point, I was like, "You know what? It's going to be all right. It's going to be more than all right." I really had the spirit of optimism. You know, I thought maybe we can sell the place in St. Bernard Parish and move to the Bywater. I enjoyed being with these people. I was thinking about that and then the little SOBs on their bicycles started making their rounds, holding people up in the neighborhood. I said, "No, I'm going back down to St. Bernard Parish. I'm not going to live like this." I went back to my house in Old Arabi. In a way, it's a typical suburban home, but since I've raised the house my kitchen window looks out over the Mississippi River.

Hart passed away in 2009. He was born on Cinco de Mayo. He passed away on Bastille Day. His whole existence was about freedom. I've got a shrine downstairs set up to him. I shouldn't say shrine, but that's what it's turning into. Fortunately, I'm not the only one. There are a number of people who have done this. It's like a cult. I still like the Bywater and Marigny. They are my two favorite spots in the city. From the French Quarter down to Arabi, this is home.

Xavier playing the trumpet inside Perserverance Hall with musicians from the New Wave Brass Band. For years, his family drove him to New Orleans from Baton Rouge to attend the program.

Xavier Michel stands outside of Perserverance Hall, No. 4, the oldest Masonic Hall in Louisiana.The lodge was built in 1820 by a membership made up of people from San Domingue (Haiti). It has deep Caribbean roots, as does Xavier's father who is from the same island. In the early 1800s, the structure must have struck an amazing pose as it is situated on the edge of Congo Square and towers 45-50 feet above its surroundings. The hall served as a music venue for public and private events, including early concerts with jazz pioneers like Buddy Petit. In 2012, it continued its musical legacy when the MFAA program relocated there for its Saturday workshops. Photographs by Bruce Sunpie Barnes.

XAVIER MICHEL

Bruce: *Xavier Michel is a young trumpet player who has grown up in Baton Rouge. His grandmother, Edna Jordan Smith, was someone I'd seen for years at second lines and musical events in the city. The founder and president of the Afro-Louisiana Historical Genealogical Society, Inc., she has organized countless events on the history of plantations and the Underground Railroad.*

Edna brought Xavier to the program about a year after it got started. He was shy but very bright eyed and trying to absorb everything going on with the way the students were interacting with the band. He didn't say very much, but when we asked him what song he'd like to play, he said, **Basin Street Blues** *right away. No hesitation. We said, "All right, you start it off." He made everyone smile, and from there it became his theme song. In this interview, Ray, Xavier and Edna talk about coming to the city to learn the music.*

The Storyville Stompers' trumpet player, Will Smith, had joined the Fairview Baptist Christian Church Band at the end of the first wave of students who had come through the program. I think Will could relate to how it was a little overwhelming for Xavier to come into something that was already established, and gave him extra lessons to help him grow. Will's logical, calm demeanor was perfect for Xavier to develop their own voice and ear in the music. He has been a classroom teacher for many years, and understands the psychology and structure needed to work with young people.

Perserverance Hall No. 4 in 2012. In the early 1960s, it was one of only a few buildings preserved when the City of New Orleans tore down blocks bounded by North Villere, Dumaine, North Liberty, St. Ann, Marais, Orleans, and Basin Streets in Tremé to build a "cultural complex." 122 families (121 of them nonwhite) were forced to relocate. In the 1998, the hall became a National Park Service site. Photograph by Bruce Sunpie Barnes.

Introduction: Family Stories

Ray: Where is your family from?

Xavier: My mom is from Baton Rouge, and my dad's family is from Cape Haitian, in the north of Haiti.

Ray: Xavier, did you ever read much about that? The revolution in Haiti with Toussaint L'Ouverture?

Xavier: No.

Ray: It's part of your culture, man. It's something you should really embrace. You'll expand a whole lot more. I read a little bit about that in college—the Haitian Revolution—and it's really interesting. You've never been to Haiti though?

Xavier: No, my dad came here around 30 years ago to become a doctor.

Ray: Your dad speaks French obviously. Do you speak some French also?

Xavier: A little. My dad speaks Haitian Creole, too. I know sometimes he thinks I don't know what he's saying but I actually do!

Ray: Xavier, from when I first met you, you're talking more now! Getting more words out of there. You were pretty shy at first.

Xavier: If you can play an instrument, you can express your whole life through a song. That's how I feel.

Ray: A good way to put it, yeah. What is music but a way of communicating?

Xavier: An international language.

Ray: You may not speak the same language as someone but once you start playing music, you'll find commonality somewhere down the line.

Ray: Did you grow up in Baton Rouge?

Xavier: Yes, around Southern University. My grandma, Enda Smith, is from New Orleans. She has more contact with people with music. I grew up listening to her tell her stories. Some of her stories are interesting, and some of them are boring.

Ray: They'll get more interesting as you get older, believe me.

Left to right: Edna's father, Ed Jordan; Edna as a young girl; Edna's mother, Christine Jordan. Photographs courtesy of Edna Smith.

Edna Jordan Smith, Xavier's grandmother: I moved to New Orleans with my mother and sister after my dad died in 1942. She got the big mighty money from the company he worked for, Standard Oil, and that's what sent her down to New Orleans. We lived on Dryades—Oretha Castle Haley now—while my mother was in the Porot's Beauty School. My grandmother called me her city child. She was born in St. Francisville, and raised my mom in Baton Rouge.

St. Francisville is more of an English area. Across the river, in New Roads, it's more French. My dad came out of St. Francisville, too. He was 25 years older than my mother. She said he had a few experiences that gave him a heart condition. One my mother would laugh at, and the other I hate to talk about.

My dad had a house on Christian Street with his first wife, Tonchie, and her sisters. Tonchie died, and he started courting a woman he knew down the street.

It was late at night when he headed home after visiting this woman's house. A piece of paper started rolling along beside him. Well, he didn't pay any mind, but then it dawned on him it wasn't windy. He decided he'd try this out. He walked a little slower. And when he did, that paper got a little slower.

Then he decided to go a little faster! And it got faster. He realized something was amiss. He got to his fence, turned toward the house, and so did the paper.

He ran into the house, and his sister-in-law and her daughter, they jumped up and yelled, "Tonchie! Tonchie is in this house!" He kept running. He ran to his bedroom, jumped into his bed. Hat on, shoes on. And when he looked back at the door, he looked right into his wife's face. They said she was as tall as the door. And this was the beginning of his swollen heart.

My dad remarried and my parents only had two of us—my sister and me. My sister was born while my parents were living on Perkins Road, which is an area that was rural outside Baton Rouge. At that time, if LSU lost a football game, black people knew to stay in the house. Those young white men would go wild. They would get in cars and roam. One night, my mother was babysitting while she was pregnant, and had to walk home. These cars were passing by. She knew they were LSU boys. They swung a sack of hard pears and struck her. They found her in the morning, but she had lost the baby. And the next one, she lost a boy. That's why she decided to come to Charity Hospital in New Orleans to have me in 1934. I was

the only one who was born in a hospital instead of at home.

My father's only brother, John, lost his first wife as well, and wound up meeting somebody else. They had three girls together, and she had one who was 14 from a previous relationship. It was the end of the Works Progress Administration (WPA), and my uncle had gotten his last check. His wife got that WPA check and said, "I'm going to cash it." She stayed gone for days. Eventually she came back, but not with any money. My uncle was sitting on the porch. He started cleaning his nails with a fish knife. She went into the house and started packing her clothes.

The daughter really felt her death. She begged her mother, "Please stay, don't go." But she kept getting ready. She came out with her bags. She stopped and turned around, "Look, Mr. John ain't no white man. I'm not afraid of him."

She walked off towards LSU. He got up. The daughter yelled for her mother to run, but she turned around and met him. He had lost his mind.

My dad was coming home from Standard Oil. A crowd was in the street, including my mother. Daddy got out, and recognized his brother. He tried to stop him, but his brother cut her jugular and she fell. A man tiptoed over to her and my mom heard him say to her, "I told you I wouldn't kill you, but some man would." Oklahoma Street was the street my uncle took and he went out to the river. He got bogged up in that river. When he looked back, he could hear those sirens coming, and that's when he tried to cut his own throat. They took my uncle in the hospital, and had to put a pipe in his throat so that he could breathe.

Days later, I was in the car with my dad. He wanted to go talk to the judge about his brother at the courthouse. The only thing the judge told him was, "I'm going to try him by the neck." My mother said that must have been the thing. I can remember him coming out screaming. All he could see was his brother hanging. But they ended up putting him in Angola. He stayed there for ten years, then he lost his mind. It was these experiences that wore my dad down.

Left: Xavier with Anthony "Tuba Fats" Lacen in Jackson Square when he was two years old. *Right:* Xavier playing the trumpet in honor of his grandfather, Ed Jordan, at the Baton Rouge National Cemetery. Photographs courtesy of the Smith family.

Leaving School

Xavier: My grandmother's worked in the public libraries for a long time and taught a lot of Louisiana history. She's also taken people on tours of the Underground Railroad, but I had a hard time in school. In third grade, my mom pulled me out of school because I wasn't doing well. I was homeschooled until eighth grade. For awhile, I went to school with seven other kids, and started doing sixth grade work in third grade. Then I stopped going to that school and went to the online school on the computer. They send you your books. You click on the things that you want to learn and they tell you which pages and how to do it. Sometimes you can have class sessions where you talk to your teacher.

Ray: How many hours a day did you work online, school-wise?

Xavier: I had 24 hours to complete my work.

Ray: So you just chop the time up as you see fit. You could just work it at your own pace then. Roughly, how many hours did you spend working?

Xavier: About five. It was boring. Just at my computer screen working. I wished I were around other kids more.

Ray: Were you being home-schooled when you first started to learn to play music?

Xavier: Yes.

Ray: What kind of experience have you had with music in your family? Does anybody else play music?

Xavier: No. My grandmother likes to dance a lot, and she's been a big part of my life in playing music, but she doesn't play an instrument.

Ray: You are the only one?

Xavier: Yes.

Ray: What would possess you to do that?

Xavier: My grandmother was reading the newspaper. When I was in Philadelphia with my dad, she called and said she saw a whole bunch of these boys playing down in New Orleans and she asked me if I wanted to play. When I came home, she took me down to the program. I never knew how to play any kind of music.

Ray: Who gave you your first horn?

Xavier: My mom.

Ray: Did you ever try another instrument? Or you just picked up the trumpet and stayed right there?

Xavier: Before I wanted to play the drums.

Ray: It was a smart move, believe me. Get rid of the

drums and pick up the horn. Definitely. I tell a lot of people you can walk into City Park and shake an oak tree and ten drummers fall out. But a good trumpet player, man, you are very much in demand. You picked a good instrument.

Xavier: Usually it is the leader of the band.

Ray: True. On stage, the trumpet pretty much runs the show. That appeals to you?

Xavier: Yes.

Ray: Have you ever worked with anyone else, taking lessons, and all of the sudden something just really clicked and you made a leap in your ability to play?

Xavier: Dr. Isaac Greggs at Southern University.

Ray: What happened?

Xavier: The way he pushed me to play. My grandma arranged for me to take lessons with him. He said he wanted me to play a C scale and wanted to know what notes were in it. I didn't know any of them. I said F and G, and he got mad. He started screaming at me, "How do you know how to play trumpet?! You don't know any notes!"

I didn't want to go back to his house because he scared me. We played a couple of notes and I didn't know any of them, and he yelled at me again. I cried a couple of times because I wasn't used to anybody being that hard on me with music. Around a couple of months, I started getting used to him screaming at me, and I started playing the notes better. He was surprised at how far I came in a year.

At the program, the first song I learned how to play was *Second Line*, by Paul Barbarin. Will Smith from your band taught me *Basin Street Blues* and *St. James Infirmary*. I started liking to play the trumpet a whole lot more playing these songs.

Ray: Will is a big help, isn't he?

Xavier: Yeah. I haven't seen him lately.

Ray: Will goes out of town an awful lot. He plays with the Preservation Hall Band. That is something you might want to catch one day, too, the Preservation Hall Band.

Left : Xavier playing the trumpet with Uncle Lionel Batiste on bass drum. *Middle:* Southern Marching Band, courtesy of the Isaac B. Greggs Collection, Archives and Manuscripts Department, John B. Cade Library, Southern University and A&M College, Baton Rouge. *Right:* Xavier and Dr. Greggs. Photographs of Xavier courtesy of the Michel family.

WILL SMITH
DELIVERY OR EXPRESSION?

Will: *I can sympathize with your mom's point of view about wanting to keep you out of school for a long time. I mean, just to look at society is scary. It's scary; however, we can't keep our children away from it. They've got to live and breathe and eat. They can't stay with us for the rest of their lives. They can't. And so you have to balance keeping them from as much negativity as you can and explaining that even in a negative circumstance, you don't have to be part of it.*

I've been teaching elementary school all over Orleans Parish for 18 years, and am cross certified in special education. I was at Helen S. Edwards in the Ninth Ward when Katrina hit. After the storm, of course, they fired everybody. Since then, I've been teaching in Jefferson Parish, and am at Vic Pitre Elementary in Westwego. It was a blessing that JP was able to accommodate some of the teachers because quite a few people from Orleans wound up working there, and all the other surrounding parishes. And a lot of people didn't come back.

Let me just brag about my relationship with my kids. See, if I felt some offense towards someone and I said, "Get him," all those kids would right now beat you down to the ground. They'd eat you like a piranha until there's nothing but bones because they know I love them, and it's genuine. But teaching has changed immensely over the last couple of years, and I don't think in any way for the better. High-stakes testing has almost been its demise.

Part of teacher's professional obligation was to present materials for kids and have them be interested and fascinated in learning for the sake of learning. Now it's strictly the test. We are only concerned about our evaluations. Three negative evaluations, you're gone. I don't care if you've been there 30 years and in 31 you could retire. You're pulling your third negative evaluation, you'll be released. If a teacher is in a subject matter that does not count towards high-stakes testing like special ed or music, the evaluation is done differently. The teacher can chart his progression, and provide a self-analysis of where he projects his students can get.

Really, right now your kid means so much less to me because I ain't got time to concentrate on the one kid. It's all data-driven down to which kids have to improve in which particular areas of which subject. This kid kept doing bad in subject-verb agreement, so that's all you're focused on for that kid, and then you got another prescription for the next kid, and that's it. It's made teaching so impersonal. Go into any school and listen to teachers talk alone. They're only talking about retirement and how to get out. I find they're strangling the zest for teaching out of us. If I can last the four years I need to retire, I'm not looking back for nothing. That's partly why the Music for All Ages program was refreshing to me. It brought out the teacher in me in the best sense of the word.

I think being part of the program was good for you, too. When you started, I could tell your spirit wasn't fully into it. You had the interest, but you were struggling. You had a little

bit of a learning curve because you came after the program was started. Some of the same trumpet players had been playing longer, and I could see you could get left out. I didn't want that discouragement to happen. It was a delicate balance too, bra, because there was a spot where everybody was ready to just show off what they knew, but I wanted to slow that down. I'm like, "But it's really not what it's about either."

Many of the kids in the program were impressing me every week. But what about the other kids? I was acutely aware of that, and I wasn't gonna allow you to feel like you didn't get to accomplish anything because all the attention was being directed to somebody else. You needed more time, more repetitions, a little more space. So I tried to do that.

I started listening to you play and allowed you to play the phrase again. See, a strict disciplinarian like Dr. Greggs is likely not to want to stop at the spot of the sheet where you are making a mistake. In a marching band, there is no room for improvisation. It's not expression. It's delivery. It's already been interpreted. It's the Pledge of Allegiance, not the funky Pledge of Allegiance. I remember when you told me you were playing A Closer Walk With Thee at church, and I was helping you with phrasing. You called me up and said, "But you gotta listen now!" You put the phone down and played the phrase for me on the phone.

When you started to play Basin Street Blues, it gave you a way to express yourself in front of the other students. The song spotlights you because it's a call and answer. The first trumpet says, "Why don't you come along with me" by himself, and then everybody else goes, "Bada dah da." You played the lead lines, and then everybody else embellishes. Playing the song gave you a voice where you could feel like, "Now I'm in the class with you all." Afterwards, I could tell your spirit was more into it. That was a huge confidence builder.

Xavier played a prelude from a dirge written by Terence Blanchard for an event at Loyola University that his grandmother, Edna, organized in honor of Solomon Northup on April 12, 2014. Solomon Northup was a free person of color who was kidnapped and sold into slavery. His story of being forced to work at a plantation about 20 miles from Baton Rouge was told in the film *12 Years a Slave*. **Left:** Xavier with the descendents of Solomon Northup. **Right:** Xavier with descendents of Samuel Bass, a Canadian carpenter who helped Solomon regain his freedom. Photographs courtesy of Edna Smith.

Xavier: Now I'm at a public school in Baton Rouge. At first, I wasn't actually used to the people—the way they behaved in the public school—but I think it's been a whole lot better since I started going to a school again. I can have a whole lot more to say.

My grandmother works for the library system, and has done programs on Haitians in Louisiana, and how people speak Creole here. One time I played the trumpet at one of the events and they gave me a hundred dollars to play my favorite song, *St. James Infirmary*.

I went down to St. James Infirmary,
and saw my baby lying there.
She was stretched out on a long white table,
So cold, so pale, and fair...lying there.

Ray: The first time somebody put that cash in your pocket: "Oh, I've found myself a new calling!"

Edna: One time, I was asked by the Louisiana State Library to come and read a story about an alligator making gumbo. I added to it, making up my own story, and brought Xavier along to play a song on his trumpet at the end.

An old alligator was traveling down Highway 1 from Baton Rouge to New Orleans on River Road. That old alligator stopped in each of the little towns to get different ingredients to make his gumbo. And by the time we got to New Orleans, *the gumbo was ready, and Xavier played* Basin Street Blues. *I had all the kids get up and I was going to help them with a second line while he was playing. Those kids....they just went on. They didn't do anything. They heard the music, but they weren't accustomed to second lining.*

Xavier: I think New Orleans is more active than Baton Rouge. Baton Rouge is more of a place that you go to retire.

Ray: Being an aspiring musician do you get a chance to hear the Southern band play?

Xavier: I've been listening to Southern's marching band a lot now.

Ray: Okay, you're making a leap into that area. One year, they brought up Southern and Grambling bands for the Mardi Gras celebration in Washington, D.C. On Saturday night, they did a battle of the bands with the two bands. It was very impressive. We felt a little intimidated after that. It was something to see. It's powerful to be around a band like that. That's one of the things that used to get me when I was a kid during Mardi Gras. That's the reason I went to the parades. I didn't care about catching throws. There's something about marching down the street, and then the drum lines. It sends goose bumps up you.

Ray: Have you developed a group of friends around music? Have you bonded with some other people musically? People you like to hang with or whatever?

Xavier: In 2011, I started playing for Roots of Music in New Orleans. I played for five Mardi Gras parades, and that was an experience I'll never forget. But at first, I didn't like it. It seemed like a lot of the kids didn't like me and I thought they cursed a lot. When I was pressured to play something, it wouldn't come out the way I wanted it to come out. I started getting used to it, and playing the songs a whole lot better. The program started becoming like family to me, and I could start to relate to the other kids.

Ray: Talking about the racial thing, do you find the music is a good way for different races to work together and actually learn more about one another?

Xavier: Yes. I never went to a mixed school. It was all black.

Ray: It goes both ways. White people have to understand also. It is: people are people.

Xavier: Not all white people are the same, like Doyle Cooper. I learned some things about playing music from them.

WILL SMITH
BEYOND PROFILING

Will: *About ten years ago, Craig Klein calls me up out of the blue and says, "Will, you know the Stompers?" I said, "Yeah, sure. Woody." The only person I knew was Woody.*

He said, "Well, look, man, they need a trumpet player. They got a good bit of work They got three gigs this weekend. You want to do them and see if you'd be interested in playing with them?"

I said, "Yeah, sure." From playing with them all these years I learned a lot about how the world hasn't changed much from when I was a kid. My whole life, my mind has never been closed by what color I am. Never. But racism still exists right now. Right now. When we play these conventions with business entities from all over the world, I'm the only black face anywhere around, and if there are any people of color, they're just the token presence. I call them my cousins. Even Woody and them laugh. I say, "Damn, Woody, they got three of my cousins at this one."

Before I joined the Stompers, I had played with all the black bands for a long time. I done played ten years with the Pinstripe. I played with the Little Rascals, the Tremé, the Algiers, the Majestic. But when I started playing with Woody, my nickname became Al Hirt. Soon as I come in the Sixth Ward, "Here come Al Hirt. Beers on Al Hirt. What's up, Al?" It took awhile for that to die. I said, "No, it's Blue Hirt, bra. Cable man's paid today," and I'd pull out the blue check from Woody. And wherever Woody needs me to play, I'm going to be there.

The Stompers were all friends for 25 years before I ever joined the band, but over time, I've developed personal friendships with each one of those guys. I got keys to our trombone player,

Uncle Gerry Dallman's house.He lives near the airport so whenever I go out of town, I just pull up and he drives me. I sleep over there. I go over there and jump in his pool.

Bruce Brackman is one of my best friends in life. I used to listen to Rush Limbaugh every day until they took him off our local station. Bruce would get in my car and say, "Why you listening to that shit?" I said, "Because it's somebody else's perspective. It doesn't mean I agree with it. But if I don't listen to it, then I don't know. How can I defend why I don't agree with him? I gotta listen to that, brah." Bruce will ask, "Can you let me out?" No.

Ray is a person who's in love with the music. It's something he does out of no kind of training, and he's refined himself to a point now where he's got his own sound on snare drum. He has distinguished himself by incorporating rimming with both sides of the stick. I think Ray's a good guy for the music. He's also a good guy for building relationships between people because he doesn't give a crap who you are. He's going to talk to you until you're looking for an escape route.

One time we had to learn a school's fight song and their alma mater for a gig. I went to Ray's house to pick up the music, and I had never been there before. I got to this really fabulous little house right on the river, and we sat there all day, man, just looking at the water, talking, and playing records.

Ray and I got to be a lot better personal friends when we went to China. The other guys in the band were tall, but I was tall and black. And so everywhere I went, they took me in the backroom. Everywhere. And I can't understand a word of what they are saying so I start singing the lyrics from Clem Tervalon's Chinatown.

I met a little girl down in Chinatown, and she asked me do I speak Chinese.
Well, I told her, "No, I don't speak no Chinese, but I'm willing to learn."
Would she teach me, please?

They're like going through everything. Digging through all my stuff. I want to say, "Yes, I'm still black. That passport is valid." At the end Ray said, "I never paid attention to profiling as much as I do now."

Left to right: Woody Penouilh, Kenneth Terry, Will Smith, Jerry Anderson, Roger Lewis, Julius "Jap" McKee, and Bruce Brackman posing in front of a picture of Danny Barker at the beginning of a BMOL parade. Photograph courtesy of the Hightower family.

OSCAR
WASHINGTON

&

AURELIEN
BARNES

241

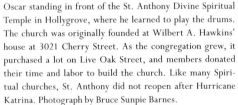

Oscar standing in front of the St. Anthony Divine Spiritual Temple in Hollygrove, where he learned to play the drums. The church was originally founded at Wilbert A. Hawkins' house at 3021 Cherry Street. As the congregation grew, it purchased a lot on Live Oak Street, and members donated their time and labor to build the church. Like many Spiritual churches, St. Anthony did not reopen after Hurricane Katrina. Photograph by Bruce Sunpie Barnes.

Inside St. Anthony, an altar with food, candles, flowers, and statues of saints. Photograph courtesy of the Washington family.

OSCAR WASHINGTON III

Bruce: *Oscar Washington is a snare and bass drummer who works as a French Market police officer. A long time member of the Doc Paulin Brass Band, he was one of the founding members of in the Pinstripe before going on to become the leader of the New Wave Brass Band. Oscar learned to play drums in the Blackhawk Spiritual Church, and he draws on the driving rhythms he learned to play in the church in how he runs his band.*

A lot of snare drummers provide the cushion for other musicians to play on, but Oscar knows how to heat the music up, and cool it down. When he talked to the students in the program, *he brought the oratory skills of a Southern preacher, speaking to them as a small congregation. He told them to take their time—they couldn't do it all in one day—but what they could learn was how to make music a full-bodied experience.*

Oscar's own inspiration came from watching his uncle, Melvin Washington, play drums at the St. Anthony Divine Spiritual Temple, and then travel with him around the city as he was invited to play in different churches that had never incorporated drums into their services. While watching Melvin transform the congregations, Oscar witnessed the power of the drums.

Introduction: St. Anthony Divine Spiritual Temple

Oscar: Playing the drums is something that was meant for me from the start. A few times in my life, I got away from it. I got away from it, but it didn't get away from me.

I learned to play at my family's church in Hollygrove, the St. Anthony Divine Spiritual Temple. The church was noted for the pastor, Bishop Wilbert A. Hawkins. There were very little flaws in him that you could see because he was a gentleman. He went about his business in an orderly manner. When you got him to laugh and smile that was a plus. He had an office up on top of the church. People would have appointments to see him on a Saturday just like they would a doctor. He would pray for them, light colorful glass candles, and give them incense to burn in their house. On the first floor, where he held services, there were altars with big human-like statues of Jesus, Mary, St. Anthony, and a big old statue of Black Hawk. Black Hawk was the Indian chief and he was the protector. People would pray with their hands on the statue.

My daddy's mother, Delia C. Washington—God rest her soul, I know she's looking down on me right now—was an usher at St. Anthony. She was from Point La Hache in Plaquemines Parish. She moved to New Orleans. Colapissa was the street I remember from a little boy, and—very, very vaguely—seeing my grandfather there. By the time I became aware of my surroundings, he left. They moved to Mistletoe Street with my two aunts. For me, that's where everything started to come to form.

After school on a Friday, I would go over to my grandmother's house, and that is where I spent my weekend. Five o'clock in the morning on Sunday, she was dressed in a starched uniform, little white hat, and pin that said "usher." We would walk the four blocks between her house and the church. Dark, dogs running out there barking at us, but she kept a grip on me to where I couldn't break loose or run. And when we got to St. Anthony's, I would try not to fall back asleep.

My grandmother's job at the church was like being the floor organizer. She fit the role. Always on time. Always great-looking. She made sure everyone was seated. If somebody got happy and in the spirit, she made sure they wouldn't do anything to hurt themselves. She comforted them, revived them, and held them until they came back. She did her job, and she did it with a lot of resilience. Rev, he made it known. "I wish all of the rest of y'all would be dedicated in your duties for this church like Sister Delia Washington!" He would say it, and I'll tell you, Grandma lived it. And you know, if she was on time, I was way early. You didn't see nobody else's child at no sunrise service.

When the words came out of Bishop Hawkins' mouth, it could hit home and a person would jump up and shout. And don't talk about when they start playing the music. The drum set, the piano, and the organ—with the tambourines—were the main instruments in a Spiritual church. Occasionally, when you would have a gospel concept you wanted to get towards, you would come with the horns. Pastor Hawkins was the key musician in the church. He was magnificent. He played the organ with the bass pedals, and he also played the drums and the clarinet. He was total. My Uncle Melvin played the drums in the church, too. He was a very well-known gospel drummer here in New Orleans.

God says he wants you to praise Him with a joyful noise. When Melvin started playing the drums fast, fast, you felt God's presence. The church fills with a spirit, and it is like something shot up inside your bones. The congregation will shout and jump around like bees swarming. I would see people who were quiet and mild mannered and all of the sudden, they are jumping up in the air. They are screaming and

Prayer candles at the F&F Botanica on North Broad Street. The store has supplied many of the Spiritual churches, and is one of the only botanicas left in the city. Photograph by Bruce Sunpie Barnes.

hollering and shaking. When the spirit would hit my grandmother, her daughters would say, "Oh Lord, look at our mama!" She would spin around, doing her holy dance with her feet going up and down. God has gotten inside of her and she felt that power.

When I was young, it would be funny to me. One time, my aunts caught me laughing. They said, "You know what? You ought to be ashamed of yourself for laughing at these people." They said, "You are going to fool around and God is going to put his hand on you and shake you up."

That scared me. I stopped laughing.

Melvin Washington remembering the Black Hawk services. Photograph by Bruce Sunpie Barnes.

The cornerstone at St. Anthony Divine Spiritual Temple. Oscar's grandfather donated the steel and tied all the iron work into the foundation. Photograph by Bruce Sunpie Barnes.

MELVIN WASHINGTON
BETTER FELT THAN TOLD

Melvin: *I was playing with a blues band at a hall in Gretna, Louisiana. I can remember, Ray Charles'* What I Say *was hot on the chart, and that's all they wanted to hear. Play it over and over and over—that number. And it was full of cigarette smoke. When I heard that voice, it came directly to me:* How can you serve two masters? *Everything—the sound—was blinded out. I stopped. I stopped the whole band. The other musicians thought there was something wrong with me. I had the sticks in my hand and I told them, "Look, this is my last night playing with you all."*

It scared me. I was trying to explain to them what happened, but they were full of that alcohol and didn't understand. I guess I was in my early 20s. I was just playing anywhere I could make money, because that's what I was living off of. Should I go further with it?

Oscar: *Sure.*

Melvin: *Playing music supported my family. At the time, we needed the money. Well, I would have to tell you about the disaster of my family and all that? Or should I leave that out?*

Oscar: *You can if you want.*

Melvin: *My daddy...I know he's deceased but well, my daddy had left the family. I was the only brother that was still at home with two sisters under me. That put me in charge, and I just took the role of...his shoes. I didn't know they were so hard to fill, but I found out. That's how I started playing music. I was playing anywhere I could make a nickel.*

Music was my inheritance. For this family to have drums in it is mostly a gift from God. I prayed a lot about it, and decided to stick only with gospel music. I used to always hear your grandmother say, "You give some and God make room for you." I had a praying mother, a really praying mother. Should I go further?

The spiritual church goes deep...it goes real deep. We were raised next to St. Anthony. Our backyard was facing the side door of the church. That's how close we were. Inside, there were saints on the wall. We did not worship those saints, but when you prayed, you gave honor to them. We believed in the nine-day candle lights. They were all white unless they had the votive lights and they had that colored glass, and it was different colors. Blue represented the Blessed Mother because she had the blue robe on and the red represented Jesus Christ. When you lit the candle you were praying to those who went to the great beyond. To the Holy Spirit.

To feel the Holy Spirit, you have to be prayed up. You don't just get on instruments and think you're going to feel it. And when I say prayed up, seriously...and like your poor parents poured their heart out to God for different challenges they had to make in life. You may not know it, but that's what a lot of these parents had to do. Poured their heart out to the All Mighty Maker. He's been a part of my life, and when I sit at a set of drums, I'm serious about what I'm doing. Once a month, we honored the spirit of Black Hawk.

Remember Me

Oscar: *Black Hawk services were always on a Thursday night. Rev used to have a black cape on and he would come out with his arms extended and spin around...ohhh boy!*

Melvin: *And our pastor had a cape with a big old cross on the back of it. He would go to the altar, raise both of his hands up and pray to our Creator to use his body, to speak through him.*

Oscar: *They had people come from all over town, with limousines, I mean it was a big thing at the time—a very big thing.*

Melvin: *People would come from all over the United States to this little church on Live Oak Street, and he would prophesize to them. When I was a little boy, during segregation time, they had just as many white people as black people coming to see Bishop Hawkins. In the Spiritual faith, they had the white ministers, too, and they came to our church as well. And that was under segregation time.*

I didn't understand it until I start getting in the Bible and reading in 12th Corinthians, First Chapter, about spiritual gifts that the Lord blesses people with. They used to put the lights out. They had a cross lit up in the center of the pulpit, and that would be the only light in the church during the séance. When they called to entertain the spirits, they played a soft hymn. Let me see if I can call it up in my memory box... mmm...mm...Remember Me:

Remember me, remember me
Oh oh, oh oh, oh Lord, re...remember me

That's when they open up. They sing that number and then they'll sing Meeting Tonight:

Meeting tonight,
Meeting tonight at the old camp ground...
Ohh, it's Black Hawk tonight,
Black Hawk on the old camp ground

The spirit would take control of Bishop Hawkins' body in the form of the dance. He'd do the Black Hawk dance in the middle of the floor. The music got louder after he started dancing around the middle of the floor, and on the drums you play the high sounding cymbals that vibrate and ring. When you hit the cymbal and on the drums, they crash together. Then the music would go low and the drum got to go down...oh, it go further now. It go deep. It's all right to share it, but would they understand it?

Oscar: *You can try to explain it.*

Melvin: *That's when he would entertain the spirit. He would turn to face the altar. He'd be down on the floor and he'd raise his hands up to the altar and pray. He asked the Lord to give him the spiritual power to get the message of Black Hawk out. A lot of people say fortune. They didn't use that word fortune, they used prophesizing, like the Scripture say:*

Great kings came before you, and he pour out his spirit on all flesh.
Your sons and daughters will prophesize to predict the future.
Your young men shall see visions,
and your old men shall dream dreams.

That's Bible.

Oscar: *It was very amazing to me for a little boy.*

Melvin: *That spirit would come in the church. Rev would*

A Black Hawk statue and candles at the F&F Botanica. Photograph by Bruce Sunpie Barnes.

Oscar and Melvin talking about drumming at St. Anthony. Photographs by Bruce Sunpie Barnes.

go round in circles with his cape on, turning around like the Indians. Then he'd stop and come down the aisle with the Indian dance and call out to a person, and tell them what's happening in their life. The spirit would bring the message and whisper it to him—whether it's danger, happiness, or sadness. We would have laying on the hands, and that comes under healing. And it is very amazing. All mighty God use people to work his purpose.

Oscar: *They are the instruments.*

Melvin: *Faith is the substance of things hoped for and evidence of things not seen.*

Oscar: *It was constant music, nonstop. You would be on the drums for awhile, and then another drum would come on for a little while. And I would just be spinning my wheels wondering, "When are they going to call me?"*

Melvin: *Something touch me, and something gets all in me, and I feel a difference. It's using me. It gets in my feet. It gets in my hand, and it looks like it takes control of my body, and I could play all night. But like they say, it's better felt than told to you.*

Drumming in the Baptist Church

Only two churches had drums—the Spiritual and the Sanctified church. The Baptist church? They'd put you out. They'd run you! It was just the organ and the piano. I started to get known for playing drums for these gospel groups that would come play from out of state at Booker T. Washington High School's auditorium. Reverend Herman Brown hired me to play behind these quartets and the choirs.

Ms. Geraldine Wright belonged to the Ebenezer Baptist Church and sang with a group called Calvacade of Gospel Stars. In the 1960s, she started to come back to St. Anthony, and that's where she saw me playing. Ms. Wright gave a program with the Cavalacade of Gospel Stars and the Ebenezer Choir, and asked me to back them up. Drums were new to the pastor Reverend Landrieu. He liked it, and asked me if I could play for his church.

The opening hymn for his broadcast was Jesus On the Mainline. *When the drums started playing with the organ and the piano, it looked like I put life in the church. The whole congregation stood up, and the choir started singing.*

They were clapping, and dancing the holy dance in the middle of the floor.

Afterwards, the choir director asked me what church I was playing for.

"St. Anthony."

He asked me did I want to play for his church. When I said yes Ebenezer became the first Baptist church to start off with drums in the city of New Orleans. Some of the deacons didn't like it. They said that was a lot of noise, but the music was too powerful. That's right, there you go. A lot of people joined from this music.

I used to pick you up on Sunday mornings in your little white suit and take you to Ebenezer with me. Look, all the ladies would come and want to talk to you. You getting all the ladies; they don't want to talk with me!

Love's Broken

Oscar: I was just so tender at that age. I was the first grandchild on both sides of the family, and I was rotten and spoiled. We lived with my mother's parents. My grandmother, Rosalie, couldn't see out of one eye. My grandfather, Cripple Sam, was in a wheelchair from a young age. He shined shoes for a living.

It was the era of the rhythm and blues bands. I was very, very into these groups. They were representing different sections in New Orleans, vying for who was the best band in the city. The school I went to was from kindergarten to the sixth grade, and at that particular time, sixth graders looked like grown adults to me. They had a group by the name of the Fabulous Phantoms and these men—sixth grade men—were so good to where in the Carrollton/Hollygrove area, they were *the* band. They would play in the school cafeteria for the dances.

I wasn't in a band, but I remember being part of school play in the Booker T. Washington Senior High's auditorium. You were under the big lights when you were at their auditorium. I had one of my worst performances there. I was a cowboy and we had little stick horses. I don't know. Something happened. Mama said, "Yeah, you missed a step. You fell off the horse." Everybody broke out laughing and I thought it was a sin for them to being laughing at me! It was one of my first experiences realizing that there might be more than one interpretation of a shared experience.

When I was nine years old, my father left. Him and my mother, they divorced. Everything happens for a reason, but when you are young, it is hard to distinguish those things because you don't know about them. All you know about is love. That is it. When love gets broken, then you are in turmoil. You are crying, and you are crying because you want your daddy. You are crying because you want your mommy and your daddy together. You are crying because what you all had as a whole has been separated.

They were big shoes to fill when Daddy left. I had to realize that the things that were easy to come by for me—the things that my daddy did and he provided—were no longer. Mama had to be the provider. She wanted me to do everything I possibly could to help her. My brother, Mark Anthony, was only three years-old. He didn't have much time in there with his daddy. He had an attitude, a serious one, that went on with him for a long period of time. My mother was basically left with my brother. He never was married. The only stint that he left home was when he went to college for a little while and then he came back.

I didn't look at my daddy as a quitter. I know situations in everyday life make people make changes that they don't want to make. No matter how hard it is and how much it hurts you to satisfy the situation, you've got to make changes. Sometimes those changes are drastic. Sometimes those changes, they never see their way right once you make them. For years, our father stayed around in the vicinity. He wound up having to get married again and having six more children. I would see him occasionally. Not on an every week basis, but I grew to get past that. I couldn't just keep leaning on what was. I went on.

My mother didn't tell me the real reason for their break up until years later. My daddy had wanted his own home, his own privacy, and she wouldn't leave her parents. What I've realized over the years was that this was just one of many untold stories that have caused congestion. The only way to relieve yourself of congestion is to have it come out. That's how I've been feeling about things in life. Family. Personal things. Music. Relationships with other musicians. It's about the truth. It's about exactly what I've seen, experienced. There's no sense of hiding. That truth is going to come out—this is what happened. It can really change your reality to know those things. Both of my parents are deceased, and so is my brother now. I am the only one left in my immediate family to tell this story. I know they are looking down on me smiling and saying, "Go ahead, tell the story and be strong telling it, because it is the truth."

You Got to Keep Up

Mark Anthony got away with not going to church. He would start whining and crying and he didn't have to go. I start whining, I have to put my clothes on and go. I didn't have a choice. One time I broke out with boils on my head. I mean, a sight, too. Like little moon craters. I said, "There's no way in the world they are going to send me to church."

"Oh well, come here." Rub some vasoline on my head, make it look shiny, and out the door I went. That was one of the embarrassing times for me, because I was in front of the girls and they were laughing. Oh boy, I must have died 20 times. I said, "This is ridiculous! I shouldn't have to go to church looking like this. Lord, why is it me that has to go through all this torture?"

The pastor's wife said, "That's okay, baby, it's going to be all right." What she said was true. Being there helped shape my life—even now and for the times to come. I had an overall vision about it: "This is the way you were taught."

I had been playing on the gumbo pot in the kitchen, and couldn't wait until my opportunity came to play at church. Eventually, Bishop Hawkins started letting me play. I had the fear that I wasn't good enough, but he had confidence in me because of my Uncle Melvin.

Being on the radio was a popular thing back in the 1960s. Broadcasters visited different churches, and we would often get on a bus and go to another church to play. They would have either a piano or organ player

Left: Oscar playing at the Faith in God Spiritual Temple. **Middle:** Oscar's mother as an ordained minister at Faith in God. **Right:** Oscar playing drums in Walter C. Cohen Senior High's marching band. Photographs courtesy of the Washington family.

there. We'd bring the drums from St. Anthony and set them up almost right in front of the pulpit where Pastor Hawkins could have eye contact with me. He would have the pocket radio in his hand, listening. When I get a beat or so behind he would pick up his hands up and let me know, "You got to keep up. You got to stay. You are losing the time." I had to push myself to stay up.

As I got better, I started to feel like I was being taken over by something. A supreme being got inside of me and was making me drum at an ease. I knew where I was going—I was right there with the band, but I was also in that zone to where the band can get on my shoulders and they can walk. I can carry them. I could stay at this pace and I won't lose no time because something is controlling me. If you want God to move inside of you, you want to feel Him, this is the way that happens.

Jazz Musicians in the Neighborhood

I was at about the tail end of segregation. I didn't become acquainted with any white musicians for a long period of time—a very long period of time. You would only see them in their territory, or parading on a main street—Canal Street or Carrollton Avenue. It was always the black musicians who I had to lean on. Mr. Percy Humphrey was my family's insurance man and when he found out that I wanted to play drums, he bought me a pair of drumsticks and he told me, "Now I got these drumsticks for you, I want you to do something with it."

Sometimes I would go with my mother to her hairdresser who had an apartment in the back of her house. She would say, "Why don't you go back there by Pops in the back. Pops plays music." He played trumpet, and asked "Well, son, what instrument do you like to play?" I said, "Oh, I like drums." He said, "Well here, this is a trumpet."

He put the trumpet in my hand and was showing me how to form my lips to blow something out. I tell you, I failed. I could not get a note out of that trumpet. But I was amazed by all of the pictures he had from the bottom all the way up to the ceiling on all four walls of the different places in the world that he had been playing the trumpet.

I didn't know who he was until later on in life. I asked her, "You remember the man that you called Pops who used to live in the apartment behind you? Do you know his name?" "Yeah, Mr. Miller, Punch Miller." He was an inspiration to me, but I didn't know the impact that he had on the music world. I didn't have much experience with jazz at that time. Most of my experience was still in the church.

The Light Came Back On

My aunts married Catholic, and left St. Anthony. Eventually my grandmother got to where she had to be cared for, and was one of the first blacks to move into the senior citizens' homes out in New Orleans East. That was the big change. Once she was unable to be at St. Anthony anymore, I stopped playing music in the church.

My grandmother Rosalie had gone on to become an ordained minister at the Israelite Spiritual Church under Bishop Johnson. She organized prayer services with a group of other women who were also ordained ministers. Since they didn't have the resources to do it on their own, they had to group up. They would go

248

Southern University's marching band, courtesy of the Isaac B. Greggs Collection, Archives and Manuscripts Department, John B. Cade Library, Southern University and A&M College, Baton Rouge.

in their building at Toledano and LaSalle. I played the whole time I was in high school from 1974 to 1978.

I had gone to a Catholic middle school, and when it came to high school, I had the opportunity to go to St. Augustine, the Catholic boys school in the Seventh Ward, but I said, "I don't know if I want to go to school around all boys. I'm just used to being around girls, and they just make the whole day better." I went to Walter L. Cohen Senior High. We had a good band director, Solomon Spencer. We called him Fess. His expertise as a band director was showcasing different types of music to his students, and you chose what best fit you. He ran a very good marching band, concert band, and a rhythm and blues band, and stressed learning how to read music.

When we were broken into sections, if one of the reserves wanted to challenge somebody who had a drum for that particular spot, then they challenge with sheet reading, rudiments, and how to dance. You had to know all three to get the position. You had to take to the nervousness and turn it into an attitude. You had to tell yourself, "Look, I'm coming to take this drum, and that's it." A lot of upperclassmen lost because the freshmen came, and, like they say, cut their head. Blew them off.

I also auditioned at Cohen to be in Southern University marching band in Baton Rouge. Southern was known as the top marching band in the land. You had other bands around the country that may have been just as good, but Southern's reign, led by Dr. Issac Greggs, was the longest standing. Should I use Julius Caesar for a start-up description for him? He was Emperor.

from house to house to build a congregation. They used to have suppers on Fridays and Saturdays, and sell fish and chicken dinners to generate money for the church.

When I was about 12-years-old, the Faith in God Spiritual Temple started in a double house on Clio Street near Simon Bolivar, and then moved around Central City, finding homes in old cornerstore buildings. My mother started full steam ahead for church, and I started going more often. I was able to revisit the earlier part of my life.

One of the deacons, John Lastie, came from a popular

musical family who were members of other spiritual churches. He came in to the church on Felicity with this old-time black drum set. It was nothing but two pieces that I could remember—bass and snare, with the side cymbal and the cymbal on the bass drum. And boy, he just thrilled me the way he beat them drums. There could have been a fire behind me, but my eyes were tuned into the drum. I would have gotten burnt up from the back.

It brought me back to when I first saw the light at St. Anthony. The light got cut off for a period of time. And here the light came back on. It was starting all over again for me. My big tenure playing drums was

When he gave me his nod, it was the beginning of a whole year of transition. My girlfriend was not in that approval stage of me leaving. We had a daughter who was newly born. Oh, she was so beautiful. That was my twin because she looks just like her father. I wanted to be in the band so much, but it was a trial.

The Human Jukebox

At Southern, band superceded everything. Band took up all your time. The halftime shows were legendary, and you had to be ready. Dr. Greggs would let you get your dinner, and then you had to go back to practice.

In *Jet* magazine, they would list the top 20 songs on the music charts, and the assistant band directors would arrange them for the band. After the whole band practiced, you had sectionals, and sectionals would take you to two or three in the morning.

Homecoming was the second best thing to being in the band. Making the band was one. Everybody came back for homecoming. Former band members came back to see how much better we were than they were. Monster crowds. Standing only. Now, the stadium is big enough to hold the capacity but back then, in 1978, it wasn't big enough.

I was playing bass drum in the reserve. On the weekends, if I wasn't going to be in the lineup, I was just worried about going home to see my daughter. Several times they were looking for me. "Where is Wash? We've got a spot for him with this game. He's got to get over here and find out what he's got to do."
"Oh, he went home."
"Ain't that something."

Doc Paulin playing the trumpet in his band. Photograph by Jeff Day.

After awhile, I didn't want to do marching band no more. It was exciting but a future was unclear. It was basically for music majors, or to be band directors. I went to a percussion class and my instructor, Mr. Dillion said, "Look, let me be honest with you. What you've accomplished is fine. It's great, but you can play with anybody else if you learn how to be a versatile drummer. Learn how to play the rest of the percussion instruments, because you never know. You may be called to play not just a snare drum or a bass drum. You may be called to play the drum set." That's what inspired me to go to Mr. Alvin Batiste. He had the jazz band at Southern University. When I got in there, it was a whole new outlook for me. I thought, "I can do this."

After the first year of college, I wanted to go back but finances were hard. I said, "Well, I got to be responsible. I got to take care of my daughter." I had to step up because everybody was looking at me. I wound up staying in New Orleans and getting two jobs—one in the morning and one overnight. It wasn't just the support for my daughter, I was helping my mother because my brother was still in school.

Dr. Greggs called my house. He said "Look, I need to see you here in two weeks." Like that. He was very demanding. He knew after your first year, you'd be ready to really take it in. But I had to get on my horses and start riding. I never got to get back to college.

I became a certified kitchen manager, and then got into security. A good friend of mine who worked for Southwest Protection Agency said, "Come on over, you'd like it. You'll enjoy this. It is easy money." From there, I moved to the City of New Orleans' French Market Operations, where I've been for almost 30 years. I thought, "Well if I come to be good at this, I can earn an income. If I get a regular job, music could be my side job."

The Doc Paulin Band

I remembered in high school, Fess would tell us, "Yeah, if you want to learn how to play traditional jazz, Ricky and Aaron Paulin's daddy's got a brass band. You need to get with them and learn how to play." Doc Paulin had six sons and all of them played music—they made up a band themselves because they all played different instruments. They told me, "Man, why don't you come out and see us play? You might want to get involved." That was my inspiration right there. I've got to hear this music that they call brass band music.

Doc Paulin had the premier band Uptown that played for a second line clubs like the Young Olympians, the Prince of Wales, and the Jolly Bunch. That is where I got my start from. All credit goes to him. For the horn players, you had to come to his house and play for him in order to get a job. He figured his sons were drummers and they knew whether you were good enough to play in their daddy's band. By me playing in high school with the sons, they said, "You can play, but you just have to learn this style of drumming. We have three bands. You can play drums in the Third Band."

The First Band was *the* band. The Second Band, they were auditioning to get into the First Band. The Third Band, we were hopefuls. Eager to the challenge, I said, "Okay, this is my break-out. I'm gonna have to make the best of it. I have to practice this to get it right."

I went to second lines and watched the older guys. On the bass drum, your left hand keeps time with the cymbal and the right hand is the beat on the one and three, and your own accents before you come back to the one. I had to incorporate this, and it wasn't easy from the start. The older guys' styles were all somewhat different. Some drummers might be playing single strokes and others might be playing double stroke. Some drummer would be rolling. I picked out what I liked and incorporated it into what I was trying to do. I would patternize a whole drumbeat, and managed to get it down. Then I got in the zone and played what was all in me.

When I got to my first gig, I was nervous. I had to worry about the way I was dressed because Doc Paulin was so strict. He was the general, you were the soldiers. At the beginning of the parade, I heard the other two bands and how good they sounded. Here I am in the Third Band, and it was like a whole different kind of pots and pans making noise. The Third Band didn't have no motivation because most of the second line was around the First Band and the rest of the people were around the Second Band. Third Band? We didn't have no followers. Doc Paulin had the First Band so trained the way he wanted, he could take his horn and walk back to play with each band and see what they were doing. I kept wondering, "Am I gonna get paid for this gig?" I was hoping we could get together to sound like something in unison.

In the First Band, Aaron Paulin played the bass drum. Ricky Paulin was originally a clarinet player, but he was playing snare. He said to me, "Look, I want to play my clarinet. That is my number one instrument. Man, we going to bring you into the First Band so you can learn the patterns that we play." After a couple of outings with them, I learned there was a few basic things that they did—when they start a song, when they change in the middle of the song, and how they end it. Once I could implement those three things, I locked up as the snare drummer. Ricky went to playing his clarinet, and Doc, he took me under his wing. I was an understudy.

Initiation

My initiation was my first road trip to a festival in Alabama. We were in the van. Doc bought this big bag of fried chicken. He held onto it and if you wanted a piece of chicken, you had to go to him to get it. Doc fell asleep up there. Next thing you know, Julius Lewis reaching over to get the bag of chicken. As he was pulling it towards the back seat, Doc snapped out of a sound sleep and grabbed that chicken. Man, we fell out! I never forget that as long as live. Julius almost had the chicken!

We were getting ready to pull up to the hotel in Dothan, Alabama. Boy, I'm wondering who am I going to be rooming with. Nobody said nothing. Everyone else in the band jumped out of that van, grabbed their stuff, and were gone. I said, "What?"
"Oh, we forgot to tell you, you rooming with the boss!"

Oh Lord! I was in that room. The chicken was in the room with us! Four o'clock in the morning, Doc was up. He was dressed. I remember jumping up and saying, "Doc, I'm running late?"
He said, "No, Oscar, you ain't running late. I'm just the boss and I got to be dressed early." That is what he told me. It was four in the morning.
I laid back down. I don't even think I went back to sleep.

When I got up, everybody is looking at me, laughing. "How you made out, man?" I said, "I was just fine. I had some chicken and you all could have come over to get it." But they were scared to knock on that door.

I became part of the Paulin family. Even with Doc's wife, I called her "Mama." He had confidence in me doing things like if I was one of his sons. When I was in my late 30s, Doc called me to come and play the gig at Blaine Kern's Mardi Gras World. I said, "Well Doc, all right, I'll bring my snare drum." He said,

"Yeah, you bring your snare drum and I got the rest of the kit to go with it." I said, "Rest of the kit?" He said, "Yeah, you are going to play the trap set with me." I said, "I never played trap set before in a jazz band. Oh my God!"

At that time, I didn't have a car. I caught the bus up to Doc's house and one thing about it, he did not want you to be late. You could not be late. You better be early! Doc had a green station wagon, and I'm loading up the bass drum, two tom-toms, cymbals and the cymbal stands thinking to myself, "Lord, what I got myself into?"

I said, "Okay, everything is loaded up, Doc."
He said, "All right. You got a driver's license?"
I said, "Yeah, Doc."
I'm driving. Oh goodness. I drove across the river. That was one feat that I accomplished. Next one was to get on the stage with all of these musicians who were older than me. I'm talking about uncle, daddy, grandpa-type age. It was a big band up there. They looked at me and said, "What you doing up here?"
I said, "I'm here to play the drums!"
I haven't hit a lick on the drums yet and I'm worried about this. Doc turned around and told me, "Roll the drums on just like that." I rolled the drums off, and he started calling songs. Jazz is a totally different style to playing gospel or rhythm and blues. I just said to myself, "Well, I've played drums before. I've played in front of people before. I've played with people before. I'm going to find my spot because I'm the drums. I'm going to get in and blend in. So be it."

Pinstripe Brass Band

If it was something that Doc didn't like, he would say, "That is bad business." Those were his favorite words. Bad Business. Look, you did what Doc said and that was it. You don't like it? Then you don't play, don't come. Doc's realm was strictly traditional jazz.

Oscar Washington playing with the Pinstripe Brass Band. Photograph courtesy of the Washington family.

He ain't playing nothing outside of it. No up-tempo songs. Some of the cats in the Second Band and his sons wanted to play street songs. He said, "You want to play that street music, you go get your own band."

That propelled us to start getting out on our own. In 1980, Herb McCarver, Brice Miller, Ricky Paulin, and I formed the Pinstripe Get Right Jazz Band. It was with the Pinstripe that I made the transition to bass drum.

We played anywhere a gig popped up, but it was the Zulu Club that really put Pinstripe on the map. Roy

Glapion, Sr. got us our first gig. From then on, Pinstripe was a mainstay with the Zulu Club. For over two decades, they booked us for every function they had, and it seemed like there was always something going on—from the balls, the parades, jazz funerals for the deceased members. As the years went on, we also started riding in the Zulu parade. They had a band float. The Pinstripe and the Sixth Ward Dirty Dozen became the two hottest bands in the street—the bands that everybody came out to see then. We made our first overseas trip to France in 1987. We were up there for 14 days. Everything was paid for, and you get paid to perform. Oh boy! You were on top of the world. You figure once you've made it overseas you have reached the mountaintop as a musician!

But my wife said to me being gone so much was really splitting our marriage up. I said, "Well, you met me playing music and you loved it, and now that I am gone on a regular basis playing music you have a problem with it." She was thinking it was other women, and it wasn't that at all. I was just going to play music. Of course, women like musicians, but you don't have to be with them just because they like you.

I wanted my wife to be happy so I stopped playing in 1989. The cats called me and asked, "What is the problem? What happened? Did somebody do you something?" I told them it was not that. For two whole years, I would go to functions where the Pinstripe was playing and the cats would look at me, "Man, we just can't believe you just stopped playing."

They asked about my wife and I got offended, and said, "Leave that alone. That is our personal situation." They said, "Man, we your friends. We come a long way with you. You know us and we know you and we just know that that is not you. God gave you that talent to play music and you are just going to stop? You are going to quit on us? You are going to quit on yourself? You quit on Him." When they told me that, it struck a nerve.

When I came home, I told my wife, "You know what, I wasted two whole years doing something I didn't want to do. That is not playing music. I had enough. I'm going back to what I love doing. If that is going to divide us, or split us, I'm sorry that has to be the reason. There might be things I didn't like about what you do, but I'm not going to tell you to stop doing it because that is what you love."

I told her I was going back to play music. I said, "Matter fact, I got a gig tonight."

We eventually wound up getting divorced. I told her that we go on. She was very angry for a long time, but we wound up being friends. I ain't never going to stop again. Only stop when I'm not here no more, and then I'm still going on. I'm going to be playing in the brass band in the sky.

Where Love Lives

I decided to remarry. My wife won't be the one to stop telling me to play music. She's the one who makes sure I remember my gigs. When I married her, she had four young kids, and I've raised them. Her second son, Steven, was the one I glued to the quickest. His biological father didn't want to be a father to him. He may have seen him twice in his entire life.

He was smart coming up all through elementary school. It was during junior high school when he made that 360 turn, and got a serious attitude towards his father. I said, "His shortcomings should be the spark for you to be a better man. If you are mad with the world because of what he didn't do, I am here to show you that you got somebody who wants you to be somebody in life."

I picked him up a Cohn trombone from the flea market. Good shape. He didn't practice. I said, "Well, ain't nobody going to play this trombone so I may as

well sell it." He told me, "Oh no, I'll sell it."

I said, "Oh no. You are either going to learn how to play it, or I'll sell my own trombone." He learned how to play. He got good at it. He went from middle school to Fortier Senior High playing the trombone. Then his school was going out of town to play and I said, "You getting ready to go?" He told me he would go if I wanted him to. I said, "Hold up. If you are not going to play this trombone for yourself, you are not doing it for me." After that, no more trombone for him.

After high school, he was in and out of jail. He wanted to keep doing wrong. I said, "You got to find a job. You got to become independent."
He told me, "I got a job."
I said, "What job you have?"
"I make money on the streets."
I said, "That is not a job. That is a hustle. You are straight up hustling. What is it really doing for you? You winning a popularity contest?"

His friends were telling him, "Come on, be with us. We love you. We got your back." He had to be torn in half. "I'm for y'all, but I also love my family here." I told him he didn't come from the streets. "This is where love lives. This is where love came for you first. And it has never left you, and it has never turned away from you."

One night, he called us in a rage. He was belligerently cursing us, saying he was coming to that house and he was going to kill both of us. I told him, "The house is not going to move. It is going to be there when you get there, and me and your mom are going to be there when you get there, too. You already made your invitation. Come on when you coming." He never showed up.

But the way Steven talked put me in another frame of mind with him. I told my wife, "You got to be prepared mentally because you know the life he live."

My wife got to the point where she said, "He is God's child. He is my child, but he is God's child. When God gets tired and ready for him, he'll come and get him." And that is what happened. His other life took him out of here. Out of this world.

On a Monday night, my wife and I were eating ice cream and all the sudden the phone rang. Let us know that Steven was shot up at Sixth and Dryades. We got up there and they wouldn't let us go see him. His brothers were both at work and when they came, I had to calm them down. Let them know it is already bad. "He already dead lying in that yard back there. There is nothing else happening right here." We all was able to leave peacefully and go on home. That was just the beginning of things. He left behind six children—all girls and one boy. Steven had so much to offer that he didn't offer. He could have made an impact.

Gospel Medley

A lot of time, I felt like I had gotten all beaten up mentally and physically because I've had to endure all life experiences myself. It hasn't been nobody to be there to lift me up. Fatherhood takes a whole person and a half. So does being a bandleader. When I started New Wave Brass Band in 1994, other musicians wanted to know why the bandleader got to get more. Because he

got to take care of more! It's like you have to go into a disciplinary role with grown men. You have to police and guard against so many attitudes.

But the gift of music is something I could fall on anytime I feel low. It is a reliever. It calms me down. It just makes me whole. In New Wave, we play a lot of gospel medleys. We will start out with *Lord, Lord, Lord*, and go into *Glory, Glory Hallelujah*, and *This Little Light of Mine*. The drums are already there. When we're in the pocket, you can hear the cats are in a spiritual zone by the way they approach their solos and riffs. It is such a powerful thing. Everything is all in unison. Everything is coming out clear. For the listener, it takes them by storm. We push the audience to let God's visitation come inside of them and just motivate them.

Left: Aurelien sitting on the steps of his family's house in Broadmoor, where, growing up, he regularly heard his father play the accordion, harmonia, drums, and piano. Before a lot of out-of-town gigs, members of Sunpie and the Louisiana Sunspots would gather at the house as well. *Above:* Aurelien dressed up to play with Young Traditional Brass Band at the Black Men of Labor parade in 2006. Photograph by Bruce Sunpie Barnes.

AURELIEN BAABA BARNES

Bruce: *My son, Aurelien, was one of my main inspirations for starting the program. We've been playing music together since he was a baby. I remember he loved to watch a Senegalese master drum video by Doudou N'Diaye Rose, and when I got him a little drum set, he would go into a trance and play on it all day long. As he got older, I taught him how to play the blues and zydeco on the piano and harmonica. I thought I might have another bluesman in our family, but when the trumpet player in my band, Eric Lucero, let him try to play his horn, he was hooked. In this interview, he talks with Oscar about taking what he learned from his family and making it is own.*

What I noticed about Aurelien in the program was how much he loved the fellowship of playing music with other young people. It is a core value to him. When he went to Lusher High School, he found a great friend in Caleb Windsay, and they now attend Tulane University together. Caleb comes from a family of world-class gospel and jazz vocalists, and has a strong understanding of harmony and musical structure. He has played in a number of brass bands around the city like the Baby Boyz, and when a group called the New Breed was being formed, he recommended Aurelien. I thought it was a great opportunity for him since he was intrigued with parades from when he was young. When I

first joined BMOL he thought it was very cool and funny to see his dad dressed up. He'd say, "That's a lot of stuff you've got laid out." Before the first BMOL second line he played in, he was extremely excited to put on the black and white, and to be part of the band.

Left to right: Aurelien as a toddler watching his father, Bruce Sunpie Barnes, play the djembe drum; Aurelien's maternal grandmother, Rosario Rodriguez, in France; Aurelien playing rubboard with his dad; Aurelien's paternal grandparents, Indiana and Willie Barnes. Photographs courtesy of the Barnes family.

Introduction: Inheritances

Oscar: Okay. Aurelien, what is your family background?

Aurelien: My mother, Maria Rodriguez Barnes, was born in France to Spanish immigrant parents who moved to France in the early 1960s. I don't really know too much about my grandpa because he, unfortunately, died before I was born, but my mom says I was named after him. My grandma is from northern part of Spain in a little village called Cevico Navero in the province of Palencia.

Growing up, my mother spoke Spanish at home with her family and French just by virtue of living in France. She also became a teacher of both of those languages, so she's been very influential on me by teaching me how to speak them. I think it is one of the biggest qualities that I have. To me, my mom is someone who I can always rely on. I think that she always had the children's best interests in mind whenever we were growing up.

For most of my childhood, she would take me to spend half the summer in France, and the other half in Spain, so that helped me learn the languages. Some of my best memories from those summers were figuring out how

to speak Spanish so that I could have friends and have a good time—be able to hang out. It's the same way for music. The best way to learn is to be put in a situation where you have to at least try to succeed, and if you don't, you're just not gonna make it too far.

Oscar: Okay, what kinds of experiences did you have with music and your family? I know you had some very interesting experiences.

Aurelien: My dad, Bruce Barnes, was born in Benton, Arkansas to parents from lower part of Arkansas. My grandpa, Willie Barnes, was a sharecropper for about 40 years of his life. I think that growing up in the American South, where conditions were never really equal for black people, had a big impact on the blues being passed down through that side of the family. That's one of the aspects that effects my playing the most today, and it's come down through family heritage.

I've grown up around music all my life. Since I can remember, my dad has been playing music. I heard music all the time in the house, particularly zydeco and blues, because he was always singing or practicing his instruments.

Oscar: I knew this would make you smile. What does it feel like playing with your father?

Aurelien: It feels kind of normal because I'm around him all the time.

Oscar: What about the first time? How did you perceive it? How did you feel because this was your first time performing with your father and you were probably a little jittery?

Aurelien: He tried to get me to come out on the stage a few times at Jazz Fest to play washboard. I just wouldn't do it when I was younger. I got all dressed up. It was too many people. I wasn't going out there. The first time I actually got on stage was overseas at a festival in Italy on Lake Como. I was about seven years old and I played percussion instruments. It was really nerve-wracking because it was my first time ever looking out at a crowd and seeing so many people watching me. But at the same time, it was exciting. When my dad introduced the band and said my name, they cheered, and after the show they came up to me because it's impressive to see such a young kid up there on the stage playing music. The same tour, I played washboard in Rapperswil, Switzerland. It got me interested in further pursuing that instrument, and I still play it today.

Having a parent who's a musician gave me insight as to how the music business works and how a musician's life is. It can get very busy, but it's not always a very

257

reliable thing, per se, because there are times when you don't get a lot of gigs. It's important to make sure that you have a consistent way of earning a living.

Oscar: What instrument do you play and why did you choose that particular instrument?

Aurelien: The trumpet player in the Sunspots, Eric Lucero, was a big inspiration to me. He played washboard as well, and when I used to think that if I was playing washboard, the next instrument should be a trumpet like him. At first, my dad got a pocket trumpet because he thought it would be easier to use, but it was actually harder. We traded that one in because I couldn't get a sound.

After the hurricane, we evacuated over to Lafayette and they had an elementary school band there. I wanted to take part in a band. We went and got my trumpet that I left at our house in the Broadmoor neighborhood of New Orleans. It was upstairs so it didn't get flooded out. I started learning the notes and was First Chair the whole time. In the band, it's the top player for that instrument in each section.

Oscar: That's the prize. You're First and you pass it down to the rest. It was the beginning of everything.

In the Pocket

Aurelien: When my dad set up the Music for All Ages program, it was my first real introduction to playing something besides elementary band music. It helped me in terms of not being scared to play, of not wanting to back down.

Oscar: It was the same with me with teaching. My first Saturday at MFAA, that stage was over limit. It had so many instruments. I said, "I wonder how this is gonna happen." They want to learn something from me. That's my purpose of being there." They're all looking at me like, "Okay, we're waiting on you." First time around, it was a little shaky for me. But then I got to feel the vibes from all of the young people sitting up there—that they are trying to really get into this groove that I'm trying to push.

Aurelien: Yeah, I remember you would get in front of the band.

Oscar: We had people in sections to work with y'all. I was in back helping the drummers. We had four other members of the New Wave Brass Band there to help the trumpet and reed players. Someone for the tubas. They showed them the fingering, and we got to a certain level where I thought, "Okay, I don't need to be back there with the drums. They got this and I can get in front of the band." I would go in there like I was directing a big orchestra. I would let them call songs they liked. I really came to like it. My theory to overcome the fear was, "I don't care about you playing bad notes. Bad notes will turn into good notes eventually."

Aurelien: That's the main thing that gets you started—if you get over that fear of bad notes.

Oscar: Witnessing the potential y'all had drove me. I said, "I got this. I'm going in there and we gonna do this." And I'm listening. I'm listening to all kinds of sounds. The trumpet players was destroyers—they were roaring. They were sounding like one.

Aurelien: We would stop, rehearse the songs, and make sure we got it down. And then once we started

Left: The Sunspots' trumpet player Eric Lucero. *Middle:* Uncle Lionel Batiste with Aurelien's mother, Maria Rodriguez Barnes. *Right:* Aurelien playing trumpet with "Kid" Merv Campbell and Xavier Michel at the MFAA program. Photographs by Bruce Sunpie Barnes.

playing, that was a whole different learning experience. You kept us on track when you conducted.

Oscar: We taught you songs that you would be expected to play if you were in a working brass band in New Orleans. There are other dirges, but *A Closer Walk With Thee* is the number one dirge for jazz funerals. It is a very complicated song because of the chord changes and the breakdown—you have to get way up, and you have to come way down.

Aurelien: At first, I could not figure out how to play it. I thought it was just random notes and a couple changes I couldn't understand. After a while, I started actually listening to the song to figure out what was going on. I'd hum it in my head, and one day I was able to play it. The beginning song is very smooth and mellow. There are certain crescendos and it picks up around the middle. If it's played right, it's a very beautiful song.

Oscar: On that song, I really had to really pay attention to the drummers. I'd say, "Look, no matter what you all do back there, watch me. Very important, very important!" I had my hands up, which meant turn the volume up. If I'd put my hands down, that means get way down under this.

Aurelien: Bring the volume down.

Oscar: I wanted to slow it down so you could just hear that they're holding the notes. When we played it together, the melody was so sweet because everybody was in the pocket. Everybody was right there. Nobody is outside; everybody is inside, and it's just some fresh air just blowing through you.

Aurelien: At Lusher Charter School, we had a big band where we played lots of big arrangements with lots of different parts, and then we had a small combo band. We were playing jazz standards—not New

Orleans jazz, but compositions by Dizzy Gillespie, Miles Davis, John Coltrane, Sonny Rollins, Quincy Jones. The band director, Kent Jordan, comes from a very musical family. It was a good experience for me because I got to play my horn every day and learned a lot of music theory and reading music that you might not get in an informal setting.

Mentors

Oscar: Who are your biggest influences and why?

Aurelien: I would have to say with traditional jazz, my biggest influence was the first person who really taught me some of the songs, and that's Kenneth Terry.

Oscar: Yes. I know him from when he first started out. He was a good strong trumpet player at that. He just came out and everybody wanted him to play. He had a Satchmo style. He would hold the trumpet with one hand, and he'd be blowing, and he might have a handkerchief in the other hand. Being the lead trumpet player, he was very clean with his approach to a song. You always knew where he was going.

Aurelien: I definitely liked his trumpet playing. It was very exciting and evoked a lot of emotion. There are a lot of trumpet players now who play lots of fast stuff—they will play very technical things and they'll sound good, but they don't really have the soul to get to a listener. There's something in his playing that when you're listening to him, it'll give you goose bumps.

Oscar: How did you learn how to solo?

Aurelien: Kenny was really the first one who taught me my first few tricks with the trumpet—like some licks to put in my solos. Hearing blues growing up helped, too, because it is a central piece of what brass band music is about, and it helps with improvisation—being able to use your imagination—because it's very based on

Members of the New Breed Brass Band opening up for Troy "Trombone Shorty" Andrews at Lafayette Square Park in 2013. Photograph by Bruce Sunpie Barnes.

feeling. It's not such a formal thing that you can teach, but you have to know the blues scale. If people figure out how to do that, you can pretty much solo. From then on, you can start to figure out notes and you might remember a little line—a series of notes that might work with a particular song—and can build on that.

Oscar: What are some of your favorite experiences playing in a traditional jazz band?

Aurelien: Playing with Mr. Benny Jones and the Tremé Brass Band at Jazz Fest. There's a feeling when you're playing something really good and you're really in that vibe, it's kind of like a tingling feeling. I don't know how to explain it—a rush of adrenaline—that's what I felt with them.

Oscar: That's a good point that you brought. It's good when you can hear those types of things coming from a younger musician. You can go anywhere once you're in that zone. After you've gotten to a certain capacity, you'll adapt this feeling. It may not hit you right away. It might take the musician a couple of songs to really warm up to good stuff like that, but then once they're on, they're on. There's no stopping them. Like you say, there's that little tingling sensation you get in there. It'll take a roof off. Oh yes. Oh yes. When my wrist is real loose, I can go there and do some things that people can't catch me doing. They can't.

The New Breed Brass Band

Oscar: How did you develop a group of friends around the music scene?

Aurelien: I think that's one of the best parts of being a musician is being able to have other people to relate musical ideas to and to really study music. One of my best friends from high school does a lot of hip-hop producing on the computer. There's a musical understanding there that we share when we're just listening to something.

I decided to stay in New Orleans for college and am sophomore at Tulane University. That's been a good move for me with music, because just as I was starting school, my friend Caleb Windsay transferred to Tulane as well, and asked me to be a part of the New Breed Brass Band. It is composed of most of the former members of the Baby Boyz Brass Band. After the Baby Boyz split, they decided to start up a new band.

Oscar: What do you learn at gigs that's different than what you learn at school?

Aurelien: Most of the time that I was in high school, I didn't play with a particular band consistently besides my dad's or at school. Now I'm in a band playing gigs several times a weekend. Most of the gigs are private events—whether it be a wedding, birthday party or somebody's retirement party. But Genard Andrews, the leader of our band, is a nephew of Troy Andrews, and so we've been able to open for Trombone Shorty and Orleans Avenue at places like the House of Blues, the Howlin' Wolf, and Tipitina's. They're usually sold out shows because Trombone Shorty is one of the biggest up-and-coming instrumental artists in the country. I think he's one of the best horn players in the

The Red Bull Street Kings competition under the overpass under North Claiborne. Photographs by Matej Slezak.

world. He has incredible range. He can play all up and down the registers. He's got great tone, and a great musical mind that has the ability to just play something that just shocks you. The shows with him are really high energy. Every time we play, we want to come at them with everything we've got. We want to prove to people that we are a legitimate contender for the top of the brass band scene.

Being in school and playing music keeps me busy, but I enjoy it a lot because it gives me an opportunity to play a lot more and to get better at what I do. I'm able to play better solos. Brass band music takes a lot of endurance and chops to play. I think it's helped me become a better trumpet player simply by the amount of performances that we have. I don't think that I'd be able to achieve that in another city as easily. And it also gives me an opportunity to sustain myself financially in college, which is a struggle for a lot of college students.

Oscar: What parts of New Orleans have you gotten to know because of music that you might have never known about?

Aurelien: I've gotten to know downtown better through second lines like Black Men of Labor, but other ones with the New Breed. Second lines are overwhelming at first. You don't really know what's going on all the time. There's lots of people. There's lots of noise going on. And when you're playing with a band that can be upwards of 10, 12 people. You have to learn how to pace yourself. You don't want to blow yourself out in the first five minutes because everything around is very loud. But once you figure out how to do it, it's really fun and exciting.

On October 26, 2013, the New Breed got to participate in the Street Kings competition under the North Claiborne bridge. Four brass bands were selected by Red Bull. It was us, the Original Pinettes Brass Band, the TBC Brass Band, and New Creations Brass Band. The stakes were high. The winner got a lot of money and a recording session out in California at the Red Bull studios. More than just the material benefits, it was definitely a big competition in terms of street credibility of who would be the hottest brass band and who got their name out the most. And so it was high

intensity. We were thinking about this competition for weeks before, and we rehearsed a lot.

They set up a stage and the crowd was pretty big. It was a free event, so it was mainly people from the Sixth Ward who had been living around there and really knew brass band music because they've been around it all their life. This was an experienced crowd. We second lined in and then second lined out, so there was a lot of dancing going on around us the whole time at that point. It felt really good when you saw a reaction from the crowd, when you saw that your music that you're playing was appreciated. We didn't know whether we'd advance to the next round. And then we did. We ended up coming in second place—a little bit controversially—to the Pinettes, the all female brass band.

Oscar: What do you think about your generation is doing with New Orleans's music that is different?

Aurelien: I think that my generation, and young people in general right now, are adding different elements to New Orleans music that may not have been seen before. There are hip-hop elements. There are some kinds of funk elements that are being added to the music now that is creating a whole new music.

Oscar: Do you figure that from your generation's standpoint that you want to upgrade brass band music—you want to put a little bit more of now into tradition?

Aurelien: I don't think it's really like an upgrade as much as it is just a new style that can coincide with the traditional jazz. If you learn how to play traditional jazz, it can really help you out in playing other styles of music proficiently. It's really the basis for a lot of other styles of music that will come after that. It's a reoccurring thing in music. You continue to adapt in music and make something new out of it.

The New Breed started off, as most modern brass bands do in the city, heavily influenced by Rebirth Brass Band. In fact, I'd almost say that most of the brass bands are all pretty much just cover bands of Rebirth. But our goal now is to kind of change that. We don't want to be exactly like the Rebirth. We want to change it up. We want to take influence from as many places as we can to add to our music so we have originals that are more influenced by jazz than just purely funk.

Oscar: What dreams about music have you been able to live out?

Aurelien: This summer I went to Switzerland to play in the JazzAscona Festival. We wouldn't have had that opportunity without a special connection with Nicholas Gilliet, the director of the festival. The first time he saw us was at a second line leaving from St. Augustine Church. He was in town to scout new talent for the festival.

It was my first trip overseas playing with my own group, not in my dad's. It felt really good. Sometimes when I play with my dad, I feel like I'm getting the opportunities solely out of being his son. And so I feel like those opportunities are almost given to me. With the New Breed, I felt like I went out and earned the trip by putting in hard work.

CALEB WINDSAY
LISTENING FOR HARMONY

Caleb: After Katrina, my mom was working at Tulane. She said, "Lusher is letting all the Tulane children enroll in their program."
I said, "No, I want to go to St. Aug or something. I want to be in the marching band."
She was like, "No, you are going to go to Lusher and you're going to get this education." I was like all right, cool, even though it's not known for music. Basically, amongst the bands Lusher is known for being a bunch of nerds.

Aurelien: That's what everyone says but that's because we get decent test scores. We first met when we were at Lusher. You were already in the jazz band, and I joined it.

Caleb: Man, all I know is I seen this kid and he had a trumpet and he was wearing soccer clothes. I was like, "What's he doing!?" Kent was telling me, "Yeah, this cat is going to be good. You got to watch out for him."

Aurelien: I knew Kent Jordan from the Louis Armstrong Camp. He recruited me into the jazz band when I first came to Lusher. I was happy to do that because I had just been learning traditional music and wanted to learn some other kinds.

Caleb: Before Katrina, I did the camp for I don't know how many years. It's actually where I met Genard, the snare drummer who plays in our band. I didn't even know that Trombone Shorty was his uncle. He was playing trombone at the time and we were trying to learn our scales, and get stuff together. Eventually he stopped playing trombone, but he's good at the drums now and that's what we really need.

Aurelien: If you look into the city, a lot of musicians who went to the camp are spread out in different places. It was a good meeting point for musicians to learn how to play and develop.

Caleb: They start out with jazz.

Aurelien: A lot of it is a listening music.

Caleb: Listening intently.

Aurelien: Bebop is like you are listening to a lecture at a university.

Caleb: So much information coming out.

Aurelien: All kinds of different ideas are coming out so you have to really pay attention to be able to understand what the person is doing.

Caleb: A lot of people aren't attracted to bebop because, to an untrained ear, it can sound like a lot of noise. If you aren't infatuated with music, you might not understand it.

Aurelien: We learned to listen and do our own arranging in Kent's program.

Caleb: He is one the best educators musically I know.

Aurelien: He's somewhere between a laid-back teacher and Kidd Jordan.

Caleb: *He knew who my mom and grandmother were. My grandmother, Topsy Chapman, is the one who taught me everything about music. When we were in Switzerland, people knew about my grandmother like it was New Orleans. She grew up in Kentwood, Louisiana and was raised on gospel music.*

My grandmother's father had been in music. He was actually learning music during the times when there was racial conflict. They wouldn't let him go in the school and learn music with the rest of the people. He got cool with this white teacher, and the teacher would say, "I'm going to open the window for you. Just stand out there and watch the class." And that's how he learned how to play music. And I'm like, "That's crazy" because if it wasn't for that teacher, we probably wouldn't have even been playing music.

Kentwood is very rural. My grandmother moved to New York to do an off-Broadway show, One Mo' Time, *and after that, her singing career took off. She does jazz standards and she still does gospel and R&B. She got my mom, Yolanda Windsay, and Auntie Jolynda Philips in it and they have a group called Topsy Chapman and Solid Harmony. You can catch them around the city. I play with her at Snug Harbor about once a month, too.*

Sometimes when we go back to Kentwood, we'll go to a service at my grandmother's church.

Aurelien: *It's the same kind of thing with my family with Arkansas. We'd only go up there for special occasions because it was pretty far away. We'd go to church in Benton, where my dad's from. The services are really long—three and a half or four hours—but they're full of music. There's drums, bass guitar, an organ, and a choir.*

Caleb: *I thought it was cool because it had a bunch of energy. The bass is driving.*

Aurelien: *Yeah.*

Caleb: *The drums are constantly moving, and the organ is*

Left to right: Joseph Bloom with Aurelien and Caleb playing for the Lusher Jazz Band. Photograph by Bruce Sunpie Barnes.

playing so much you can't keep up with it, and the people are like, "Yeah!" I think that's how we feed into how we play now because if nobody is feeling involved, I'm going to be feeling like I'm not involved. If I'm not feeling the crowd's energy, it's going to be dead to me. I need to see y'all moving. Y'all need to clap your hands or something!

I've been watching that with my grandmother's band.

Aurelien: *Do you think you had an advantage in terms of what you hear since you've been around it your whole life?*

Caleb: *I felt like it was built in me. Before I had to figure out music; it was happening up here [tapping on head]. My mom would be singing in the car, and I'd hum the three or the five. And she'll be like, "Hold on, you're singing harmonies. How do you know about that?" I must have picked it up from listening to them. She started showing me chord changes, and how chords work together.*

Aurelien: *I noticed that with your brother, Mike. We'd be in math class and we'd be humming a song, and he'd hit some note that was supposed to be hit but I didn't know he knew about that!*

Baby Boyz to New Breed

Caleb: *I was with the Baby Boyz since 10th grade. I knew Glen Hall III and Desmond from the Project Prodigy music program, and had met Genard at the jazz camp. I felt like I fit right in with them, and was used to playing a lot of music. I think I made the wrong choice to go to Louisiana State University for college because I lost the music outlet. It was so big, and I felt alone. I tried out for the marching band, and I could have made it but I didn't know how to do the military style marching because Lusher didn't have a marching band. I would practice in my dorm room and would be playing so many brass band records because I would be missing it so much. Soul Rebels, Trombone Shorty, Shamaar Allen. I*

263

Caleb and Aurelien perform with the New Breed at a Money Wasters parade in the Sixth Ward. Photographs by Bruce Sunpie Barnes.

had to come back home, and I had to come play music. This is what I loved to do.

I decided to transfer to Tulane. When I got home, the Baby Boyz were going through a transition. Glen Hall III was starting to do his own thing with a stage band, and we could tell that's where his heart was. We were like, "You know what? We're going to do this and you do that." There's no hard feelings. And that's how we formed the New Breed, but we needed a trumpet player.

Everybody was like, "Man, we don't really know a trumpet player who really knows the music. We don't have time to teach somebody from the ground up." I was like, "You know what? I know a trumpet player."
They was like, "Man, you don't know no trumpet player."
I'm like, "Watch, I'm going to call him." It happened from there.

You bring things to the band that other people aren't bringing. I remember when you were into Outkast's Morris Brown. We listened to it together, and. I was like, "Man, that's crazy. The time signature keeps changing. You be listening to that?!" And then when you play, we can hear you are incorporating things like that, which is cool because we're trying to do as a band is to raise the expectations of a brass band. What people expect now is not what we would like. It's not a good image. Most venues would not like to hire brass bands because they think we're wild. Right now people don't really respect brass bands as a culture, and as an art from. We don't want to be looked at as deviants.

Aurelien: And the way that translates to music is we are trying to create a more polished sound. It's definitely going to be funky. You're not going to get around that, but we're trying to add something to it. We want to play music where if people want to replicate us, they actually have to pick up their horns and work on stuff. We want music enthusiasts to understand our ideas.

Caleb: That's why we've been doing a lot of arranging. If you are playing the same part all the time, it gets wack. We want to keep a fresh sound.

Aurelien: That's what Big Paul told me the other night when we were at the Blue Nile. He's like, "Man, y'all's arrangements! It's refreshing to hear that because a lot of brass bands don't focus on that too much." If all the parts are tight, and everything is working in the harmony, it sounds a lot better than if people are just blasting notes.

Caleb: We can play traditional jazz—that's basically what we did in Switzerland with a bunch of Louis Armstrong songs, but we're trying to do it all. We don't want to put ourselves in a box and get stuck there. We want to explore the universe through music. Each song will have a part where we are featuring an instrument. But we are moving it all around. We don't want people to get too stuck on seeing the trumpet always playing the melody.

Aurelien: I think you are one of the most soulful trombone players, like Gregory Veils of the Rebirth Brass Band. You know what rhythm to play—that's the most important part when you are playing funky stuff, you are going to play around the blues scale but the rhythms is what makes you distinguished in your solos.

Caleb: That's something I had to learn from Greg, too. He would always tell me, "Man, why are you trying to play everything you know?"
And I was like, "Why not? I know it."
He said, "Man, slow down. Take your time. You don't have to play everything you know. Just play one little riff, and then the next time play something else." And then I started hearing rhythms and little hooks that would capture people's attention, and I'd start incorporating that into the background while one of them are playing a solo.

Aurelien: We've been trying to incorporate different chord changes not the typical ones that you expect.

Caleb: We are bringing organization to it. The Dirty Dozen's got to be the most organized as far as brass bands we are looking up to. They got arrangement and musically, they're it.

Aurelien: Yeah.

Caleb: Musically, they got it going on.

Aurelien: In order to get your name out, you have to play parties. If you distinguish yourself in quality from other brass bands, people are going to start talking about you because they can notice it. They really know the music, and when they hear something good, they'll spread your name around, and you start to get better gigs. I think it's pretty good that in one year we made it all the way to Switzerland.

Caleb: I didn't know you spoke all these languages. We get over there and you're talking French to the people, and I'm like, "Man?!?"

Aurelien: I think after the Switzerland trip we became a lot closer musically as a band. People are starting to get used to each other's playing styles and we know what to expect from each other. It's starting to translate into our music because the more you play with somebody, the more in sync it's going to be.

Caleb: The parades help, too. I'd been to them a few times but it wasn't like every week I was going to second lines. After I started really playing the music, that's when I started going out there. I think we played four of them last year. Those same parades called us back for this year and we've got new parades from those parades.

Aurelien: When you are at a second line, whenever I hear the music and I see the whole scene going on, I always get goosebumps. "Ooohh!" That's one particular kind of spirit.

Caleb: When you are playing a second line, it's like organized chaos. Everybody's doing something totally different. It's so raw. You can play something and I'll ask you what you just played and you will already have forgotten. You don't even remember what you just played a second ago. It's crazy. It feels so good, and it fits.

Aurelien: After a second line, especially if I've been playing for four hours, I just have bass lines stuck in my head all day. Just bass lines from the tuba.

Caleb: It's crazy because when you are playing you don't even realize how far you're walking until you are done walking. I really walked that far?!

One thing you can expect, the club is always going to be sharp. They are going to have suits on and they are going to be looking elegant and fancy. There will be other people who are coming out who are in different second line clubs and they'll wear be in matching T-shirts, and then you got bands like us. We'll go out there and wear our New Breed T-shirts and other bands like TBC will wear theirs just to represent and show people this is what we do. We're not playing today, but we're going to wear these t-shirts. And then to people who don't have anything to represent, they represent themselves. So they dress however they want to dress.

Aurelien: That can range from zero to—

Caleb: A hundred.

Aurelien: A lot of clothes.

Caleb: It's addictive. I was ready to go this Sunday and somebody told me it was cancelled, and my heart was hurt. The whole summer I can't wait for second line season.

Nine Times Social and Pleasure Club's parade in November of 2013 was one of the first parades the New Breed played for. The Ninth Ward always makes a strong showing. Photographs by Bruce Sunpie Barnes.

THADDEAUS
RAMSEY

&

JULIUS
LEWIS

Thaddeus Ramsey in front of his grandparents' house in the Faubourg Marigny. Photograph by Bruce Sunpie Barnes.

Thaddeus with his younger brother Jawansey and grandfather Ashton Ramsey at the MFAA program. Photograph by Bruce Sunpie Barnes.

THADDEAUS RAMSEY

Bruce: *Thaddeaus "Peanut" Ramsey is a bass drummer with the Young Fellas and Stooges Brass Bands., who is currently studying music at Texas Southern University. I remember when he was five years old running around with his grandfather, Ashton Ramsey, to all kinds of cultural events in the city. He used to carry a small African drum with him that he beat on. His grandfathe played with the Dirty Dozen Kazoo Band and taught black history classes for Tambourine and Fan. Over the last few decades, Ashton has developed an important career as a folk-art historian, making elaborate Carnival suits, paper hats, and jazz funeral collages, which have been featured at the Ogden Museum of Southern Art as part of an international art biennale of contemporary art, Prospect 2, as well as the Jazz and Heritage Festival every year.*

When I would be at the Backstreet Cultural Museum in Tremé with the Northside Skull and Bone Gang, an old black Carnival group that masks on Mardi Gras day as skeletons, Thaddeaus would play drums with us, and his grandfather would say, "He's going to be a real musician." When I started the program, he was one of the first students I wanted to recruit. I got

lagniappe because his grandfather also brought his younger brother, Jawansey "NouNou" Ramsey, along as well.

Thaddeaus was a solid musican on the bass drum. He picked up on rhythms extremely fast. He had a deep understanding of how everything should work. I really enjoyed watching him learn from people like Uncle Lionel Batiste, Oscar Washington, and Anthony Bennett. In a short period of time, he was playing like a grown man. He learned how the bass drum keeps everyone in the band together.

When we were working on the book project, we asked Thaddeaus if he wanted his talk to be with saxophonist Julius Lewis from the New Wave Brass Band. With his typical easy demeanor he said, "Sure." It took them awhile to connect because Julius was struggling with health issues, but once they got together things flowed very easily. It was clear that it was the right combination. As it turned out, they played with many of the same musicians.

Introduction: Let's Roll

Julius: Where did you grow up?

Thaddeaus: I grew up in New Orleans in the Bywater/Marigny area, at my grandparents' house.

Julius: Did somebody in your family play music?

Thaddeaus: My grandfather played with the Dirty Dozen Kazoo Band. He played cowbell and also the kazoo. And my older cousin Mr. Walter Ramsey plays tuba and is the leader of the Stooges Brass Band.

Julius: You play in them now, too? You are with the Stooges?

Thaddeaus: Yes, sir.

Julius: Y'all should be getting pretty good now, y'all have been around. What is your grandfather's name?

Thaddeaus: Mr. Ashton Ramsey.

Julius: Tell us about him.

Thaddeaus: As far as my life, and music-wise, he's the man who pushed me to be the person I am now. He is my idol, and the man who I ask for help if I need something.

Julius: What's his personality and some of the things he did that stood out in your mind?

Thaddeaus: My grandpa is an artist. He does paper mache and collages. He used to work as custodian, but now works with elderly people. He'll go help them at their house. That's how we got our income with that.

Every December, he starts to work on his Mardi Gras costume. He'll have boxes of stuff, and a suit laying in the middle of the floor with like words on it. When I was young, I was shocked. I'd think, "What he was cutting all these magazines and newspapers out for?" When I got that age to really catch on, I could see what he was doing.

Wherever my grandpa brought me, I went. That's how it was. We looked forward to Carnival. We'll go sit by the lot right next to the Candlelight in Tremé. Other family will come pass through. The baby dolls, the skeletons. A few Indian gangs, and my little brother, Jawansey, masks with Mr. Bruce as a skeleton in the Northside Skull and Bone Gang. For jazz funerals, my grandpa will make a collage on a suit he wears or on a plastic board. They are pictures of the fun times he had with the people.

Julius: Scenes from the street.

Thaddeaus: Sometimes on this collage, he'll cut letters out of newspapers. He'll make glasses out of signs that get put out for elections. He cuts designs out of voting signs, carves out names, and glues it to the glasses.

Julius: Did your grandfather like second lines?

Thaddeaus: Yes! He brought us to second lines every Sunday. They would call to let him know, and he'd say, "They got a second line in the Sixth Ward. Put your clothes on. They about to roll!" He rode my sister and me around on a big pedal bike.

We'll be down there before it got started, and I was excited. Never knew who I was gonna see out there—friends, family. My grandpa had a cowbell with the

One of Ashton Ramsey's Carnival suits made with found objects. Photographs courtesy of Ashton Ramsey.

screw in the middle of it. We'd follow the band and he'll just ring the cowbell to the beats. And he had a triangle. He switches up on different songs. I used to watch him.

Julius: He had quite an influence on you, huh? That must have been pretty cool.

Thaddeaus: Yes.

Julius: You hung with him more than anything. That's all right. You grew up quick.

Portrait of Ashton Ramsey, by Bruce Sunpie Barnes.

ASHTON RAMSEY
FOUND INSTRUMENTS AND ART

Ashton: You've lived with me here a good while, but I grew up in the Seventh Ward. I was born in 1934. Back then, it was hard to find a place to live when you got boys and girls. Most houses were shotguns with two or three rooms and a kitchen with a wood stove. You had to have a front room. You had to have a place to receive guests and wake the dead. At our house at 2424 Annette Street, my brothers and I slept in a bed and we took a bath in a Number 2 tub. Yeah. We had to warm the water. You wash my back, I'll wash your back. You laugh. All my grandkids laugh, but I tell y'all, that was real life. Now, you see, y'all have the good life.

When I was growing up, I didn't know none of my grandfathers. I didn't have that opportunity. All I knew was my daddy's mom. She had been a slave. She lived around the corner from us on St. Anthony Street, and my aunties lived on both of those streets, too. My mama's mom, I only saw a picture of her. She was an Indian from Houma.

My mother was red and had hair way down to her waist. She was different from the rest of her family, but they love them some Margueritte. Yeah. When Margueritte had eight children, those brothers would come by my mama's house and bring food, bring money. They took care of us. When they were getting together and they didn't want you to know, they'd be talking that old talk, that Creole.

Thaddeaus: Your mom?!

Ashton: Yes indeed. The whole family.

Thaddeaus: Not while I was around!

Ashton: Oh no, man. You came in the 1990s, she talked that Creole a long time ago. I didn't understand it. All the people they grew up with and knew, they spoke Creole, too, you see.

Where we was living at, all those people were carpenters. They were yellow people with "good" hair. That was their language. See, that's how they grew up.

The Dirty Dozen

When Carnival came around, everybody had to do something. It's not like now where everybody's standing around looking. I got hooked up with the Batiste family—Uncle Lionel and them. Their band was mostly voice. Uncle Lionel was the banjo player and lead vocalist, but they passed around the songs. Everybody would sing something. I played the tambourine and the kazoo. It was exciting. Besides Carnival, when a baby had a christening in the neighborhood, we would perform. We'd start around the corner and collect people. You'd have all kinds of people as the word got out, "The kazoo coming, the kazoo coming!" We'd go there and play spirituals. There were so many songs that aren't played now that it makes me sad. But see, back then, everybody was in church.

And then the Dirty Dozen band came along and took the place of the kazoo band. I started going with them, getting jobs and all that, bringing them to stores to buy music. We bought John Coltrane and Dizzy Gillespie—that was bebop. We used to sing, too, when the Dozen first got together. Before it got educated and started playing technical music.

We'd go over by Charles and Kirk Joseph's house over on North Dorgenois and Elysian Fields. Their father, Mr. Frog, would say, "Man, what's wrong with y'all, man. Y'all don't sound like nothin! Y'all get yourself together!" We practiced in a little building in the back of the house. It was a place where we could sit down and play music.

And then we started playing back there by Darryl on St. Anthony and Rocheblave in barroom on a Wednesday. Baseball was the thing, and the band would dress up as women. We'd parade to Hardin Park, and have people waiting for us to pass. That wasn't my shot. I never wanted to see myself dressed up as no woman, but it was so much fun. When the people saw us, it was a happy thing. We brought joy.

People call me Triangle Man at second lines, but when I started off, I made a lot of things. Blow that whistle, and they'd jump off the roof. I played the kazoo. I got all kinds of bells. I cut the broom handle off to make different kinds of percussion. When we went to Darryl's, I had a stand with a big cymbal on it, and I'd play that cymbal.

In the 1980s, I was with the band in Tremé, and they said, "Ramsey, listen, man, we got to let you go. We are going a different way so we aren't going to need you to play percussion no more." That's all right. That's quite all right. They went on, and I'm glad for them. I think I recorded the songs Little Liza Jane and Feet Don't Fail Me Now. I continued to play percussion with different brass bands. I played with the Olympia and the Chosen Few. I played with Rebirth, New Birth, Lil Rascals, Tornado Brass Band.

I was all right with the music, and all of that, but I have hypertension and I wasn't eating proper. I was a gardener. I was working mostly by myself out there in that hot sun. I'd knock off work, go in the street, be out to two in the morning, get up at six o'clock, be on the job at seven, not eating. Only drinking coffee. My weight got down to like 130 pounds, and my clothes were just hanging on me. Business started to change, too. See, when I started I trimmed around the fences and the beds by hand, but then the weed eater came up. Where I was spending hours on a yard, two people could do now in 20 minutes.

I decided I wanted to get out. I had a friend who knew one of the School Board members and he spoke to him about getting me a job. In 1990, I became a custodian at Walter C. Cohen High School. I started working there, and couldn't spend those nights on the street. I had to come home. During Carnival time, I was talking with the children at the school about masking and all that, and decided to make a costume to show

Left: Black and white collage, courtesy of Ashton Ramsey. *Right:* Ashton Ramsey on St. Bernard Avenue getting out ahead of the parade with the police detail. Photograph by Bruce Sunpie Barnes.

them. The first year I masked, it was caution tape and buttons with a black suit. I wore it to school for the children, and oh Lord, they just flat out loved it: "Oh, Mr. Ramsey!"

All through the next year at Cohen, I was finding these barrettes all in the yard, all in the desks in the classrooms. The girls would leave their rollers and combs. I thought, "This could be a good idea." For Carnival in 1991, that's what I did. I put all of those clips and things that I had collected on a suit and it was a hit. Oh yeah, it was a hit!

I decided to be like the Mardi Gras Indians, every year, I made a new suit. I used to wear my costume for Mardi Gras, Super Sunday, and then my birthday is in May, and I wore it in May. One time, I was cleaning out a closet at the school and I found all these beautiful long stemmed roses, so I brought that home, and put them on a white suit I had. Over the years, I've made more statements, too. I made one for the earthquake in Haiti, and another one called "Black and White" about race and music in America.

I like art, so once I started, I ended up making collages for funerals, too. I keep folders of pictures I collect of different musicians. When Antoinette K-Doe died, I did a collage for her with pictures that I kept over the years with her and her husband, the R&B singer Ernie K-Doe. Right now, I've got a stack of pictures about Fats Domino. He's put in the paper more than anybody else. There are very, very few pictures of Dave Bartholomew. I've got a bunch of photographs of Pete Fountain when he had a bunch of hair on his head. I'm not wishing that the man die, but I've got that.

Since 1998, my suits and collages have been exhibited at the Jazz Fest. I wasn't interested in it at first, because of the custodian job, but when I did start, it was all right. I felt this is a way for people to see myself around the world, and you wouldn't believe, I've taken pictures with kings and queens, standing next to each other, hugging like we are brother and sister.

Left Thaddeus with his grandfather in front of the Tremé Community Center. *Right:* And playing the drum with Chief Arvol Looking Horse of the Sioux Nation during a procession to Congo Square for White Buffalo Day. Photographs courtesy of Ashton Ramsey. *Middle:* Thaddeaus' brother, Jawansey Ramsey, at Uncle Lionel Batiste's funeral. Photograph by Bruce Sunpie Barnes.

Lil Stooges

Thaddeaus: When we were growing up, the Lil Stooges used to practice upstairs at my grandparents' house. Walter started the band with his friends when they were in high school. Some of them went to Kennedy, and some of them went to St. Augustine together.

Julius: You got a chance to see them behind the scenes. When a band gets to practice together all the time, you can come up to the same level and work together. There are several bands—Hot 8, Stooges, Rebirth—who got that sound and you're going to enjoy whatever they do. On the traditional side, the Paulin Brothers have their own little sound, Tremé, the Storyville Stompers. Everybody has their own little thing. If you practice as a unit, you are hard to beat.

Thaddeaus: They used to come over twice a week to practice and chill, joke around. I used to be in the room where they were playing.

Julius: When we were in high school, we had Sound Corporation. We used to practice after school at my house and we got really popular with it. The kids hanging out, listening.

Thaddeaus: I used to listen to the Lil Stooges, and be like, "Wow, they playing all this!" My grandfather always told me to get in there and try. He had a lot of pride in my sister, my little brother, and me about what we did. He volunteered at my elementary school, Lorainne Hansberry. One day after school he took me into the cafeteria and Mr. Mitchell, the band director, had the horns laying on the table. I was like, "I want to play the trumpet." And that's how it went. We had to do a Mardi Gras Extravaganza parade, and I was the lead—and only—trumpet.

We were dressed in our school uniforms. It started in the front of the school and went around the block. I felt nervous at first. Being at a parade, you'll feel the vibe, but it's nothing like when you are doing it. Generating a parade—the feel—is way different. You see everything that's going on, and you feel like everyone is looking at you. Afterwards, the band director for Douglass High School walked up to me. Said I sounded nice. I should keep it up. I was like, "Hey, I could do this more often."

Julius: Where were you during Katrina?

Thaddeaus: The storm had hit my sixth grade year. I evacuated to Atlanta with my cousin Walter. He got the Stooges to come to this one house, and they were trying to put something together in clubs there. Then I flew out to Fort Worth, Texas and stayed with my mom, sister, and younger brother in an apartment.

Julius: You missed this place?

Thaddeaus: Yes! It was hard. Couldn't go to no second lines out there. I was just stuck on radio. At school, they had a music program where we played songs with concert bells.

Julius: And you moved down the street?

Thaddeaus: This was sitting at a table.

Julius: Sitting still.

272

Thaddeaus: You had to hit the bell every time it was your turn on the song.

Julius: Each of one of y'all were responsible for how many bells?

Thaddeaus: One.

Julius: One bell?

Thaddeaus: Yes.

Julius: That was a good learning experience, huh? Patience was tested.

Thaddeaus: They were just playing it straight off the sheet with no feeling or nothing. I was telling them about New Orleans music—how we do brass band music down here. I played the tambourine, and they were shocked, "How you know to do that?" I was like, "Dang, y'all don't know how to play a tambourine? Y'all don't know how to play a drum?"

Julius: I know that made you feel even better about getting home, so that you can get back into the feel of the music.

Thaddeaus: I only stayed out there for one school year. And that was it. I had to come back. I left my mom in Texas. She wanted me to stay but she knew what it was. I just missed home. I had to come back down to stay with my grandfather. The year after that, she came back, too.

On the Drum Line

Julius: What kind of music did you play when you got back?

Thaddeaus: Back in New Orleans, I liked to get on my bike and ride around to listen to music. I'd ride

towards Douglass to hear their band practice or go hear the kids from NOCCA play more modern jazz. Every other Sunday, my grandpa took us to the drum circles at St. Augustine Church. You'll have New Orleans style music—one song you'll have Mardi Gras Indian music. Next song you'll have like second line music. It'll be drumbeat and everybody'll just put their own feel. It was something I could do.

I used to see Mr. Bruce at the drum circles and around the Backstreet Cultural Museum across the street from the church. One day he told my grandfather, "We got a program coming up. I think you should bring your grandson along." I went the first week, and I liked it ever since. Wake up early in the morning. Ride the bike to the National Historic Park and see kids my age and younger playing their horn.

I met Jeremy Jeanjacques there, and started seeing him more in the neighborhood. I said, "Hey, I've seen you before." He became my best friend. His mother was over the Color Guard at McDonogh 35. She was like, "Oh, boy, we could use you at McDonogh 35."

"Oh, really?" She helped me do the paperwork to get in.

Julius: Did you play music in high school?

Thaddeaus: I played sousaphone at McDonogh 35.

Julius: Okay, a good band over there. You were marching in the band, too?

Thaddeaus: I marched in their band for four years. I wanted to get on the drum line. Drum sticks, mallets always caught my attention. In school, with the pens and pencils beating out on the desk. After school, at the bus stop, on the sidewalk. People said, "You should be a drummer."

"I should, huh?" Took it in for consideration.

But the band director said, "Oh, man, we've got so many drummers. Everybody coming here want to be a drummer." Then my friend Jeremy was like, "Hey I heard you played tuba before—you actually kind of nice." They gave me the mouthpiece and the horn. I was like, "Oh man, I don't want to hold this heavy instrument!" But once I started learning stuff, I became attached to the sousaphone.

My section leader was a big guy. Probably like 280. I'm a freshman. He pressured me. It was hard on me but that made me a better player at the end of the day. What I noticed, you'll never learn as quickly as if you're with pressure. You get ranked about what you know—how to play your horn. It was my first year so I was in the middle or at the back, but as the year went on, I made my way to the front.

Julius: At Cohen, each section would pair off and we'd give each other the chords. Somebody would hold the chords in rhythm and somebody played up and down—soloed. You did that?

Thaddeaus: Yeah.

Julius: A lot of fun. On the bus. Right before a parade. A little camaraderie. Each section had their own sound and then we'd get together and have one big sound.

Thaddeaus: At school, we used to have battles sitting around the tables. We'll have another table right behind us. Somebody will come out with the beat. A friend'll start rapping. Somebody else from another table will say, "Well, you get your drummer. I got my drummer."

I got known as someone who could handle the beat. Other kids be like, "Come on, what you got? What you got? I know you got a beat! You got something!"

I had a lot of audience. We're thinking we going hard.

Top: The New Orleans Young Traditional Brass Band in Albany, Georgia. Photographs courtesy of Ashton Ramsey.
Bottom: Mark "The Missing Link" Smith playing the sousaphone with the Pinstripe Brass Band at an Avenue Steppers second line circa 1982. Photograph by Michael P. Smoth © The Historic New Orleans Collection, 2007.0103.4.426

Every day at first and second lunch we used to meet in the courtyard and beat on the vending machine and make up songs that come on the radio—bounce, rap, R&B. If somebody came up with a song, I put a beat to it and rolled from there. We used to have a lot of friends come over and dance. The cheerleaders would come up and do a beat to their song or their cheer.

Bands Out of High School

Julius: When I was in school, brass bands weren't such a big thing—it was more rhythm and blues. The brass bands were always there, but they weren't as popular as they are now. The R&B bands were where all the horns were. We'd have these bands with these eight-piece rhythm sections with anywhere from three to six horns.

Thaddeaus: They had a lot of brass bands that were coming out of the high school marching bands. Easton and St. Augustine had bands coming out. Out of 35 came the Baby Boyz and 21st Century. And the school has their own the Three to Five Brass Band.

Julius: The style of music is changing a lot. It's trying to co-exist with an old culture.

Thaddeaus: Some of the guys in the bands want to learn our generation of music over the traditional brass band music. They criticize the traditional, "What we need to learn this for?" But I look at it like this, "How you expect to go forward if you don't know where you come from?"

Julius: One of the guys that I used to play with in the Pinstripe, Mark Smith, was really the one of the main ones who started the funk with the tuba. Tuba Fats started it, but Mark took it from there.

Thaddeaus: They call him the Link.

Julius: What I noticed about him was his memory. You could call anything, and he could play it.

Thaddeaus: Mark crazy.

Julius: You are going to get the real him.

Thaddeaus: Loose. Real loose. When the Young Traditional band went to Albany, Georgia to play a parade, it was us and the Link. It was different. We were used to living in the inner city and this was more rural. The president of the university was crazy about us. It was my first time being in that kind of parade. Everybody lined up on the side and you just walk. Nobody following you. We waited for an hour and a half for the Homecoming queen to come and they had cars and all that, but the parade only lasted twenty minutes. It was just like riding around the block compared to the second lines. But it was fun to experience something new.

Julius: And it's the most exciting thing they've seen in their whole life.

Thaddeaus: We're coming down the street with our traditional song and Mark just come on out with the funky song. He started turning around with the tuba, dancing and hollering, "Whoo whoo!" Singing.

Julius: I remember one time the Paulin Brothers went to Philadelphia and we all paired up when we got to the hotel. Mark was left with Doc.

Thaddeaus: That's like a negative and a positive.

Julius: Doc was all right but you ain't gonna do nothin. We were just starting to go out. Doc was sitting down on a little bench outside of the hotel with Mark. He had to be inside for eight o'clock. Getting ready to go to bed. Mark was so disciplined, we had to crack up. We pulled off waving.

Thaddeaus: When we were playing with the Young Traditional, one of the trumpet players, John Michael Bradford, wanted to learn funk music. We went by Kenny Terry's house on the weekends and he'd teach us some numbers. His son, Sam Jackson, played snare drum and also tuba. Sam had a friend named Marshan Bowden who could play sousaphone, and we had a back groove. We had a trumpet, and Jeremy played trombone. I was like, "Let him get his chance." Might be able to do a little something. We practiced wherever we could. My house. Sam's house. The park. We called ourselves the Young Fellas Brass Band.

I remember I got a phone call one night. "Hey, you feel like making some money? Come meet us on Frenchman Street; we could hit out here to however late we want to." I was like, "I'm not doing anything. I'll be right on the way!"

Julius: So was it true?

Thaddeaus: Yeah it was true! It was like a big party scene on Frenchmen every night. We got us some fans that come see us. Every night, people come out to see the Young Fellaz.

Julius: I heard that the tourists on Bourbon Street pushed the locals to Frenchmen Street. Bourbon Street became too touristy. The music, the loudness, all the "I bet I can guess where you got those shoes." Frenchman was a bit slower for the locals even though, for people in other parts of the world, it's moving pretty fast.

Thaddeaus: Some of the younger brass bands still play out on Bourbon Street, but I'd rather stay with Frenchmen.

Thaddeaus playing with the Young Fellaz Brass Band on the corner of Frenchmen Street. Photographs by Bruce Sunpie Barnes.

Tuba and Bass

Julius: What instrument do you play now?

Thaddeaus: I transitioned from sousaphone to bass drum when I started playing with the Stooges.

Julius: Oh, okay. You like the rhythm section. The heartbeat. The tuba is basically the same beat as the bass drum. You must be looking for that pocket. You know that drum is one of, if not the most important, instrument in the band.

Thaddeaus: Can't run without it.

Julius: Keeping time is everything. You get some of those snare drums, and their timing is not there until the bass drum comes in.

Thaddeaus: Before I hit the cymbal, the song may start out off with the snare drum doing a roll. Their roll might be off if I don't lock the groove in with the cymbal.

Julius: Different snare drums have different techniques. By themselves, they are like any other musician in not keeping good time. The bass drummer is very important for that. He comes in and it's like, "Okay, that's where we are."

Thaddeaus: When I first started sitting in with the Stooges, they wanted a more of an up-to-date beat. It was hard for me cause all I knew was the traditional beat. In the middle of the song, I would start playing it without knowing that I'm doing it.

Julius: I'm a horn man, as you know, but how does the drum change from traditional to funk—how does the beat change?

Thaddeaus: Traditional, you have a swing feel. It's like a church feel.

Julius: The guy I play with hits on the "and" between the three and the four count. That's how he plays, and it's weird. He doesn't come down on the beat—he's on the up beat but it's still funky. The old musicians used to do the songs how they felt. Nobody knew how they were going to do it. If he was gloomy, you got the gloomy version. They really expressed themselves.

Thaddeaus: I remember at the Music for All Ages program, some days, Uncle Lionel would be there, then the next week the Stompers or Oscar with the New Wave. All of those people, they had their own style, and their own ways of playing a traditional song.

Uncle Lionel didn't have regular bass drums like we have. I want to say there is one that is white coated, and it gave him a unique sound. I think that's what made me who I am, from listening to him. Unc, he taught me where the feeling should go between the three and the four. It was more of a listening thing with him. Like his licks. He would do a roll on the four. He didn't hit the cymbal, he hit the other side of the bass drum. And I took that from him. The guys in the Stooges will hear it and say, "That's that Uncle Lionel. That's that old man beat."

I tell them, "Yep, you're right!"

Julius: What are you doing to make the Stooges the Stooges?

Thaddeaus: For the Stooges, at a parade, it's all about the crowd—however the second line is feeling. If the people on the sidewalk are not dancing, then the people inside the rope aren't happy. You want to keep pleasing them. The club trusts you will make them shine.

Julius: Do y'all have a regular gig?

Thaddeaus: We try to have a show every Thursday. It used to be at the Hi-Ho Lounge on St. Claude Avenue and now it is at the Rock Bottom, Uptown on Tchoupitoulas.

Julius: What?! I didn't know that. That's a good bar because that's a second line bar. It's home of Prince of Wales. You just play the drums or you get involved in the other parts of the band?

Thaddeaus: Well, me on the back row, I dance with the music. We have a dance called *Wind It Up for Michael Buck*. It's a little two step—two steps to the front, two to the back and then you just wind it up. It's a little dance that everybody in the band can do. It ain't too complicated. The crowd do it after they see us do it the first time. After they see us do it, they be right on with it.

Julius: I'm going to ask you this question: What do you think could be done about sharing the market between the traditional bands and the new bands? Seems like when they have Battle of the Bands, why do they only have the funk bands? They have these events but they never have a traditional band there. I don't see what the problem would be. If they get booed, they get booed, but I doubt it. I'm just wondering what you think.

Thaddeaus: I think it's because we rarely see a traditional band on the street on a Sunday. So whatever what people see, that's what they like.

Julius: That's what I'm saying. Okay, y'all got everything on a Sunday but the traditional got everything in the Quarters. What can we do to bridge that gap? You hardly ever see a funk band at Preservation Hall. It's New Orleans music and it needs to be preserved too. That's something I've been asking around about.

Thaddeaus: I feel like we should be in Preservation Hall, because it is New Orleans music but it's just our feel separated from their feel.

Julius: I agree. So you think we need to go ahead and spread the word? If you talk to your people and I talk to my people?

Thaddeaus: We can work something out.

Streetlights stream through Thaddeaus' bass drum while he plays in front of Cafe Brazil on the 500 block of Frenchmen.
Photograph by Bruce Sunpie Barnes.

Right: Portrait of Julius Lewis by Bruce Sunpie Barnes. *Above:* Musicians gather in front of Bethlehem Lutheran Church in Central City before Julius Lewis' funeral service on October 12, 2013. Photographs of the funeral and procession by Rachel Breunlin.

JULIUS LEWIS

Bruce: *Julius Lewis was an alto and tenor saxophone player who got his start with a high school R&B group called Sound Corporation, and later in life came into brass band music with the Doc Paulin and Pinstripe Brass Bands. Working at Tulane and Loyola's chemistry departments for years, he was also a founding member of the New Wave Brass Band.*

In the program, Julius taught the reed section, working with the clarinet and saxophone players. He came every week dressed in black and white, often arriving early and staying late to help students learn the correct musicality. During the program, he shared how reed instruments should harmonize melodic lines with the main melody of a song. In demonstrating how to do this, he taught the students how to play their role in the collective sound that is created in a traditional brass band. In short, it was the lessons in how to be a role player in a group of musicians.

In the middle of working on the book, Julius passed away unexpectedly. We had talked about where he would like to be photographed for the introduction to his life history, but hadn't had a chance to do the photo shoot yet. When his family decided to have his funeral service at Bethlehem Lutheran Church, we thought it was a special way to pay tribute to his musical history because he helped start the church band in the late 1960s that is still an important part of the congregation today. In the pages that follow, we wove Julius' life history through his family and friends' memories of him that were shared at his service, as well Reverend Patrick Keen's eulogy. In his jazz funeral, Julius' hope that he shared with Thaddeus—for brass band musicians of different generations to continue coming together—was realized as members of the MFAA program played a heart-felt tribute to the spirit and love that was shared in making music together. In New Orleans, music is truly for all ages.

Introduction: The Lewis Family

Curtis Lewis: *My brother Julius was my lifetime brother, my partner in music, and my wingman.We were born just a year and a half apart. So close he couldn't even be the special baby of the house before I came home from the hospital. My mama said, "Julius, come see your little brother." Julius walked over, looked at me, threw his cap on the bed, and walked away. Mama said, "This is going to be a long life."*

Julius: My family was the third family to move into the new section of the Magnolia that the Housing Authority of New Orleans built with the Housing Act of 1949. 3214 Clara, apartment C. I had two brothers and three sisters. We stayed in the Magnolia for 10 years and then my mom urged my dad to buy a house, and we moved to 2817 Baronne.

Curtis: *Growing up, I would get all his hand-me downs. Sometimes our clothes would get mixed up, and he would say, "Mom! Curtis wearing my underwear!"*

Julius: My mother Beatrice was a country girl from Scotlandville, Louisiana. She was a beautiful dark-skinned woman. At that time, people from the city considered anybody coming from any other place a little slower than we were. But my mother had a bit of intelligence. She had gone to Southern University for two years. She enjoyed being here. During World War II, she worked in the factory doing ironwork when the men left. She used to brag on that all the time—how it was until they came back. Everywhere you went, it was women running the country.

She was the reader and the businesswoman in the family, and I think I got the love of music from her. On the weekends, she played Martha and the Vandellas and songs like *Wang Dang Doodle* and *C. C. Rider* on a record player that looked like it was a suitcase. The speakers came off the side with a nice bass. They were real fancy. Not until the weekends, though. She wouldn't

blast it no other time.

Curtis: *In our eight-room shotgun house, Julius and I shared the same bed. We were excited when our daddy bought us new bunk beds.*

Julius: My dad, Julius, was from downtown New Orleans around Orleans Avenue. He had every color in the rainbow in his family, but he was a bright-skinned Creole guy. I'm a dark-skinned person, but I never really paid attention to it. Some people have a complex in our race if they're dark but I never did. One thing I got to say about my dad is that he was a quiet man. He was quiet, but he took care of business. I think I take after him with that.

My dad only went to eighth grade. During World War II, he was stationed in Pearl Harbor. When he came out of the military, he did carpentry, bartending, and was a bouncer for Dooky Chase's.When we were kids, he worked for Sears and Roebuck as a maintenance man, but I didn't know that until I was a teenager. He dressed like you'd think he was going to an office job. He'd have his nice slacks and shirts, hats. He'd make all of that effort to leave the house and put on the uniform at work, and then change again before he'd come back. That was his way. Back in that era, blacks had to prove themselves and try to keep an image. It wasn't okay for us to slip.

My dad was a walker. He didn't even want a car. He liked to participate in what men did in those time; he did a little drinking and some gambling. All of that was supposedly supplementary income—sometimes it worked, sometimes it didn't. He was a member of the Jolly Bunch. From the Magnolia project, my dad walked me down to Basin Street to second lines and had me dance.

We were familiar with brass band instruments from growing up around second line parades, and watch-

Musicians from the Paulin Brothers, New Wave, the Bone Tone, and Red Hot Brass Bands perform at the beginning of Julius' service.

ing Doc Paulin's band stop at the corner barroom near our house. I remember my friends, Gregg Stafford and Mark "The Link" Smith, used to get together and march around the Magnolia project. Link would put on that Zulu grass skirt for the impromptu second line and come back with a crowd.

The Carter G. Woodson Band

Curtis: *In the seventh grade, Julius came home with this huge baritone horn case. The band director at Carter G. Woodson Middle School, Mr. Harris, had convinced him to play it.*

Julius: Over the summer, I was supposed to take private lessons with Mr. Harris and be ready for the band in the fall. I took the horn home and started playing...basketball. I didn't think about that horn until a week before school opened. It was dusty and I was scared. Mr. Harris embarrassed me and got me with the baton. I got on the horn and made a sound out of fright. He let me know that my position was pretty shaky. It was on me. I actually started practicing.

Curtis: *Julius carried his case about eight blocks from our* house to Woodson and back. He was happy to carry it because he said it was building his arm muscles and he was developing an egg. He would change to the tenor saxophone, which had an even bigger case. I would see him performing in those crimson and gold uniforms and I wanted to be a part of that.

Julius: When Mr. Harris came out of the Army, he swore down that he would take the project kids and make then into champs. We did that. All it took was for me to play my part one time and get everything right. Mr. Harris said, "Good tenors." That's all I needed right there. He ain't have to call my name or nothing.

Curtis: Woodson had some vocational training, and since carpentry ran in our family, my parents urged me to take industrial arts. I was in Mr. Benjamin's class. He was in charge of making paddles for teachers, and he cursed like a sailor. Mr. Harris came down to the shop room one day to order a new paddle, and Mr. Benjamin made it. Mr. Harris walked around chatting with us. When he got to me he said, "You look like a trumpet player. Come up to the band room and see me."

I said "What?!" I think Julius put the bug in his ear. I practiced and got pretty good on the trumpet.

Julius: Under Mr. Harris, my brother came in and out of nowhere bumped the guy for First Trumpet so they had two first trumpets. He was noticed more than I was as far as a young musician with potential. He was powerful. He still is. I brought him on a gig when he was here a few months ago and the guy wanted to hire him.

Gregg Stafford: I'm quite indebted to Julius because when I first started playing the trumpet, Julius and Curtis were at Woodson and were two of the most intelligent, well-advanced musicians in the band. You could put anything before them and they could read it. They were playing symphonic music at 12 years of age.

Julius: There was a program called *A Night of Music and Drama.* The band would be in concert form, and we would have the Woodson choir. I played tenor in all the concert pieces. I think it helped me play harmonies. The tenor part is not a lead part that everyone is familiar with. When you first start, you can't really tell where it fits until the rest of the music comes in because it's a second or third part. But if you put all three parts together, it is a pretty sound. The other parts are there to support that top. With the concert music, it's flowing. The harmonies cross. In an interview with Delfayo Marsalis, Mr. Harris said he'd never forget the piece we played, Ralph Vaughn Williams' *English Folk Song Suite.* It was a hard piece of music. It had three movements to it, and we knew that thing back and forth. I wish I had the recording he made. You wouldn't believe it's a bunch of middle school kids. He had us playing college level music.

Saxophones in High School

Curtis: When I got to the eighth grade, and Julius was in the ninth, we joined an R&B band called the Blue Pearls. We were hiding our faces and playing in nightclubs. Mr. Harris would fuss about it, but our parents were supportive of us. And then Julius went to Cohen High School and joined the band.

Julius: By the time I got to Solomon "Fess" Spencer, he was kind of old and he was cranky, but he still put out a good product. His arrangements were so fast. We wouldn't even get a sheet of music. He'd do it on the board. "This your part, this your part, this your note. Now, let's go." He was also an excellent alto saxophone player. Sometimes he just would stand in front of the class and start wailing. I respected him very much, and I wished I could sound like him when I was in school.

Cohen was integrated in the late 1960s. We had one white student. The thing I remember about the integration was when we played Mardi Gras's parades, how dangerous it was. We had 80 members of the band, but at Mardi Gras, we had 30. I'd be one of those. We had to talk about how we were going to deal with the violence before we left. "All right, this is what we're going to do." Everybody put the biggest guys on the end, put the littlest guys in the middle. Most of our classmates would follow us through the whole parade. Like other black bands in the city, they tried to protect us.

I became known as one of the reliable players in the marching band. When I got the uniform in the junior year, Fess made me wait last. Then he gave me the best uniform he had. Cohen was a little, ten-minute walk from my house and I used to strut all the way up with my band uniform on while everybody's saying, "Hey, how you doing?" Sticking my chest out. Yeah, man. That's a great feeling.

Curtis: Under Fess, Julius switched to the alto saxophone. He bragged about his little brother coming next year to cut some heads. He also met the members of the Sound Corporation, featuring the Soul Impressions. I auditioned and was quickly accepted into the band, too.

Julius: When I got to be a senior, Fess gave me the raggediest uniform. No crotch. All crooked. Too big. He was sending a message.

He didn't like the fact that I was using his horn in Sound Corporation. In fact, one time he showed up on a gig at the Nightcap on Carondelet and Louisiana Avenue. When I stepped off the stage, he was standing right there, and said, "Give me my horn."

I said, "I'm not going to be able to finish the gig." He knew that. He was just razzing me. He just wanted to show me the power he had. I didn't let him know where we was playing at after that.

Curtis: The years at Cohen would be exciting and busy.

Julius: We were young, and it wasn't always about money. In fact, we played for a dance in the gym. We packed that place for four hours. It was dripping. We thought the roof was leaking, but that was just perspiration from the crowd. We raised money to pay for my whole senior class's budget, which was $60 a head. We had good hearts, but it was a time in my life when some people were very critical.

Curtis: Julius and I would form a church band in this very church.

Julius: My family's Lutheran. Martin Luther split off from the Catholics back in the day and created the Lutheran religion. We're so similar, except for some of the burning of the incense and other rituals. The music was like Catholic music, too. You almost needed a degree to sing the hosannas in weird keys.

Bethlehem Lutheran, this quaint, two-story brick church, on Washington and Dryades, was around the corner from our house. Curtis and I were altar boys and were in the choir. But once we started playing in an R&B band, when we'd walk into church, people in the congregation would say, "Oh, those Lewis boys."

And then we got Reverend Orval Mueller. He was German-American. I loved that guy. We had a lot of youngsters who wanted to do stuff, not just sit in church. He was open to the kids. When we wanted to start a band, he said, "Yeah, okay."

We played songs like *Jesus' Love*, by Lionel Richie. We did some hymns, but we funked them up with the drum and the guitar, and did solos with the horns. We were swinging it. I think that it kind of woke the church up. It gave the patrons something to talk about.

Curtis: Julius' fiancé, Odilee, was in the church band with us. Even though we have all grown up, I'm glad to say they still have the band today.

Julius: Odilee's mother was the secretary of Woodson, and the editor of the society column for the *Louisiana Weekly*. She has some awesome interviews with Louis Armstrong and other big time people. I met her through church, and she joined the public school at Cohen. We wound up going to the prom together, and then we split for many years. We just recently found each other again.

Finding Confidence in Myself

After high school, Sound Corporation had dreams of Motown, but because of the Martin Luther King era, I think the adults in our lives wanted us to just make sure we concentrated on academics rather than music. I think it screwed us around because we were ready to be good musicians. Instead, I went to Southern University. I was planning on playing in the band, but my dad got diabetes. The discipline that it took to live with it, he couldn't do it. He got a sore on his foot that turned bad, and it just went all the way up until he had to get the leg amputated. He still lived for a few years after that, but he wasn't the same.

I came home to support my mother. I worked at D.H. Holmes, a department store on Canal Street, for about a year and a half. I didn't like it, and decided to join the Air Force. I tried to get Curtis to join with me but he was busy. He wasn't ready. I had to fill out a "dream sheet" that says where you want to go. You can either pick a base or you can pick a state and get lucky with whatever base is in the state. Being down in the South, I always heard how nice California was. Even back then, they were ahead of us with race relations. They didn't discriminate as much. I ain't gonna say "at all," but that's why I chose California.

And I got it. From 1974 til 1979, I was stationed at Travis Air Force Base, an hour's ride from San Francisco when Harvey Milk was a member of the Board of Supervisors. I did a little music playing in the Air

1972 EASTER

Julius and Curtis Lewis playing with their band at Bethlehem Lutheran in the late 1960s. Photograph courtesy of Julius Lewis.

Force. In the late 1970s, the synthesizer came out, and it reduced the size of these big rhythm-and-blues bands. Sly and the Family Stone was one of the favorite groups we used to listen to. He had at least five or six piece rhythm section. Three or four horns. He started playing with a synthesizer and got rid of his horns. Soon a lot of us were knocked off the stage by the synthesizer.

The military solidified my feelings about race relations. We were all just what they called us: slime, green slime. They made us cut our hair the same. It gave you the opportunity to find out who you were. When out here sometimes it wasn't fair, in there, everybody lined up, started at the same spot, and went at the same time. In those circumstances, you can measure up to see how you fit in with everybody else. I always had confidence in myself. That's how I wound up there. But then, you find out more about yourself. "Okay, I can hang with these guys." You're not sure until you do it.

When I came out of the Air Force in 1980, I started

working at Tulane University. I was the supervisor in the chemistry department, where they had a big research program. I used to get some help from the professors because I was learning on the fly. Part of my job was also to keep rare chemicals in stock. I had an $80,000 budget, and relationships with scientific companies. I was also in charge of setting up the experiments for all the different labs. I had one of the biggest waste pickups out of the whole state. I stayed there 13 years.

Gregg Stafford: When we were in our 20s and 30s, Julius and I used to carouse around a lot. We double dated young ladies together. Almost every week, Julius would come around my apartment with a bridal magazine. I said, "What you got this for, Julius?" He said, "You need to think about getting married." I said, "No, not right now." But I would go by his apartment and bring a bridal magazine for him. We'd go back and forth about it.

Denise Lewis: Growing up, some of us in the Lewis family did not have our father so we relied on our uncles. We spent a lot of weekends with them. When I was younger, I got something that's plagued our family—rheumatic arthritis. In the third grade, it was so bad I couldn't walk. At one point, it went into my eyes and I couldn't see.

One afternoon, it was so bad that my grandma called Julius off the job to come get me. Well, Julius took the time with me. He gave me a book called The Lion, the Witch and the Wardrobe. *He told me to read it and he expected a full report on it. I ended up being held back that year, and during that time, he taught me everything from long division to geography. He prepared me so well, I graduated from high school a year early.*

The Paulin Family

Curtis: When Julius started working at Tulane, I had been playing a few gigs with the Doc Paulin Brass Band and introduced him to some of the band members.

Julius Lewis (*saxophone*) playing with the Paulin Brothers Brass Band at the Old U.S. Mint. Photograph by Bruce Sunpie Barnes.

Ricky Paulin: We all started together in my father's band from real young.

Julius: Doc Paulin had a parade with three or four different churches, and he needed just as many bands. I got in the Third Band. When I met him, Doc was in his 70s, and he was still a vibrant man. He was a realist and a little bit before his time, because he wasn't gonna let anybody mistreat him. He was a black Creole from Wallace, Louisiana. He was the son of a slave, I believe, and he saw a lot of the injustices after Emancipation. He didn't want to be a part of that, so he moved to New Orleans, and joined the military.

When Doc started playing in brass bands in the city, he got disgusted with how the cut wasn't right, and started his own band. He got his wife and created a band with his sons. He used to treat the band members like they were in the military. That's why a lot of band members right now like him because he whipped them

into shape. He was demanding, but he was only trying to teach you how to be a man—an honorable person.

I loved to talk to him because he was pre-TV and pre-telephone. He told us about booking gigs when he was a young man, and how he had to walk to tell each member the date. If the gig was on a Saturday, he'd do that at the beginning of the week in order to give the musician time to let him know if they could make it. If they couldn't, then they had to walk to him and to let him know or send someone that day. One time I went to his house right off the corner of Seventh and Liberty. He had a thick book tattered with musicians' names listed. His last days, he was writing his autobiography, and still booking gigs.

Ricky: Julius was one of those people who was a real asset to the band because he had abnormal hearing—he could hear all kinds of things.

Julius: I came in from rhythm and blues, but I didn't know much about the structure of traditional brass band music. It took me some years to figure it out. I was used to having a piano back up, a guitar holding the chords. In a brass band, none of that stuff was there. I found out the saxophones were the ones that had to play the chords. The trombones would be countermelodies to the saxophones. Doc would be on top playing the regular melody on the trumpet, but then you had all that movement and harmony underneath, and that's what was so outstanding. As long as we had those harmonies, we could do whatever rhythm we wanted to complement the music.

Ricky: Julius put together all kinds of background riffs while the melody was doing something else and we'd go: "That's it, that's it."

Julius: When you are listening to the music, you tap your feet to certain things. I notice that when we get a nice jumpy riff, people are on that riff. When music has that movement, you never get tired of it.

At one time Doc had all the Uptown parades. And then the music changed, and he wasn't as popular with them anymore. I went through that period with Doc. I was a young man, playing that old music, and they had the youngsters running away from us. Rebirth was just getting big and the funkiest thing we had was, *Go to the Mardi Gras.* That wasn't getting it no more. People wanted the other stuff, and Doc refused. He stayed true to the traditional.

I had gone against the tide, because I had played a lot of funk with rhythm and blues. What I saw in the Paulin's thing was challenging to me. With rhythm and blues, everything is, "This is what your part is, this is your part." With jazz, you have more freedom, but at the same time, you can't clutter it up because of that freedom. That's why I stayed so long, trying to learn the art form.

Sometimes in a band, the different instruments can go separate ways—that's what the Olympia used to do with countermelodies—but you have to know what you are doing. If there are four countermelodies going at the same time, you've got to stay in your lane. You don't want to clash. I notice that a lot of brass bands sound good at the beginning of the music, but somewhere they get a cacophony. You just hear a lot, and it ain't clear what it is. The musicians are jamming but it seems like their hearing has turned off. I think that's a little out of control, so what I like to do is give the music form. I go back to one simple riff that I started with at the beginning. You have to be mindful of when to do it. If you can form it up like that, you can bring everybody back to end the song together.

Making Others Sound Good

Curtis: The Doc Paulin Band was the beginning of a long legacy. Julius would take the ball and run with it, and started playing with the Pinstripe, Oscar Washington's New Wave, and Louis Lederman's Bone Tone Brass Band, to name a few.

Julius: I was playing with the Paulins when I got offered to play with the Pinstripes, too. Mark Smith is one of the innovators of the brass band music. Like Kirk Joseph, he was one of the first ones to bring in funk. Pinstripe was very well known for that. And for years, they ruled the streets with Mark on tuba. For four years, I played with them. We'd have second lines on Sundays, and gigs after the parade. Herbert had that club on Washington and Freret. Every Sunday we had that from nine to one. That thing used to be jumping, especially when they had a parade pass earlier by Kemp's.

Oscar Washington and I were still a part of the Paulin's Brothers Brass Band, but we weren't playing many gigs. It was suggested that Oscar start New Wave as a branch of the band. One year, we went on a trip, and I think Oscar decided he wanted his own independence.

"Bringing him on down." The band playing slow hymns and dirges as the body exits the church.

He wanted his own band and sound, so the band split. I stayed with both. I was worried because I knew I was in the middle, but I'm a good diplomat. I became Oscar's right-hand man. We are still together.

Oscar Washington: We come from one big family in music. There is no separation because it is a talent that God has given us, and he wants us to express to bring other people together. I'm thinking Julius did his job, and he did it well.

Ricky: We always pray before we play. He was always there saying, "Give God the glory."

Louis Lederman: I originally met Julius when we were in the Down and Dirty Brass Band, and then when I formed my own band, I invited him to come play with us. He was always an unbelievable asset to my efforts to play traditional New Orleans jazz. I will never ever forget, whenever I had a gig, I would always put in the song list a spiritual medley of Lord Lord

Lord *and* Jesus On the Mainline. *I always counted on Julius to take the vocals, and he brought it on home.*

Oscar: *He loved those spiritual songs, those hymns. And I guarantee you, he would sing with fire and soul and make everybody break it down—just get under him and listen to him. That's when you pay respect for another musician. When you say, "Let's make sure he's heard."*

Julius: It takes a lot of discipline to give way and enjoy actually making other people sound good. It takes a long time to figure that out sometimes. Everybody thinks they're playing if they're wailing. You ain't listening to the guy next to you. You're wailing, he wailing. Several times I've seen this on TV with the New York musicians. You might have some top-notch musicians in the band, but they don't sound as good as they should because they're not gelling. You could take a family band like the Paulins, and they'll scare the hell out of some of these other bands, because we play together all the time.

Louis: *Julius wasn't just someone who I hired for gigs. He truly became one of my best friends.*

Ricky: *He was a good listener. If you had a problem, you could go to him and he wouldn't give you advice unless you asked him. He wouldn't say, "Oh man, you need to do this." No, he didn't do that.*

Julius: In 1993, I went from work one day to take a physical. They told me I had to come back and they were going to put me in the hospital. I had a 900-sugar level. I went into denial. I took the prescription and didn't fill it.

Around the same time, Tulane was downsizing, and offering a severance package to people who wanted to resign. I thought, "Okay, I can go out and play music." Once I did that, Loyola University asked me to come work for them, doing the same thing but without the big research budget. I stayed over there a few more years, and then I finally left after we came off a big old

trip from overseas.

Ricky: *We'd get on that plane to go to Europe and Julius would say, "I feel different, man. I feel free." The whole trip is like that—leaving your worries and cares at home, and enjoying the scenery and culture while playing music.*

Julius: It's kind of scary because you're programmed to work. That's what's in your mind. At first, you feel like, "Well, who am I?" All kinds of crazy negative thoughts go through your mind, until you can realize that you can make the most out of retirement. You just have to formulate it. It's not gonna happen instantly. It took years for me to get comfortable. I don't just sit around and play checkers.

Gregg: *When I moved back Uptown, Julius would stop by with a six-pack of beer and we'd sit and talk. Come to find out, we never agreed on anything.*

We would meet in different festivals all over the place. The

284

Louis Lederman playing the snare drum coming out of the church. Louis passed away a number of months after Julius on August 14, 2014.

last one was in Italy. We would meet every morning to have breakfast and disagree with each other. Julius said, "Don't come over here with all that foolishness. I let you have the last word in America, I'm not going to let you have it in Italy."

Odilee: As good as he is on that saxophone, he makes an effort to practice three or four times a week.

Julius: When you practice, you come to a point where you think you got a song. But you don't. You got it for now. You don't know the song until you own it. If I'm still stumbling, I don't know the song. I have to go and work the kinks out. Boredom is your best teacher. Once you get bored with a song, then you go, "Well, let me try it this way." You open a window and you go in there, and then there's another window. You finally figure out a way to put it all together. Now, I get on my keyboard, and I'm figuring a lot of things out with the chords—extending them, going down.

Gregg: One time Julius invited me over to the house, "I want to show you what I've been doing...arranging some music on the piano." I looked at some of the music he was writing and I said, "Julius that doesn't look right."
"What do you mean that doesn't look right?"
"The timing is not right."
"Well, let me introduce you to something. This is an eraser. That's what it's made for."

Julius: When I'm practicing, I think about the terminology from my chemistry days—saturated solution. That's what happens when you take a beaker of water and you keep putting salt in it until it can't take anymore. And what happens is a grain of salt pops out.

Catie Rodgers: I first met Julius when Louis Lederman called me for a funeral at Greenwood Cemetery, and then we played another funeral at St. Louis Cemetery. Sometimes when you get out there on the street, everybody's blowing, and it's all out. But Julius played with class and love, and Julius listened. You would play something and then he'd play it in his solo, you know. He encouraged younger musicians to listen to each other and get a conversation going.

Playing When Sick

Curtis: I remember finding Julius one evening sitting on a bench bent over and throwing up. He was developing some really serious issues.

Julius: I went on until I got congestive heart failure. I can see how people give up.

Curtis: He called me one day and expressed remorse towards life, and the will to go on. I had been living in North Carolina, so I got in my car and drove 16 hours to New Orleans to see him.

Julius: You have to want to live. I had to stop being afraid of it and started working with it. Your body is always trying to heal itself and all you can do is assist it. I don't just get up out of the bed and go anymore. I'm a long way from that now. I have to do all kinds of stuff before I leave out the door, but you adjust.

Curtis: Julius would discuss his health and he would say it was always improving. He would never tell us how he really felt.

Julius: Playing the horn sick isn't easy. I don't want anyone to know I'm sick when I'm playing. That's personal. Recently, Odilee lost her husband and I lost my friend. She tells me she was all over the place she was trying to find me, and tracked me down. I really love her, and we've decided to get married. She's been there for most of my life. I want to thank her for being so supportive of me.

Curtis: Julius went peacefully sitting on the sofa with his Saints hat on getting ready to go to a gig. Farewell, Julius, my loving brother, my partner in music, my wingman. God bless you.

Oscar: And I'd like to give my praise and strength to the family that you just lost a loved one, but who didn't love him better than God. Nobody can dodge this—we all have to take it. And I'm going to pray for you and love this situation even more because you know he is going to be with his Maker.

Gregg Stafford (*trumpet*), Catie Rodgers (*trumpet*), Oscar Washington (*snare*), and Ricky Paulin (*clarinet*) playing before Julius' procession begins.

Julius' Eulogy

Reverend Keen: *We have a Psalm that we sing here that says* Open Our Eyes. *If you call upon him, He will show up. Is there a witness here?*

Congregation: *[Clapping]*

Reverend Keen: *Somebody said he's an old time God. Yes, he is. Yes, he is. I need a launching pad to begin this eulogy for a great man. And what better launching pad to begin this accession than the Psalms. And not just any Psalm, but I would go to the 105th Psalm that says:* Make a joyful noise unto the Lord.

Congregation: *Yes, yes, yes.*

Reverend Keen: *Isn't that just what Julius wanted? To serve the Lord with gladness and to know that He is our God above all gods, a King above all kings. Make a joyful noise, and that's what we've done here today. And the beautiful thing is, I don't have to be here long because his life has already been lived, his eulogy has already been spoken. He lived his eulogy.*

Congregation: *Yes.*

Reverend Keen: *My job is easy. Amen. Well done, my good and faithful. I can hear Julius right about now leading that band around the heavenly throne. I got a bright crown waiting for me in that New Jeruselum. My soul looks back and wonders how I got over.*

It's about celebrating life. Let me tell you something people, too many times we go around faking it. There is no reason to fake it. It is what it is. Let me say that one more time. It is what it is. The problem in the church today is that we want to present ourselves as more holy than we really are. We don't have to have it all together, not as much as we would like to sometimes.

Left: For Julius' jazz funeral, the musicians paraded in a traditional lineup with sousaphones in the front. *Middle:* Julius' fiance Odilee walking with the hearse after they cut the body loose. *Right:* Julius' brother, Curtis, dancing one last dance.

I'm glad to have gotten a chance to get to know Julius even though it was brief. Odilee brought him to church a few weeks ago wanting to introduce him to the place that he started from. He played in this congregation years and years ago. She wanted to introduce him to this ministry and did he have a good time? Yes he did. It's good to come back home. But it's good to have a home to come back to.

As I've heard the stories about his legacy, I heard the story of how he had a special place in his heart for children. God honors that. I just heard a story about a young man whose mother was involved in the music industry here, and as this young man was exposed to music, he wanted to hang with the second line musicians, and he was a brother of another mother, of another hue, if you understand what I'm saying. But that makes no difference. I understand that Julius spent a lot of time working with him and encouraging him: Are you practicing? Are you going up and down your scales? Are you putting the time in? That young man was here today. That young man was standing over here with the other musicians playing on that tuba. That young man is standing back there now. Doyle, raise your hand.

Congregation: [Clapping]

Reverend Keen: That's just one story. I could tell you another story, about how he took care of children in the family. When Mama couldn't be there, on more than one occasion, he stood in as their daddy. When the family had a need, this man stood up, and did the job that was needed to be done.

Every now and then, we need to have our memories stirred up so we can have our faith stirred up. Our faith will be stirred up today when we remember that the God he served is the same God that's available to us. No, he wasn't in church every Sunday. We don't have to make up nothing. You see, the fact is I don't have a heaven or hell to send anybody to, but I know that I serve a God that sits high and serves low, and he touches the heart of everyone.

One thing I do know is that he knew that his Redeemer lived. Did you not hear the testimony that witnessed before you that said before he played a note, he prayed? He knew his Redeemer lived. They also gave witness that of all his favorite songs—and he knew classical, he knew blues, he knew jazz, and rock and roll—his favorite brought him back to his foundation. Gospel music. So his spirit was saying, "Give me that old time religion, it's good enough for me." And so we say goodbye, a final farewell, to Julius Walter Lewis, Jr., we say: Sleep on, servant. You've earned your rest from this world, but your labor will not cease because you're working in glory.

Congregation: Yes.

Reverend Keen: Ahh, y'all didn't hear me today. I said: He's working in glory! Whether you believe it or not, I believe that God has raised him up to higher heights, and now he is starring in the brass band in glory. So we say to you: God bless you. And keep you. May the Lord make a space to shine his graciousness on you. May the Lord look upon you with favor, and give you His peace. In the name of the Father, the Son, and the Holy Spirit. And God's people said:

Congregation: Amen.

Catie: Doyle Cooper's mom, Leslie, needed a band to fill in for the Red Hot Brass Band at the French Market, and asked me if I could do it. I was playing more modern music, and the only guys I know who played the traditional songs played with Louis Lederman, and the Paulin Brothers, so I called them up, and I was really surprised they said yes. It was a blessing to get more time with Julius. After saying goodbye to him, I'm going to do what everybody's going to do—I'm going to miss him. But I'm going to try to do what he taught me—to reach out, reach out while you are playing.

Edward Reed (*tenor saxophone*) Julius Lewis (*alto saxophone*), Percy Johnson (*trumpet*), Oscar Washington (*snare*), and Herbert McCarber III (*sousaphone*) playing with the New Wave Brass Band in the French Quarter in 2012. Photograph by Bruce Sunpie Barnes.

The All Around Brass Band was formed from the next wave of students to come out of the MFAA program. *Left to right:* Emmanuel Mitchell, Jr., Israel Mitchell, Keith Hart, Jr., and Jawansey "NouNou" Ramsey. Photograph by Bruce Sunpie Barnes.

END NOTES

All interviews in Talk That Music Talk *were conducted by Bruce Sunpie Barnes and Rachel Breunlin between March 2012 and October 2014. The interviews were transcribed, and then Rachel edited them into narratives and conversations. For the primary oral histories, we often did three to four follow-up sessions to co-create the text—reading the pieces together and then building out the storylines, developing musical connections, and making links to the broader cultural and political landscape of New Orleans.*

While there is an incredible body of literature on the history and ethnography of jazz, as well as other important topics such as the Civl Rights Movement, these end notes are directed specifically to the autobiographies and oral histories we wove through the book and sources we consulted for captions.

P. 10. On creating literature from the spoken word: *Mr. Jelly Roll: The Fortunes of Jelly Roll Morton, New Orleans Creole and "Inventor of Jazz."* Berkeley: University of California Press, republished in 2002: xiv.

P. 12. A good introduction to Seydou Keita's work is Elizabeth Bigham's article in *African Arts:* "Issues of Authorship in the Portrait Photographs of Seydou Keita." Vol. 32, No. 1 (56-67+94-96).

P. 19. Rahsaan Roland Kirk on jazz funerals can be found as a prelude to *New Orleans Fantasy Part II: The Black and Crazy Blues* on Hyena's 2002 release of *The Man Who Cried Fire.*

P. 21-22. Interviews with Louis Armstrong can be found in the Hogan Jazz Archive's oral history collection. Item Numbers 47-49 Digitized Box 2 (ID 933-935) and 51-52 Digitized Box 2 (ID 937-938). Listening to one after another, it is striking how he returns to the same stories about growing up in New Orleans.

Many of the same stories also appear in his unpublished writings, which are heavily referenced in Lawrence Bergreen's 1998 biography, *Louis Armstrong: An Extravagant Life.* New York: Broadway Books. Bergreen writes of Armstrong's childhood: "It was, by all externals, a wretched childhood, yet Louis was obsessed with it and returned to it throughout his maturity as the wellspring of his identity, of his music, and of jazz itself" (2). His discussion of Congo Square and connection to Africa can be found on page 11-12.

P. 22. History of Peter Davis can be found in a 2011 article, "Louis Armstrong and the Waifs' Home," by Will Buckingham in *The Jazz Archivist* Vol. XXIV: 2-15.

P. 22. On reducing chaos to form through jazz, see Ralph Ellison's "Living With Music" from *The Collected Essays of Ralph Ellison* published in 2002 in the United States by Modern Library: 229.

P. 29. Douglas Redd's reflections about Tambourine and Fan are from Kalamu ya Salaam's 2006 DVD, *Talking with Douglas Redd,* 95 min. New Orleans: Ashe Cultural Center.

P. 31. Danny Barker's recordings of Mardi Gras Indian songs, *Tootie Ma Is A Big Fine Thing* and *Corrine Died on the Battle Field* were developed from recordings he did in 1947 with Ray "Hatchet" Blazio, Ray's Uncle Howard, and other Mardi Gras Indians from the Seventh Ward. The songs were recently recorded by Tom Waits and the Preservation Hall Jazz Band on a 2010 album, *Preservation: An Album to Benefit Preservation Hall and the Preservation Hall Music Outreach Program,* released by Preservation Hall Recordings.

P. 43. Billie Holiday first recorded *Strange Fruit* in 1939. It was released as a single by Commodore. For more on the significance of the song, see David Margolick's 2000 book, *Strange Fruit: Billie Holiday, Café Society, and an Early Cry for Civil Rights.* Philadelphia: Running Press.

P. 46. For more on the significance of the Dew Drop Inn in the Civil Rights Movement in New Orleans see Elizabeth Manley's 2014 article, "'Cream With Our Coffee': Preservation Hall, Organized Labor, and New Orleans Musical Color Line, 1957-1969," in *Working in the Big Easy: The History and Politics of Labor in New Orleans,* edited By Thomas J. Adams and Steve Striffler. Lafayette: University of Louisiana at Lafayette Press: 131-162.

P. 53-56. Danny Barker's edited interview comes from an oral history conducted by Richard B. Allen in New York City on June 30, 1959 found in the Hogan Jazz Archive's Oral History Collection, Item 18 (ID 75 and 76) and a transcript from an interview conducted for the movie *Red Beans and Ricely Yours* in the summer of 1990, which is Item 22 at the Hogan Jazz Archive.

P. 56. Kid Ory's first band can be found in *Hear Me Talkin to Ya: The Story of Jazz As Told By the Men Who Made It,* edited by Nat Shapiro and Nat Hentoff. New York: Dover Publications: 28.

P. 59. Anthony "Tuba Fats" Lacen's story of joining the Fairview comes from his oral history with Mick Burns, published in 2006 as part of *Keeping the Beat On the Street: The New Orleans Brass Band Renaissance.* Baton Rouge: Louisiana State University Press: 35.

P. 89. On listening to each other, see Sidney Bechet's 2002 *Treat It Gentle*. United States: Da Capo Press: 177.

p. 93. Excerpts of an interview with Chester Jones come from an oral history conducted by William Russell and Richard B. Allen on July 10, 1961. It is archived at the Hogan Jazz Archives Oral History Collection, Item 30 Digitized (ID 450-452).

P. 100-101. Uncle Lionel Batiste's interview is a compilation of two oral histories that are part of the New Orleans Jazz National Historical Park and the New Orleans Jazz Commission of New Orleans' collection housed at the Hogan Jazz Archive. Videotape 9 was conducted by Jack Stewart on September 6, 2001 as part of the New Orleans International Music Colloquium, and Videotape 10 was conducted by Barry Martyn on April 17, 2004.

P. 116. For background information on Economy Hall, see Norman R. Smith's 2010 book, *Footprints of Black Louisiana*, published by Xlibris in the United States: 100-101.

P. 124. An excerpt of an interview with Placide Adam comes from an oral history conducted by Barry Martyn on February 8, 1999. It can be found on Videotape 1 of the New Orleans Jazz National Historical Park and the New Orleans Jazz Commission of New Orleans' oral history collection housed at the Hogan Jazz Archive.

P. 141. Alphonse Picou telling the story of his legendary clarinet solo on *High Society* can be found in *Hear Me Talkin to Ya: The Story of Jazz As Told By the Men Who Made It*, edited by Nat Shapiro and Nat Hentoff. New York: Dover Publications: 23-24.

P. 144. Excerpts of interview with Louis Cottrell, Jr. from an oral history conducted on July 12, 1974, can be found in the Hogan Jazz Archive's oral history collection, Item 55.

P. 145 Excerpt of an interview with Pete Fountain on July 31, 1974 can be found in the Hogan Jazz Archive's oral history collection, Item 23.

P. 161-162. Edited interview comes from an oral history with Waldren "Frog" Joseph conducted by Barry Martyn on August 9, 1999. It can be found on Videotape 58 of the New Orleans Jazz National Historical Park and the New Orleans Jazz Commission of New Orleans' oral history collection housed at the Hogan Jazz Archive.

P. 169-170. Edited interview with Milton Batiste comes from an oral history conducted by Tad Jones on February 5, 2002. It can be found in the Hogan Jazz Archive's oral history collection, Item 35 Digitized Box 4 (ID 1442-1446).

P. 192. The goals of the New Orleans Free School, written by Robert Ferris, can be found in his 2012 memoir *Flood of Conflict: The New Orleans Free School*, published in the United States by Aero.

P. 206. History of the merging of the black and white musicians unions can be found in Manley 2014.

P. 216. Meschiya Lake's reflections on the pull to New Orleans comes from her website: meschiya.com/about. Last accessed on November 1, 2014.

P. 220. The story of Werlein's music contest that launched the music program in the public schools of New Orleans can be found in the New Orleans Jazz Club's *Second Line* Winter 1990. Vol. XLII, No. 1: 12-14.

P. 224. On the confusion between the origins of jazz and the New Orleans redlight district, Storyville, see Bechet 2002: 54.

P. 228-230. An excerpt of an interview of Hart McNee by Henry Griffin appears with permission from StoryCorps. The entire interview is included in StoryCorps' archive at the American Folklife Center at the Library of Congress.

P. 232. For more information about the history of Louis Armstrong Park, see Michael Crutcher's 2010 *Tremé: Race and Place in a New Orleans Neighborhood*. Athens: University of Georgia Press: 39.

INDEX

Crowding around the band, a second line goes by Louis Armstrong Park in Tremé. Photograph by Bruce Sunpie Barnes.